PRIVACY, SECURITY, AND CYBERSPACE

Editor

Palmiro Corti

scitus
academics

Privacy, Security, and Cyberspace
Edited by **Palmiro Corti**

This Book is Printed on Acid-Free Paper. ♾

ISBN: 9781681178516
Library of Congress Control Number: 2017948878

SCITUS Academics LLC,
616, Corporate Way, Suite 2, 4766,
Valley Cottage, NY 10989

www.scitusacademics.com

Notice

Printed in United States of America.

Preface

New technologies provide the development sector with powerful tools to carry out its work more effectively, but they also introduce risks. Access to information technologies – such as mobile phones, the internet, social networking sites and video – can play a critical role in helping people hold governments and development agencies accountable. There is a growing understanding that privacy is an essential component of security. In order to decrease the probability of having data breaches, the design of information systems, processes and architectures should incorporate considerations related to both privacy and security. Cyber crime is only likely to increase, despite the best efforts of government agencies and cyber security experts. Its growth is being driven by the expanding number of services available online and the increasing sophistication of cyber criminals who are engaged in a cat-and-mouse game with security experts. Technical innovation throws up new online dangers. For example, the migration of data to third-party cloud providers has created a centralization of data and therefore more opportunities for criminals to misappropriate critical information from a single target attack. Similarly, the emphasis on mobile services has opened up corporate systems to more users—multiplying the opportunities to penetrate security measures.

This volume 'Privacy, Security, and Cyberspace' provides a better understanding of the risks, perceptions, and myths that surround cybersecurity by looking at it from different levels of analysis. It addresses topics ranging from phishing and electrical-grid takedowns to cybercrime and online freedom, sharing illustrative anecdotes to explain how cyberspace security works. This book is premised on the belief that computer science-based approaches, while necessary, are not sufficient to tackle cybersecurity challenges. Instead, scholarly contributions from a range of disciplines are needed to understand the varied aspects of cybersecurity. Policymakers and strategists will find this book to be an invaluable resource in their efforts to ensure national security and answer concerns about future cyberwarfare.

Table of Contents

CHAPTER 1

Web Search Query Privacy, an End-User Perspective

Kato Mivule

Department of Computer Science, Norfolk State University, Norfolk, USA

ABSTRACT

While search engines have become vital tools for searching information on the Internet, privacy issues remain a growing concern due to the technological abilities of search engines to retain user search logs. Although such capabilities might provide enhanced personalized search results, the confidentiality of user intent remains uncertain. Even with web search query obfuscation techniques, another challenge remains, namely, reusing the same obfuscation methods is problematic, given that search engines have enormous computation and storage resources for query disambiguation. A number of web search query privacy procedures involve the cooperation of the search engine, a non- trusted entity in such cases, making query obfuscation even more challenging. In this study, we provide a review on how search engines work in regards to web search queries and user intent. Secondly, this study reviews material in a manner accessible to those outside computer science with the intent to introduce knowledge of web search engines to enable non-computer scientists to approach web search query privacy innovatively. As a contribution, we identify and highlight areas open for further investigative and innovative research in regards to end-user personalized web search privacy—that is methods that can be executed on the user side without third party involvement such as, search engines. The goal is to motivate future web search obfuscation heuristics that give users control over their personal search privacy.

Keywords: Web Queries, Web Search Privacy, User Profile Privacy, User Intent Privacy

1. INTRODUCTION

Search engines have become a useful part of a daily routine when it comes to searching for information on the Internet. However, the issue of privacy remains a major concern, due to the capability of search engines to retain user search logs. While search engine query log retention abilities might offer better personalized search results, user privacy is never guaranteed. Another challenge is that due to the enormous computation and storage power of search engines, query disambiguation keeps improving, making it problematic for users to reuse the same obfuscation techniques over time. Although research in web search query obfuscation has gained the attention of researchers [1] [2] [3] [4] [5] , studies have noted that web search query confidentiality continues to be a difficult pro- blem, mainly due to the monetization of search results by search engines [6] [7]. For instance, on the rationale for retaining user web search query logs, search engine companies offer the following rationale for doing so [8] : (i) Enhancing ranking algorithms, (ii) Query fine-tuning, (iii) Improving personalized query results, (iv) Combating fraud and abuse, (v) Enabling shared data for research, and (vi) Enabling shared data for marketing and other commercial purposes. It is interesting to note that each of the mentioned reasons for retaining user search query logs is a privacy concern. Even when organizations claim to privatize web search query logs, errors can still be made; as was the case with the 2006 AOL scandal in which a user was re-identified and traced to their geo-location after an anonymized set of web search query logs was published [9] [10].

Therefore, the user-based privatization techniques that do not require third party intermediaries are urgently needed as another layer of protection. Moreover, from a policy point of view, researchers have highlighted a number of relevant issues, important for gauging privacy guarantees when it comes to implementing web search query obfuscation methods. For example, Cooper (2008) noted that web search query obfuscation techniques could be judged using the following criteria [8] : (i) Effectiveness of the method to protect user privacy, (ii) Effectiveness of the procedure to conserve the usefulness of query results, and (iii) How effectively the user can have control to implement the privacy technique. As noted by Cooper (2008), the reasons given by search engines for retaining user web search query logs, are often wanting, with no user confidentiality guarantees. As a contribution, we identify and highlight areas open for further investigative and innovative research in regards to personalized web search privacy—that is methods that can be executed on the user-side without third party involvement such as, search engines. The goal is to motivate future web search obfuscation heuristics to give users control over their personal search privacy. The central question being asked by this study is if it is possible to generate web search query obfuscation methods that can be executed on the user-side without third party collaboration. For trusted privacy, users require techniques executed on the user side of the machine without involving untrusted third parties, such as search engine providers. This study reviews material in a manner accessible to those outside computer science with the intent to introduce knowledge of web search engines to enable non-computer scientists to approach web search query privacy innovatively. To reach readers outside computer science but interested in web search privacy, we have broken this article down

into a review of web search engine mechanisms and suggested areas for further study. Therefore this study reviews web search engines with respect to web search queries and user intent privacy. While a number of cryptographic and anonymous web browsing techniques, such as Tor, have been suggested [11] [12] [13] [14] , this article emphasizes privatized web search querying techniques that do not necessarily involve cryptographic and other third party anonymous web browsing methods. The rest of the paper is organized as follows. Section 2 reviews search engines and web search queries. Section 3 identifies areas for further research. Section 4 concludes the article.

2. THE WEB SEARCH ENGINE

This section presents an overview on how search engines work; an essential foundation for formulating end-user personalized web search privacy techniques. A basic understanding of web search engine mechanisms is necessary, for example, for data privacy curators to formulate new web search query obfuscation methods with enhanced query result usability when compared with existing methods.

2.1. How Web Search Engines Work

A web search engine is a software tool used to search for information on various subjects on the Internet, and returns the most relevant search results to the user. A typical search engine works by providing the following functionality, as illustrated in Figure 1 [15] [16] [17]. It is important to note that each component of a search engine is a privacy concern as search engines maintain logs of user interactions with these components. While the explicit mechanics of how search engines work is beyond the scope of this paper, we endeavor to cover the web search query functionality of the search engine in greater detail since given that our concern is the privacy of search queries:

- Web crawling—Web crawling involves a software agent that is given starting URLs and downloads every webpage by following each URL link. The URL of every downloaded webpage is stored and the document saved in a repository.
- Indexing web pages—Every downloaded webpage is indexed and stored in a repository. Each word on the downloaded page is stored, given a word identifier, sorted; and the webpage is given a document identifier.
- Web search querying—Search terms from the user are converted to word identifiers and the indexed documents are searched until a match occurs.
- Relevant search results—The search engine employs techniques and metrics, such as user profiling, user intent estimation, and Page Rank to return the most relevant search results to the user. A rank computation of the matching documents to the query is performed, and the top-k document results are returned; where k represents the number of documents returned.

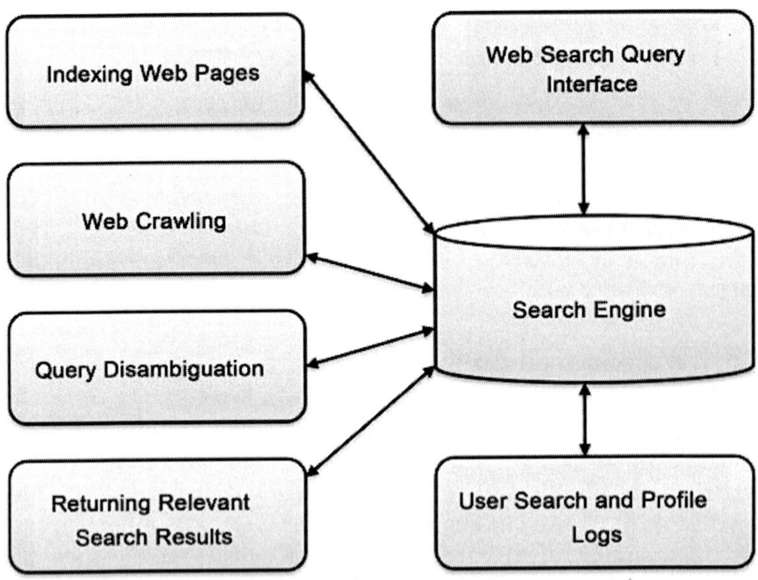

Figure 1. Typical search engine functionalities.

2.2. Web Search Engine Data Structures

- Web search engines include the following data structures for enhanced functionality, a key consideration for researchers when creating query obfuscation techniques to implement privacy [16] [18] [19] :
- Repository—The repository contains the full compressed HTML of every webpage, with its URL and a given document identifier.
- Document Index—The document index contains every webpage or document indexed sorted by document identifiers and a URL list containing the URLs.
- Lexicon—A lexicon is maintained with a list of every known word; Google's lexicon contained 14 million words by 1999.
- Hit Lists—Hit lists keep track of every occurrence of a word in a document.

2.3. Web Search Engine Navigation

Another area of concern in regards to end-user privacy is web search navigation. Search engines seek to profile users so as to correctly target advertisements and maximize revenue. When a user enters a search query, the search engine returns results that can be categorized in two of the following groups [20] [21] :

- Paid search results—These are targeted results based on user profiles, intent, and query search terms, generated and paid for by advertisers, as illustrated in Figure 2. User profiles in this context are behavioral profiles of the user generated from web browsing history and patterns over time, and thus a major privacy concern since they would collectively reveal a user's intent [22].
- Organic search results—These are general results returned by the search engine based on the user query, as shown in Figure 2.
- Organic search results can be further divided into these categories [20]
- Meta-search results—These are a combination of search results collected from a group of search engines.
- Grouped search results—These are retrieved results after result clustering and classification.
- Personalized search results—These search results are generated using user search query logs, browsing history, user profiles, and usage records.

- Natural Language search results—These search results involve question answering in a natural language.
- Image search results—These search results involve a return of image and multimedia to search queries.

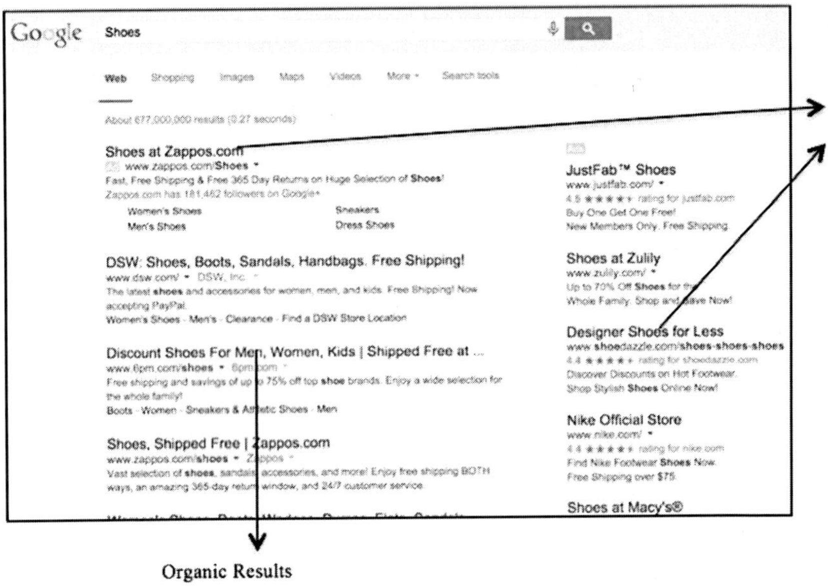

Figure 2. Paid search and organic search results.

2.4. Paid Search Engine Results Process

When a user executes a web search query, search engines provide advertising in the form of texts and images on the search results pages, as in Figure 2. Paid search results are often driven by user query inputs. For example, if a user searches for "Toyota", paid search results would include ads about where to buy a Toyota. Paid search results generally depend on the following [23] :

- The advertiser—These are entities that provide the advertisement source; the ads are usually temporal and thematic in nature, for example, a Samsung ad during the Christmas holidays would include Christmas sales.
- The search engine—The search engine acts as a middleman, targeting advertiser ads to specific audiences and users, based on data collected

from user profiles, query, and browsing history. If a user's search history includes a large amount of queries on cars, then the search engine would target "Honda" ads when the same user searches for "Honda".

- Users—Users are visitors who utilize the search engine to query for information; search engines largely seek to understand user intent so as to correctly target advertisements to the right audience.

Paid search results could be used as one aspect in monitoring the effect of implemented web search query privacy, since advertisements are always targeted to specific users based on their profiles and search queries.

2.5. Ranking Factors

Search engines return user query results based on relevance. Relevance is affected by the search results' importance. Factors that might influence search results' importance include the following [20] [24] :

- The webpage—how frequently a word is used on a specific page.
- The website—the worth and authority of the website—e.g. New York Times vs. a blogger page.
- Click-through data—the number of clicks on a page—higher is better.
- Social reference—how frequently a website is mentioned on social media.
- Geographical Location—search engines tend to return local answers for local questions.

Factors, such as click-through-data and geographical location, are used in the generation of user-profiles by search engines, and therefore need to be given consideration when formulating end-user web search obfuscation methods.

2.6. User Profile Generation

Another essential aspect of search engines that requires privacy research attention is the generation of user profiles, mainly used for targeting advertisements and improving relevant search results. Search engines generate user profiles by employing these two methods [25] [26]:

- Click logging—the search engine tracks each URL from the search query results based on user browsing clicks. Click logging is used to build a user web search profile and to infer user intent by the search engine to reduce irrelevant results. The method works best when a user repeats the same query a number of times or refines the query.

- Profile generation—search engines employ user personal information, query history, browsing history, click-through history, bookmarks, download history, etc., in the generation of a user web profile.

2.7. Web Search Queries

The purpose of search engines is to provide functionality for users to query for information on the Internet. Insight into the workings of web search queries is fundamental for developing effective obfuscation techniques. Web search queries are words, phrases, or descriptions that a user inputs in a search engine that are matched against documents indexed and stored by search engines, to return results relevant to users [27]. Web search queries can be in the form of hyperlinks, but differ from basic database search queries in that they do not use strict syntax rules, as in SQL [28]. There are three main web search queries categories [29] [30] [31] :

- Informational queries—web search queries concerned with larger general topics, and return large related result numbers, e.g. "cars" and "travel".
- Navigational queries—these queries are concerned with finding a single website or webpage of particular inquiry, i.e. "Twitter" and "Yahoo Movies".
- Transactional queries—these query types indicate the user seeks to make an online action like an item purchase, downloading music, or viewing a movie; e.g., "buy a Toyota 2014".

2.8. Ranking Factors

The three main categories of web search queries could further be broken down into the following types of queries:

- Boolean queries: Boolean queries involve the use of logical operators in the query construction. The two common Boolean logical operators include the AND logical operator, which returns restrictive and exclusive search results, and the inclusive OR operator. Boolean search queries have been found to be non-intuitive and difficult for users to employ [27].
- Faceted queries—Another category of web search queries consists of faceted queries, in which the query is divided into subjects in combination with Boolean operators, with the goal of the user viewing

all the documents. An example would be, {Car AND Fuel}, {Toyota OR Honda}, {Camry and Civic} [27].

- Concept-based search query—Concept-based search queries employ semantic concepts and ideas rather than keywords in the composition of queries to retrieve documents in the same concept area [31].
- Single and Multi word sense queries—Single word sense queries are composed of a word but with wide-ranging contextual meanings. Multi word sense queries are made up of multiple single-word sense queries, providing better context to meaning than a single word query [33].
- Keyword-based queries—Keyword queries are composed of words or terms that tend to be short, ambiguous, and focused on a particular entity or subject. Examples include, {Toyota, Honda, Sales}. However, keyword-based queries can have several acceptable inferences, and various interpretations, generating a large set indicating what that particular query could mean [34] [35].
- Single and multi word queries—Single word queries are composed of only one term, while multiple have many search terms. Single and multi word search queries might not be entity specific as keyword-based queries [36].
- Context queries—these are queries where the search is done in context with information, such as the user's profile, search history, browsing habits, query features, user background, user interests, etc., used to disambiguate the query and return results relevant to the user [37].
- Natural language queries—natural language queries are composed of search terms in the form of real questions in the user's natural language, without the use of query syntax and special formats. i.e. a user could query, "what is the circumference of the Earth?" [27] [38].

Web search queries tend to be brief, vague, consist of subtopics, and generalized into two major groups—faceted and ambiguous queries [30] :

- Faceted queries: Faceted queries can be composed of subtopics, but are non-ambiguous, clear, and return precise and relevant results to the user.
- Ambiguous queries: Queries usually have more than one meaning, and so the search engine returns results that might not be relevant to the user.
- A categorization of ambiguous queries is needed to obfuscate web search queries, as noted by Song's taxonomy (2007) [39] [40] [41] :
- Category A: Ambiguous Queries—queries consisting of one or more search terms where each term has multiple meanings. Ambiguity

results from the multiple meanings, i.e. "bank" could be a financial institution or riverbank.

- Category B: Broad Queries—these query types are composed of different subtopics a user might search for. Examples include, "race cars". Ambiguity is caused by the vagueness of the topic and subtopics. For example, a user might have differing meanings for keywords, "race" and "cars".
- Category C: Clear Queries—these are queries composed of keywords with a very narrow and specific meaning. Examples include, "Harvard University". Clear queries return numerous search query results with a higher degree of quality than the ambiguous and broad queries.
- Under the natural language processing (NLP) queries category, Wu et al. (2014) further categorized question retrieval queries into two major groups [42] :
- Short queries: these are NLP type queries in which the questions being asked by the user are very short, unclear, and ambiguous, thus making it difficult to correctly pinpoint user intent.
- Long queries: in this group of NLP queries, the question asked by the user is long and complete, often resulting in precise and relevant search results.

2.9. Semantic Search

An important aspect of web search queries lies in semantic search. Semantic search is concerned with meaning, the understanding of an expression, insinuation, and/or inference, highlighting the relationship between similar keywords and phrases in a web search query [43]. Search engine organizations spend considerable effort in employing semantic search techniques to efficiently pinpoint user intent, return relevant results, and better target advertisements. Thus, for effective web search privacy and query obfuscation, proposed frameworks must take into consideration query semantics to enhance user privacy. The following are some of the relevant semantic search characteristics:

- Disambiguation: Semantic search goes through disambiguation, to remove any ambiguity and multiple word meanings, to return the most probable search term meaning [44] [45].
- Generation of relevant results: To generate relevant web search results, semantic search systems take into consideration the context of the search, location, intent, word alternatives, word substitutes, and generalized and specific word concept equivalents [46].

- Natural Language Processing: In semantic search, Natural Language Process- ing linguistic components, such as, homonymy and synonymy, are employed in efforts to better understand the meaning of a user query, to accurately predict user intent, and return relevant query search results [44].

2.10. Word Sense Disambiguation

Word sense disambiguation is a computational process of finding the contextual meaning of words, a problem that researchers have noted to be intractable, as are other difficult problems in artificial intelligence [47]. Word sense disambiguation requires external repositories of knowledge, such as thesaurus, ontologies, and corpora to get the right context and sense of words [47] :

- Thesaurus—a text repository that offers synonyms, which are similar word meanings, and antonyms, which are opposite word meanings.
- Ontologies and Lexicons—these are descriptions of concepts of particular subjects of interests, taxonomies, and semantic relations, such as WordNet.
- Corpora—this is a collection of texts for studying language representations.

External knowledge repositories are crucial to effectively understand user intent and enhance personalized search results. However, the use of word sense disambiguation repositories, such as thesaurus, ontologies, and corpora, is also vital for web search query obfuscation during the query formation and reformation process. The challenge is to formulate queries so that user intent is protected, but with less disambiguation to retrieve relevant search results and thus improve usability.

2.11. The Word Net Database

WordNet is a commonly used external repository of knowledge, employed in the process of query refinement and keyword reformation to get the appropriate word meanings. The following is a description of the possible semantic relations that could be derived when using WordNet, with applications in query disambiguation, and, more importantly, query obfuscation insofar as this study is concerned [48] :

- Synonym—these are words with same meaning. For example, search can be replaced with investigate.

- Hyponym—the first word is an exact occurrence of the second word. For example, crimson and red.
- Hypernym—the second word is an exact occurrence of the first word. For example, Tablet and iPad.
- Meronym—the first word is a component part of the subsequent word. For example, foot and leg.
- Holonym—opposite to meronyms, the second word is a component part of the first word. For example, keyboard and keys.

2.12. Web Search Query Disambiguation

Web search query disambiguation involves the reformation and refinement of query search terms to remove ambiguity, better predict user intent, and return the most relevant search results to the user. Web search query disambiguation involves the following techniques [43] :

- Manual query modification—the user makes modification to the query by adding or removing search terms.
- Query expansion modification—search terms are added to the original query with the use of semantics.
- Query trimming modification—some query search terms are removed to improve query results.
- Conjunction and disjunction modification—the conjunction (AND) is used in the query to combine search terms and return exclusively unambiguous results; the disjunction (OR) is used to return inclusively generalized results.
- Substitution modification—query search terms are replaced with similar search terms using semantic techniques.
- Graph-based modification—graph theory techniques are used so documents are viewed as nodes in the graph, and query search terms are employed to return semantically relevant and related documents in the graph.

2.13. Web Search Query Reformation

As mentioned earlier, one of the most essential search engine tasks is to understand user intent and yield search results that are most pertinent to the user. Therefore, understanding query reformation provides a facet into how search engines "think", in regards to capturing user intent. To achieve this, search engines employ web search query improvement techniques, in which user queries are refined and modified to accurately capture user intent. However, search engines also take advantage of and store web search query reformations performed by the user, to correct errors, typos, and for modifications of the query for personalized results. While search engines might return better and more specific search results to the user, web search query reformation could be used as an attack against web search query obfuscation [49] [50] [51] [52]. When a user modifies an obfuscated query, it might be possible for the search engine to deduce the real query from dummy queries in such instances. Therefore, it would be essential to understand and consider query reformation techniques, and design suitable web query obfuscation methods. A taxonomy of web search query reformation was compiled by Huang and Efthimiadis (2009), on how search engines could use such categorization to improve web search results [53]. Huang and Efthimiadis (2009), outlined 13 categorizations of query reformation that a search engine could use to detect, estimate user intent, and offer better search results [53] : Word rearranging—words in the initial query are reordered but unchanged in the reformulated query. Whitespace and punctuation—whitespaces and punctuations are changed or removed in the reformulated query. Deleted words—some words are deleted from the initial query but the same words are kept in the reformed query. Supplemented words—extra words are added to the initial query. URL removal—the URL is removed from the query. Stemming? word stems are altered in a query. For example, jumping over boxes to jump over a box. Acronym formation—the query words are transformed into an acronym. For example, the United States of America is altered to USA. Acronym expansion—the modified query will have an expansion of the acronym that appeared in the initial query. Substring—the subsequent query is a rigid prefix or suffix of the initial query. For example, food restaurant is changed to food rest. Superstring—the subsequent query contains the initial query as a prefix or suffix. For example, food rest becomes food restaurants. Abbreviation—matching words in the initial query are a prefix of every word in the subsequent query. For example, higher sec is changed to high security. Word replacement—words in the initial query are replaced with semantically related words in the subsequent query. Spelling correction—the Levenshtein distance algorithm is used to predict the spelling correction a user would do in the subsequent query, by counting the number of characters between the two queries. If the Levenshtein distance is equal or less than two, the swapping takes place. For example, corection is replaced with correction. In so far as search query obfuscation is concerned, Huang and Efthimiadis (2009) observed that there exists classes of query reformations that are difficult for classifiers to detect [53]. These involve: Queries with semantic rephrasing—the more complex a query is rephrased, the harder it is to classify. Multi-reformations—reformation techniques used to modify the query. Classifying multi-reformation queries is difficult because they lack a commutative property. Subsequent queries can yield different results from the initial query [53].

2.14. User Intent Based Query Temporality

Generally search engines track users by generating a behavioral user profile based on the user's search history, using techniques such as, cookie tracking, browser preferences, IP address geo-location, and URL clicks [22] [54] [55]. However, one way to understand user intent in web search queries is to study time-related search words and search phrases in a submitted query. Since user intent can be deciphered by looking at the temporality of a web search query, temporality must be considered for better search query privacy. The intent of a query, as related to time, can be categorized as follows [56] [57] [58] :

- Implicit temporal intent—in which the user specifies no time data in the query phrase. For example, the "Olympics".
- Explicit temporal intent—whereby the user makes specific time reference in a query. For example, the "2016 Olympics".
- Queries with implicit temporal intent can be further broken down according to the following classifications [56] :
- Atemporal?queries that lack time information, e.g., "Olympic games";
- Temporal unambiguous—queries with specific time related information. For example, the "2012 Olympics";
- Temporal ambiguous—queries with unclear multiple time requests, i.e., a query, "Isaac Newton", may return his birthday and discovery times.

2.15. Search Query Classification and Paid Ads

Another aspect important for web search query obfuscation is query classification. Web search query classification is an ongoing research challenge that involves the grouping of user queries into specific categories so as to better predict user intent, retrieve the most relevant webpages for the user, and direct web advertisements to the appropriate audiences [23] [59] - [65]. It is estimated that the most popular queries only involve between 2.4 and 2.7 words, making it difficult to disambiguate and pinpoint user intent, due to the small amount of information contained in the queries [23]. The main goal of web search query classification is to disambiguate queries, pinpoint user intent, and accurately direct paid search results to users [23]. However, Gabrilovich et al. observed that the problem of query classification remains intractable due to the short composition of queries. Moreover, Gabrilovich et al., pointed out that since search engines catalog huge quantities of information and, in so doing, become storehouses of knowledge, it therefore makes sense to use web query search results to get an understanding which can lead to query interpretation [23].

3. AREAS FOR FURTHER INVESTIGATIVE STUDY IN WEB SEARCH PRIVACY

This section identifies areas for further study and investigative research. While some ongoing research covers potions of the proposed study areas listed below, we believe that the identified areas need further investigation, given the intractability and complexity involved in query ambiguity and disambiguation, and the trade-offs required to find the right balance between privacy and usability. The context here is that research could focus on non-cryptographic solutions that do not require the use of third party applications. Under the web search engines and web search query mechanism, we identified the following privacy challenges, as summarized in Table 1.

- Web search engine navigation privacy: Further study is needed into holistic privacy and usability techniques that take the web search engine navigation process into account, including, (i) query formulation, (ii) result selection, (iii) result navigation, (iv) and query reformulation.

- Employing paid and organic search results to enhance privacy: Studies could include how to use paid and organic search results as a measure of obfuscation effectiveness. For instance, if paid results accurately mirror the real query instead of the dummy query then we can infer that the search engine has deciphered and separated dummy queries from real queries.

- Precision and recall: Questions, such as how to improve the precision and recall of noisy web search queries with respect to user expectations and results, warrant further studies. A fruitful approach could involve the application of new or innovative statistical models and empirical application results.

- Obfuscated user profile generation: Investigations could be made into whether it is possible to generate pseudo-user profiles while offering more personalized search results. This line of research has the potential to offer privacy with improved usability for obfuscated user profiles.

- Web search query obfuscation: This remains an open area for further investigation. One study area asks how to generate privatized web search informational, navigational, and transactional queries with better usability. Transactional queries would be of most interest, especially with applications to transactional databases, such as Amazon and social networks.
- Types of search queries: Another open area ripe for study and investigation is the obfuscation of different types of queries. For example, studies could include obfuscating Boolean queries, privatizing keyword queries, a hybrid of concept such as keyword queries for obfuscation, and, most challenging, how to obfuscate natural language queries when real questions are asked.
- Semantic search and word sense disambiguation: While some significant work has been done, it remains open to further investigation due to the challenges involved in query disambiguation. Questions include how to find a balance, with trade-offs, between ambiguity and disambiguation needs during the query obfuscation process. Other investigations could focus on using mathematical and statistical modeling, natural language processing, graph-theory, and machine learning techniques for usability-aware web search query obfuscation.
- Privacy in web search query reformation: There is not much research in privacy in web search query reformation. Search engines spend considerable effort disambiguating queries, and data mining user intent, with every query reformation. More studies are needed on how to achieve privacy during web search query reformation. Questions could include how web search query reformation methods could be used in conjunction with privacy methods to implement obfuscation techniques pre or post reformation. These techniques could be broken down into off-line vs. real time obfuscated query reformation.
- Privacy of user intent in temporal queries: Temporal queries are vulnerable to information leakage due to date and time information in the query search terms. However, not much work has been done with respect to implementing privacy and obfuscation techniques for temporal queries. This is another area for investigation and study, with consideration to the usability of obfuscated temporal queries. If a user intended to search for "Honda 2015", in the original query, how would usability be attained in an obfuscated "Honda 2014" query?
- Web search query classification: Another area of study that has captured the interest of researchers, and is worth further investigation, is the classification of web search queries with the goal of capturing user intent. However, the classification of web search queries remains a challenge when privacy is considered. For example, is there a way to

obfuscate queries using both semantics and different query classifications?

Table 1. A summary of web search engine and query privacy challenges.

Web Search Engine and Query Functionalities	Privacy and Usability Challenges
1. *Web search engine navigation privacy*	Holistic privacy and usability approach to web search navigation using query formation and reformation plus result selection and navigation.
2. *Paid and organic search results*	Employing paid and organic search results as a measure/indicator of web search query obfuscation.
3. *Precision and recall*	Using precision, recall, and Page Rank to measure web search query obfuscation and usability.
4. *User profile generation*	Generation of obfuscated user profile with an acceptable level of search result usability.
5. *Web search queries*	Privacy and usability approaches to informational, transactional, and navigational queries.
6. *Types of search queries*	Privacy and usability methods, including hybrids—e.g. Boolean, concept and keyword queries.
7. *Semantic search and word sense disambiguation*	Privacy and usability approaches to semantic search using statistical, natural language processing, graph theory, and machine learning models.
8. *Web search query reformation*	How to achieve privacy and usability during web search query reformation. How can a user correct their query without revealing their intent?
9. *Temporal queries*	How can an acceptable level of usability be achieved with obfuscated temporal queries?
10. *Query classification*	How to obfuscate user intent with query classification. Methods to obfuscate search queries using both semantics and different classifications.

4. CONCLUSION

In this survey, we presented an overview of web search querying from the privacy perspective and identified areas that need further investigation insofar as web search query privacy is concerned. Covering all areas of web search querying is beyond this study's scope, but an effort was made to highlight key essentials to the formulating end-user search privacy techniques. An example of an area not covered in depth is the study of mathematical and statistical models for web search query and related obfuscation techniques, a subject left for further study. A second goal for this study was to review the material in a manner accessible to those outside computer science. The intent was to introduce knowledge of web search queries and search engines to enable non-computer scientists to approach web search query privacy innovatively. While there has been considerable research interest in web search query obfuscation, web search privacy remains a challenge with no proposed generalizable solution. Future work will include the study of mathematical and statistical models for web search query and related obfuscation techniques as we identified in the area that need web search query privacy innovation. Solutions tailored to specific domains might be more appropriate. For example, a specific search query obfuscation method for healthcare systems might not work well when making queries into social media postings. Additionally, addressing challenges of web search query privacy and usability in terms of human computer interaction will have to be considered for future work. For instance, one question could focus on how additional delay in processing web search query results after obfuscation could affect people's willingness to make the tradeoff between privacy and usability. Finally, researchers need to consider the computation and storage power of intelligent search engines. Search engines store search query logs and over time with ever-improving disambiguation and semantic techniques. It is believable that search engines can decipher user intent and separate dummy queries from real queries in many circumstances. Privacy researchers have to have techniques that can operate in the context of a smart search engine?one that combines artificial intelligence, natural language processing, high performance computing, etc. to decipher user intent. Research into obfuscation techniques that take into consideration such search engine dynamics are needed to further advance the web search query privacy domain.

ACKNOWLEDGEMENTS

We would like to acknowledge the Department of Computer Science at Norfolk State University for making this work possible.

REFERENCES

1. Zheleva, E.G. (2011) Privacy in Social Networks: A Survey. In: Social Network Data Analytics, 277-306.
2. Gotz, M., Machanavajjhala, A., Wang, G., Xiao, X. and Gehrke, J. (2012) Publishing Search Logs—A Comparative Study of Privacy Guarantees. IEEE Transactions on Knowledge and Data Engineering, 24, 520-532. https://doi.org/10.1109/TKDE.2011.26

3. Chen, T., Boreli, R., Kaafar, M.A. and Friedman, A. (2014) On the Effectiveness of Obfuscation Techniques in Online Social Networks. In: Privacy Enhancing Technologies, Vol. 8555 LNCS, 42-62.
4. Ruiz-Martínez, A. (2012) A Survey on Solutions and Main Free Tools for Privacy Enhancing Web Communications. Journal of Network and Computer Applications, 35, 1473-1492. https://doi.org/10.1016/j.jnca.2012.02.011
5. Toch, E., Wang, Y. and Cranor, L.F. (2012) Personalization and Privacy: A Survey of Privacy Risks and Remedies in Personalization-Based Systems. User Modeling and User-Adapted Interaction, 22, 203-220. https://doi.org/10.1007/s11257-011-9110-z
6. Pang, H., Xiao, X. and Shen, J. (2012) Obfuscating the Topical Intention in Enterprise Text Search. IEEE 28th International Conference on Data Engineering (ICDE), 1-5 April 2012, 1168-1179. https://doi.org/10.1109/icde.2012.43
7. Hillard, D., Schroedl, S., Manavoglu, E., Raghavan, H. and Leggetter, C. (2010) Improving ad Relevance in Sponsored Search. In: Proceedings of the third ACM International Conference on Web Search and Data Mining—WSDM'10, ACM, New York, 361-370. https://doi.org/10.1145/1718487.1718532
8. Cooper, A. (2008) A Survey of Query Log Privacy-Enhancing Techniques from a Policy Perspective. ACM Transactions on the Web, 2, 1-27.https://doi.org/10.1145/1409220.1409222
9. Arrington, M. (2006) AOL Proudly Releases Massive Amounts of Private Data. Techcrunch.com.
10. Barbaro, M. and Zeller Jr., T. (2006) A Face Is Exposed for AOL Searcher No. 4417749. The New York Times, p. C4.
11. Gao, X., Yang, Y., Fu, H., Lindqvist, J. and Wang, Y. (2014) Private Browsing: An Inquiry on Usability and Privacy Protection. Proceedings of the 13th Workshop on Privacy in the Electronic Society, Scottsdale, 3 November 2014, 97-106. https://doi.org/10.1145/2665943.2665953
12. Danezis, G. and Diaz, C. (2008) A Survey of Anonymous Communication Channels.
13. Reed, M.G., Syverson, P.F. and Goldschlag, D.M. (1998) Anonymous Connections and Onion Routing. IEEE Journal on Selected Areas in Communications, 16, 482-494. https://doi.org/10.1109/49.668972
14. Ren, J. and Wu, J. (2010) Survey on Anonymous Communications in Computer Networks. Computer Communications, 33, 420-431.https://doi.org/10.1016/j.comcom.2009.11.009
15. Gordon, M. and Pathak, P. (1999) Finding Information on the World Wide Web: The Retrieval Effectiveness of Search Engines. Information Processing and Management, 35, 141-180.
16. Brin, S. and Page, L. (1998) The Anatomy of a Large-Scale Hypertextual Web Search Engine. Computer Networks and ISDN Systems, 30, 107-117.
17. Ozcan, R., Altingovde, I.S., Cambazoglu, B.B., Junqueira, F.P. and Ulusoy, Ö. (2011) A Five-Level Static Cache Architecture for Web Search Engines. Information Processing & Management, 48, 828-840.
18. Chakrabarti, S., Berg, M. and Dom, B. (1999) Focused Crawling: A New Approach to Topic-Specific Web Resource Discovery. Computer Networks, 31, 1623-1640. https://doi.org/10.1016/S1389-1286(99)00052-3
19. Barroso, L.A., Dean, J. and Holzle, U. (2003) Web Search for a Planet: The Google Cluster Architecture. IEEE Micro, 23, 22-28.
20. Levene, M. (2010) An Introduction to Search Engines and Web Navigation. Wiley, Hoboken. https://doi.org/10.1002/9780470874233
21. Jansen, B.J. and Molina, P.R. (2006) The Effectiveness of Web Search Engines for Retrieving Relevant Ecommerce Links. Information Processing & Management, 42, 1075-1098. https://doi.org/10.1016/j.ipm.2005.09.003
22. Chen, Y., Pavlov, D., Canny, J.F. and Ave, H. (2009) Large-Scale Behavioral Targeting Categories and Subject Descriptors. Proceedings of the 15th ACM SIGKDD International Conference on Knowledge Discovery and Data Mining, Paris, 28 June-1 July 2009, 209-218. https://doi.org/10.1145/1557019.1557048

23. Gabrilovich, E., Broder, A., Fontoura, M., Joshi, A., Josifovski, V., Riedel, L. and Zhang, T. (2009) Classifying Search Queries Using the Web as a Source of Knowledge. ACM Transactions on the Web, 3, Article No. 5.https://doi.org/10.1145/1513876.1513877
24. Nunney, M. (2012) SEO Made Simple, Wordtracker's Free SEO Guide.
25. Speretta, M. and Gauch, S. (2005) Personalized Search Based on User Search Histories. Proceedings of the 2005 IEEE/WIC/ACM International Conference on Web Intelligence, Compiegne, 19-22 September 2005, 622-628.https://doi.org/10.1109/WI.2005.114
26. Sugiyama, K., Hatano, K. and Yoshikawa, M. (2004) Adaptive Web Search Based on User Profile Constructed without Any Effort from Users. Proceedings of the 13th Conference on World Wide Web, New York, 17-20 May 2004, 675-684. https://doi.org/10. 1145/ 988672.988764
27. Baeza-Yates, R. and Ribeiro-Neto, B. (1999) Modern Information Retrieval. ACM Press, New York.
28. Lee, W.M. and Sanderson, M., (2010) Analyzing URL Queries. Journal of the Association for Information Science and Technology, 61, 2300-2310.https://doi.org/ 10.1002/ asi.21407
29. Broder, A. (2002) A Taxonomy of Web Search. ACM SIGIR Forum, 36, 3-10. https://doi.org/10.1145/792550.792552
30. Ullah, M.Z. and Aono, M. (2014) Query Subtopic Mining for Search Result Diversification. IEEE International Conference of Advanced Informatics: Concept, Theory and Application (ICAICTA), Vol. 1, Bandung, 20-21 August 2014, 309-314.
31. Zamora, J., Mendoza, M. and Allende, H. (2014) Query Intent Detection Based on Query Log Mining. Journal of Web Engineering, 13, 24-52.
32. Egozi, O., Markovitch, S. and Gabrilovich, E. (2008) Concept-Based Information Retrieval using Explicit Semantic Analysis. ACM Transactions on Information Systems, 29, Article No. 8.
33. De Luca, E.W. and Scheel, C. (2013) Disambiguate Yourself. Translation: Computation, Corpora, Cognition, 3, 75-86.
34. Demidova, E., Zhou, X., Oelze, I. and Nejdl, W. (2010) Evaluating Evidences for Keyword Query Disambiguation in Entity Centric Database Search. 21th International Conference on Database and Expert Systems Applications, Bilbao, 30 August-3 September 2010, 240-247. https://doi.org/10.1007/978-3-642-15251-1_19
35. Pound, J. and Hudek, A.K. (2012) Interpreting Keyword Queries over Web Knowledge Bases. Proceedings of the 21st ACM International Conference on Information and Knowledge Management, Maui, 29 October-2 November 2012, 305-314.
36. Liu, B. (2007) Web Data Mining. Springer-Verlag, Berlin Heidelberg.
37. Croft, W.B. and Wei, X. (2005) Context-Based Topic Models for Query Modification.
38. Hristidis, V. (2009) Natural Language Queries Information Discovery on Electronic Health Records. CRC Press, Boca Raton.
39. Liu, Y., Song, R., Zhang, M., Dou, Z., Yamamoto, T., Kato, M., Ohshima, H. and Zhou, K. (2014) Overview of the NTCIR-11 IMine Task. Proceedings of the 11th NTCIR Conference, Vol. 14, Tokyo, 9-12 December 2014, 8-23.
40. Luo, C., Liu, Y., Zhang, M. and Ma, S. (2014) Query Ambiguity Identification Based on User Behavior Information. In: Jaafar, A., et al., Eds., Information Retrieval Technology, Springer International Publishing, Basel, 36-47.
41. Song, R., Luo, Z., Wen, J.-R., Yu, Y. and Hon, H.-W. (2007) Identifying Ambiguous Queries in Web Search. Proceedings of the 16th ACM International Conference on World Wide Web, Banff, 08-12 May 2007, 1169-1170.https://doi.org/10.1145/1242572.1242749
42. Wu, H., Wu, W., Zhou, M., Chen, E., Duan, L. and Shum, H.-Y. (2014) Improving Search Relevance for Short Queries in Community Question Answering. Proceedings of the 7th ACM International Conference on Web Search and Data Mining, New York, 24-28 February 2014, 43-52. https://doi.org/10.1145/2556195.2556239
43. Mangold, C. (2007) A Survey and Classification of Semantic Search Approaches. International Journal of Metadata, Semantics and Ontologies, 2, 23. https://doi.org/ 10.1504/IJMSO.2007.015073

44. Manning, C.D. and Schutze, H. (1999) Foundations of Statistical Natural Language Processing. MIT Press, Cambridge.
45. Guha, R., McCool, R. and Miller, E. (2003) Semantic Search. Proceedings of the 12th International Conference on World Wide Web, Budapest, 20-24 May 2003, 700-709. https://doi.org/10.1145/775152.775250
46. Bonino, D., Corno, F., Farinetti, L., Bosca, A., Torino, P. and Duca, C. (2004) Ontology Driven Semantic Search. Transactions on Information Science and Applications, 1, 1597-1605.
47. Navigli, R. (2009) Word Sense Disambiguation. ACM Computing Surveys, 41, Article No. 10. https://doi.org/10.1145/1459352.1459355
48. Miller, G.A. (1995) WordNet: A Lexical Database for English. Communications of the ACM, 38, 39-41. https://doi.org/10.1145/219717.219748
49. Dang, V., Croft, W.B. and Croft, B. (2010) Query Reformulation Using Anchor Text. Proceedings of the 3rd ACM International Conference on Web Search and Data Mining, New York, 4-6 February 2010, 41-50. https://doi.org/10.1145/1718487.1718493
50. Song, Y., Zhou, D. and He, L. (2012) Query Suggestion by Constructing Term-Transition Graphs. Proceedings of the 5th ACM International Conference on Web Search and Data Mining, Seattle, 8-12 February 2012, 353-362.https://doi.org/10.1145/ 2124295. 2124339
51. Gupta, M. and Bendersky, M. (2015) Information Retrieval with Verbose Queries. Proceedings of the 38th International ACM SIGIR Conference on Research and Development in Information Retrieval, Santiago, 9-13 August 2015, 1121-1124. https://doi.org/10.1145/2766462.2767877
52. Bing, L., Lam, W., Wong, T.-L. and Jameel, S. (2015) Web Query Reformulation via Joint Modeling of Latent Topic Dependency and Term Context. ACM Transactions on Information Systems, 33, Article No. 6. https://doi.org/10.1145/2699666
53. Huang, J. and Efthimiadis, E.N. (2009) Analyzing and Evaluating Query Reformulation Strategies in Web Search Logs. Proceeding of the 18th ACM Conference on Information and Knowledge Management, Hong Kong, 2-6 November 2009, 77-86. https://doi.org/ 10.1145/1645953.1645966
54. Hannak, A., Sapiezynski, P., Kakhki, A.M., Krishnamurthy, B., Lazer, D., Mislove, A. and Wilson, C. (2013) Measuring Personalization of Web Search. Proceedings of the 22nd International Conference on World Wide Web, Rio de Janeiro, 13-17 May 2013, 527-537. https://doi.org/10.1145/2488388.2488435
55. Liu, F., Yu, C. and Meng, W. (2004) Personalized Web Search for Improving Retrieval Effectiveness. IEEE Transactions on Knowledge and Data Engineering, 16, 28-40. https://doi.org/10.1109/TKDE.2004.1264820
56. Campos, R., Al, J. and Jorge, A.M. (2011) Using Web Snippets and Web Query-Logs to Measure Implicit Temporal Intents in Queries to Cite This Version: Using Web Snippets and Query-Logs to Measure Implicit Temporal Intents in Queries. ACM SIGIR 2011 Workshop on Query Representation and Understanding, New York.
57. Lin, S., Jin, P., Zhao, X. and Yue, L. (2014) Exploiting Temporal Information in Web Search. Expert Systems with Applications, 41, 331-341.https://doi.org/10.1016/ j.eswa.2013. 07.048
58. Xu, Z., Liu, Y., Mei, L., Hu, C. and Chen, L. (2014) Generating Temporal Semantic Context of Concepts Using Web Search Engines. Journal of Network and Computer Applications, 43, 42-55. https://doi.org/10.1016/j.jnca.2014.04.002
59. Jansen, B.J., Booth, D.L. and Spink, A. (2007) Determining the User Intent of Web Search Engine Queries. Proceedings of the 16th ACM International Conference on World Wide Web, Banff, 8-12 May 2007, 1149-1150. https://doi.org/10.1145/1242572.1242739
60. Ortiz-Cordova, A. and Jansen, B.J. (2012) Classifying Web Search Queries to Identify High Revenue Generating Customers. Journal of the American Society for Information Science and Technology, 63, 1426-1441. https://doi.org/10.1002/asi.22640
61. Rose, D.E. and Levinson, D. (2004) Understanding User Goals in Web Search. Proceedings of the 13th ACM International Conference on World Wide Web, New York, 17-20 May 2004, 13-19. https://doi.org/10.1145/988672.988675

62. Beitzel, S.M., Jensen, E.C., Frieder, O., Grossman, D., Lewis, D.D., Chowdhury, A. and Kolcz, A. (2005) Automatic Web Query Classification Using Labeled and Unlabeled Training Data. Proceedings of the 28th Annual International ACM SIGIR Conference on Research and Development in Information Retrieval, Salvador, 15-19 August 2005, 581-582. https://doi.org/10.1145/1076034.1076138
63. Agrawal, R., Yu, X., King, I. and Zajac, R. (2011) Enrichment and Reductionism: Two Approaches for Web Query Classification. Proceedings of 18th International Conference on Neural Information Processing, Vol. 7064, Shanghai, 13-17 November 2011, 148-157.
64. Broder, A.Z., Fontoura, M., Gabrilovich, E., Joshi, A., Josifovski, V. and Zhang, O. (2007) Robust Classification of Rare Queries Using Web Knowledge. Proceedings of the 30th Annual International ACM SIGIR Conference on Research and Development in Information Retrieval, Amsterdam, 23-27 July 2007, 231-238. https://doi.org/10.1145/1277741.1277783
65. Cao, H., Hu, D.H., Shen, D., Jiang, D., Sun, J.-T., Chen, E. and Yang, Q. (2009) Context-Aware Query Classification. The 32nd International ACM SIGIR Conference on Research and Development in Information Retrieval, Boston, 19-23 July 2009, 3-10.

CHAPTER 2

Architecture and Knowledge-Driven Self-Adaptive Security in Smart Space

Antti Evesti [1,*], Jani Suomalainen [2] and Eila Ovaska [1]

[1]*VTT Technical Research Centre of Finland, Kaitoväylä 1, 90571 Oulu, Finland*

[2]*VTT Technical Research Centre of Finland, Vuorimiehentie 3, 02044 Espoo, Finland*

ABSTRACT

Dynamic and heterogeneous smart spaces cause challenges for security because it is impossible to anticipate all the possible changes at design-time. Self-adaptive security is an applicable solution for this challenge. This paper presents an architectural approach for security adaptation in smart spaces. The approach combines an adaptation loop, Information Security Measuring Ontology (ISMO) and a smart space security-control model. The adaptation loop includes phases to monitor, analyze, plan and execute changes in the smart space. The ISMO offers input knowledge for the adaptation loop and the security-control model enforces dynamic access control policies. The approach is novel because it defines the whole adaptation loop and knowledge required in each phase of the adaptation. The contributions are validated as a part of the smart space pilot implementation. The approach offers reusable and extensible means to achieve adaptive security in smart spaces and up-to-date access control for devices that appear in the space. Hence, the approach supports the work of smart space application developers.

Keywords: architecture; authentication; authorization; ontology; self-adaptation

1. INTRODUCTION

The smart space trend has initiated several research projects and publications, from technologies to applications. Smart spaces—such as smart homes, smart buildings and smart cities—offer available information and devices for end-users' purposes without a pre-defined configuration or application behavior. Smart spaces are dynamic, and moreover, utilized technologies are heterogeneous. Consequently, it is not possible to envision all the possible situations where the smart space application will be utilized, which creates a challenge for software designers. Self-adaptation is a possibility to respond to this challenge by postponing decision making from design-time to runtime. Self-adaptation is a software's capability to configure and tune its functionality at runtime, in order to tackle changing situations. Challenges related to smart space security are complex—due to the dynamicity and heterogeneity of smart spaces. Firstly, the required security objectives vary between situations, e.g., sometimes integrity is the essential security objective but in other situations the user's privacy is the first priority. Secondly, the security needs of a smart space application vary between situations. For instance, an application utilizing entertainment or critical control information has variable requirements for security effectiveness, *i.e.*, for the security level. Thirdly, smart spaces change continuously, as new devices appear and leave. These devices must be able to use the smart space's available security mechanisms. However, the same security mechanisms are not applicable in all smart spaces. For example, one smart space may support only one particular authentication mechanism while another provides three different mechanisms.

These challenges demand an adaptive security solution that is able to change and modify the used security mechanisms autonomously at runtime. The importance of self-adaptation in smart spaces is also recognized in [1]. A reference model called MAPE-K (Monitor, Analyze, Plan and Execute) has been introduced as a solution for self-adaptation. This model is generic, *i.e.*, it can be applied for various quality and functionality adaptations, and thus it was selected as the reference model for security adaptation in this work. In the MAPE-K model, the Monitor collects information that is analyzed to recognize adaptation needs. Thereafter, the Plan phase creates an adaptation plan for execution. These four phases constitute an adaptation loop supported by knowledge. Currently, several security-adaptation approaches exist [2,3]. The first survey reveals that the existing security-adaptation approaches concentrate on specific security objectives. The second survey shows that the existing approaches have a lack in the adaptation loop coverage, *i.e.*, the approaches do not define the whole MAPE loop. Moreover, Yuan *et al.* note that the abstract architecture for security adaptation is not presented in the existing approaches [3]. These architecture-level problems complicate the reusability and extensibility of the existing security-adaptation approaches. The MAPE-K model separates knowledge from the adaptation loop. However, existing security-adaptation approaches do not support this separation but utilize hard-coded adaptation decisions, which is not sufficient in dynamic smart spaces. Moreover, smart spaces require flexible access control, which is able to handle the situations when new devices and information constantly appear in the smart space. However, the existing approaches are not able to offer this flexibility for dynamically changing access control needs.

This paper concentrates on architecture, knowledge and access control problems. Hence, the paper makes the following contributions: (1) Architecture for the security-adaptation loop is defined and mapped to the MAPE model. Hence, the architecture covers all the adaptation phases in a clearly defined form. The adaptation loop selects from the security mechanisms and configures the parameters of those mechanisms at runtime. (2) The knowledge is mapped to the security-adaptation architecture, in order to encompass the knowledge part of the MAPE-K reference model. In our solution, knowledge is made accessible to the security adaptation by means of ontologies. Compared with the existing approaches, our solution is novel because it makes it possible to minimize the amount of hard-coded knowledge and supports knowledge addition and modifications. (3) A runtime security-control model for dynamic authorization and access control is defined. The security-control model defines how shared information is effectively secured and controlled in smart spaces.

The novelty of contributions comes from the integration, which builds up the consistent security-adaptation architecture. The architecture covers all adaptation phases from monitoring to execution with dynamic access control. In contrast to the existing approaches, knowledge is separated from the architecture, and mappings from the architecture to knowledge are presented. Thus, the presented security adaptation does not require hard-coded rules for the analysis and planning phases because ontologies form the knowledge for the adaptation. Finally, the whole approach is validated as part of the wider smart space pilot implementation.

Background information and related work are described in Section 2. The whole adaptation approach is presented in Section 3. Section 4 describes the implementation of the approach by means of a use case. A discussion of the approach and future research are summarized in Section 5. Finally, the Conclusions Section closes the paper.

2. BACKGROUND AND RELATED WORK

2.1. Smart Spaces

Smart spaces are physical spaces where devices cooperate and share information to intelligently provide services for the users. Cook *et al.* define a smart environment as one that is able to acquire and apply knowledge about the environment and its inhabitants in order to improve their experience in that environment [4]. The terms smart space and smart environment are widely used interchangeably—this article uses the term smart space.

Cooperation and information sharing requires that devices and Smart Space Applications (SSAs) are able to interoperate. This interoperation is able to occur at different levels, which are called interoperability levels, defined in [5,6]. The presented interoperability levels from bottom to top are Connection, Communication, Semantic, Dynamic, Behavioral and Conceptual interoperability. The Connection interoperability level focuses on network connectivity, whereas the Communication level focuses on data syntax. However, these two lower-most interoperability levels are out of the scope of this paper. The Semantic interoperability level concentrates on understanding data from the communication level. Next, the Dynamic level focuses on context changes and the Behavioral level matches actions together. Finally, the Conceptual interoperability level focuses on abstracting; representing easy-to-use knowledge to the other interoperability levels, and making deductions based on data, context and actions. Thus, conceptual interoperability creates meaning from the information, context and behavior in the smart spaces. Hence, this is the level where the "smartness" is built for the smart space.

The SSA consists of a set of software agents that communicate and share information with each other. Therefore, the deployment of the SSA can be distributed to several smart space devices, *i.e.*, agents of the SSA are executed in different devices instead of one centralized device. These agents and the composed SSA act in dynamically changing smart spaces, which may offer a huge amount of information. Context-awareness is a means to handle this information flow in order to provide reasonable information and services for the user. Similarly, security in smart spaces requires context-awareness in order to provide reasonable security for different situations and actions. From the interoperability-level viewpoint, SSAs and context-awareness occur at the Dynamic and Behavioral levels.

Establishing a smart space requires an appropriate infrastructure—in this paper, the Smart-M3 concept [7] will be utilized. In the Smart-M3, the Semantic Information Broker (SIB) forms a backbone for the smart space. The SIB takes care of information sharing between agents—called Knowledge Processors (KPs). Agents are able to make queries and subscriptions, and insert semantic information in the SIB. Consequently, various devices are able to interoperate, *i.e.*, share semantic information, by means of the SIB and agents inside devices, as illustrated in Figure 1. The SIB utilizes semantic web technologies—especially Resource Description Framework (RDF) [8] and SPARQL query language. From the interoperability-level point of view, the SIB embodies the Semantic Interoperability level. In the Sofia project [9], three different Smart-M3 concept implementations were made for different usages. This paper utilizes the implementation called RIBS [10], which contains mechanisms to secure communication and is able to work in resource-restricted devices—such as a WLAN access point.

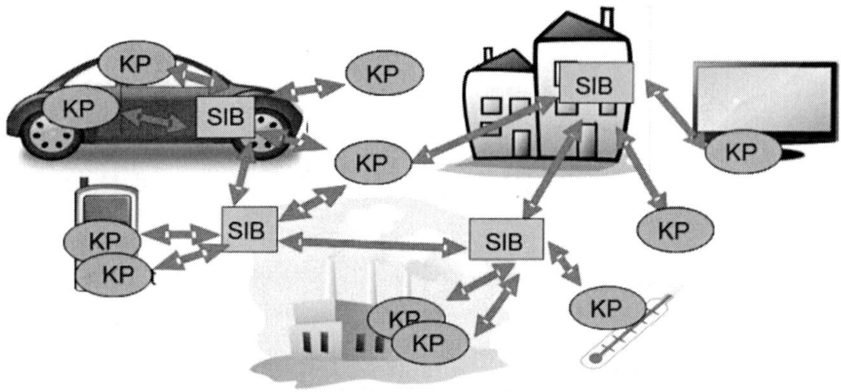

Figure 1. Smart spaces formed by Semantic Information Brokers (SIBs) and Knowledge Processors (KPs).

Security challenges caused by the dynamicity and heterogeneity of smart spaces are mentioned above. Moreover, traditional security challenges, e.g., key exchange and resource restrictions, are present in the smart spaces. Similarly, openness and free utilization, which are characteristics of smart spaces, affect security. Nevertheless, this paper focuses on security challenges due to dynamicity and heterogeneity by presenting a security-adaptation approach with a dynamic access control.

2.2. Security Adaptation

Kephart *et al.* define autonomic computing as computing systems that can manage themselves by using high-level objectives given by administrators [11]. The autonomic element contains the MAPE-K control loop composed of the Monitor, Analyze, Plan and Execute phases, supported by Knowledge. A similar structure is also applied in [12,13] as a reference model for autonomic computing. However, the names of the phases vary. For instance, Dobson *et al.* use the terms Collect, Analyze, Decide and Act [12]. In contrast, Psaier *et al.* define a control loop that joins the Analyze and Plan phases into one Diagnosing phase [14]. The loop concentrates on self-healing, which is a form of autonomic computing.

However, in this paper the MAPE-K loop will be utilized as a reference architectural model. The terms autonomic computing, self-management and self-adaptive are utilized interchangeably for instance in [13,15]. This article utilizes the term self-adaptive and its short-form adaptive to refer to software's ability to adapt itself at runtime. Adaptability has been defined as the ability of software to adapt its functionality according to the environment and user [16]. From the security viewpoint, functionality means security mechanisms intended to support the required security objectives.

Elkhodary *et al.* survey four approaches to adaptive security in [2]—namely Extensive Security Infrastructure [17], Strada Security API [18], Willow Architecture [19] and the Adaptive Trust Negotiation Framework (ATNAC) [20]. Moreover, the recent survey from Yuan and Malek [3] compares over 30 self-protection approaches. The extensible Security Adaptation Approach (ESAF) distinguishes security mechanisms from the application to the middleware layer [21]. Hence, the application communicates the required security to the middleware without any knowledge of the used security mechanism. In contrast, Context-sensitive adaptive authentication utilizes context information to replace static authentication mechanisms [22]. Hence, in situations where a lower authentication level is sufficient it is possible to utilize other attributes, e.g., location-based authentication, instead of passwords. The GEMOM (Genetic Messaging-Oriented Secure Middleware)—covered also in [3]—offers self-healing and adaptation features to ensure optimal security strength and uninterrupted operation in changing environments and threats [23]. The GEMOM applies the Monitoring part of the MAPE-K model by means of security measuring [24].

In the security adaptation, the Monitoring phase utilizes security measuring or observes events that affect security. Security measures can be produced by means of the decomposition approach, where security objectives are divided into smaller parts until the measurable components are found [25]. Garcia *et al.* presented a similar technique for generic software measurement in [26] by categorizing measures as Base Measures, Derived Measures and Indicators. Base Measures represent raw measures, which are further composed into Derived Measures. Indicators are on the highest abstraction level—and are able to compose Base Measures, Derived Measures and other Indicators. Figure 2 illustrates the structure of these measures.

The indicator for the particular security objective is on the highest level. The Indicator is derived from the Derived measures, Base Measures and other indicators. Structuring measures hierarchically ensures that measures can be reused and extended. Hence, security measures will be applied to Monitoring in this article. The Monitoring phase uses base measures. The results of the base measures are composed in the Analysis phase to reveal the current security level.

The Analyze phase utilizes monitoring results. However, it is not enough to know the current security level but the required security level also has to be known. The required security level can be defined at design-time, or alternatively, the Analyze phase can reason the required level at runtime. Deciding on an appropriate security requirement set is a challenging task. Defining security requirements for design-time purposes is extensively covered in [27]. The presented security requirements engineering framework takes into account assets, threats, business goals, and system context. All these aspects can be modeled in order to achieve the most extensive security adaptation approach.

For example, Salehie *et al.* [28] concentrate on the variability of assets and how this affects security, and how adaptive security is able to deal with these challenges. This is an important viewpoint and starts from assets, which initially set the requirements for all security. It is said that an asset is an entity that someone places value upon [29], and thus, it needs protection. However, we do not model requirements and assets in this granularity. On the contrary, we will utilize context information to recognize the importance and role of handled data, *i.e.*, asset value, which in turn leads to required securities.

Many uncertainties relate to security, and thus, getting accurate numbers to describe security for adaptation purposes is challenging. Sahinoglu [30] utilizes variance values to cover uncertainties in risk analysis. Similarly, in security adaptation, results from monitoring and analysis contain variance in some range.

Uncertainties affect the achieved security and the recognized adaptation need but uncertainties do not affect security adaptation architecture or the utilization of knowledge itself. Thus, these uncertainties are out of the scope of this article.

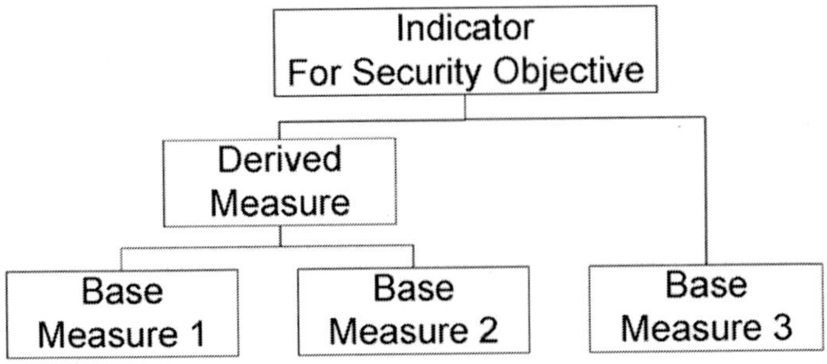

Figure 2. The Structure of Measures.

2.3. Adaptation Knowledge from Ontologies

The MAPE-K model does not define how the knowledge has to be offered. However, in order to follow the separation of the concerns principle, we introduce knowledge as a separately identifiable architectural element by utilizing ontology orientation to represent a self-sufficient model of security concepts. Ontology can be defined as a shared knowledge standard or knowledge model, defining primitive concepts, relations, rules and their instances, which comprise topic knowledge. It can be used for capturing, structuring and enlarging explicit and tacit topic knowledge across people, organizations and computer and software systems [31]. Several security ontologies have been listed in [32]. In addition, our earlier work [33] compared security ontologies from the runtime applicability and measuring viewpoints. Ontologies, designed for runtime usage, often concentrate on the service discovery and matchmaking, e.g., ontologies in [34,35]. However, these ontologies do not cover security measuring. In contrast, Savolainen *et al.* [36] present a security taxonomy for design time usage, which also contains a high-level security measuring part. At the moment, the most extensive security ontology is proposed by Herzog *et al.* [37], known as Ontology of Information Security (OIS). The OIS contains over 250 concepts, which describe security threats, countermeasures, assets and security goals, *etc.* In this paper, security goals and countermeasures are called security objectives and mechanisms, respectively. The OIS lists the following security objectives: confidentiality, integrity, availability, authentication, accountability, anonymity, authenticity, authorization, correctness, identification, non-repudiation, policy compliance, secrecy and trust. Nevertheless, the OIS does not contain a security-measuring part. In contrast, Garcia *et al.* presented the measurement terminology in an ontology form called Software Measurement Ontology (SMO) in [26]. Consequently, we have combined the Information Security Measuring Ontology (ISMO) from OIS and SMO in [38]. The ISMO makes it possible to present security measures via a common vocabulary and map defined measures to security concepts, e.g., security objectives and mechanisms. In the ISMO, security measures are defined in detail—containing descriptions on how the particular measuring has to be performed and how the base measures can be further combined into indicators. Hence, the ISMO offers knowledge for design-time and runtime purposes, e.g., what kind of measuring probe to implement at design time and how to utilize measuring results at runtime. This paper utilizes knowledge from the ISMO. Furthermore, context knowledge is vital for security adaptation, in order to describe an environment and user actions. For this purpose, we utilize the Context Ontology for Smart Spaces (CO4SS) [39] in this paper. In [40] we defined the taxonomy of context information for security. The taxonomy maps security-related context information to physical, digital and situation context levels. The physical context describes an infrastructure where the SSA is running. The digital context presents the role of the smart space, e.g., public space. Finally, the situation context describes the user's role and activity within the smart space. Moreover, the role of the exchanged/stored data is described in the situation context.

Our earlier work in [41] presented ontology-based security adaptation. In that work, risk-based security measures were stored in the ontology to support security monitoring. Moreover, the ontology contained knowledge about how much each security mechanism decreases the particular security risk, which supports the Planning phase. In [40] we presented a micro-architecture for security adaptation. However, in that architecture the ontology usage was tightly coupled inside the architecture. In this article, the architecture is developed towards the MAPE-K reference model and the ontologies will be separated out to their own interoperability level, *i.e.*, to the Conceptual level.

2.4. Access Control over Semantic Information

To control access to shared semantic information, fine-grained authorization models have been introduced for RDF. These approaches include approaches where access control is implemented as an additional layer on top of the repository, as in [42], and approaches where access-control information has also been integrated into repositories. In the triple-level access control [43], RDF resources are protected with access-restriction properties. Essentially, these properties are links to access policy graphs that specify the owner of the RDF resource as well as those predicates to which this protection applies.

Some researchers have proposed models where RDF-level access control decisions are implicitly derived from existing higher-level policies and context information. The policy-based access control model [44] uses metadata to define permit or prohibit conditions. Jain and Farkas [45] introduce an access-control model where RDF class hierarchy is utilized to manage and derive access control policies. Flourish *et al.* [46] propose a high-level policy-specification language for annotation RDF triples with access-control information. Moreover, approaches for access-control reasoning, based on concepts and their relations represented by ontologies, have been introduced by Kim *et al.* [47] and Cho *et al.* [48].

However, none of these reasoning solutions are directly applicable for smart spaces. In smart spaces, access control is enforced by information-brokering devices, which are not aware of application-specific policies. Also, semantic reasoning for real-time security control is a challenging task as the reasoning problems are, at the worst case, only solvable in exponential time with respect to the input size [49,50]. Consequently, to enable real-time security enforcement, efficient and scalable solutions are needed. These solutions should enable smart spaces to support different reasoning applications, which may be based on expressive and complex security ontologies.

Our earlier work defined solutions [10,51] for securing communication between smart space devices and controlling information sharing. In [51], we proposed an RDF node-level access-control model for a semantic information broker. The model is simpler than other RDF access-control models as each security policy can be expressed using a single RDF triplet and, in an optimized implementation, be presented with a single bit. In this article, the model is formally defined and generalized, and its granularity is enlarged to protect semantic relationships in addition to semantic information.

2.5. From Quality Variability to Quality Adaptation

In our approach, building a capability for quality adaptation begins at design-time. Consequently, our earlier work combines quality-, model-, and knowledge-driven software development. Our previous work presented the quality-variability model [52]. The variability model defines binding times for variations, *i.e.*, design, assembly, start-up and runtime, which defines the latest time point when quality can be changed. This work concentrates on the situation where security variation occurs at runtime—called security adaptation. Quality variability is closely related to architectures, and thus, the approach for the knowledge-based quality-driven architecture design and evaluation was presented in [53]. The approach contains three steps: (1) Modeling the quality requirement. (2) Modeling the software architecture and transforming the requirements to the models. (3) Quality evaluation. Steps one and two are divided into the knowledge and software engineering processes, whereas step three is divided into the quantitative and qualitative evaluation processes. In that study, quality ontologies for reliability and security were utilized as a knowledge base. Now, we will also bring ontology-based knowledge from design-time for automatic runtime usage.

Lastly, the design steps to produce an application with security adaptation features were presented [54]. The following steps were recognized: (1) Required security objectives—defines all security objectives for the application. (2) Adaptive security objectives—selects objectives, which will be adapted at runtime. (3) Mechanism variants for the selected objectives—selecting security mechanisms and their parameters, which can be adapted at runtime. (4) Measurements for triggering adaptation—selecting security measurements to monitor the adaptation needs of the selected security objectives. (5) Architecture design—designing the selected security mechanisms and measurements into the application architecture in a way that supports runtime adaptation. The contribution of this paper relates to step five, *i.e.*, presenting security-adaptation architecture and mapping it to the knowledge retrieved from the ontologies.

3. THE CONCEPT FOR ADAPTIVE SECURITY

The security-adaptation approach is presented in this section. Firstly, we give an overview of the approach, and thereafter, each part of the approach is presented in its own sub-section. The approach is not bound to any particular security objective or security mechanism. Nevertheless, the approach contains all the necessary components required to build adaptive security for smart spaces. The presented concept is instantiated by means of a case study in Section 4. The case study illustrates the approach from the authentication and authorization viewpoints.

The adaptation approach combines solutions from different interoperability levels. Figure 3 illustrates the proposed solutions—mapped to the interoperability levels and design-time and runtime phases. Sub-Sections 3.1–3.3 concentrate on these levels one-by-one.

Knowledge, required in security adaptation, is set on the Conceptual interoperability level. The knowledge is described with ontologies—namely the Information Security Measuring Ontology (ISMO) and the Context Ontology for Smart Spaces (CO4SS). Hence, security- and context-related knowledge is offered to other interoperability levels from the Conceptual level at runtime. Ontology-based knowledge ensures that smart space applications (SSA) are able to understand security and context situations in a uniform way. Moreover, the architect utilizes knowledge from ontologies at design-time to implement the appropriate monitoring probes and adaptation actions for the SSA, *c.f.*, connections from ontologies to Monitoring probes and Adaptation actions in Figure 3. In other words, these components are specific for the designed SSA. In contrast, the Analyzer and Planner components search required knowledge at runtime.

The security-adaptation loop—based on the MAPE reference model—and the SSA are located on the Behavioral and Dynamic interoperability levels. The architect designs and implements the required software components at design-time. These components are as follows: Pure application logic, monitoring probes, security mechanisms with adaptation actions, analyzer and planner. The adaptation logic is located in the Planner component. However, the architecture does not dictate the utilized adaptation logic, *i.e.*, the internal functionality of the Planner component. The plan phase is described in Subsection 3.2.3. At runtime, the SSA utilizes monitoring probes to observe security and context changes. The Analyzer component analyses the consequences of the changes based on knowledge retrieved from the ontologies at runtime. Sequentially, the Plan component creates an adaptation plan for responding to changes. Finally, the adaptation plan is enforced by the executors. In the security adaptation these executors are the selected security mechanisms. For example, "a new mobile device has arrived in the smart space" is a change observed by means of monitoring. The SSA analyzes the security consequences of a new device and decides how to adapt to this change. Adaptation actions can, e.g., affect information sharing on the semantic level or reset the communication parameters.

On the Semantic interoperability level, the RIBS constitutes the smart space infrastructure. The RIBS takes care of information sharing between smart space devices and SSAs. Hence, various devices are able to interoperate via the RIBS by sharing semantic information, which is presented by means of RDF. The Semantic level has to contain security solutions, which protect and control the sharing of semantic information. Therefore, we propose a semantic level security-control model to enable efficient access control. The security-control model enables SSAs to prepare security policies so that the RIBS does not have to support complex ontologies or perform runtime security reasoning. Applications requesting and providing information must unambiguously define the semantics of shared information. However, the presented dynamic access control ensures that variations are handled at runtime, without design-time rules.

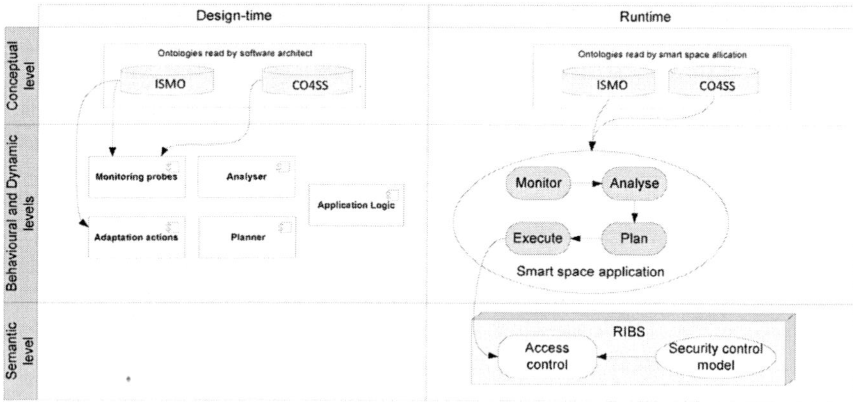

Figure 3. Interoperability levels and proposed solutions.

At this point, it is necessary to emphasize the difference between semantic and conceptual interoperability levels. However the semantic technologies, *i.e.*, RDF and OWL, are applied on both levels the difference comes from the abstraction level of the knowledge. The Semantic level contains separated pieces of information, e.g. temperature is minus five or a password length is seven characters. In contrast, the Conceptual level makes it possible to deduct the causes of the semantic information, e.g., water will freeze or the authentication level is low.

3.1. Security Adaptation Concepts from Ontologies

The right knowledge is an essential part of the security adaptation. In our solution, knowledge will be offered from the Conceptual interoperability level by means of ontologies. Ontologies make it possible to update and extend the existing knowledge. Moreover, ontologies support reusability and offer knowledge in a machine-readable form. Knowledge requirements for the security adaptation are threefold, *c.f.*, Figure 4. Firstly, security knowledge is needed to describe security mechanisms, security objectives, threats and their relationships. Secondly, measuring concepts are needed to monitor the achieved security, *i.e.*, the current and/or past security. Thirdly, context knowledge is needed to describe the state of the smart space from situational, digital and physical viewpoints. The situational context is intended to describe the user's role in the smart space and the role of the exchanged/stored data. In contrast, the digital context depicts the role of the smart space. Lastly, the physical context presents the execution platform and smart space infrastructure. The knowledge is arranged in two separate ontologies, *i.e.*, ISMO [38] and CO4SS [39], which together contain over 300 concepts and their connections. The ISMO describes security and measuring knowledge, while CO4SS contains context knowledge.

Figure 4 summarizes the main dependencies of these ontologies, and thus, it contains only the main concepts. The additional concepts and connections are presented in Figure 6, Figure 7, Figure 8, Figure 9, Figure 10 in Subsection 3.2. It is notable that the content in Figure 4 is laid in the conceptual level in Figure 3 (the highest level). The context knowledge from the CO4SS sets the required security objectives and levels. For example, dealing with professional information in an office environment has different security requirements than handling the same information in a public environment, which may contain additional threats. The ISMO describes which security mechanism supports the particular security objective and how the security objectives mutually relate. However, the applicable mechanisms depend on the physical context of the smart space, which describes the execution platform and operating system. For instance, the used operating system supports only a particular security mechanism, therefore, in Figure 4 the Physical context is connected to Security mechanisms with an offers connector.

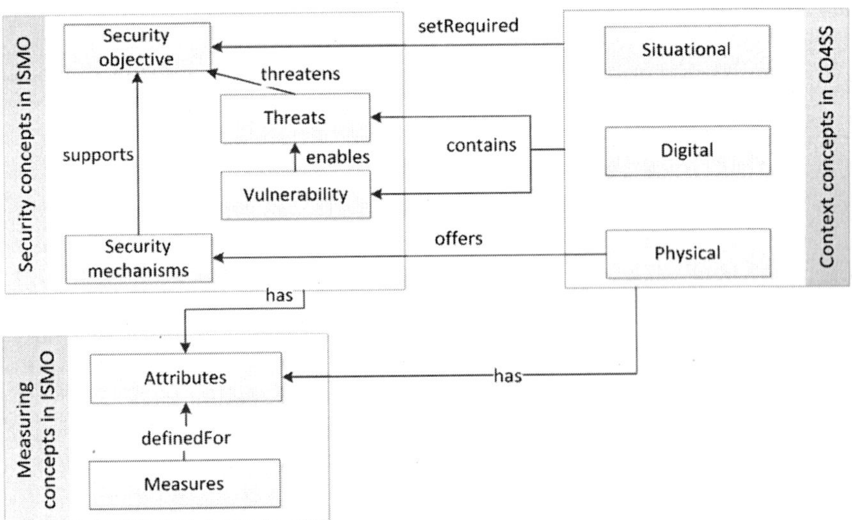

Figure 4. Dependencies of security and context ontologies.

Triggering the security adaptation requires that both security and context concepts are monitored. The monitoring focuses on measurable attributes (attribute), and thus, security and context are connected to the Attribute, *c.f.*, Figure 4. In Figure 4, the connections to Attribute start from the

Security concepts and Context concepts frames, which means that all of those concepts can contain measurable attributes. Examples of attributes are a key length from the security side and the number of smart space devices from the context side. Naturally each attribute contains its own measures.

Figure 3 shows that knowledge from ontologies is utilized at design-time and runtime alike. At design-time, the software architect implements a set of monitoring probes, which require knowledge of the measures. Moreover, the architect searches which security mechanisms to implement from ISMO. Additional details of the design-time use of ISMO are presented in [38,53]. At runtime, the SSA automatically utilizes knowledge from the ISMO. The application has to know what measures to utilize, how to analyze results, and finally, how to create an adaptation plan. These knowledge requirements are described in detail in the following sections.

Smart spaces create a need to update knowledge every now and then. There can be several reasons for updates: new security mechanisms appear, vulnerabilities are found, the threat landscape changes or the execution environment changes. The SSA has to be aware of these changes, which is ensured by up-to-date knowledge. Utilizing ontologies as the knowledge source offers an advantage from a knowledge updating and enhancement view point. ISMO and CO4SS are presented in an OWL format, and thus, updates can be made to ontologies without modifying SSAs, which only retrieve knowledge from ontologies.

3.2. Architecture for Security Adaptation

The security-adaptation approach follows the MAPE model. The Monitor phase collects information by means of monitoring probes. The Analyze phase calculates the security level achieved, reasons the required security level, and calls the Plan phase if the required securities are not achieved. The Plan phase creates a plan to adapt, and finally, the Execute phase enforces the adaptation plan. The following descriptions of these phases show, how they utilize knowledge from the Conceptual interoperability level. Figure 5 presents a legend for figures used in the next sections.

3.2.1. Monitor

The Monitor phase gathers information from the environment and the SSA itself. The purpose of monitoring is to collect those small information pieces, which are then utilized to reveal an adaptation need. The target of monitoring can be at any level—from a low-level network technology to a high—level description of the user situation. These monitoring targets are called attributes-the encryption key length and the number of unknown devices in the smart space are examples of monitored attributes. Monitoring utilizes security measures, and thus, the measuring related terminology is utilized in the Monitoring phase. The Monitor phase uses Base measures to collect raw data by means of Monitoring probes. It is notable that Figure 4 presents the Measure concept, and the Base measure is one subclass of the Measure.

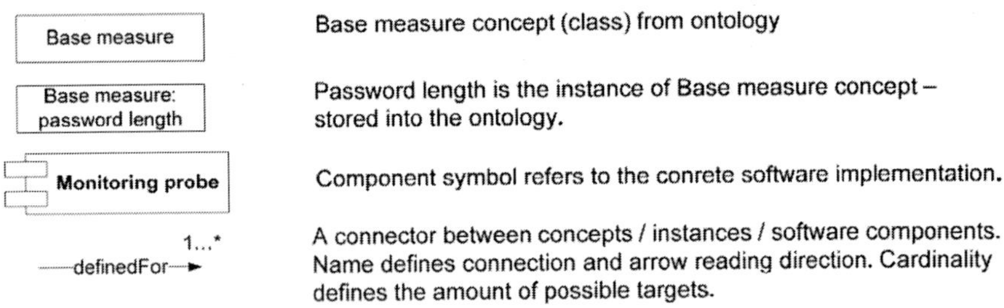

Figure 5. Symbol definitions.

At design time, the software architect implements Monitoring probes into the SSA and environment based on the Measurement method descriptions from the ISMO, *c.f.*, Figure 6. If the architect creates a new Base measure and Monitoring probe, knowledge about what attribute the probe measures is added into the ISMO. The Monitoring probe is a concrete code snippet, which is able to observe the particular attribute, e.g., by retrieving a key length from the utilized encryption library. In other words, the Monitoring probe is the implementation of the Measurement method. Each Monitoring probe is intended to observe only one attribute from the environment or SSA. Therefore, implemented probes can be easily reused.

Figure 6 depicts knowledge from the ISMO, *i.e.*, the Conceptual level, and its relation to the SSA and the environment in the Monitoring phase. The SSA and environment contain several attributes and each attribute has its own Monitoring probe implementation. At runtime, the ISMO provides knowledge about useful Base measures.

The environment contains several probes but only a certain set is needed in each particular situation. For instance, in a situation where communication integrity is not needed it is useless to utilize integrity-related Base measures. Hence, the knowledge from the ISMO reveals which probes to use. Consequently, it is vital that the ISMO contains the connections depicted in Figure 6 because that information shows what attribute each probe is able to measure.

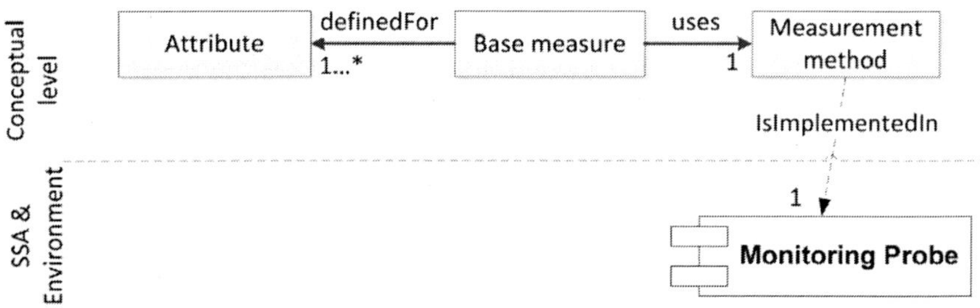

Figure 6. Knowledge from the Information Security Measuring Ontology (ISMO) for the Monitoring phase.

3.2.2. Analyze

The Analyze phase reveals the current security levels for the required security objectives and decides which levels are sufficient for the current situation. Hence, the Analyze phase combines the Base measure results from the Monitoring phase to Indicators. The Indicator presents the security level of the security objective in that particular smart space situation. In other words, Base measures indicate that some changes have occurred in the smart space, whereas, the Analyze phase reveals the consequences of these changes, *i.e.*, it builds a meaning for the information in that situation.

The ISMO contains Derived measures and Indicators, which combine the Base measure results. Base measures, Derived measures and Indicators are sub-classes of the Measure concept, depicted in Figure 4. The ISMO follows a terminology defined in [26], and thus, Derived measures use the Measurement function and Indicators use Analysis models to perform the combining process. The Measurement function can be a simple mathematical operation, e.g., base_measure_1 + base_measure_2. In contrast, Analysis models contain more complex structures including conditional clauses and Boolean operations. For instance, the result from the Analysis model can be the integrity level of communication.

Figure 7 shows concepts for the Analyze phase from the ISMO. Each indicator has Analysis models, which use Base measures, Derived measures and Indicators. Every Security objective has its own Indicator—e.g., authentication is a security objective, which has an Indicator called the authentication level. However, the Indicator is able to use several Analysis models, depending on the situation in hand. For example, a different Analysis model has to be used when authentication is based on fingerprints, passwords or a multi-factor authentication mechanism. In the multi-factor authentication case, the Analysis model, which combines analysis models from a single mechanism, is applied. Therefore, each Analysis model has a property that binds it to the security mechanism—from the above example, multi-factor authentication is seen as an individual security mechanism. Similarly as the Base measures, Indicators are also defined for Attributes. At design-time, the architect brings the Analyzer component into the SSA and the Analyzer component searches knowledge from the Analysis models to calculate security-level indicators for the SSA at runtime.

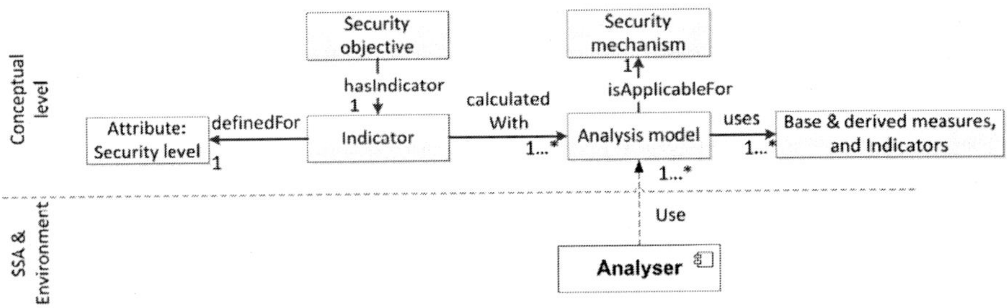

Figure 7. The concepts from the ISMO for the Analyze phase.

The security level indicators are compared to the required security levels. As depicted in Figure 4, the context information sets the required security objectives and levels. In [40], we defined the context concepts, which affect the required security as follows: (i) The user's role in the smart space. (ii) The actions performed in the smart space. (iii) The role and importance of the data. (iv) The role of the smart space. Furthermore, user preferences are able to affect the required security level.

Figure 8 shows the context information rules that define the required authentication level for different situations. However, the rule sets are an example—not the extensive rule sets to define authentication requirements. In these rules, the role of the smart space, *i.e.*, Private, Public or Office, constitutes the main categorization between the rule sets. In the private smart space, e.g., home smart space, the role of the data and its importance define how strong authentication has to be used. Thus, in a situation where the user consumes entertainment data—like news—authentication level 1 is sufficient. However, in a situation where the high importance level control information is handled, e.g., a home alarm system, authentication level 4 is required. In contrast, in public smart spaces, like freely available smart city services, authentication is not required at all. Finally, in an office smart space the user's action is also taken into account in the rules.

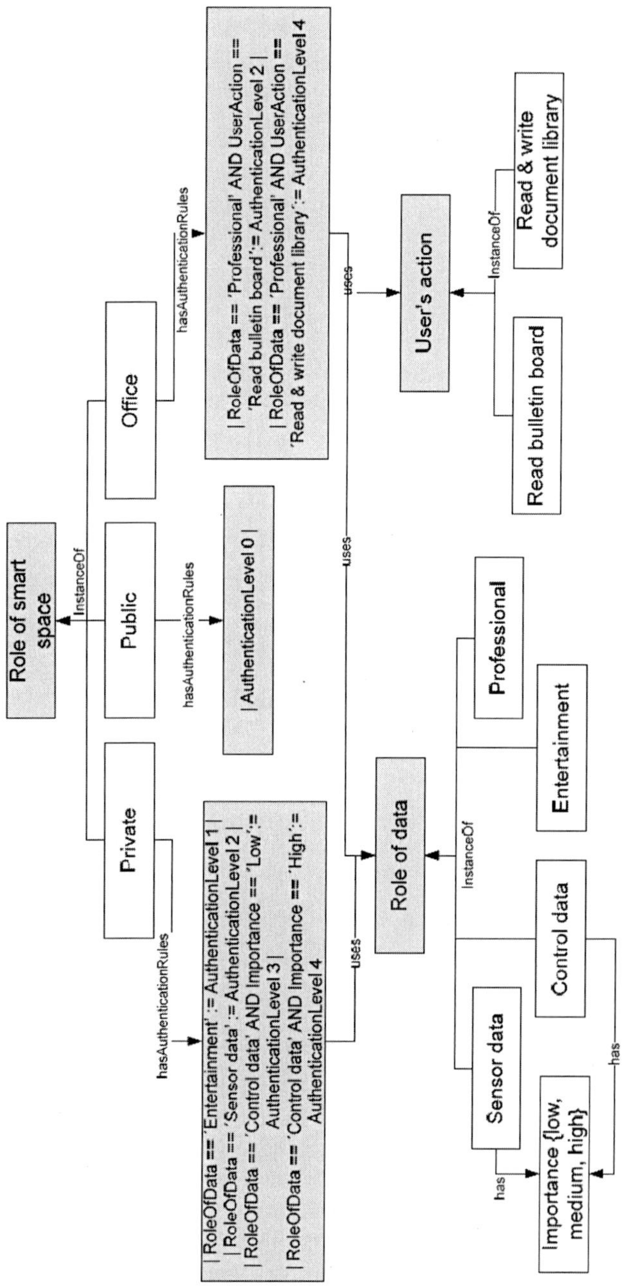

Figure 8. An example of context information to define security objectives and levels.

Similar context-based rule sets can be defined for other security objectives, *i.e.*, confidentiality, integrity, availability, *etc*. Based on these rules, the SSA is aware of the required security objectives and levels in different situations.

The final step in the Analyze phase is to compare the Indicator results to the required security objectives and levels. If some indicators show that the required security level is not achieved, the Planning phase will be triggered.

As a whole, the Analyze phase requires a lot of knowledge, which is available from the ontologies. Based on the knowledge, the SSA builds an individual view point of the environment and achieved security. In order to produce the correct results, knowledge maintenance is important. Analysis models and the rule sets for the definition of requirements can be added and updated without modifying the application logic. The utilization of ontologies makes this flexibility possible, *i.e.*, the knowledge is not hard coded inside the application.

3.2.3. Plan

The Plan phase decides how to adapt the SSA when the required securities are not achieved. The Plan phase uses the results from the Analyze phase as input information, *i.e.*, (i) the unfulfilled security objective. (ii) The current and required security level. (iii) The used security mechanism. Furthermore, ontologies offer knowledge to make an adaptation plan. In some situations, only certain security mechanisms are supported, and thus, the Plan phase has to take these restrictions into account.

We have recognized three alternative ways to create the adaptation plan:

1) SSA utilizes pre-defined configuration alternatives.

2) SSA searches alternative security mechanisms or individual attributes to adapt, based on knowledge from the ISMO.

3) SSA asks the user how to proceed.

The first one is the simplest case. At design-time, the architect implements configuration alternatives inside the SSA. Thus, the Plan phase selects one of these pre-defined configurations at runtime. Naturally, dynamism is restricted in this alternative. However, this is enough for simple devices and applications. As an example, for a situation where the required level of communication confidentiality is not achieved, the pre-defined configuration can be *"Start to use the TLS connection"*.

The second planning alternative changes the security mechanism or adapts individual attributes. When changing the whole security mechanism, the Planner component searches alternative mechanisms from the ISMO. In the ISMO, each security mechanism contains a link to the supported security objectives. For the required security objective, the ISMO can contain several security mechanisms. However, it is probable that only few of those are applicable in the current situation. For instance, the user's device supports fingerprint authentication but the smart space infrastructure does not offer this possibility. Hence, the adaptation plan has to take into account these restrictions from the context information. Alternatively, the Planner component can adapt individual attributes. To achieve this, the SSA searches the causes for the current security level by means of the same Analysis model, which showed that the adaptation was needed. In other words, the Analysis model is used to search Attributes, which have affected the current security level. Therefore, the SSA knows which attribute to adapt in order to affect the security level. Figure 9 illustrates this alternative—colored rectangles refer to the concepts presented in Figure 4. The Analysis model uses Base measures to observe Attributes. If the Attribute can be adapted its *adaptableWith* property shows an action for how to adapt the Attribute. The smart space may contain attributes that affect the achieved security level but all of these cannot be adapted. For instance, if the smart space contains an external threat that cannot be removed other attributes have to be adapted to mitigate threat effects. Finally, the Planner component decides on the adapted Attribute and the Action to be performed. To make this decision the Planner component may utilize goal, constraint or utility function based decision-making. At the moment, our approach is clearly goal orientated, *i.e.*, the context sets the required security objectives and levels (goals) and the purpose of the planning is to find a configuration that satisfies the goal.

However, the decision-making algorithm is out of the scope of this paper but the architecture does not restrict decision-making algorithms utilized internally in the Planner component. When the Planner has to take trade-offs into account more sophisticated decision making will be needed, for instance for utility functions.

The third case is for a situation where the SSA is not able to create an enforceable adaptation plan. The following reasons can lead to this alternative: (i) The required knowledge is not defined in the ontologies. (ii) Knowledge is available but creating an adaptation plan would consume too many resources. Therefore, the only way to proceed is to give a warning message to the user and ask for instructions on how to continue.

From these alternatives, the second one is the most dynamic and autonomous without hard-coded adaptation plans. Hence, it is the preferred alternative.

3.2.4. Execute

The final step in the adaptation is the Execute phase, where the created adaptation plan is executed. In other words, it is the straightforward realization of the adaptation plan. At design-time, the software architect has to design variation points inside the SSA. The variation point ensures that it is possible to adapt security mechanisms and attributes at runtime. Figure 9 contains the Action to adapt concept. From the Execute phase point of of view the action is a component, which modifies the related Attribute. Figure 10 shows a runtime situation, where the Planner component calls the Executor and offers the adaptation plan. Based on the adaptation plan the Executor signals an implementation component.

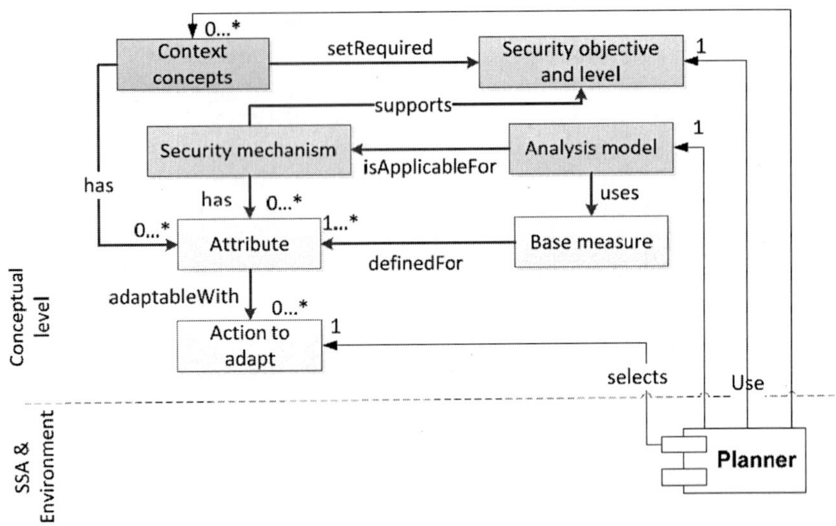

Figure 9. Planning using an Analysis Model.

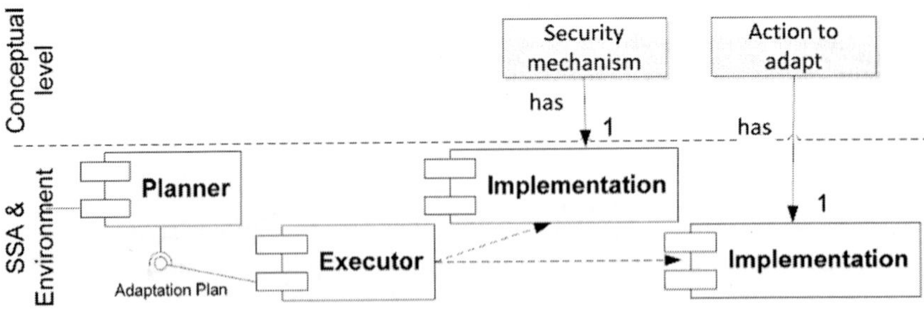

Figure 10. Execute phase.

The execution can affect different layers in a device where the SSA is running. Moreover, the execution can indirectly affect the whole smart space infrastructure. For example, when the SSA adapts a communication protocol the application has to establish a new connection to the smart space infrastructure by using new parameters or a new mechanism. The execute phase can, for example, control how information can be shared by defining security policies according to the Security Control Model described in the next section.

3.3. Runtime Security Control Model

Security knowledge in the conceptual interoperability level provides a means to present security policies, which control the behavior of smart space devices and applications. However, analyzing and planning access-control decisions at runtime, when information is queried and modified, can be computationally costly. In smart spaces the information is shared using SIBs, which are unaware of applications' conceptual policies and hence unable to enforce these policies. SIBs can be assumed to be aware only of a minimal set of standard security primitives, which are associated to information elements instead of the meaning of this information. In addition, as smart space devices may have limited computing capabilities, solutions based on cryptography are often unfeasible. Therefore, efficient solutions are needed to protect information sharing and to control information access in a fine-grained manner at the level of semantic data.

This subsection generalizes and formalizes our previously presented RDF access control approach [51] into a conceptual security control model. The control model has been verified with RDF but it can be applied to any information presentation system, which is based on subject-predicate-object triples. It specifies how access-control policies and security control information over resources are structured and presented. Runtime costs are minimized by requiring that each policy is presented with a single information triple. The security control model is based on context and security measurement concepts, which are used to authorize actions. Hence, the model can be applied efficiently and flexibly in various dynamic security-control situations.

Figure 11 depicts the security relationships in the security control model. The model has a relationship with three software components, presented in the top-right corner of the figure. *Smart space applications* insert, query, modify or subscribe to information resources. The *access control* component authorizes and controls these operations. Application specific *security adaptation* components administer the behavior of the access-control component. This administering is done by controlling the relationships between resources as specified by the security control model.

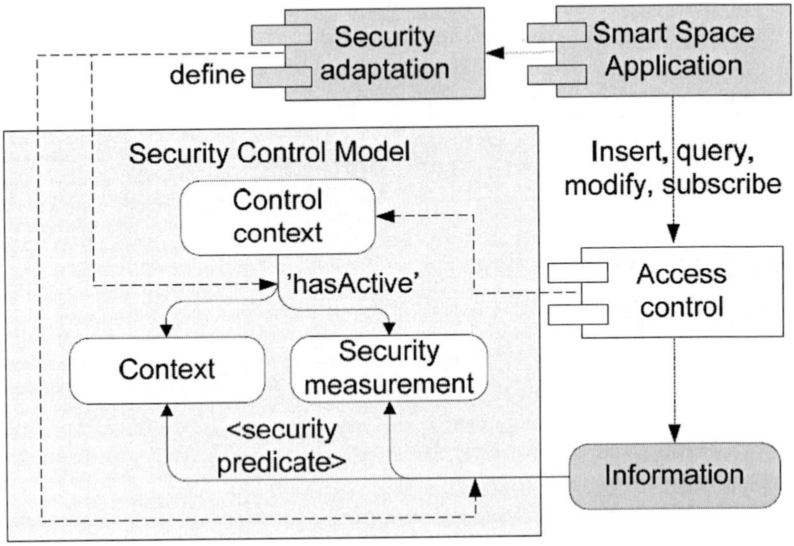

Figure 11. Runtime security-control model for smart spaces.

Each piece of information, *i.e.*, each *information* resource, can have a relationship with one or several *context and security measurement* resources. Each relationship presents one access control statement and is described using triplets in the form: "*Information, SecurityPredicate, Context/Measurement*". *Security predicates* are properties that define authorizing or accounting relationships for the security control. Predicates, which are to be used when authorizing transactions, are presented in Table 1. Predicates for accounting can be found inTable 2. *Context/measurement* refers to any resource that the security adaptation component selects based on the ontologies and policy information from the conceptual level.

When the SSA queries or modifies information, only some contexts and measurements are active. The access control component uses resources, which are active for the application in the current situation. Active resources are found through the *control context* concept, which can be realized as a resource. Security adaptation components define which measurement and context resources are active with triplets: "*ControlContext, 'hasActive', Context/Measurement*". Determination of what resources are active is a dynamic and constantly running process, which may involve different security-adaptation applications. ControlContext resources are fixed in the sense that the access control and security adaption components must know them. For instance, each SSA that is connected to a SIB and has an open communication socket may have a dedicated ControlContext resource. In this case, the active resources could be URIs representing the end-user's identity or security level. These URIs can be resolved and activated by the security adaptation component in the Monitor and Analyze phases, when the user authenticates.

3.3.1. Authorization Predicates

An important use case for the security-control model is authorization over resource access. Policy predicates enabling authorization are defined in Table 1. The granularity of the security-control model protects individual resources and also semantic relationships because of control over access to the resource properties. The security-control model supports the use of allow and disallow policies.

Different policies can be used in conjunction to the set conditions of the authorizations (e.g., a user can access information but only if a contextual requirement is met). To prevent contradictory behavior due to the simultaneous use of allow and disallow policies, the proposed approach is that 'disable' policies override "allow" policies.

The security control model enables efficient runtime access control. An access-control component does not need to do heavy reasoning at the time applications are querying or modifying information, instead, security adaptation Analysis and Planning phases can be done in advance when adaptation-triggering events occur.

The access control component needs to locate the relevant security relationships, presented with triples, between context or measurement resources and a target sources. When an SSA queries or modifies information, the access control component checks whether there are active policies allowing or denying the action.

When the amount of active and authorizing context and measurement resources is n, the access control component must do at most 2*n truth queries ("is there an allow or deny relationship between the active resource and the accessed resource?") to resolve the authorization of a transaction on a target.

The access control component must also find active resources for each used control context resource. Implementations may further speed this up by keeping the list of control context specific active resources in the cached memory.

Table 1. Authorisation policy predicates.

Predicate	Description
GetAllowedFor	Authorizes reading a URI or literal value
SetAllowedFor	Authorizes modifying a URI or literal value
PropertyCreationAllowedFor	Authorizes adding a new URI or literal node under the URI node
PropertyRemovalAllowedFor	Authorizes the removal of a URI or literal node from the URI node
UseAsPropertyAllowedFor	Authorizes use of this node under other URI nodes
GetDisabledFor	Prevents reading a URI or literal value
SetDisabledFor	Prevents modifying a URI or literal value
PropertyCreationDisabledFor	Prevents adding a new URI or literal node under the URI node
PropertyRemovalDisabledFor	Prevents the removal of a URI or literal node from the URI node
UseAsPropertyDisabledFor	Prevents the use of this node under other URI nodes
IsAuthorisedBy	Sets a node under access control and specifies authority. There may be several authorities in one broker.

Table 2. Predicates for access control accounting.

Predicate	Description
HasBeenAuthoredBy	Identifies a resource's author
HasAddedPredicate	Identifies authors who have added predicates under the resource
IsSignedWith	Link to a signature proving authenticity and the origin of the resource
HasSecurityContext	Link to any security measurement or context resource which was active when the data was stored (needed to verify e.g. trustworthiness of data)
IsAuthorisedBy	Specifies the authority that controls security. If such relationship to a known security authority is missing, access can be directly authorized without any other checks.
CanBeMonitored	Allows or disallows logging (e.g. due to performance or privacy)
HasBeenReadBy	Identifies contexts (users) where data has been successfully queried
HadInvalidReadAttemptBy	Identifies contexts (users) with rejected read requests
HadInvalidWriteAttemptBy	Identifies contexts (users) who have made rejected write requests

3.3.2. Accounting Predicates

In addition to authorization, the security control model supports other real-time security control situations. Table 2presents predicate definitions for access accounting activities, which are needed to determine the authenticity or trustworthiness of information. The table defines the relationships for accounting predicates, which are used to log access requests, both successful and unsuccessful. This information is needed, e.g., when trying to detect malicious or harmful modifications and intrusions and when reasoning which nodes may have been potentially compromised due to harmful information. The table also lists *IsSignedWith* and *HasSecurityContext* predicates, which users can use to verify the authenticity and trustworthiness of information. Trustworthiness may depend on context or measurement, which were active when the information was stored.

4. IMPLEMENTATION OF ADAPTIVE SECURITY

4.1. Case Description

The validation was based on a use case from the smart space pilot—called Seamless Usage of Multiple Smart Spaces (SUM-SS) [55]. The SUM-SS pilot combines four smart spaces, *i.e.*, smart personal space, smart home, smart office and smart city. An end user facilitates information from these smart spaces via his/her mobile phone, which constitutes his/her personal smart space. In the personal smart space, the user is able to store information from other smart spaces, like calendar information and documents from the office space. The home smart space offers capabilities to monitor energy consumption; control light and wall sockets and control home automation via the Lon network etc. The smart city offers public information and facilitates everyday life in an urban environment—for instance, by offering information on parking areas and traffic jams. Furthermore, mobile devices and televisions are able to consume entertainment content from a cloud, which is supported by the Cam4Home platform [56]. Consequently, the SUM-SS pilot opens up possibilities to select a smart space use case for the validation purposes. Hence, the use case selected for the validation purposes concentrates on illustrating the following issues:

1) The SSA running in an end user's mobile phone utilizes the adaptation loop to ensure an appropriate authentication level in different situations.
2) Security- and context-related knowledge is retrieved from ontologies.
3) RIBS controls access over shared information by using the security control model.

Use case description: The homeowner leaves the home in the morning, by car. During the drive she wants to check that the front door of her house is locked properly. The owner is able to check a lock status via her mobile phone without any additional authentication.

During the working day, a maintenance man arrives on the front door of the house and rings a doorbell. The doorbell sound is played in the owner's mobile phone and a video stream from the front door of the house is delivered. Hence, when she recognizes the maintenance man at the door, she is able to open the door remotely. However, her current authentication level is not strong enough for the remote door opening, and thus, re-authentication is requested.

After a while, the maintenance man is ready and leaves the house. The owner is informed and she locks the front door again. Now the time has passed and the authentication level is dropped. Nevertheless, re-authentication is not needed because the door can be locked with a lower authentication level.

The home owner arrives home and opens the front door locally by utilizing the NFC (Near Field Communication) feature of her mobile phone. The mobile phone authenticates the user and then the mobile is authenticated through NFC. Inside the house, the owner adjusts the lighting—and the earlier achieved authentication level is enough for these actions. After a while, the owner wants to turn down the heating system in the house. However, controlling the home automation system is a critical action and too much time has passed from the last authentication. Thus, authentication with a stronger authentication level is required.

4.2. Case Implementation

Figure 12 shows the deployment of the use case from the security adaptation viewpoint. The use case implements user authentication in an adaptive manner by using password-based authentication. Our previous demonstration utilized a gait-based authentication [57]. The construction contains six nodes, *i.e.*, homeowner's mobile device, RIBS, smart door, lighting, Lon server and the maintenance man's mobile device. The main actions in the use case are performed with the homeowner's mobile device Nokia C7. Hence, it contains application logic agents to retrieve and insert information into the RIBS. These agents are implemented with Qt C++. In this case, the adaptation will be performed from the homeowner's viewpoint, and thus, adaptation-related components are located in her device. The smart door node contains lock, camera and doorbell agents, which offer related functionalities. Similarly, the lighting node and the Lon server node contain agents to utilize those devices. The RIBS is executed inside a WLAN access point—in order to offer a good connectivity. The RIBS supports the Transport Layer Security (TLS) protocol [58] to secure communication between agents and the RIBS. The last node is the maintenance man's mobile device that contains a visitor agent. The visitor agent makes it possible to ring the doorbell that is available publicly from the home smart space.

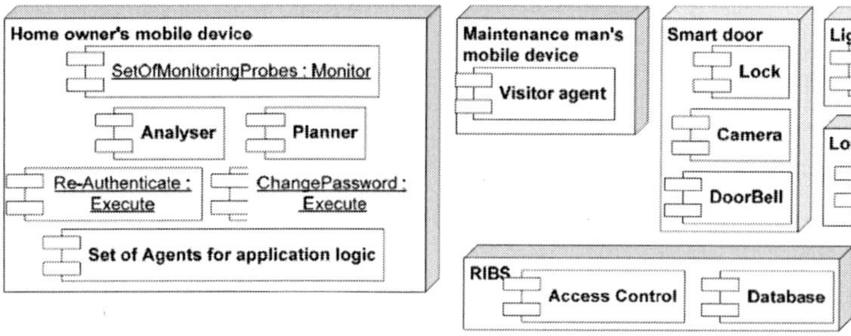

Figure 12. The deployment of the use case.

Monitoring probes are components that implement measurement methods for base measures (*c.f.*, Figure 6). For password-based authentication the use case utilizes the following base measures: (1) Password length. (2) The number of special characters in the password. (3) Password usage time. (4) Session duration. The change of these base measures is informed to the Analyze component. Naturally, Base measures 1 and 2 change when the password is changed. In contrast, Base measures 3 and 4 change constantly, and thus, the changed values are informed to the Analyze component at a certain intervals.

The Analyze component combines the monitoring results to authentication level indicator by means of the Analysis model (*c.f.*, Figure 7). The Analyzer component retrieves the right analysis model from the ISMO. Analysis models are described by a natural language, which combines English and Boolean algebra. We made this decision in our previous work [38] in order to facilitate the preparation of Analysis models. Thus, Analysis models can be modified and added without experience of ontology query languages. The Analysis model utilized in this case is presented in Figure 13. The analysis model uses four base measures—either directly or via the Password type indicator—as depicted in the figure. Moreover, the figure presents Monitoring probes, which implement measurement methods for base measures.

The above-presented Analysis model produces the achieved authentication level. Moreover, the Analyze component analyzes the current situation in order to decide the required authentication level. For this purpose, rules presented in Figure 8 are utilized.

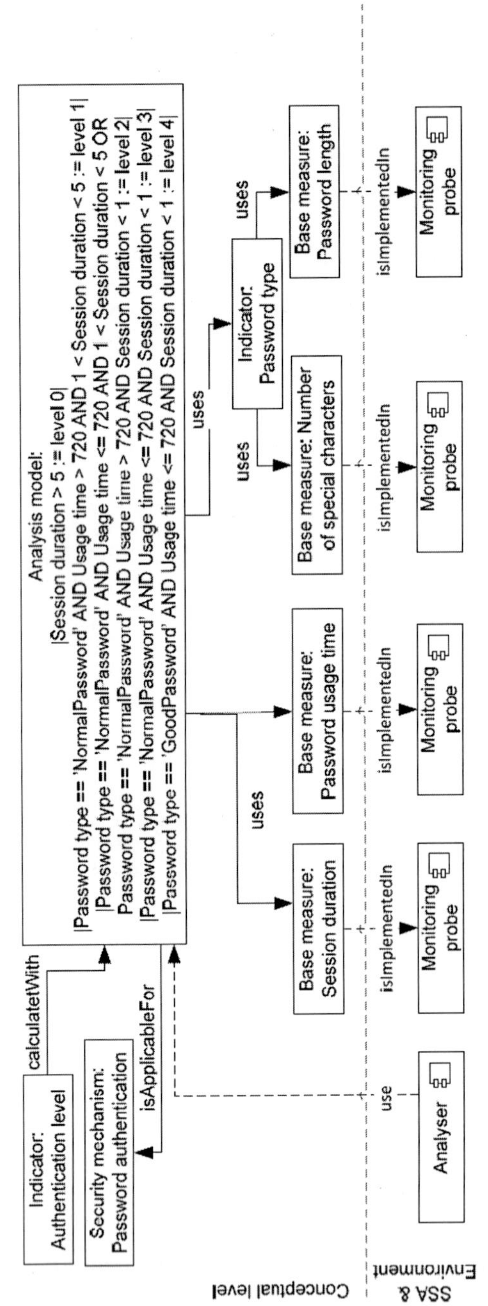

Figure 13. Analysis model used in the use case.

Table 3 summarizes user actions, situations and the achieved and required authentication levels. The achieved authentication level means the level before adaptation. Hence, Actions 1, 3 and 5 do not require adaptation because the achieved level is higher than the required level. Other actions require adaptation and the Planner component is called.

The Plan component selects how the adaptation is performed. In this case, the Planner component searches the causes of the current security level from the analysis model (*c.f.*, Figure 9). Figure 14 lists the attributes of password authentication. In the ISMO base measures from Figure 13 are connected to these attributes by means of a *definedFor* property. Now there are two possible ways to adapt. Firstly, the re-authentication of the user affects the session duration attribute. Secondly, calling the change password function affects password usage time—and depending on a new password—the length and number of special characters attributes. Based on this knowledge, the Planner component selects an appropriate action to adapt.

Table 3 listed user actions. Action numbers 2 and 4 are handled with re-authenticate adaptation. The user action number 6 leads to the change-password adaptation action because the one-month usage time, *i.e.*, 720 h, boundary has been exceeded.

Table 3. Achieved and required authentication levels in different situations.

Action	Situation and Input Information for the Analysis Model	Achieved Auth. Level	Required Auth. Level
1. Check the lock status	Check the lock status Normal password selected 708 h ago. Session duration: 2 h	2	0
2. Open the front door	Remote opening Normal password selected 710 h ago. Session duration: 4 h	2	3
3. Lock the front door	Remote locking Normal password selected 712 h ago. Session duration: 2 h	2	1
4. Open the front door	Local opening Normal password selected 719 h ago. Session duration: 7 h	0	3
5. Modify lighting	Local modification Normal password selected 719 h ago. Session duration: 0.02 h	3	1
6. Modify home automation	Local modification Normal password selected 721 h ago. Session duration: 2 h	1	2

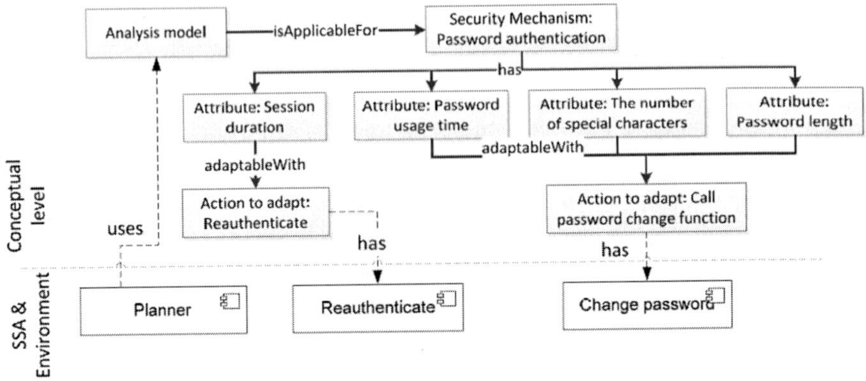

Figure 14. Actions to adapt different parameters.

Lastly, the Execute component performs the created adaptation plan. Both adaptation actions also have an effect outside of the homeowner's device: It requires re-authentication into the RIBS or calling the password-change function from the RIBS. However, in both cases the initiative for these actions is made in the Execute component inside the homeowner's device.

Figure 15 shows the screenshot of the ISMO in the Protégé ontology tool. The screenshot contains concepts instantiated for the use case purposes. The ISMO is also available in web: https://sofia-community.com/projects/sontologies/—needs registration. The page contains ISMO and links to imported ontologies.

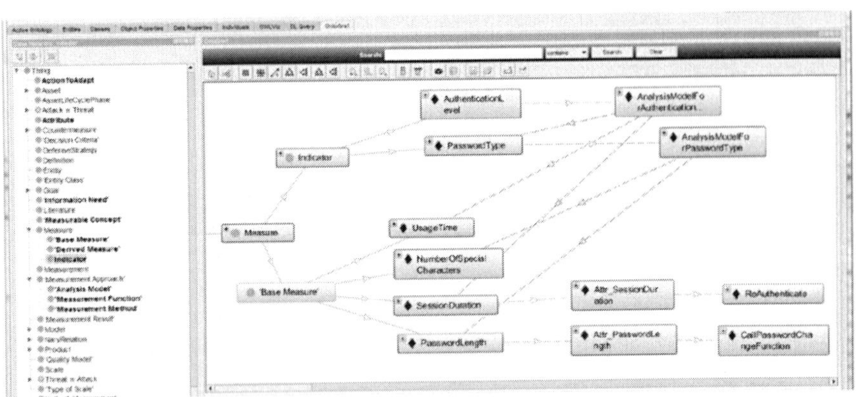

Figure 15. ISMO in Protégé.

The RIBS is responsible for enforcing access control over brokered information. It enforces that only authenticated and authorized users can insert and modify information. The authorization checks follow the runtime security-control model, as illustrated in Figure 16. The agents in the homeowner's terminal are responsible for administering the authorization policies, which are stored in the RIBS for each RDF resource. When a user is authenticated, appropriate context and measurement resources are activated. In the use case, the maintenance man is mapped to a visitor context and the homeowner is mapped to a resource, which represents owner's identity. Further, all users are mapped to security measurement resources, which describe the authentication level. When users query or modify information, the SIB checks whether these active RDF resources authorize access to the requested resources. All authenticated users are given access to non-critical information inside the home e.g., the lighting. The homeowner has access to every piece of information. However, access to the most critical information requires that the owner have a sufficient authentication level.

The RIBS has been optimized to provide fast and low-power consuming information access. The implementation indexes all incoming RDF data, and thus, enables RDF URIs as well as literals to be directly addressed. Relationship information is stored to a three-dimensional (subject-predicate-object) array, *i.e.*, to a bit cube. As security policies are presented with a single bit, which is either on or off, they can be quickly checked and the amount of required memory will not increase even when the security configuration becomes more complex.

4.3. Lessons Learned

Implementing and performing these use cases showed several advantages from the presented approach. Firstly, all knowledge is retrieved from ontologies. Thus, content from the analysis model (*c.f.*, Figure 13) and rules for setting the required authentication levels (*c.f.*, Figure 8) do not need to be coded into the SSA. Hence, knowledge can be modified and extended without coding work. Secondly, adaptive user authentication enhanced usability. However, as the authentication level decreased the user was able to perform Action 3 (see Table 3). In contrast, using a static authentication requires that all actions be set as equally critical, which in turn means that all actions require the highest authentication level. Thirdly, from the implementation view point the presented adaptation loop clearly defined the required components. In addition, knowledge—required in each component—was defined explicitly. Therefore, the approach description can act as an implementation guideline. Finally, the security-control model in the RIBS supported flexible access control. The access control information is described in the RIBS as RDF information, and thus, separated access-control lists are not needed.

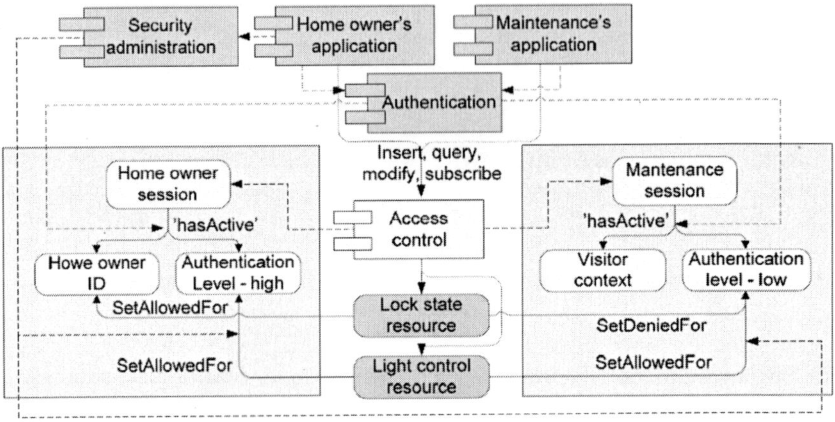

Figure 16. Examples of authorizing relations in the runtime security-control model.

However, improvement ideas are also recognized. The first consideration relates to the selected security objective—in the use case user authentication was in the focal point. Supporting other security objectives does not require changes to the adaptation approach and utilization of knowledge from the ontologies. Nevertheless, the content of the ontologies has to be extended with new knowledge related to security objectives. This knowledge does not need to be created from scratch but the existing knowledge has to be described in a machine-readable form by means of the ontologies. The second issue relates to the definition of the Analysis model. During the case implementation it was noticed that defining the Analysis model is a complex and time-consuming task—although only three variables were used. Thus, automation is needed in the future in order to define extensive analysis models.

5. DISCUSSION

5.1. The Advantages of the Approach

Achieving security in smart spaces requires dynamic security solutions. The presented adaptation approach for security ensures that the achieved security corresponds to each situation faced in the smart space. Further, the introduced security-control model ensures the appropriate information access in changing smart spaces. Thus, the introduced security-adaptation approach offers several advantages:

Firstly, the approach is generic—security objectives and mechanisms can be freely selected. Hence, the approach is able to offer adaptation for one security objective, or alternatively, a set of security objectives can be implemented in an adaptive manner. Similarly, the adaptation approach is independent on the used security mechanism.

Secondly, the adaptation approach is based on knowledge from ontologies, which cover the knowledge part of the MAPE-K model. This separation of concerns, *i.e.*, separation of generic knowledge from application logic, improves reusability. The knowledge can be updated and extended easily and quickly without modifying the SSA. Moreover, the ontologies ensure that there is a uniform way to present security terminology.

Thirdly, the commonly known MAPE model ensures that the required components are clearly defined, *i.e.*, Monitoring, Analyzing, Planning and Executing. Clearly defined components support reusability, which facilitates the architects' work. The Monitoring utilizes security measures and the Analysis utilizes extendable analysis models. In each phase the required knowledge is retrieved from the ontologies.

Fourthly, smart spaces consist of devices and applications that can enter and leave the space at any time. Various situations require dynamic access-control policies that are enforced automatically. The security-control model provides an approach for enforcing the access control for different situations. The model is expressive but still straightforward, and hence, more suitable for runtime enforcement than the previous RDF level access-control proposals.

5.2. The Challenges of the Approach and Future Research

Firstly, the use cases showed that creating analysis models is a complex task. Therefore, a tool, or at least guidelines, for the analysis model definition is needed in the future. The tool has to present the possible variables and their value ranges. In addition, the tool has to check that contradicting analysis models are not created.

Secondly, in the future mutual relationships between security objectives have to be taken into account during the Analyze and Plan phases. The ISMO already contains basic connections between security objectives, e.g., authorization demands identification. Therefore, analysis models have to notice these dependencies when recognizing adaptation needs. Similarly, the Plan phase is able to utilize this knowledge when searching applicable adaptation actions. For instance, the need to adapt authorization causes the utilized identification scheme to change. Furthermore, trade-offs and dependencies on other qualities like performance, reliability and usability are topics for future research.

Thirdly, the performance cost of the approach is a natural question. However, end users were not able to recognize decreased performance during the case study. It is clear that the performance overhead can be noticed if a huge amount of base measures and complex analysis models are used. Therefore, it is important to adjust the analysis models and the number of base measures for device resources. The performance penalty caused by the RDF access control depends on the amount of requested RDF resources. In a performance test case with the RIBS implementation, the average request times were around one per cent longer when compared to a case where all requests were authorized without any checks [51].

The last issue relates to the security of the adaptation approach. It is possible that an attacker may try to modify some parts of the adaptation loop in order to attack the smart space. For instance, manipulating the Monitoring or Analyzing parts might mean that a decreased security level is not recognized. Or alternatively, the Plan phase may create an inappropriate adaptation plan, which is advantageous for the attacker. Hence, it is extremely important to protect these components and ensure the authenticity and integrity of knowledge.

5.3. The Maturity of the Approach

The approach was developed during a three-year research project. The development was performed incrementally by utilizing different use cases and smart space set-ups. In previous cases, we have experienced different adaptation ideas and worked on different phases of security adaptation. Table 4 summarizes the previous validation cases.

6. CONCLUSIONS

In smart spaces, it is not possible to take all the security requirements into account at design-time. Hence, this paper presented a self-adaptation approach for smart space security. The presented approach contains an adaptation loop the Monitor, Analyze, Plan, and Execute model—in a clearly defined form. The monitor phase utilizes monitoring probes to observe security-relevant attributes from the smart space and smart space application. The monitored results are analyzed in order to reveal if the required security is not achieved. The Plan phase creates an adaptation plan, which will be enforced in the Execute phase. The adaptation approach requires a lot of knowledge, which is retrieved from the ontologies. The utilization of ontologies ensures a flexible and extensible way to manage and use knowledge in machine-readable form. The ISMO provides security- and measuring-related knowledge and CO4SS offers context knowledge. For access control, the security-control model was presented, which utilizes context information and provides dynamic access control. Hence, the security-control model provides a flexible and efficient mechanism to control information sharing in smart spaces.

Table 4. Previous validation cases.

Validation Case	Description
Risk-based security adaptation in a greenhouse [41,57].	A greenhouse with a shopping area constitutes a public smart space. In the smart space threats increase the risk levels and security mechanisms decrease risks. Hence, the monitoring concentrates on recognizing threats. In this case, confidentiality and integrity were considered. Furthermore, users authenticated by means of gait information identified from the measurements of acceleration sensors inside the mobile phone.
Adaptive user authentication [38].	The first case that utilized knowledge from the ISMO. It adapts user authentication by monitoring authentication-related measures: password length, age, variation of characters and session duration. Important information was available only when an acceptable authentication level was reached. The user's re-authentication was requested when the session duration was exceeded.
Role- and popularity-based access-control simulations [51,59].	Controlling access to information according to the user's role or popularity of information. Popularity is a measure that indicates how many readers or how many authors an RDF resource has. These adaptation cases were simulated with the smodels logic solver.
Adding new knowledge into the ISMO [54].	The paper and related case example showed how easily knowledge in the ISMO can be extended. Moreover, design steps to develop adaptive security were presented.

The presented approach was validated by means of a use case. The use case illustrated (i) all the phases of the adaptation loop, (ii) how ontologies offer knowledge for adaptation at runtime, (iii) that access control enforced the semantic information. The advantages of the presented approach are evident. Firstly, the approach is independent of security objectives and mechanisms. Second, the approach provides a reusable architecture to develop adaptive security applicable for different kinds of smart spaces. Thirdly, the components for the security adaptation are clearly defined, which help in adopting the approach. Finally, the utilization of ontologies ensures that knowledge can be updated and extended easily.

In the future, new and wider analysis models are needed. Thus, a tool will be developed for defining a wider set of analysis models for various security objectives.

ACKNOWLEDGMENTS

This work has been carried out in the SOFIA ARTEMIS project (2009-2011) and SASER-Siegfried Celtic-Plus project (2012-2015) funded by Tekes (the Finnish Funding Agency for Technology and Innovation), VTT Technical Research Centre of Finland and the European Commission.

REFERENCES

1. Conti, M.; Das, S.K.; Bisdikian, C.; Kumar, M.; Ni, L.M.; Passarella, A.; Roussos, G.; Tröster, G.; Tsudik, G.; Zambonelli, F. Looking ahead in pervasive computing: Challenges and opportunities in the era of cyber–physical convergence. *Pervasive Mob. Comput.* **2012**, *8*, 2–21.
2. Elkhodary, A.; Whittle, J. A Survey of Approaches to Adaptive Application Security. In Proceedings of the International Workshop on Software Engineering for Adaptive and Self-Managing Systems, Minneapolis, USA, 20–26 May 2007; pp. 16–23.
3. Yuan, E.; Malek, S. A taxonomy and survey of self-protecting software systems. In Proceedings of the IEEE Software Engineering for Adaptive and Self-Managing Systems, Zürich, Switzerland, 4–5 June 2012; pp. 109–118.
4. Cook, D.J.; Das, S.K. How smart are our environments? An updated look at the state of the art. *Pervasive Mob. Comput.* **2007**, *3*, 53–73.
5. Ovaska, E.; Salmon Cinotti, T.; Toninelli, A. Design principles and practices of interoperable smart spaces. In *Advanced Design Approaches to Emerging Software Systems: Principles, Methodologies, and Tools*; Liu, X., Li, Y., Eds.; IGI Global, 2011; pp. 18–47.
6. Pantsar-Syväniemi, S.; Purhonen, A.; Ovaska, E.; Kuusijärvi, J.; Evesti, A. Situation-Based and Self-Adaptive Applications for Smart Environment. *J. Ambient Intelligence and Smart Environ.* **2012**, *4*, 491–516.
7. Honkola, J.; Laine, H.; Brown, R.; Tyrkkö, O. Smart–M3 information sharing platform. In Proceedings of the IEEE Symposion on Computers and Communications, Riccione, Italy, 22–25 June 2010; pp. 1041–1046.
8. RDF Primer. 2004. Available online: http://www.w3.org/TR/rdf-primer/ (accessed on 23 November 2012).
9. SOFIA Smart Objects For Intelligent Applications. 2012. Available online: http://www.sofia-project.eu (accessed on 23 November 2012).
10. Suomalainen, J.; Hyttinen, P.; Tarvainen, P. Secure information sharing between heterogeneous embedded devices. In Proceedings of the 4th European Conference on Software Architecture: Companion Volume, Copenhagen, Denmark, 23–26 August 2010; ACM, 2010; pp. 205–212.
11. Kephart, J.O.; Chess, D.M. The vision of autonomic computing. *Computer* **2003**, *36*, 41–50.

12. Dobson, S.; Denazis, S.; Fernández, A.; Gaïti, D.; Gelenbe, E.; Massacci, F.; Nixon, P.; Saffre, F.; Schmidt, N.; Zambonelli, F. A survey of autonomic communications. *ACM Trans. Auton. Adapt. Syst.* **2006**, *1*, 223–259.
13. Salehie, M.; Tahvildari, L. Self-adaptive software: Landscape and research challenges. *ACM Trans. Auton. Adapt. Syst.* **2009**, *4*, 1–42.
14. Psaier, H.; Dustdar, S. A survey on self-healing systems: approaches and systems. *Computing* **2011**, *91*, 43–73.
15. Huebscher, M.C.; McCann, J.A. A survey of autonomic computing—degrees, models, and application. *ACM Comput. Surv.* **2008**, *40*, 1–28.
16. Matinlassi, M.; Niemelä, E. The impact of maintainability on component-based software systems. In Proceedings of the 29th Euromicro Conference, Belek-Antalya, Turkey, 3–5 September 2003; IEEE, 2003; pp. 25–32.
17. Hashii, B.; Malabarba, S.; Pandey, R.; Bishop, M. Supporting reconfigurable security policies for mobile programs. *Computer Networks* **2000**, *33*, 77–93.
18. Hu, W.; Hiser, J.; Williams, D.; Filipi, A.; Davidson, J.W.; Evans, D.; Knight, J.C.; Nguyen-Tuong, A.; Rowanhill, J. Secure and practical defense against code-injection attacks using software dynamic translation. In Proceedings of the 2nd international conference on Virtual execution environments, Ottawa, Canada, 14–16 June 2006; ACM, 2006; pp. 2–12.
19. Knight, J.C.; Strunk, E.A. Achieving critical system survivability through software architectures. In *Architecting Dependable Systems II*; Lemos, R., Gacek, C., Romanovsky, A., Eds.; Springer: Berlin Heidelberg, 2004; pp. 51–78.
20. Ryutov, T.; Zhou, L.; Neuman, C.; Leithead, T.; Seamons, K.E. Adaptive trust negotiation and access control. In Proceedings of the 10th ACM Symposium on Access Control Models and Technologies, Stockholm, Sweden, 1–3 June 2005; pp. 139–146.
21. Klenk, A.; Niedermayer, H.; Masekowsky, M.; Carle, G. An architecture for autonomic security adaptation. *Ann. Telecommun.* **2006**, *61*, 1066–1082.
22. Hulsebosch, R.; Bargh, M.; Lenzini, G.; Ebben, P.; Iacob, S. Context sensitive adaptive authentication. In *Smart Sensing and Context*; Kortuem, G., Finney, J., Lea, R., Sundramoorthy, V., Eds.; Springer: Berlin Heidelberg, 2007; pp. 93–109.
23. Abie, H.; Savola, R.M.; Bigham, J.; Dattani, I.; Rotondi, D.; Da Bormida, G. Self-Healing and Secure Adaptive Messaging Middleware for Business-Critical Systems. *Int. J. Adv. Se.* **2010**, *3*, 34–51.
24. Savola, R.; Abie, H. Development of measurable security for a distributed messaging system. *Int. J. Adv.* **2009**, *2*, 358–380.
25. Wang, C.; Wulf, W.A. Towards a Framework for Security Measurement. In Proceedings of the 20th National Information Systems Security Conference, Baltimore, Maryland, USA, October 1997; pp. 522–533.
26. García, F.; Bertoa, M.F.; Calero, C.; Vallecillo, A.; Ruíz, F.; Piattini, M.; Genero, M. Towards a consistent terminology for software measurement. *Inf. Softw. Technol.* **2006**, *48*, 631–644.
27. Haley, C.B.; Laney, R.; Moffett, J.D.; Nuseibeh, B. Security Requirements Engineering: A Framework for Representation and Analysis. *IEEE Trans. Softw. Eng.* **2008**, *34*, 133–153.
28. Salehie, M.; Pasquale, L.; Omoronyia, I.; Ali, R.; Nuseibeh, B. Requirements-driven adaptive security: Protecting variable assets at runtime. In Proceedings of the 20th International Requirements Engineering Conference (RE), Chicago, USA, 24–28 September 2012; IEEE, 2012; pp. 111–120.
29. ISO/IEC 15408-1:2009 Standard, Common Criteria for Information Technology Security Evaluation – Part 1: Introduction and general model, International Organization of Standardization. 2009.
30. Sahinoglu, M. Security meter: a practical decision-tree model to quantify risk. *Security Privacy* **2005**, *3*, 18–24.
31. Zhou, J. Knowledge Dichotomy and Semantic Knowledge Management. In Proceedings of the 1st IFIP WG12.5 Working Conference on Industrial Applications of Semantic Web, Jyväskylä, Finland, 25–27 August 2005; Springer: US, 2005; pp. 305–316.
32. Blanco, C.; Lasheras, J.; Valencia-García, R.; Fernández-Medina, E.; Toval, A.; Piattini, M. A systematic review and comparison of security ontologies. In Proceedings of the 3rd

International Conference on AvailabilitySecurityand Reliability, Barcelona, Spain, 4–7 March 2008; IEEE, 2008; pp. 813–820.

33. Evesti, A.; Ovaska, E.; Savola, R. From security modelling to run-time security monitoring. In Proceedings of the European Worshop on Security in Model Driven ArchitectureCTIT Centre for Telematics and Information Technology, Enchede, Netherlands, 23–26 June 2009; pp. 33–41.
34. Kim, A.; Luo, J.; Kang, M. Security Ontology for annotating resources. In Proceedings of the On the Move to Meaningful Internet Systems 2005: CoopIS, DOA, and ODBASE, Agia Napa, Cyprus, 31 October–4 November 2005; Springer-Verlag: Berlin Heidelberg, 2005; pp. 1483–1499.
35. Denker, G.; Kagal, L.; Finin, T. Security in the Semantic Web using OWL. *Inform. Sec. Tech. Rep.* **2005**, *10*, 51–58.
36. Savolainen, P.; Niemelä, E.; Savola, R. A taxonomy of information security for service centric systems. In Proceedings of the 33rd EUROMICRO Conference on Software Engineering and Advanced Applications, Lübeck, Germany, 27–31 August 2007; IEEE, 2007; pp. 5–12.
37. Herzog, A.; Shahmehri, N.; Duma, C. An ontology of information security. *J. Inform. Sec. Privacy* **2007**, *1*, 1–23.
38. Evesti, A.; Savola, R.; Ovaska, E.; Kuusijärvi, J. The Design, Instantiation, and Usage of Information Security Measuring Ontology. In Proceedings of the 2nd International Conference on Models and Ontology-based Design of Protocols, Architectures and Services, Budapest, Hungary, 17–22 April 2011; IARIA, 2011; pp. 1–9.
39. Pantsar-Syväniemi, S.; Kuusijärvi, J.; Ovaska, E. Supporting Situation-awareness in Smart Spaces. In Proceedings of the International Workshops, S3E, HWTS, Doctoral Colloquium, Held in Conjunction with GPC 2011, Oulu, Finland, 11–13 May 2011; Springer-Verlag: Berlin Heidelberg, Germany, 2012; pp. 14–23.
40. Evesti, A.; Pantsar-Syväniemi, S. Towards micro architecture for security adaptation. In Proceedings of the 4th European Conference on Software Architecture: Companion Volume, Copenhagen, Denmark, 23–26 August 2010; ACM, 2010; pp. 181–188.
41. Evesti, A.; Ovaska, E. Ontology-Based Security Adaptation at Run-Time. In Proceedings of the 4th International Conference on Self-Adaptive and Self-Organizing Systems, Budapest, Hungary, 27 September–1 October 2010; IEEE, 2010; pp. 204–212.
42. Dietzold, S.; Auer, S. Access control on RDF triple stores from a semantic wiki perspective. In Proceedings of the Scripting for the Semantic Web Workshop at 3rd European Semantic Web Conference, Budva, Montenegro, 11–14 June 2006; CEUR Workshop, 2006; pp. 1–9.
43. D'Elia, A.; Honkola, J.; Manzaroli, D.; Salmon Cinotti, T. Access Control at Triple Level: Specification and Enforcement of a Simple RDF Model to Support Concurrent Applications in Smart Environments. In Proceedings of the 11th International Conference, NEW2AN 2011, and 4th Conference on Smart Spaces, ruSMART 2011, St. Petersburg, Russia, 22–25 August 2011; Springer: Berlin Heidelberg, 2011; pp. 63–74.
44. Reddivari, P.; Finin, T.; Joshi, A. Policy-based access control for an RDF store. In Proceedings of the Policy Management for the Web, Chiba, Japan, 10–14 May 2005; pp. 78–81.
45. Jain, A.; Farkas, C. Secure resource description framework: an access control model. In Proceedings of the 11th symposium on Access control models and technologies, Lake Tahoe, California, USA, 7–9 June 2006; ACM, 2006; pp. 121–129.
46. Flouris, G.; Fundulaki, I.; Michou, M.; Antoniou, G. Controlling access to RDF graphs. In Proceedings of the Future Interner - FIS 2010, Berlin, Germany, 20–22 September 2010; Springer: Berlin Heidelberg, 2010; pp. 107–117.
47. Kim, J.; Jung, K.; Park, S. An Introduction to Authorization Conflict Problem in RDF Access Control. In Proceedings of the Knowledge-Based Intelligent Information and Engineering Systems, Zagreb, Croatia, 3–5 September 2008; Springer: Berlin Heidelberg, 2008; pp. 583–592.

48. Cho, E.; Kim, Y.; Hong, M.; Cho, W. Fine-Grained View-Based Access Control for RDF Cloaking. In Proceedings of the 9th International Conference on Computer and Information Technology, Xiamen, China, 11–14 October 2009; IEEE, 2009; pp. 336–341.
49. Bock, J.; Haase, P.; Ji, Q.; Volz, R. Benchmarking OWL reasoners. In Proceedings of the Workshop on Advancing Reasoning on the Web: Scalability and Commonsense; CEUR Workshop Proceedings: Tenerife, Spain, 2008; pp. 1–15.
50. Dentler, K.; Cornet, R.; Ten Teije, A.; De Keizer, N. Comparison of reasoners for large ontologies in the OWL 2 EL profile. *Semantic Web* **2011**, *2*, 71–87.
51. Suomalainen, J.; Hyttinen, P. Security Solutions for Smart Spaces. In Proceedings of the 11th International Symposium on Applications and the Internet, Munich, Germany, 18–21 July 2011; IEEE, 2011; pp. 297–302.
52. Niemelä, E.; Evesti, A.; Savolainen, P. Modeling quality attribute variability. In Proceedings of the 3rd International Conference on Evaluation of Novel Approaches to Software Engineering, Funchal, Madeira, Portugal, 4–7 May 2008; pp. 169–176.
53. Ovaska, E.; Evesti, A.; Henttonen, K.; Palviainen, M.; Aho, P. Knowledge based quality-driven architecture design and evaluation. *Inf. Softw. Technol.* **2010**, *52*, 577–601.
54. Evesti, A.; Ovaska, E. Design Time Reliability Predictions for Supporting Runtime Security Measuring and Adaptation. In Proceedings of the 3rd International Conference on Emerging Network Intelligence, Lisbon, Portugal, 20–25 November 2011; IARIA, 2011; pp. 94–99.
55. Sofia Pilot Brochure. 2012. Available online: http://www.slideshare.net/sofiaproject/sofia-project-brochure-pilots-set(accessed on 23 November 2012).
56. Cam4Home Project. Cam4Home. Available online: http://www.cam4home-itea.org/ (accessed on 8 May 2012).
57. Evesti, A.; Eteläperä, M.; Kiljander, J.; Kuusijärvi, J.; Purhonen, A.; Stenudd, S. Semantic Information Interoperability in Smart Spaces. In Proceedings of the The 8th International Conference on Mobile and Ubiquitous Multimedia, Cambride, UK, 22–25 November 2009; ACM, 2009; pp. 158–159.
58. Dierks, T.; Rescorla, E. The Transport Layer Security (TLS) Protocol Version 1.2. 2008. Available online: http://www.ietf.org/rfc/rfc5246.txt (accessed on 23 November 2012).
59. Suomalainen, J. Flexible Security Deployment in Smart Spaces. In Proceedings of the International Workshops, S3E, HWTS, Doctoral Colloquium, Held in Conjunction with GPC 2011, Oulu, Finland, 11–13 May 2011; Springer: Berlin Heidelberg, Germany, 2012; pp. 34–43.

CHAPTER 3

BangA: An Efficient and Flexible Generalization-Based Algorithm for Privacy Preserving Data Publication

Adeel Anjum[1,*] and Guillaume Raschia[2]

[1]*Department of Computer Science, Comsats Institute of Information Technology, Park Road Chak Shahzad, 44000 Islamabad, Pakistan*

[2]*Laboratoire LINA, Ecole Polytechnique, University of Nantes, 44306 Nantes, France*

ABSTRACT

Privacy-Preserving Data Publishing (PPDP) has become a critical issue for companies and organizations that would release their data. *k*-Anonymization was proposed as a first generalization model to guarantee against identity disclosure of individual records in a data set. Point access methods (PAMs) are not well studied for the problem of data anonymization. In this article, we propose yet another approximation algorithm for anonymization, coined *BangA*, that combines useful features from Point Access Methods (PAMs) and clustering. Hence, it achieves fast computation and scalability as a PAM, and very high quality thanks to its density-based clustering step. Extensive experiments show the efficiency and effectiveness of our approach. Furthermore, we provide guidelines for extending BangA to achieve a relaxed form of *differential privacy* which provides stronger privacy guarantees as compared to traditional privacy definitions.

Keywords: data privacy; generalization; *k*-anonymity; differential privacy; Bang file

1. INTRODUCTION

1.1. Motivation

Data privacy protection is no longer discretionary. The information surge has made the retrieval of public and private information of individuals a part of day-to-day life. Many critical services, e.g., health care, typically gather this information for improving the quality of services; however, given the co-dependency of the Internet and information systems, sensitive data is under the radar of theft and corruption.

Organizations may release their microdata for the purpose of facilitating useful data analysis and research. For example, patients' medical records may be released by a hospital for research purposes. Releasing this kind of data about individuals without risking their privacy is an important problem. To avoid personal identification, many organizations usually remove the uniquely identifying information like *name* or *SSN* from the published data. However, this sanitization of data might not be helpful in guarding the secrecy of given individuals, as it may still be possible to link released records back to their identities by matching some combination of attributes like *age*, *zip code* and *sex*, coined *quasi-identifier* or *linking attributes*. These attributes can be used to infer the sensitive attributes, e.g., *disease* for any individual.

1.2. Basic Requirements

The type of attacks mentioned in Section 1.1 gave rise to the need for robust sanitization methods to publish sensitive individual data keeping their privacy intact. The seminal *k*-anonymization paradigm [1] was proposed to achieve this goal by means of a *generalization model*. Basically, anonymization based on generalization consists of decreasing the accuracy of values from quasi-identifiers. For instance, the 44100 Zip code would become 44xxx and 70 pounds would be said to range between 50 and 80 pounds.

Table 1 provides an example of a public release of six medical records following three-anonymity, i.e., each public record is identical on quasi-identifiers (Age, Zip and Gender) with at least two other records. For instance, records 1, 2, 3 from Table 1 belong to the same equivalence class and are indistinguishable one with each other. The pattern of the class is

(Age = (48–62), Zip = 441xx, Gender = *). Similarly, records 4, 5, 6 form the second equivalence class.

Table 1. Three-Anonymous public release.

Id	Age	Zip Code	Gender	Disease
1	(48–62) (62)	441XX (44120)	*(F)	Flu
2	(48–62) (51)	441XX (44190)	*(M)	Flu
3	(48–62) (48)	441XX (44100)	*(M)	HIV
4	(59–77) (59)	444XX (44470)	*(F)	Flu
5	(59–77) (77)	444XX (44420)	*(M)	Gastritis
6	(59–77) (66)	444XX (44420)	*(M)	HIV

1.3. Typical Use Case

The sanitized release must support exploration, analysis and scientific studies. The very first and popular processing of sanitized release is to search and filter tabular data by means of *point queries* and *window queries.* A point query retrieves the records where the predicate matches the exact value e.g., find an employee whose SSN is "3456". In other words, point query relates to an exact point in an *n*-dimensional space. A *window query or range query* retrieves all of the records where some value is between an upper and lower boundary e.g., list of all employees with age between 23 to 25. The result of a window query is a set of points matching a specified range or window. Indeed, regular database records can be geometrically interpreted as points in a multidimensional space where each dimension is a column of the raw table. Point coordinates are then defined by the attribute values. Transformation is obvious for numerical and ordinal variables. Categorical variables could also be equipped with a total ordering, except that without any native ordering, the process is driven by the application domain and background knowledge. Thus, database queries are transformed into queries against a *set of points*.

Once the microdata is sanitized, its records become *hyper-rectangles* in a multidimensional space, where each dimension is a field in the set of quasi-identifiers. For instance, sanitized records from Table 1 are cuboids in the three-dimensional (3D) space (Age, Zipcode, Gender) as shown in Figure 1. As a point query example Q1, user would filter data to retrieve possible patient's record designated by Age = 62 AND Zip Code = 44120 AND Gender = F. For sanitized release, Q1 can be expanded for Zip Code and Gender. For instance, Zip Code can be replaced with its value in the increasing levels of its Value Generalization Hierarchy i.e., Zip Code = 44120 OR Zip Code = 4412X OR Zip Code = 441XX OR Zip Code = 44XXX OR Zip Code = 4XXXX OR Zip Code = *. Similarly, Gender = F or *. Consequently, the result set for Q1 is comprised of 1, 2, 3 from Table 1. Similarly, a window query Q2 for Zip Code IN [4442X, 4447X] AND Age ≥ 50 AND Gender = * is comprised of the result set 4, 5, 6 from Table 1.

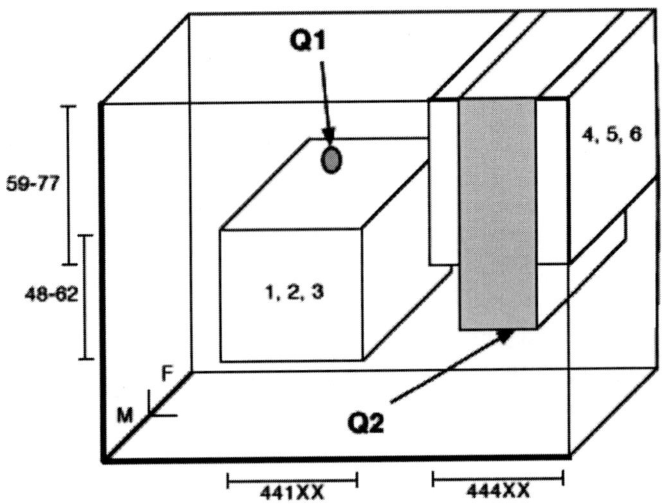

Figure 1. Three-dimensional (3D) spatial representation of the anonymous public release from Table 1 with point query Q1 and window query Q2.

To achieve such a querying scenario, the sanitized records are mutually disjoint spatial objects with a *rectangular extent*and window queries are *orthogonal range queries*. Any record that overlaps/lies within the query region is a member of the result set. There exist many efficient algorithms and data structures [2] to compute such orthogonal range queries against the spatial representation of the anonymous database. Furthermore, since any orthogonal range query can be decomposed into several one-dimensional (1D) range queries, it is easy to manage filters on the tabular representation of the public release within a basic spreadsheet or web-client technologies as well. Query Q2 over Table 1 gives an example of such straightforward decomposition. These practical features are very useful in lots of iterative exploration processes that would support analysis and scientific studies. *Then, we argue that the axis-parallel* *rectangular coding of anonymous records is a strong requirement for a generic Privacy Preserving Data Publishing PPDP task.*

Other kinds of window queries are defined by the shape of the query region: sphere, half-space, simplex, and polytopes. Sphere range queries, so-called *nearest-neighbor queries*, have been extensively studied, and there also exist efficient algorithms to compute such popular queries especially on rectangular objects. However, none of these range queries satisfies the decomposition property that makes anonymous releases human-friendly under tabular representation. To sum-up the above discussion, we argue that every PPDP task should meet at least the following theoretical and practical requirements in order to be valuable for the end-user:

- Indistinguishability principle—to achieve generalization;
- Mutually disjoint equivalence classes—to preserve quality of the anonymous public release;
- Multidimensional point partitioning—to support point and range queries on the anonymous public release;
- Hyper-rectangular coding of equivalence classes—to allow decomposition of orthogonal range queries.

1.4. Related Work

It is worth noticing that public release with one single equivalence class described on each dimension, by every domain, is obviously k-anonymous ($k \leq n$ the number of records), but it is definitely useless for the end-user. Thus, the main challenge of k-anonymization is to compute a public release where the information loss has been minimized, in the sense of a general criteria by means of popular utility metrics such as *discernibility penalty* [3], *Kullback–Leibler (KL)-divergence* [4] and the certainty metric proposed in [5]. This optimization problem was proved to be NP-hard [6].

Hence, many approximation algorithms have been proposed in the literature since the seminal work of Sweeney [1]. Fung et al. [7] provide a detailed survey on the approximation algorithms for k-anonymity. Usually, the Mondrian approach [8] is thought of as the baseline algorithm since it has many interesting properties that we could expect from such algorithms: local recoding and multidimensional partitioning. Mondrian iteratively operates a binary partitioning of the data space until every block contains between k and 2k−1 data points. Actually, Mondrian builds a *kd*-tree over the raw data and publishes bounding boxes of the leaves as equivalence classes of the anonymous release. Construction has time complexity $O(N \log(N))$, where N is the number of records in raw data.

Following the geometric representation of the data, Iwuchukwu et al. [9] propose using a bulk-loading implementation of an R+-tree, one of the most popular spatial access methods for databases, to compute the *k*-anonymous release. It outperforms Mondrian thanks to buffering and efficient bottom-up index construction algorithm, and it scales up to very large data sets. Furthermore, the hierarchical structure of the R+-tree natively supports $(B^{\ell}k)$-anonymity for all levels ℓ in the tree, with B the fanout parameter. With an ordered leaf scan, it could support (cK)-anonymity as well, for all c in N. Time complexity remains in $O(N\ log(N))$, and I/O cost for external computation is in $O(\frac{N}{B} log(\frac{N}{B}))$.

Since the R+-tree bulk-loading algorithm is applied on a set of points rather than a set of spatial objects with an extent, it is actually a variant of a *kd-B*-tree structure where hyper-rectangles have been shrunk to the minimum bounding boxes (MBB) of the subset of points in each equivalence class. It is important to note that a *kd-B*-tree is a bucket-oriented variant of a *kd*-tree, where the fanout of each node is defined by a parameter B that usually fits the disk block size. Therefore, many good features of the R+-tree approach makes it the reference algorithm for *k*-anonymization up until now.

Many works also proposed point partitioning structures in low dimension (2–3D) for privacy preserving location-based queries [10,11,12,13]. In this application domain, privacy is related to instant location of users and queries as well. Popular approaches design an anonymizer that dynamically provides a Cloaking Region to the Location-Based Service. For that purpose, Gruteser et al. [11] implements a *kd*-tree, whereas Mokbel et al. [13] uses a variant of a Point Region (PR) quadtree in *Casper*. Ghinita et al. [10] accommodate partitioning structures from kd-tree and *R*-tree to hash a database of Points Of Interest (POI) and answer approximate nearest-neighbor queries in a Privacy Information Retrieval (PIR) approach (*a PIR protocol allows a user to fetch a tuple from a database while concealing the identity of the tuple from a database server*) [14]. They also consider Hilbert space filling curves to map 2D points to single-dimensional data structures like B+-trees to index POIs. Actually, they argue that their PIR approach is independent from the partitioning structure as far as it provides at most N−−√ buckets within up to N−−√ POIs each. Other work [15] focused on geo-privacy in the sense of privacy-preserving location data publishing. In this context, a space filling curve was also employed to order both data points and POIs on the map. Quad-trees and space filling curves do not scale for higher dimensions, and the latter cannot guarantee non overlapping bounding boxes in the worse case. Furthermore, Arribas et al. [16] and Erola et al. [17] propose anonymizing high dimensional set valued data via microaggregation.

The short review states that every approach to geo-privacy accommodates in memory and implements well-known structure for multidimensional point data partitioning. k-anonymity was also studied from the cardinality constraint clustering point of view. On one hand, the anonymization algorithms were proposed [18,19,20] that achieve good quality, whereas neither they scale up in the size of the data set, nor they meet the basic orthogonal range query requirement since patterns are spheres (centers and radius) of each cluster. On the other hand, many grid clustering techniques ([21,22] for a short excerpt) have been proposed. However, none of them are as fast and scalable as Point Access Methods (PAM) since external storage support and dedicated insert-delete-search operations are missing. Then, PAMs remain the preferred logical structures for the anonymization of very large data sets.

1.5. Synopsis

The k-anonymity model proposed by Samarati and Sweeney [23] provides a practical solution for Privacy Preserving Data Publication (PPDP) and has been studied extensively for the last two decades. Anonymization via generalization and/or suppression is able to protect the privacy of individuals, but at the cost of information loss especially for high-dimensional data. This is due to the fact that generalization based k-anonymity is impeded by the curse of dimensionality as shown by Aggarwal [24]. Furthermore, in order to achieve an effective generalization, the tuples which share the same set of quasi-identifiers ought be close to each other so that the generalization may not lose too much information. Nevertheless, high-dimensional data forces greater amount of generalization to satisfy basic requirements for k-anonymity even for relatively smaller values of the parameter k. Hence, it is important to consider deeply the trade-off between privacy and information loss. Thus, the motivating question in this context is *how to minimize the information loss in the course of generalization, especially for high-dimensional data*.

Since the emergence of k-Anonymity, many generalization models have been proposed, e.g., ℓ-diversity, t-closeness, that tend to overcome the inherent problems with k-anonymity. Recently, Differential Privacy (DP) has emerged as a de facto standard in the domain of PPDP. Though DP has originally been proposed in the context of statistical disclosure control, it has gained much anticipated popularity in Privacy Preserving Data Mining (PPDM) and PPDP due to the fact that it promises strong privacy guarantees as compared to the techniques proposed previously. Quite recently, there is an encouraging trend of combining DP style privacy with generalization based approaches. Specifically, the works in [25,26,27] provide interesting directions to achieve DP for k-anonymity based generalization approaches since *Differentially Private* k-anonymous release has an effective privacy vs. utility trade-off.

This article presents *BangA*, a new generalization algorithm that meets generic PPDP features and that offers several new desirable features in regard to many other existing approaches, and especially compared to the R+-tree based anonymization algorithm [9].

Though BangA generalization algorithm can be extended to achieve any generalization mode, e.g., ℓ-diversity or t-closeness, we implement BangA to achieve a k-anonymous public release for the following reasons:

- k-anonymity is conceptually simple;
- k-anonymity does not enforce any constraint on the distribution of sensitive information in a public release [25]. This is one of the main reasons it can be extended to achieve more stronger notions of privacy e.g., *differential privacy* (DP).

The article is organized as follows: Section 2 discusses the main recipe for BangA. Section 3 and Section 4 explain how the raw data can be transformed to anonymous public release using BangA. Section 5 evaluates the effectiveness of the proposed approach.

2. GENERAL OVERVIEW

2.1. Preliminaries

In this section, we provide the basic definitions of some important concepts.

Definition 1. *(Quasi-identifier (from [28])). Consider a set of attributes* $A=A_1, A_2,\ldots,A_n$ *sampled from a general population. The set of attributes* $QI_1,\ldots,QI_w \in A$ *is said to be a quasi-identifier if these attributes can be used via linking to uniquely identify an individual from the general population.*

Definition 2. *(k-Anonymity from [1,28,29]). Let R be the data set and* QI *be the set of all quasi-identifiers in it. R satisfies k-Anonymity, if for a record* $t \in R$, *there exist at least* $k-1$ *other records* $t1,t2,\ldots,tk-1 \in R$ *such that* $t[QI]=t1[QI]=\ldots=tk-1[QI]$ *for all* $QI \in QI$, *where* $t[QI]$ *corresponds to the projection of t on the members of QI.*

Definition 3 (X-Equivalence relation $\sim$). *Let R be a table with schema* R(X,Y). *The X-equivalence relationship* $\sim X \subseteq R \times R$*is defined as:* $\forall t,u \in R$, $t \sim Xu \leftrightarrow t[X]=u[X]$.

For a tuple $t \in R$, the X-equivalence class of t, denoted $[t]_{\sim X}$, contains similar values on each component of X. In what follows, we refer to this QI-equivalence class as an equivalence class defined by a QI-equivalence relation.

Since the quasi-identifiers are susceptible to linking attacks, the table R is not released directly; it is first processed through a *sanitization mechanism* and then resulting table R^* is published.

There exist various sanitization mechanisms in the literature e.g., *generalization, suppression, bucketization*, etc. Since we employ generalization (generalization substitutes a specific value with a more general *less precise* value while preserving the data "truthfulness") as a sanitization mechanism, we provide below a definition of a generalization mechanism to achieve R^*.

Definition 4 (Generalization mechanism A). *Given a micro-data table R, a generalization mechanism is a bijective function* A*defined as follows:*

$$\begin{array}{llll} \mathcal{A}: & R\langle ID, QI, S\rangle & \rightarrow & R\langle ID, QI, S\rangle \\ & \mathrm{I}(R) & \longmapsto & \mathcal{A}(\mathrm{J}(R)) = \mathrm{I}(R^*) = \\ & & & \{\langle t[ID], v, t[S]\rangle \mid t[QI] \preceq v \wedge t \in R\}, \end{array} \quad (1)$$

where $J(R)$ is a generalized table of R, and v is a generalized value of $t[QI]$ according to any pre-defined partial order over QI. For the sake of simplicity, we denote in the following by R the instance $I(R)$ of R, and by R^* the instance J(R)that is a generalized version of R.

Note that such $a \preceq$ partial order is basically a containment relationship. In addition, $A(R)$ is not unique since there exist many different ways to generalize $t[QI]$ and the $A(R)$ enumeration is properly combinatorics. Then, regular approaches try to optimize a utility-based objective function in the generalization mechanism. This is the underlying reason why the k-anonymization based generalization mechanisms have been proven to be NP-hard [4].

We have employed global recoding as proposed by LeFevre et al. [30]. There are several advantages of the global recoding scheme:

- The strategy has conceptual simplicity.
- It is usually tractable to obtain an optimal solution [3].
- Finally, the inferences among the remaining attributes stay uniform with the original data set.

2.2. Overview of BangA

Figure 2 overviews the major steps involved in BangA from raw data to the anonymized release. It is important to mention here that BangA does not provide a straightforward implementation of Bang clustering. It redefines the main steps in bang clustering (e.g., the density index calculation (see Section 4.1)) to achieve high quality public release. It is also worth mentioning that the original definition of Bang clustering is not focused on releasing the data for specific purposes. Thus, we have significantly molded the original Bang clustering to fit into our problem.

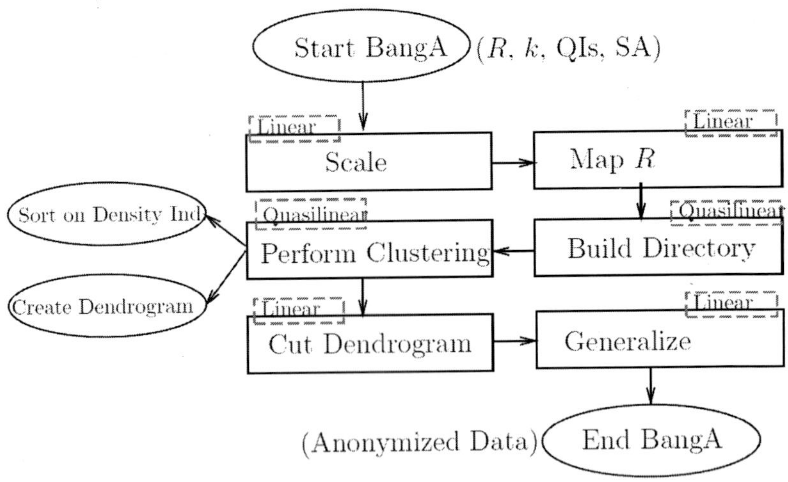

Figure 2. BangA: A big picture.

BangA consists of a six step process with an overall quasilinear complexity. The complexity of each phase is depicted in Figure 2.

BangA relies on an index structure, a so-called BANG file [31]. It operates on the axis-parallel space partitioning by means of nested hyper-rectangles rather than disjoint hyper-rectangles only. This singular feature allows for improving expressive power of patterns compared to *kd*-B-trees, including variants like R^+-tree. Consequently, it has a simple splitting strategy as scales are pre-defined over each dimension, thereby substantially increasing the efficiency of the algorithm. BangA starts by mapping the *n*-dimensional raw data to the unit hypercube [0,1]n where the BANG file is going to be defined. The Bang file stores the data points in the underlying space by a tree structure known as *bang directory*. This structure, which is governed by scales, partitions the *n*-dimensional space into so-called *block regions* or *blocks*. BangA is also able to provide multi-granular anonymous release. It performs a density-based clustering step on blocks of the BANG file to build a dendrogram. Then, a cut in the dendrogram could yield to the required equivalence classes that can be generalized to achieve high quality public releases and provide very flexible settings within one single run.

To sum up, various practically useful features of our approach are given below:

1) Spatial indexing technique—to leverage 30 years of research and experience in effective and efficient external multidimensional partitioning data structures built from very large data sets;
2) BANG file revisited—to accommodate a well-studied logical structure to the generalization problem;
3) Axis–parallel coding of equivalence classes—to ease orthogonal range queries for the end-user;
4) Nested hyper-rectangles—to improve quality of the anonymous public release keeping the axis-parallel coding feature up;
5) Grid-based partitioning—to make the computation faster and to control the privacy requirement by means of knowledge about the data;
6) Density-based clustering of blocks—to enforce quality of the anonymous public release in the process of block merging;
7) Multi-granular anonymization—to allow different settings for the k value with a single run of the algorithm.
8) Methodology for point and orthogonal range queries on non hyper-rectangular tabular data—to support exact match and basic range searching against anonymous public releases into spreadsheets.

Features 1, 3 and 7 are shared with at least the R+-tree based approach, whereas features 2, 4, 5, 6 and 8 are unique to BangA.

3. FROM RAW DATA TO THE BANG DIRECTORY

3.1. Data Space Partitioning

3.1.1. Mapping *n*-Tuples to the Unit Hypercube [0,1]n

The very first step of the overall anonymization process in BangA is to map n-dimensional raw data to the unit hypercube $[0,1]n$ where the BANG file is going to be defined. Records are n-tuples $\langle xi \rangle 1 \leq i \leq n$ over the set of quasi-identifiers, and each field value xi is an element of an attribute domain Di. Mapping records $[0,1]n$ consists of normalizing all the n domains. The operation becomes independent from the kind of variable. For instance, a straightforward linear transformation could be used for interval variables. Ratio and additive variables are also easy to manage. Ordinal variables, isomorphic to the natural numbers, could be handled as well, whereas nominal variables would require more effort to achieve the mapping, especially to define an ordering. Here, the application domain supports the definition of the right ordering. Samet reminds reminders in the introduction of his book [32] Page 479 that "it should be clear that finding an ordering for the range of values of an attribute is not an issue; the only issue is what ordering to use!" Then, any background consideration should be made, e.g., reasoning from domain taxonomies, to help finding the right ordering for categorical values.

The second strong requirement of the user-defined mapping to $[0,1]n$ is to provide a partitioning of domain Di within 2^{li} ranges, $li \geq 1$. The li parameter set up the resolution of the dimensional scale that will be used for space decomposition into the BANG file. Similarly, the unit interval $[0,1]$ is partitioned on the ith dimension into equal-sized ranges $[\frac{k}{2^{l_i}}, \frac{k+1}{2^{l_i}}]$, $0 \leq k \leq 2^{li}$ that map to the 2^{li} ranges from Di. Since there is no constraint on the mapping from $\Pi 1 \leq i \leq n Di$ to $[0,1]n$, background knowledge could be incorporated into scales in order for instance to fix undesirable data distribution or to emphasis portions of the data space in the transformation.

3.1.2. Grid Partitioning and Resolution

The n scales define a grid on the multidimensional data space as shown by Figure 3 for a two-dimensional space. Furthermore, as many grid-based structures, the BANG file divides the data space within a hierarchy of regions, where the leaves are the finest grained grid regions corresponding to the grid resolution. The BANG file performs iterative binary partitioning to develop the hierarchy from the entire data space (root) to the grid regions (leaves). Scales are used as partition lines for regular decomposition and the process is *cyclic through the dimensions.*

Each region in the hierarchy, including grid regions, is identified by a unique pair (r,ℓ), where r is the region number and ℓ is the granularity or level number. A key feature of the BANG file [31] is the region numbering scheme. It relies on a *bitstring* representation of regions that provides very efficient search facilities.

Figure 4 shows the numbering scheme. The outermost region is not given any identifier, whereas each non-root block region is identified by (r,ℓ), with *r* being the value of a string of binary digits, e.g., **010** is assigned to region (2,3). Each subspace of a binary partitioning is given value 0 (left/below part) or 1 (right/above part) and regions are identified by the sequence of values of binary partitioning.

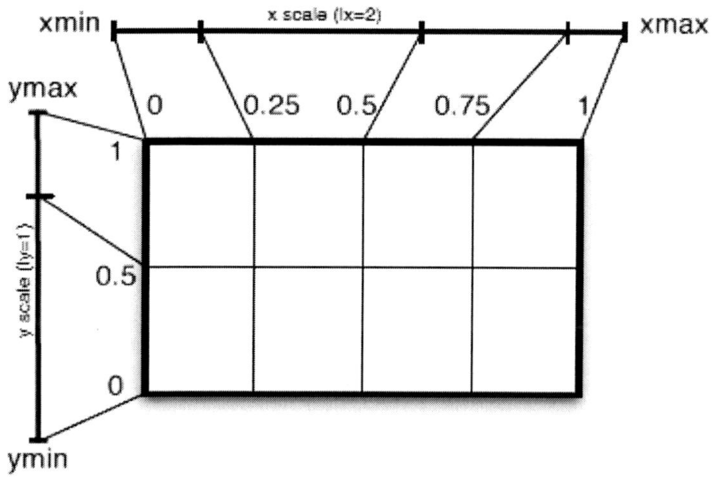

Figure 3. Grid partitioning of the data space by means of regular decompositions following dimensional scales.

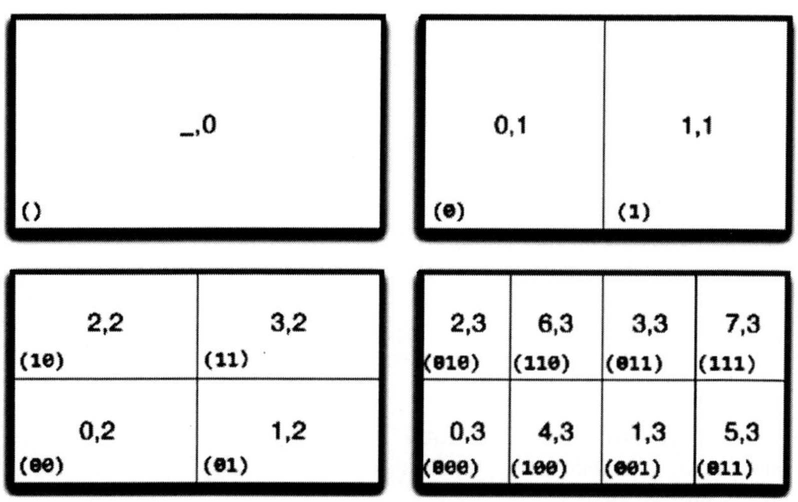

Figure 4. Block region numbering scheme.

3.1.3. About Shape

The BANG file relies on two axioms stated by Freeston [31]:

- The union of all sub-spaces into which the data space has been partitioned must span the data space.
- If two sub-spaces into which the data space has been partitioned intersect, then one of these sub-spaces completely encloses the other.

The second axiom states the existence of *nested regions* in the data space partitioning. Hence, the BANG file removes the requirement that the portions resulting from decomposition of the underlying space that are spanned by a region be hyper-rectangles.

The consequence is that the sub-space spanned by a bucket of point data, a so-called *a block*, is a combination of an enclosing region minus a set of enclosed regions. Then, it could be either a hyper-rectangular region or an axis-parallel concave portion of the space or even a disjoint set of sub-blocks.

In the following, we denote by X a hyper-rectangular region of the space given by the regular decomposition of the BANG file. The block enclosed into X is itself denoted by $[X]$. For instance, on Figure 5, the block [A] is assigned to region A and is defined as the sub-space spanned by region A minus regions B, D and G. Only the innermost regions, e.g., C, E, $F$and G in Figure 5, coincide with their corresponding blocks $[C]$, $[E]$, $[F]$ and $[G]$, respectively. Otherwise, the general definition of a block is as follows:

$$[X] = X - \bigcup_{Y \in \mathcal{H}_X} Y, \qquad (2)$$

where $\mathcal{H}X$ is the set of pairwise disjoint X-enclosed regions at the first level.

For the sake of simplicity, we also use $[X]$ to denote the data bucket from which points lie into the sub-space spanned by block $[X]$. Thus, $[X]$ is a subset of points and a complex shape as well, depending on the contextual meaning and without any ambiguity. The advantages of the block definition compared to hyper-rectangle-based *kd-B*-tree structures are a better observation of inherent clusters into data and also a higher filling rate of buckets.

A building algorithm as described by Freeston [31] guarantees the balance among buckets by redistribution, thereby making way for clustered value sets.

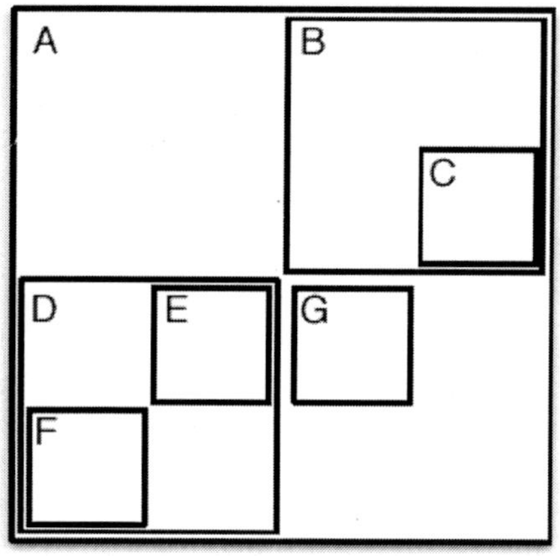

Figure 5. Example of a two-dimensional (2D) data space partitioned with the BANG file into seven nested block regions *A, B, C, D, E, F, G.*

3.2. Mapping Scheme

Both insertion and searching into the BANG directory require mapping data point coordinates to a block where the point lies by the way of the enclosing region number. To this end, the BANG file defines a set of hash functions [31] from data point coordinate $\langle x_i \rangle 1 \leq i \leq n$ to region number *r* at scaling level *ki*, by means of enclosing region coordinate $\langle d_i^{k_i} \rangle_{1 \leq i \leq n}$

$$d_i^{k_i} = \frac{\lfloor 2^{l_i}.x_i \rfloor}{2^{l_i - k_i}}, 0 \leq k_i \leq l_i. \tag{3}$$

Then, the convenient bit-string representation of region numbers allows for concatenating dimensional $d_i^{k_i}$ coordinates at levels k_i to one single $(r, \ell = \sum_i k_i)$ value. Let's take the following example:

$$d_1^2 = (10)_2, \qquad\qquad r = (101|011|10|0)_2$$
$$d_2^4 = (0110)_2,$$
$$d_3^3 = (110)_2,$$

Using such a numbering scheme, a data mapping function is defined with the help of following rules:

1) Level *k*+1 is created by splitting each region in a specific dimension.

2) The total number of regions for the level 1 is 2*k*.

3) The region (r,1) can be split into (r,k+l) and (r+2k,k+1).

4) Region numbers r and $r+2k$ are two possible extensions of the binary representation of r by one bit (the most significant).

5) The value space of a scale is doubled, if the splitting level in dimension i increases from k_i to k_i+1. This indicates an extension by one bit.

The value points can now be mapped to a unique region number by performing a simple concatenation of binary representation of the scale values. This efficient mapping is valid if regular decomposition of the space is cyclic through the set of dimensions. Offsets correspond to different dimensional scales depending on each attribute domain. It is important to mention here that the categorical values are first transformed into numerical values before mapping. We follow the same mechanism as adopted by Iwuchukwu et al. [9]. Mapping is depicted in Algorithm 1.

Algorithm 1: Mapping Scheme [33]

```
Data: r = 0; offset = 1; s = 0
Result: Region numbers
initialization;
while s < k do
    i = s mod n + 1;
    j = s div n + 1;
    if k[i] >= j then
        r = r + offset * b[i, k[i]-j];
        offset = offset * 2;
        s = s + 1;
    end
end
```

3.3. BANG Directory

Despite historical proximity with the Grid file and its variants, the directory of the BANG file is a tree rather than an array (grid). It follows Samet's claim [32], who states that the BANG file is a variant of the *kd*-B-trie, that is, a *kd*-B-tree with regular decomposition. Figure 6 shows an example of a BANG tree directory from partitioning of Figure 5. Blocks are in the leaves, whereas inner nodes contain entries of the form (subspace spanned by a child node, reference to child node). The subspace spanned by a child node is defined as an outermost hyper-rectangle and zero or more nested regions to remove. On Figure 6, we denote by *X* a simple hyper-rectangle (region) and X! a complex shape built as follows:

$$X! = X - \bigcup Y, \tag{4}$$

where *Y* is an *X*-nested region that occurs in the path from the root to the current node. For instance, the root of the BANG tree directory from Figure 6 contains two entries: *D* and *A*!. *D* is the sub-space spanned by the left child node, whereas *A*!=*A*−*D* is the sub-space spanned by the right child node. Note that the second *A*! of the tree is defined as follows:

$$A! = A - (B \cup D). \tag{5}$$

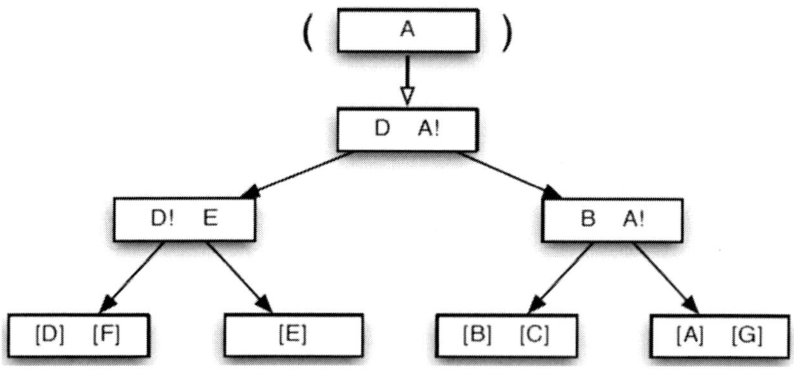

Figure 6. BANG directory of partitioning from Figure 5 represented as a *kd*-B-trie with fanout *B*=2.

The partitioning algorithm is simple yet efficient. As any *kd*–B-tree, its time complexity is *O*(*NlogN*). For external data, I/O cost still remains in $O(\frac{N}{B}.log\frac{N}{B})$ with *B* the disk block size. It performs incremental insertion of data points in a top-down manner. The enclosing grid region identifier is first computed thanks to the mapping scheme discussed before. The all path up to the root (the entire space) is also retrieved. Then, the BANG directory is searched for the smallest recorded region that encloses the data point. It is then assigned to the corresponding bucket.

When data bucket overflows, the algorithm operates splitting to balance the distribution of points between buckets. When a bucket *A* overflows, the value space is split and a new bucket *B* is created, and those records that lie in one half of the space are moved from the old bucket to the new one. Splitting is done by iteratively halving the space spanned by points in the bucket until the best balance is achieved. It gives birth either to a buddy region or to a newly enclosed region. Further details on splitting strategies can be found in [34]. The iterative halving strongly differs from the R^{+}-tree splitting strategy. Indeed, the BANG file operates from the entire space to blocks (top-down), whereas the R^{+}-tree operates from points to blocks (bottom-up). This distinct feature will be discussed further in the Performance section (see Section 5.2).

Finally, in order to first encompass anonymity requirements, and then to obtain the highest quality partitioning for the anonymization process, we set up the minimum filling rate to the lowest page size (M) value, depending on the grid resolution. Then, splitting is performed whenever the bucket size reaches $2M+1$. The second parameter B (the fan-out of the tree directory) is set to the page size such that it allows for building an external tree structure that scales up to potentially any size of data sets.

4. FROM BANG DIRECTORY TO ANONYMOUS PUBLIC RELEASE

We chose to achieve k-anonymity, based on the Bang$A$ generalization algorithm, and this optional post-processing step merges buckets from the BANG file to build equivalence classes of the anonymous release with the desired parameter $k \leq M$. Although the brute BANG directory already achieves very high quality in the public release thanks to non hyper-rectangular blocks, this additional processing increases the usefulness of the anonymous public release for higher k values. Actually, it could be performed on any other axis-parallel partitioning for anonymization and can be performed independently to any PAM algorithm, e.g., the R^{+}-tree approach.

4.1. Density-Based Clustering

BangA performs a density-based clustering on data buckets in a way similar to BANG- clustering [33]. BANG-clustering is a grid clustering approach that relies on a main memory kd-tree accommodated from the BANG file. It is a direct descendant from GRIDCLUS [34], itself based on the Grid file.

The algorithm computes a density index for each block assigned to a data bucket, and it creates a dendrogram by merging neighbor blocks having the closest density indices. However, BANG-clustering as well as GRIDCLUS compute density indices for each block $[X]$ by means of card([X]), the number of data points it contains, and $V(X)$, the spatial volume of the enclosing region only. This approach does not leverage the non hyper-rectangular blocks built by the BANG file. Thus, we refine the previous proposal and define the spatial volume $V([X])$ of a BANG directory entry [X] as follows:

$$V([X]) = \prod_{1 \leq i \leq n} e_X^i - \sum_{Y \in \mathcal{H}_X} \prod_{1 \leq i \leq n} e_Y^i, \tag{6}$$

where $X - \bigcup H_X\, Y$ is the block where the data points from [X] are located, and X and elements of H_X are hyper-rectangular regions. The e_α^i are extents of the region α on the ith dimension.

The density index $D([X])$ of block [X] is then given by the ratio:

$$\mathcal{D}([X]) = \frac{card([X])}{V([X])}. \tag{7}$$

Next, the algorithm performs a sort on blocks according to their decreasing density. The ranking of blocks supports the construction of a *dendrogram* obtained by merging iteratively pairs of *neighbor* blocks with the highest density indices, creating new clusters otherwise. Neighborhood is defined as a shared (n−1)-dimensional hyperplane between two block regions. The algorithm is detailed in [34].

4.2. Multi-Granular Anonymity

BangA allows multi-granular anonymity in a single run. However, instead of working directly on the index structure, we leverage the above *dendrogram* by means of computation of a cut. The main purpose is to allow the end-user to set the $k$value on the fly, without the need for scanning raw data. For the basic k=M setting, leaves of the dendrogram are straightforwardly the equivalence classes for the anonymous public release thanks to the filling requirements on the BANG file. The process to find a required cut in dendrogram is linear in the worst case to the number of nodes because a single path in the tree from the root is a local decision i.e., does the child node of the current node fulfill the cardinality constraint? If yes, we have the desired result; otherwise, the dendrogram traversing continues until cardinality constraints are met. Optimizations such as top-down/bottom-up crossing paths are still possible, but the procedure is already simple and fast (negligible cost compared to the rest).

If we consider higher *k* values, then we could perform a top-down depth-first traversal of the dendrogram until we reach maximally specialized *k*-filled blocks in each and every branch. The result cut draws the anonymous public release. Since we compute the cut on the dendrogram rather than on the index structure (*kd-B*-trie), then the *k* value is not restricted to $M\ell$ settings. Indeed, the approach gives BangA the ability to perform cM-anonymity, for any natural number *c*.

In R^+-tree based approach [9], this feature is offered thanks to an ordered leaves scan of the *kd-B*-tree that gives low quality releases compared to BangA since adjacent leaves could be merged even if they belong to very different branches of the tree, which are the bottom line for any clustering technique.

4.3. BangA and Other Syntactic Generalization Models

Though we employed BangA to achieve *k*-anonymity generalization model, it can be directly exposed to any sophisticated syntactic generalization model e.g., ℓ-diversity [29] and *t*-closeness [35]. As its R^+-tree counterpart, BangA would be able to incorporate constraints from the definition of the various existing generalization models in its anonymization process. The only accommodation would be to redefine the assignment and splitting strategies such that both resulting blocks satisfy the generalization model.

For instance, to make the anonymous release ℓ-diverse, it requires that at least ℓ sensitive values are “well represented” in each equivalence class. Thus, BangA would incorporate checking on sensitive values in its splitting decision to only create new ℓ-diverse blocks from old ones. In addition, it would add constraints on assignment of a new point into an existing block such that the resulting block still satisfies the ℓ-diversity; otherwise, the algorithm would locally redistribute points into blocks.

Then, in order to improve the utility of a final ℓ-diverse release, there can be several possible ways of switching the points in the blocks so as to keep the generalization to minimum.

4.4. Compaction Procedure

Iwuchukwu et al. [9] propose a compaction procedure that simply shrinks the envelope of each block to its MBB as shown in Figure 7. The R^+-tree approach natively computes such MBBs for every block. Consequently, the average volume of the blocks is minimized.

However, BangA operates a top-down decomposition of the space such that the union of all the blocks spans the entire space. Obviously, a compaction of each block would yield to a more accurate anonymous public release, and would still increase its quality w.r.t the R^+-tree numbers. Thus, it can be considered as a straightforward improvement of BangA, even if computation of non hyper-rectangular "MBB" , e.g., those on Figure 8 must be carefully defined.

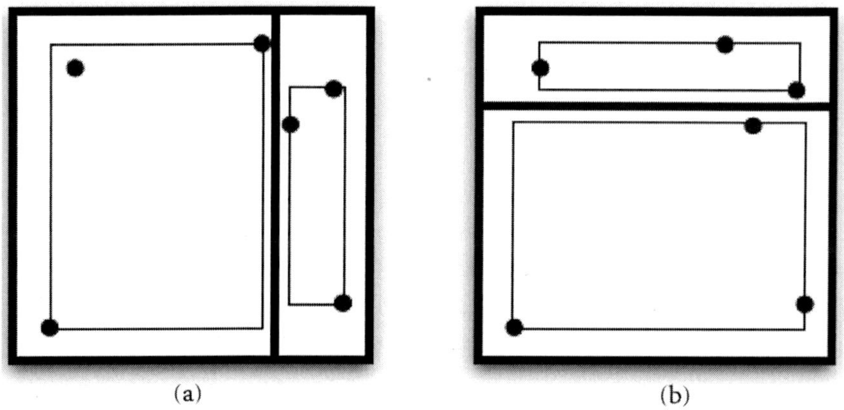

Figure 7. Low quality binary partitioning of a set of six points into blocks of at least three points, following either (**a**) *X*-axis; or (**b**) *Y*-axis.

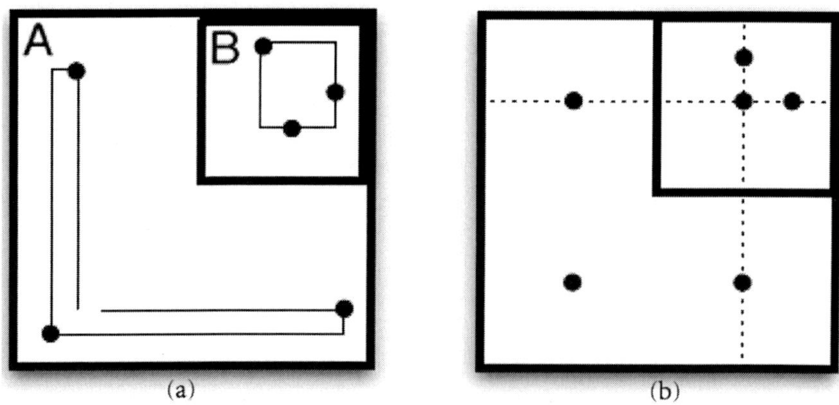

Figure 8. BANG file (NHR, non-hierarchical routing) partitioning with cardinality constraint (≤3 points), (**a**) on points from Figure 7; and (**b**) where HR partitioning fails.

5. EXPERIMENTAL VALIDATION

This section provides an extensive experimentation on BangA generalization algorithm to achieve *k*-anonymous public release.

5.1. Preparation and Settings

We conducted experiments on two data sets for the empirical evaluation of BangA. Efficiency and effectiveness were addressed according to time cost of the computation and quality of the public release, respectively. We also implemented R^+-tree approach for *k*-anonymization espoused in [9] for comparison with BangA, since it is commonly admitted that it is the reference algorithm. Though we had no access to the source code, we implemented the closest possible solution for the given approach strictly observing the requirements in [9] and adopted the same architecture than BangA for the sake of equity in the comparison analysis.

We used the popular "Adults" data set taken from the U.C. Irvine Machine Learning Repository. This data set, also known as "Census Income" data set, contains the data about individuals in the USA. We purged all records with missing values and were left with a table containing 1 million tuples. We used the attributes *Age*, *Zipcode* and *Education level* as quasi-identifiers. The second data set was "Voter list" taken as is from the experiments conducted by Sweeney [1] in her seminal work on *k*-anonymization. It contains 54,803 records (tuples with missing values are already removed). We used *Age*, *Zipcode* and *Salary* as quasi-identifiers. For stress testing and to study the behavior of both the approaches for high dimensional data, we used a third data set named "Customer" that was synthetically generated using a data generator tool (Datanamic data generator: [36]). This data set contains 1 million tuples with 15 attributes and all of them are used as quasi-identifiers.

To conduct the experiments in a real database environment, we first populated a PostgreSQL database with all three of the data sets. For convenience and code efficiency, data has been normalized (see Section 3.1) on the database level using advanced query facilities provided by PostgreSQL DBMS. We also used database statistics for query optimization. We applied R^+-tree and BangA approaches on all the quasi-identifiers of Adults, Voter list and Customer data sets. In the R^+-tree approach, the anonymization process is followed as in [9]. The algorithms are developed in C_{++} and are tested on a system with 4GB RAM and a Windows 7 operating system (Microsoft Corporation, Redmond, WA, USA).

5.2. Performance

Execution time of R^+-tree and BangA was measured on Voter list, Adults and Customer data sets—thus from 50 K to 1 Million records. Block size and page size was set to five, in order to evaluate the performance of each algorithm under stress of very small bucket and fan-out values. Many runs with different settings have been done and results always confirm those presented here. In this experiment, we evaluated the BangA algorithm with *dendrogram* construction, against the brute R^+-tree construction, i.e., w/o leaf scan or cut extraction.

Results are presented in Table 2. It shows a 50% lower time cost in favor of BangA compared to R^+-tree for the Voter list data set, and the difference still increases for large data sets like Adults since it spends up to 36% less execution time for the public release computation. For high dimensional data in Customer data set with 15 quasi-identifiers, BangA simply outperforms R^+-tree based anonymization, as the latter is unable to cope with such high dimensional data. In order to make a verifiable comparison of both approaches, a set of 1 million tuples with seven quasi-identifier attributes was randomly sampled from the Customer data set (having 1 million tuples and 15 quasi-identifier attributes). With a slightly large number of quasi-identifiers, results in Table 2 indicate substantially lower time cost in favor of BangA compared to R^+-tree. This shows that whatever the number of dimensions, BangA out performs its counterpart.

Table 2. Time cost (in seconds) of BangA and R^+-tree with B = 5 and M = 5.

Data Set	Size	Quasi-Identifiers	R^+-Tree	BangA
Voter list	54,803	3	6 s	3 s
Adults	1 million	3	91 s	55 s
Customer	1 million	15	Out of memory	240 s
Customer	1 million	7	1214 s	112 s

We did not compare the efficiency of BangA with previous proposal such as Mondrian [8], since experiments in [9] have shown that R^+-tree anonymization outperforms all of the previous algorithms. Thus, these experiments validate the very good behavior of BangA regarding performance and scalability. Moreover, the second storage structure of the BANG file guarantee that it could handle very large data sets without any drop in the performance.

The second result is as follows: we could argue that bottom-up spatial indexing is not systematically more efficient than top-down approach as conjectured in [9]. This result is given by our own experiments comparing in the same running environment R^+-tree approach (bottom-up) with BangA (top-down). Following the usual analysis on spatial access methods, we claim that the performance is mainly dependent from the splitting strategy. In BangA, we use regular decomposition following the grid, whereas the original R^+-tree grows by means of a quadratic procedure comparing pairwise distances of elements in an overflowed bucket. These strategies determine a constant factor (w.r.t. N) in time complexity that makes the execution time slower for the R^+-tree as shown on Table 2.

We also empirically evaluated the influence of input parameters on the process. We compared *fine-grained* and *coarse-grained* block sizes both for the R^+-tree and BangA. The results indicate that varying the M parameter, for a given output $k$value, does not affect the quality of data, but it reduces the execution time of both algorithms, as there would be less partitions in both cases. For instance, to build a 100-anonymous release, it is fast and safe to set $M = 100$ and to build the public release as the set of leaves of the tree directory. However, in this case, the construction of any k-anonymous release, $k< 100$, requires a new run. Thus, for a generic anonymization process, it is much better to set M to a quite small value and to then perform a cut in the the dendrogram given an online k parameter.

5.3. Quality of the Public Release

Since the k-anonymity problem relies on the trade-off between privacy of individuals and utility of the public release, we computed and compared quality of the public releases built, respectively, with BangA and with the R^+-tree, by means of several measures of information loss. The main idea is to evaluate the extent to which the data set has been distorted when generalizing records. We adopted generic quality measures, i.e., measures that do depend on the application domain or on a specific usage of the public release. Then, we first followed the experimental protocol described by Iwuchukwu et al. [9], with three different measures: *discernibility penalty* [3], *KL-divergence* [4] and the certainty metric proposed in [5].

We conducted experiments on the Adults and Customer data sets. Results for Adults data set are presented on Figure 9, Figure 10 and Figure 11 for certainty metric, discernibility penalty and KL-divergence, respectively. Roughly speaking, all of the experiments show that BangA provides higher quality public releases than the R+-tree since BangA curves systematically remain lower than those from the R^+-tree and quality measures are actually "penalty" measures.

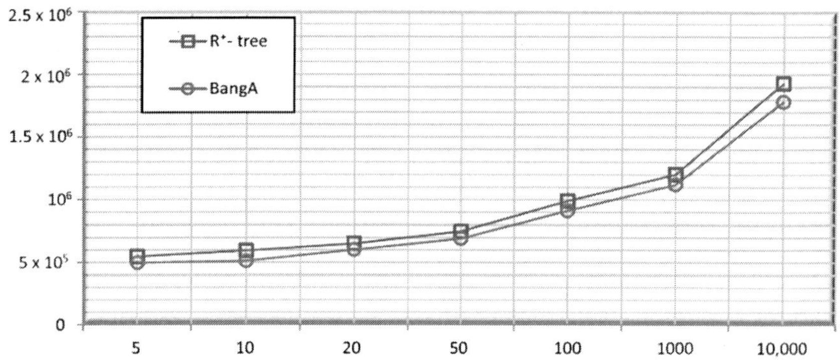

Figure 9. Certainty penalty (*Y*-axis) according to *k* parameter (*X*-axis) in 5, 10, 20, 50, 100, 1000, and 10,000 on a log-linear scale.

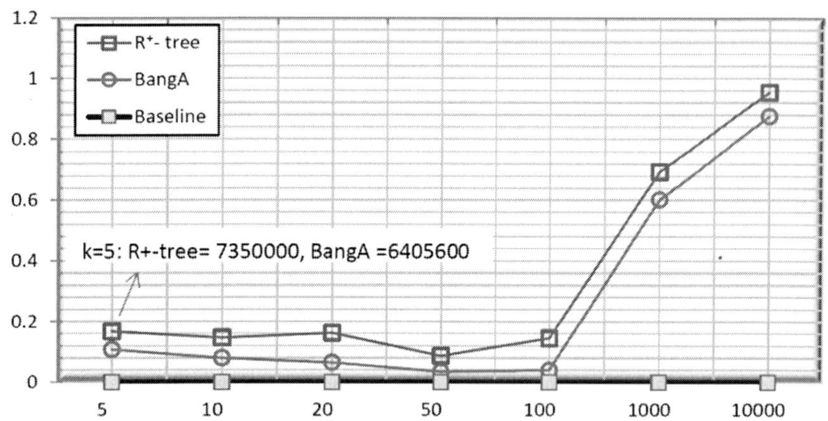

Figure 10. Discernability penalty (on *Y*-axis, normalized by log ratio on baseline) according to *k* parameter (*X*-axis) in 5, 10, 20, 50, 100, 1000, and 10,000.

Next, curves are all increasing since the higher the *k* parameter, the lower the overall quality. We could notice that the gap between the R^+-tree and BangA increases with *k* in the discernibility penalty. Here, we face the usefulness of the density-based clustering of BangA since merging elementary blocks give birth to very accurate equivalence classes even for higher k values, compared to the R^{+}-tree. To focus on specific values rather than analysis trends in large scale curves, we consider numbers for k=100 since it represents a descent rate of 0.01% of the size of the data set. Here, we observe 5% better quality in CM, 8% in DP an 9% in KL-divergence always in favor of BangA. For instance, in Figure 10 and Figure 11, we normalized the values, respectively, for KL-divergence and DCP for R^{+}-tree and BangA w.r.t. baseline values (original values are marked for k=5,1000 in Figure 11 and for k=5 in Figure 10) in order to highlight the gain achieved by BangA over R^{+}-tree based anonymization. These values are prototypical of the average gap between BangA and R^{+}-tree with a varying k value. Moreover, if we consider the baseline of DP, then the improvement of BangA with respect to the R^{+}-tree is more than 48%. Finally, it is worth noticing that CM is not designed to take into account non hyper-rectangular blocks since it aggregates dimensional range values. Thus, we only computed estimated values based on enclosing regions for BangA.

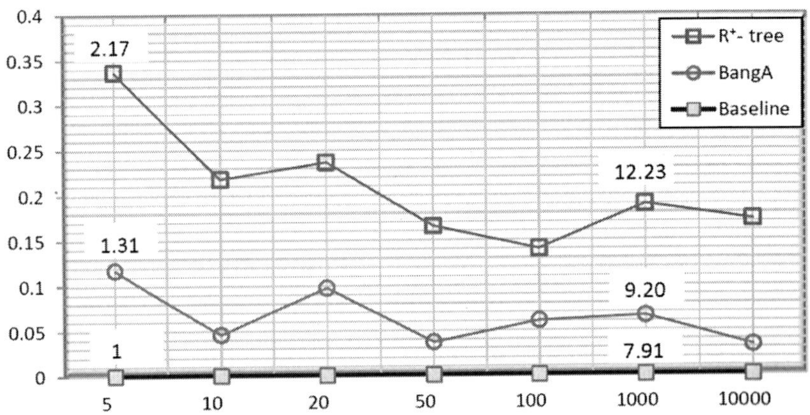

Figure 11. KL-divergence (on Y-axis, normalized by log ratio on baseline) according to k parameter (X-axis) in 5, 10, 20, 50, 100, 1000, and 10,000.

5.4. Query Accuracy

Apart from studying the quality of data through "penalty" measures and KL-divergence metrics, the utility of the anonymized data is also studied in terms of *relative query error*. In this section, we focus on *point and window queries* as they are important building blocks for statistical analysis and many data mining applications (e.g., association rule mining and decision trees).

This approach aims at measuring the utility of a sanitized release in terms of accuracy in answering aggregate queries. For answering the aggregate queries, the "COUNT" operator is considered in which the query predicate includes quasi-identifier attributes. Let R be a table with q quasi-identifiers, $QI_1,...,QI_q$, where $D(QI_i)$ denotes the domain of ithquasi-identifier. Then, the queries are of the form:

- **SELECT COUNT**(*) **from** R
- **WHERE** $qi_1 \in D(QI_1)$
- **AND** ... **AND** $qi_q \in D(QI_q)$

The predicate of a query contains two important parameters: (1) the query dimensionality parameter q; and (2) the query selectivity θ. The query dimensionality parameter q indicates the number of quasi-identifiers used in the predicate. The query selectivity θ indicates the number of values for each attribute A_j, $1 \leq j \leq n$. Query selectivity is usually obtained as follows:

$$\theta = \frac{|T_Q|}{|R|}, \tag{8}$$

where $|T_Q|$ is the number of tuples in the result set obtained from Q on R and |R| is the number of tuples in data set. The error for the query Q, denoted Error(Q), is the normalized difference between the result set from the evaluation of Q on raw and sanitized data, respectively. Then, the query error is calculated as follows:

$$\text{Error}(Q) = \frac{\text{sanitized\_count} - \text{actual\_count}}{\text{actual\_count}}, \tag{9}$$

where the result from the COUNT query on R is denoted by *actual_count* and on R^* as *sanitized_count*.

We used the randomly sampled Customer data set containing 1 million tuples and seven quasi-identifier attributes for these experiments.

The point queries are relatively easier to handle. The window queries are of the form:

- **SELECT COUNT**(*) **from** R
- **WHERE** $R.QI_1 \geq qi_1$ **AND** $R.QI_1 \leq qi_2$

- **AND**
- ...
- **AND**
- $R.QI_7 \geq qi_7$ **AND** $R.QI_7 \leq qi_7$

The above mentioned seven-dimensional query is dynamically created by using the upper and lower bounds on the range of each participating attribute. These bounds are defined as follows:

A *COUNT* query Q on the anonymized data set R^* fetches the count of tuples matching the query Q. For point query, the result set contains those tuples with the lowest value on the region level.

A window query Q returns a count of the records in R^* that matches Q. A tuple $t \in R^*$ is said to be a matching tuple for Q if the region spanned by t and the query Q have a non-null intersection i.e., t must intersect Q on all quasi-identifier attributes.

We conducted the experiments using query dimensionality parameter. The query error rate is calculated using Equation (9). We considered 300 randomly generated queries for conducting these experiments and calculated the average relative error.

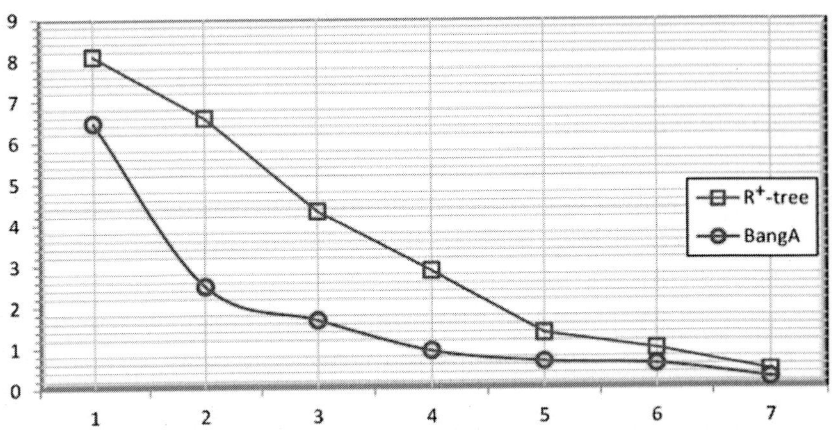

Figure 12. Error (Y-axis) for point queries according to varying query dimensionality (X-axis).

For these experiments, we anonymized the Customer data set on all seven quasi-identifiers and varied the query dimensionality parameter i.e., the number of *QI* attributes in query predicate. The results for point and window queries with varying query dimensionality are shown in Figure 12 and Figure 13. As the query dimension increases, average relative error rate decreases. Thus, the anonymized data performs better for queries with a larger query dimensions. BangA tends to be more stable than an R^{+} based approach showing less relative error rate for any query dimension.

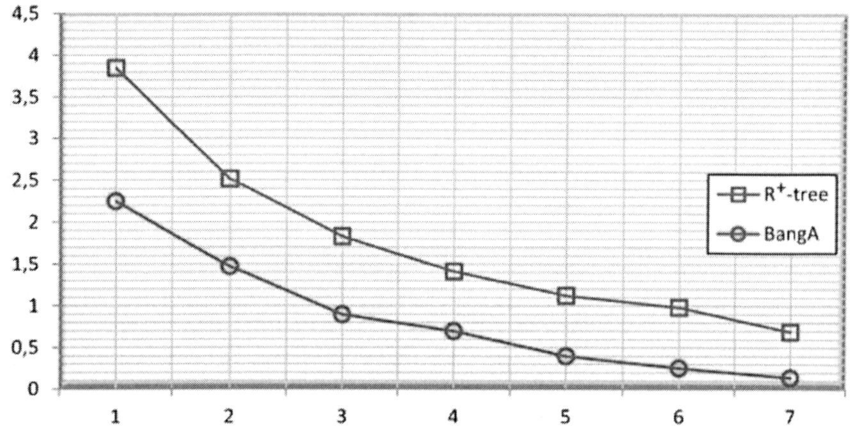

Figure 13. Error (*Y*-axis) for window queries according to varying query dimensionality (*X*-axis) with dimensions = 7.

6. CONCLUSIONS

In this communication, we proposed a new generalization algorithm called BangA. Based on the BANG file indexing structure, it performs very well and provides non hyper-rectangular blocks assigned to the equivalence classes of the public release. Furthermore, BangA allows for incorporating background knowledge in the dimensional scales that are used for regular decomposition. A post-processing step provides a density-based clustering of the blocks in order to achieve a high quality anonymization regardless of the *k* value, and, since the result of such post-processing is a dendrogram, then it offers the opportunity to build on demand *k*-anonymous release without reconstructing the dendrogram again. Along with the usual benefits, BangA can easily be extended to adopt the compaction procedure to achieve better utility of data. In addition, BangA can incorporate other generalization models like *ℓ*-

diversity by making slight adjustments in its assignment and splitting strategies.

As described in Section 4.3, BangA can be directly applied to any syntactic generalization model. Quite recently, DP has emerged as a state-of-the-art semantic privacy paradigm that offers strong theoretical privacy guarantees. Due to its inability of achieving practical implementation, there is a surge of works nowadays that tend to combine the practicalness of syntactic approaches with the effectiveness of DP. Since BangA performs very efficient multidimensional partitioning to achieve high quality generalization, inspired by Gehrke et al. [26] DP relaxation, as a future work, we may adopt the following framework for achieving DP:

- random sampling,
- regular generalization mechanism with multidimensional partitioning,
- Laplace mechanism for blocks with small counts.

BangA has been proved to manage sanitization with a generalization mechanism in a very efficient way and with a high quality output. Then, we legitimately propose to settle a sanitization process to achieve crowd blending with BangA.

ACKNOWLEDGMENTS

This research is supported by HEC Pakistan and Laboratoire LINA, University of Nantes.

REFERENCES

1. Sweeney, L. Achieving *k*-anonymity privacy protection using generalization and suppression. *Int. J. Uncertain. Fuzziness Knowl.-Based Syst.* **2002**, *10*, 571–588.
2. Agarwal, P. Range Searching. In *Handbook of Discrete and Computational Geometry*; CRC Press, Inc.: Boca Raton, FL, USA, 1997; Volume 2, pp. 809–838.
3. Bayardo, R.; Agrawal, R. Data privacy through optimal *k*-anonymization. In Proceedings of the 21st International Conference on Data Engineering (ICDE 2005), Tokyo, Japan, 5–8 April 2005; pp. 217–228.
4. Kifer, D.; Gehrke, J. Injecting utility into anonymized datasets. In Proceedings of the 2006 ACM SIGMOD International Conference on Management of Data, Chicago, IL, USA, 27–29 June 2006; ACM: New York, NY, USA, 2006; p. 228.
5. Xu, J.; Wang, W.; Pei, J.; Wang, X.; Shi, B.; Fu, A. Utility-based anonymization using local recoding. In Proceedings of the 12th ACM SIGKDD International Conference on Knowledge Discovery and Data Mining, Philadelphia, PA, USA, 20–23 August 2006; ACM: New York, NY, USA, 2006; p. 790.

6. Meyerson, A.; Williams, R. On the complexity of optimal *k*-anonymity. In Proceedings of the Twenty-Third ACM SIGMOD-SIGACT-SIGART Symposium on Principles of Database Systems, Paris, France, 14–16 June 2004; ACM: New York, NY, USA, 2004; pp. 223–228.
7. Fung, B.; Wang, K.; Chen, R.; Yu, P.S. Privacy-preserving data publishing: A survey of recent developments. *ACM Comput. Surv. (CSUR)* **2010**, *42*, 14.
8. LeFevre, K.; DeWitt, D.; Ramakrishnan, R. Mondrian multidimensional *k*-anonymity. In Proceedings of the 22nd International Conference on Data Engineering ICDE'06, Atlanta, GA, USA, 3–7 April 2006; p. 25.
9. Iwuchukwu, T.; Naughton, J. *K*-anonymization as spatial indexing: Toward scalable and incremental anonymization. In Proceedings of the 33rd International Conference on Very Large Data Bases, VLDB Endowment, Vienna, Austria, 23–27 September 2007; pp. 746–757.
10. Ghinita, G.; Kalnis, P.; Khoshgozaran, A.; Shahabi, C.; Tan, K. Private queries in location based services: Anonymizers are not necessary. In Proceedings of the 2008 ACM SIGMOD International Conference on Management of Data, Vancouver, BC, Canada, 9–12 June 2008; ACM: New York, NY, USA, 2008; pp. 121–132.
11. Gruteser, M.; Grunwald, D. Anonymous usage of location-based services through spatial and temporal cloaking. In Proceedings of the 1st International Conference on Mobile Systems, Applications and Services, San Francisco, CA, USA, 5–8 May 2003; pp. 31–42.
12. Damiani, M.; Bertino, E.; Silvestri, C. The probe framework for the personalized cloaking of private locations. *Trans. Data Priv.* **2010**, *3*, 123–148.
13. Mokbel, M.; Chow, C.; Aref, W. The new casper: Query processing for location services without compromising privacy. In Proceedings of the 32nd International Conference on Very Large Data Bases, Seoul, Korea, 12–15 September 2006; pp. 763–774.
14. Chor, B.; Goldreich, O.; Kushilevitz, E.; Sudan, M. Private information retrieval. In Proceedings of the 36th Annual Symposium on Foundations of Computer Science, Milwaukee, WI, USA, 23–25 October 1995; pp. 41–50.
15. Krishnamachari, B.; Ghinita, G.; Kalnis, P. Privacy-Preserving Publication of User Locations in the Proximity of Sensitive Sites. In *Scientific and Statistical Database Management*; Springer: New York, NY, USA, 2008; pp. 95–113.
16. Navarro-Arribas, G.; Torra, V.; Erola, A.; Castellà-Roca, J. User *k*-anonymity for privacy preserving data mining of query logs. *Inf. Process. Manag.* **2012**, *48*, 476–487.
17. Erola, A.; Castellà-Roca, J.; Navarro-Arribas, G.; Torra, V. Semantic Microaggregation for the Anonymization of Query Logs. In *Privacy in Statistical Databases*; Springer: Berlin/Heidelberg, Germany, 2010; pp. 127–137.
18. Aggarwal, G.; Feder, T.; Kenthapadi, K.; Khuller, S.; Panigrahy, R.; Thomas, D.; Zhu, A. Achieving anonymity via clustering. In Proceedings of the Twenty-Fifth ACM SIGMOD-SIGACT-SIGART Symposium on Principles of Database Systems, Chicago, IL, USA, 26–28 June 2006; ACM: New York, NY, USA, 2006; pp. 153–162.
19. Byun, J.; Kamra, A.; Bertino, E.; Li, N. Efficient *k*-anonymization using clustering techniques. In Proceedings of the Advances in Databases: Concepts, Systems and Applications, Bangkok, Thailand, 9–12 April 2007; pp. 188–200.
20. Chiu, C.; Tsai, C. A *k*-anonymity clustering method for effective data privacy preservation. In Proceedings of the Advanced Data Mining and Applications, Harbin, China, 6–8 August 2007; pp. 89–99.
21. Pilevar, A.; Sukumar, M. Gchl: A grid-clustering algorithm for high-dimensional very large spatial data bases. *Pattern Recognit. Lett.* **2005**, *26*, 999–1010.
22. Wang, W.; Yang, J.; Muntz, R. STING: A statistical information grid approach to spatial data mining. In Proceedings of the International Conference on Very Large Data Bases, Athens, Greece, 26–29 August 1997; pp. 186–195.
23. Samarati, P.; Sweeney, L. Generalizing data to provide anonymity when disclosing information. In Proceedings of the ACM SIGACT SIGMOD SIGART Symposium on Principles of Database Systems, Seattle, WA, USA, 1–3 June 1998; Volume 17, p. 188.
24. Aggarwal, C. On *k*-anonymity and the curse of dimensionality. In Proceedings of the 31st international conference on Very Large Data Bases, VLDB Endowment, Trondheim, Norway, 30 August–2 September 2005; pp. 901–909.

25. Li, N.; Qardaji, W.; Su, D. Provably Private Data Anonymization: Or, k-Anonymity Meets Differential Privacy. Available online: https://www.cerias.purdue.edu/assets/ pdf/ bibtex_archive/2010-24.pdf (accessed on 29 December 2016).
26. Gehrke, J.; Hay, M.; Lui, E.; Pass, R. Crowd-Blending Privacy. In *Advances in Cryptology–CRYPTO 2012*; Springer: Berlin/Heidelberg, Germany, 2012; pp. 479–496.
27. Soria-Comas, J.; Domingo-Ferrer, J.; Sánchez, D.; Martínez, S. Enhancing data utility in differential privacy via microaggregation-based *k*-anonymity. *VLDB J.* **2014**, *23*, 771–794.
28. Sweeney, L. *k*-anonymity: A model for protecting privacy. *Int. J. Uncertain. Fuzziness Knowl. Based Syst.* **2002**, *10*, 557–570.
29. Machanavajjhala, A.; Kifer, D.; Gehrke, J.; Venkitasubramaniam, M. l-diversity: Privacy beyond *k*-anonymity. *ACM Trans. Knowl. Discov. Data (TKDD)* **2007**, *1*, 3.
30. LeFevre, K.; DeWitt, D.J.; Ramakrishnan, R. Incognito: Efficient full-domain *k*-anonymity. In Proceedings of the 2005 ACM SIGMOD International Conference on Management of Data, Baltimore, MD, USA, 14–16 June 2005; ACM: New York, NY, USA, 2005; p. 60.
31. Freeston, M. The BANG file: A new kind of grid file. *ACM SIGMOD Rec.* **1987**, *16*, 260–269.
32. Samet, H. *Foundations of Multidimensional and Metric Data Structures*; Morgan Kaufmann: Burlington, MA, USA, 2006.
33. Schikuta, E.; Erhart, M. The BANG-Clustering System: Grid-Based Data Analysis. In *Advances in Intelligent Data Analysis Reasoning about Data*; Springer: Berlin/Heidelberg, Germany, 1997; pp. 513–524.
34. Schikuta, E. Grid-clustering: An efficient hierarchical clustering method for very large data sets. In Proceedings of the 13th International Conference on Pattern Recognition, Vienna, Austria, 25–29 August 1996; Volume 2, pp. 101–105.
35. Li, N.; Li, T.; Venkatasubramanian, S. *t*-closeness: Privacy beyond *k*-anonymity and *l*-diversity. In Proceedings of the IEEE 23rd International Conference on Data Engineering, ICDE 2007, Istanbul, Turkey, 16–20 April 2007; pp. 106–115.
36. Datanamic Data Generator. Available online: http://www.datanamic.com/datagenerator/ index.html (accessed on 31 December 2016).

CHAPTER 4

Program Counter Encoding for ARM®Architecture

Seho Park, Yongsuk Lee, Gyungho Lee

Department of Computer Science and Engineering, Korea University, Seoul, Korea

ABSTRACT

ARM® is the prevalent processor architecture for embedded and mobile applications. For the smartphones, it is the processor for which software applications are running, whether the platform is with Apple's iOS or Google's Android. Software operations under these platforms are prone to semantic gap, which refers to potential difference between intended operations described in software and actual operations done by processor. Attacks that compromise program control flows, which result in these mantic gaps, are a major attack type in modern software attacks. Many recent software protection schemes for servers and desktops focus on protecting program control flows, but there are little protection tools available for protecting program control flows of mobile applications for ARM processor architecture. This paper uses a program counter (PC) encoding technique (PC-Encoding) to harden program control flows under ARM processor architecture. The PC-Encoding directly encodes control flow target addresses that will load into the PC. It is simple and intuitive to implement and incur little overhead. Encoding the control flow target addresses can minimize the semantic gap by preventing potential compromises of the control flows. This paper describes our efforts of implementing PC-Encoding to harden portable binaries in ELF (Executable and Linkable Format).

Keywords: Compiler, Control-Flow Integrity, PC-Encoding, Software Security, ARM®

1. INTRODUCTION

Software security has become an increasingly important concern with the prevalent use of the Internet. With the looming popularity of the Internet of Things (IoT), this concern is becoming even more prevalent with respect to every aspect of modern life. A variety of security techniques have been researched and developed at the software level, and some of these have been adopted in practice. There are many researches focusing on control flow hardening for server and desktop environments, but there are relatively fewer studies about hardening the program control flow for embedded and mobile devices, i.e., tend to concentrates on Intel's x86 architecture. Attackers, however, are continually capable of finding vulnerabilities, and while the success of the attacks is, more or less, dependent on the same techniques of the past, the incidence rates that are being documented make a cause for a greater alarm; furthermore, the number of vulnerabilities that are utilized for the attacks is increasing, and the risks inherent in the security vulnerabilities have become even more serious.

A major portion of the vulnerabilities allows a memory overwrite, which in turn causes a program control transfer that is contrary to the intentions of the original programmer. The existence of this semantic gap, i.e., the potential difference between the intended operations described in software and the actual operations performed by a processor, is from the existence of a memory overwrite vulnerability.

There have been a variety of techniques for the prevention of arbitrary memory overwrites, along with schemes for the prevention of the activation of injected attack codes, e.g., the numerous variations of DEP (data-execution prevention) [1] [2] [3] [4] ; however, the incidence of software attacks that utilize the memory overwrite is ongoing. ROP (return-oriented programming) [5] is a recent attack method that allows a code-reuse attack without an injection of attack code; the code reuse attack utilizes a memory overwrite to activate the preexistent code in memory to start an attack [6] [7] [8] [9] [10]. Note that a memory overwrite is essential for not only traditional code-injection attacks [11] , but also for recent code-reuse attacks that seek to divert program control flows from the intended operations that are described in software [12].

To protect the control flow from the software attacks, we need to enforce the integrity of the control flows through an examination of the destinations of all the control flow transfer instructions to confirm their legitimacy. Conceptually, one can generate a control-flow graph (CFG) for a program under protection and check at runtime to see whether the program execution actually follows the CFG. Even without a contemplation of the accuracy of the CFG, a couple of issues arise from this conceptual control flow validation scenario such as CFG granularity and the representation and storage of the CFG. System-call-level CFG was utilized during the early days of the technology to reduce the overhead of the CFG representation and storage, and also to enable access to the CFG at runtime [13] ; however, such a coarse-grain CFG often fails to catch a compromised control flow because many hundreds or thousands of instructions can exist between the system calls.

The CFI (control-flow integrity) [14] [15] [16] is one of the early proposals for checking and validating each control-flow transfer at the fine-grain machine instruction level, whereby the destinations of all the indirect branch instructions are forcibly checked. The full CFG, comprising a pair of IDs, the branch-instruction address ID and its target address ID, for all the indirect branch instructions is generated by a binary patch, and each control-flow transfer is checked at run time per the CFG. Even if the CFG is limited to statically linked procedures, however, it is still very difficult to draw a fully accurate CFG in practice. Also, there is a not so trivial overhead for representing and accessing the CFG. CFI implementations in general utilize the fact that a code region is safe from a memory overwrite, and the instruction addresses and target addresses are also coalesced together to make the CFG representation compact and fast to access. There have also been some CFI-implementation methods with a looser notion of CFG for the ease of the deployment and a lesser performance overhead [17] [18] ; although, the coalesced address ID and the looser notion of the CFG will result in more of the semantic-gap potential, thereby reducing the robustness of the protection [19].

PC-encoding can protect the general indirect-branch instructions as the CFI does, but without the requirement of CFG generation [20] [21] [22]. Instead, PC encoding encodes the target address at its definition and requires a proper decoding of the target address for a legitimate control-flow transfer. PC encoding has little room for the semantic gap because the CFG is not generated as an approximation of what is described in the program, but the program itself acts as the CFG; furthermore, unlike randomizing the instruction set architecture [23] or the program code [24] , checking the legitimacy of each control-flow transfer requires only a couple of machine instructions without a need to access the memory for the CFG. PC encoding ensures a minimal performance degradation.

This paper describes our efforts to implement PC-encoding for hardening the portable ELF (executable and linkable format) binary. ARM® processor stores the return address at *lr* (link register) when it uses a *bl* (branch link) instruction to call a function. In the function prologue, PC encoding encrypts the *lr* and *fp* (frame pointer register) before pushing into the stack. At the function epilogue, the *fp* and *pc* (program-counter register) are restored after decrypted from the stack. Our LLVM (low-level virtual machine)-based PC-encoding compiler provides control flow protection without significant overhead for programs that run under the ARM®-processor architecture [25]. Compared to other software based control flow hardening schemes, PC-encoding makes a suitable fit for the relatively simple architectural environment of ARM®.

The remainder of the paper is organized as follows: Section 2 discusses the basics of PC encoding. The process of applying PC encoding for the ARM-Linux- ELF binary is described in Section 3. Section 4 presents the performance-test results from the Gem5 simulator. Also discussed is a comparison of PC-encoding with a typical CFI implementation. This paper concludes in Section 5 with a discussion of the limitations of our current PC-encoding implementation for ARM® processors.

2. BACKGROUNDS

A program control flow is dictated by program data that is loaded to the program counter at runtime, which we call *PC-bound* data. The basic idea of PC encoding involves the checking of the integrity of the PC-bound data. PC encoding ensures the integrity of the program control flow by protecting the PC-bound data; it encodes the PC-bound data at their definition and during its use, decoding is performed with a secret key. PC encoding provides a sound solution for hardening the program control-flow for embedded platforms because it only incurs a small performance penalty. Data encoding/decoding computation can also be simplified, whereby simple encoding/decoding operations that can be completed in one or two cycles may be employed, e.g., exclusive-or. Also, a compatibility issue is non-existent because the memory layout does not need to be changed; moreover, cooperation with a non-hardened binary is feasible.

Software operations are prone to the semantic gap, which refers to potential difference between intended operations described in software and actual operations done by the processor. The semantic gap always exists in a sense that actions done by the processor do not have exactly the same semantics of the program code in high level languages. But only the semantic gaps related with program control flow may cause a critical vulnerability. As an example, consider functions like *strcpy()* or *memcpy()* have been used for copying data to a specified variable. Programmer using these functions may intend to copy some data to a specified variable but without a consideration about the actual actions of the processor. A compiled instruction sequence using the functions may not include a logic for checking the size of data to copy, causing a PC-bound data located next to the local variable for the data copy be overwritten. Also, note that the processor executes one instruction at a time, independent from other instructions. As a result, the processor is not aware of the context for each instruction and may execute the instructions out of context if the PC-bound data is compromised.

PC encoding encodes the destinations of indirect jump instructions including return addresses on stack, function addresses on GOT, function pointers, and exception handlers. It is, however, impossible to overwrite the hardcoded destination of a direct jump, and direct jumps are therefore excluded from the scope of PC encoding. Figure 1(a) shows the normal code parts of an object file. A memory-overwrite attack can occur during the execution time of {*Some code*}. If an attacker contaminates the PC bound data during the Some-code execution, the *"movpc, PC-bound data"* instruction will take the control flow to an illegal location. Figure 1(b), however, shows a hardened case. Due to the key value, the PC-bound data is already in an encoded state during the Some-code execution, so an attacker cannot overwrite the intended-value to PC-bound data properly; the key value must be known by an attacker for a successful attack.

In general, the key must be stored in a recoverable point at the time of verification, and the memory is one of the typical places used for the key storage; however, if the key is stored in the memory, the key itself can be vulnerable to a memory-overwrite attack. This dilemma can be found in a number of protection schemes; for example, StackShield copies the return address of the function to a specially reserved and managed area called Global Ret Stackor Shadow RET Stack [26]. Stack Shield then performs an integrity check through a comparison of the two values at the functions epilogue; however, the Shadow RET Stack is also stored in the dynamically-writable memory area, and it can still be a target of a memory-overwrite attack. Some schemes are therefore supported by low- level software like a kernel to ensure a read-only property of the key storage. These solutions maintain the key storage as a read only area during a code execution that is under protection, and they temporarily change the storage permission into a writeable form at the time that the PC-bound data is defined, e.g., the *mprotect()* function can change the memory permission dynamically, but this function can also be the victim of an RTL attack [27] [28] [29] [30] [31]. As a result, the *mprotect()* function can become a more serious vulnerability. More- over, the frequent changes of the memory permission cause a critical performance penalty.

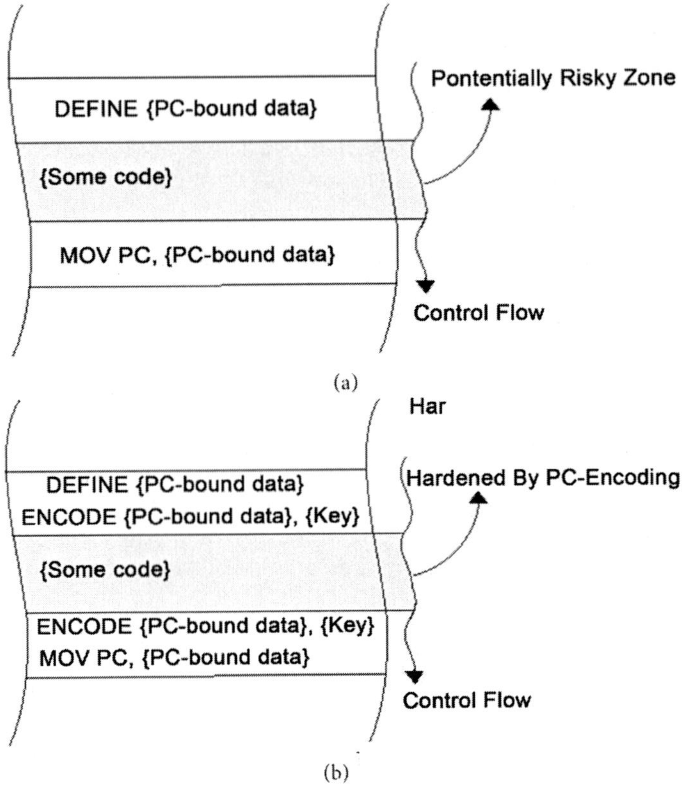

Figure 1.PC-encoding concepts.

The key value used in this paper is the self-address of the PC-bound data. The self-address is the address of the memory location containing the PC-bound data. The self-address does not require any additional storage, and it is always available as a part of the value-address pair. Therefore, it is possible to extract the key easily at the moment of the decoding or the encoding of the target addresses. Also, it is not possible to compromise the self-address with a memory- overwrite attack because the address is not in the memory. The memory layout for different address spaces can be allocated with some level of randomness in the ASLR environment [31] [32] , and the allocation order of the function frames on the stack space can vary depending on the dynamic execution flow of the process.

One can apply PC-encoding to all indirect calls including calls and returns; however, it is difficult to locate the exact locations of all indirect calls with the exception of a few stylized cases such as GOT entries, function returns, and exception handlers. This paper focuses on a basic implementation under the ARM®-processor environment. In consideration of the fact that call/return pairs are the most frequent indirect branches, this paper focuses on the encoding and decoding of the return addresses for our first realization of the PC-encoding compiler for ARM® processors.

A variety of high-level languages such as C, C++, Fortran, and Ada can benefit from PC-encoding. PC-encoding adds an instrumentation of a few instructions into a binary executable. There are three ways one can add new instructions for the instrumentation into a binary executable. The first is a runtime modification (binary editing); however, with the binary editing at run time, it is possible to damage the functionality of the binary executable. Nevertheless, the technique may have the highest utility in the sense that it is independent of the languages that the code is written in. The second way is a binary patch. A binary patch is also of a high utility because it requires no source code. With this technique, it is possible to insert a protection patch by using only the executable binary without a dependence on the type of high-level language; however, a relocation of the addresses related to the inserted code patch can be a difficult problem to handle, and many clues for an understanding of the programmer's intent disappear from the binary executable. The third way is a compile-time modification. Generating additional code regarding a security mechanism at the compile step has a disadvantage, though, due to a dependency on the type of underlying high-level language. However, it can add the instrumented protection in a relatively reliable way due to its use of an internally-validated library. This leads to a guarantee of the functionality of the instrumented program.

In this paper, we have applied our PC-encoding technique at the compile time under the LLVM compiler infrastructure. The aim of the LLVM is to facilitate developing a compiler in a way that is independent from specific high-level languages and processor architecture. The LLVM frontend is separate from the code generation for an elimination of the dependency upon a specific high-level language. This frontend converts a high-level language code into an intermediate language code called the *LLVM IR*, e.g., the Clang is a typical frontend for the C language. By utilizing these features, codes that have been written in a variety of high-level-language types can be easily hardened with the PC-encoding technique.

3. IMPLEMENTATION

In the call/return convention under ARM®-processor architecture, ARM® processor stores the return address at *lr* (link register) when it uses a *bl* (branch link) instruction to call a function. In the functions prologue, the *lr* and *fp* (frame pointer register) are pushed into the stack. At the functions epilogue, the *fp* and *pc* (program-counter register) are restored. Figure 2 shows an implementation overview of generating the hardened ARM-Linux-ELF binary via PC-encoding. This walk through is consisted of three steps. In step 1, the written code is converted from a high-level language to the LLVMIR code. In step 2, the hardened- assembly file is created with an LLVM IR file. The LLC is a tool that can convert LLVM IR files into a specified architecture-assembly file. It is possible to adjust options to make the assembly files of other architectures; for this paper, an assembly file for ARM® processors was constructed. In step 3, it is possible to determine the appropriateness of the patches or to collect the number of added instructions by analyzing the assembly file; then, step 3 converts the assembly file into a binary object file using the ARM®-processor assembler.

In step 2, a modified LLC named LLC.PCE is used for the implementation. The LLC.PCE applies PC-encoding to the LLVM IR file regardless of the high level language used. In the LLVM, the ARM Frame Lowering class is responsible for the code generation of the function frame in the ARM environment. The emit Prologue and the emit Epilogue functions of the ARM Frame Lowering Class were edited for the PC-encoding.

The general prologue and epilogue that the gcc compiler generates for the ARM environment are below:

Prologue:

pushfp,lr *//Save frame pointer and return*

add sp,sp,$n *//Allocate space for local variables*

Epilogue:

movsp,fp *//Move stack pointer to stack base*

popfp,pc *//Restore frame pointer and return*

In the above code, the *lr* register is stored on the stack in the prologue, suggesting that the *lr* register can be overwritten by a memory-overwrite attack. PC-encoding inserts encoding and decoding instructions for the protection of the *lr*, as follows:

Prologue:

eorlr,lr,sp *//Encode return address*

pushfp,lr *//Save frame pointer and return*

add sp,sp,$n *//Allocate space for local variables*

Epilogue:

movsp,fp *//Move stack pointer to stack base*

ldrlr,[sp,#4] *//Load return address at lr*

eorlr,lr,sp *//Decode return address*

strlr,sp *//Save decoded return address*

popfp,pc *//Restore frame pointer and return*

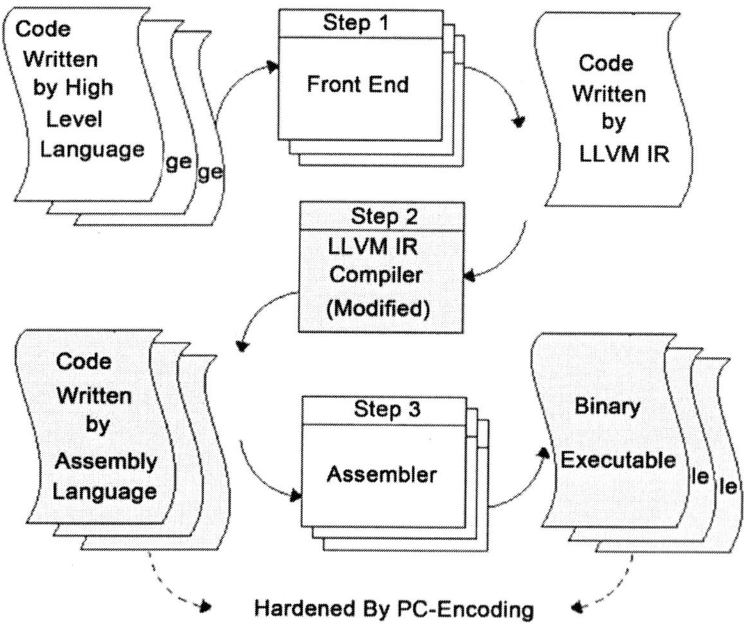

Figure 2. Implementation overview.

In the above code, four instructions are added for PC-encoding. In this case, it is inevitable to have a memory access at the decode because of "*pop fp, pc*". The return address moves directly to the PC register *p c*, but the PC-encoding must decode the return address before this action. The decode process must therefore be accompanied by a memory access. At the function exit, the main intention of a programmer is just "return to the caller": The specific status of the registers and the memory are not always a part of the programmer's consideration. However, it is possible to manipulate the return address by using a frame-pointer overflow. *If* we follow *gcc* style of prologue and epilogue, compiler and its library do not correct this potential semantic-gap source. Furthermore, since the *fp* register is pushed to the stack, this can also be compromised by a memory overwrite attack. Both the *lr* and *fp* registers must therefore be encoded for the full protection of the return process in the gcc version.

To avoid the problem of additional memory access and the issues with the frame pointer, we have used the features in LLVM. Compilers do not always need to make the prologue-epilogue in gcc style as previously shown. LLVM can create a different prologue-epilogue form as follows:

Prologue:

Pushlr *//save return address*

add sp,sp,$n *//Allocate space for local variables*

Epilogue:

addsp, sp, $n *//Mov stack pointer to base*

poplr *//Restore return address*

movpc,lr //Return to caller

In the above code, an *fp* register is not utilized. The offsets are calculated based on the sp instead of the *fp* when the local variables or function parameters are accessed; furthermore, the return address is restored at *lr* before it moves into *pc*. As a result, it is possible to remove a memory access during the decode process. PC-encoding implemented without the additional memory access is as follows:

Prologue:

eorlr,lr,sp *//Encode return address*

pushlr *//Save encoded return address*

sub sp,sp,$n *//Allocate space*

Epilogue:

add sp,sp,$n *//Move stack pointer to base*

poplr *//Restore return encoded address*

eorlr,lr,sp *//Decode return address*

movpc,lr//Return to caller

The two added eor instructions have no memory reference; as a result, we can protect the return with just two register-to-register instructions. Encoding the target addresses can avoid the unintended control transfer because it allows the control transfer to only a target address that is legitimately decoded, avoiding the potential semantic gap.

The PC-encoding implementation depends on a trust worthy low-layer software like the OS kernel. If the code is contaminated by an arbitrary memory- overwrite attack, it is not possible to protect the PC-bound data with PC-en- coding; however, this does not mean that PC-encoding needs special functions like *mprotect()*.

4. PERFORMANCE

By comparing the efficiency of the PC-encoding technique with a typical implementation of the well-known CFI [14] , it is possible to illustrate the performance-overhead potential. One can patch the code with the ARM®-processor assembly to enforce the CFI as shown in Figure 3.

When the CFI is implemented on the ARM® processor, the caller needs one instruction and the recipient of the call needs three additional instructions; regarding the latter, one of the instructions is a memory reference instruction, while another is a conditional branch instruction. A memory reference instruction will take longer than the others, and a conditional branch instruction also may cause more cycles due to branch misprediction than those required by a normal command; consequently, a relatively large performance degradation may incur. Table 1 shows the number of instructions between the CFI and the PC- encoding.

```
caller:
blcallee        //Call the callee
b next          //Bypass the ID
[AABBCCDD] //block ID
next:
.
callee:
pushlr          //Save return address
sub sp,sp,$n    //Allocate space for local variables
.
add sp,sp,$n    //Move stack pointer to base
poplr           //Restore return address
ldr r3,[lr,#4]  //Obtain ID of return block
cmp r3,AABBCCDDh //Check validation
bne error label // Error handling
movpc,lr  //Return to caller(next)
```

Figure 3. Example instrumentation for CFI.

ROP [28] is one of the latest powerful code-reuse attacks that can bypass the existing defenses such as DEP, ASLR, and ASCII-Armor [30]. Attackers can gather fixed-position code parts that are called gadgets, and these fixed-position addresses can be selected without a containing NULL byte. By using these *gadgets*, the attacker can perform a desired operation without executing any code in the NX (non-executable) area. The overwrite attack and the advanced RTL attack that jumps to fixed PLT entries use some of these ROP gadgets, whereby an attacker can seize the control of a system more easily.

These advanced memory-overwrite attacks typically start from the contamination of one PC-bound data. Canary and ASCII-Armor can be effective against a linear memory-overwrite attack (smashing attack), but there are many ways to overwrite the PC-bound data without smashing. An arbitrary overwrite attack can bypass defenses such as Stack Guard [33] because the guard is separate from the return address. PC-encoding, however, protects the target directly; the target address and its protection are integrated together as a single data. This integrated way provides a useful form of protection regardless of whether the attacker uses a pointer for an indirect overwrite or just performs straight smashing. PC-encoding technique can therefore prevent the first intended jump using the target PC-bound data; meanwhile, the ROP-attack sequence that occurs after the overwriting of the first PC-bound data is blocked by the PC-encoding environment.

PC encoding also provides additional benefits against ROP. PC encoding can eliminate the ROP gadgets by inserting a decode instruction in front of the return instructions. Typical gadgets in a pattern of *pop-pop*-ret will be transformed into a *pop-pop-eor-ret* pattern, and an attacker should therefore be able to guess the key for the use of the gadgets. In the Intel x86 architecture, the insertion of instructions into the gadgets may cause a side effect of unexpected instructions that can be exploited for an ROP attack, because the unaligned instructions that are different from the programmer's intention can be fetched and executed with the Intel x86 architecture. But only the 4 byte aligned instructions are executable with the ARM® processor, meaning that the insertion of instructions for the elimination of a gadget can be a more reliable and clear solution under the ARM® architecture.

Table 1. The number of instructions in the CFI and PC encoding.

	added instruction	of memory access	conditional branch
CFI	4	1	1
PC-Encoding	2	0	0

Among the potential gadgets-instruction sequences ending with the following indirect branch instructions: *b; bl; bx; blx; bxj* and *pop {pc, ...}* or *mov pc, {reg/mem}*, PC encoding removes the gadgets that use the *"pop {pc, ...}"* or *"mov pc, {reg/mem}"* instruction. However, binaries that are compiled by the LLVM rarely have the *"pop {pc,...}"* instruction because the LLVM compiler does not use the *"pop {pc,...}"* instruction as a return instruction.

The *"b, bl, bx, blx, bxj"* gadgets are not removed by the current PC-encoding implementation reported in this paper, as the implementation in this paper covers only the return-address cases; therefore, attacks that use other PC-bound data can still succeed. Our future implementation will be able to handle all of the indirect branches in accordance with the use of our PC-encoding compiler under the Intel x86 architecture [21] [22].

The CFI is also capable of protecting the control flow from advanced attacks and can remove ROP gadgets; however, the CFI has a compatibility problem regarding the binary objects that are created separately due to a global ID-match- ing problem. For example, the CFI can cause a problem when a program tries to jump to the non-hardened block from a hardened block; in this case, the ID of the CFI verification codes regarding a proper jump are mismatched because the non-hardened block has no ID for the block entry. But there are no such issues with the PC-encoding environment because the definitions and verifications of the PC-bound data are usually in the same block; also, there is no need for the PC-encoding technique to maintain global IDs during the process.

Table 2 shows the performance results for SPEC2006 benchmark binaries that have been hardened by PC encoding. The simulations were performed with the default SE mode of the Gem5 simulator [34]. The SE mode of the Gem5 can simulate most Linux system calls, and it shows that the performance overhead is under 2%; also, the numbers of encode/decode instructions that were added by our PC-encoding compiler are shown in Table 2.

The numbers of encoding and decoding instructions are not the same because a must-terminate epilogue terminates the process directly without the execution of a return instruction, and a function may have multiple epilogues upon the receipt of branch instructions. Unfortunately, the SE mode of Gem5 does not simulate all of the Linux system calls, and only a few of the binaries can be simulated properly on the Gem5. For example, the bzip2software that is used for compression needs to call a *utime()*, which is a system call that is not included in theGem5; therefore, the bzip2 execution cannot be finished properly on the Gem5.

Table 2. Performance results.

Name	Simulated instructions (million)		Overhead (instruction)	Overhead (tick)
	Normal	PC-encoding		
mcf	8953	9128	1.95%	1.93%
sjeng	33,823	34,170	1.02%	1.00%
Name	Input		Added instructions	
			Encode	Decode
bzip2	dryer.jpg		110	120
mcf	test/input.in		24	24
sjeng	test/test.txt		141	144

5. CONCLUSIONS

This paper presents a practical guide for the implementation of a PC-encoding compiler under the ARM®-processor architecture. The ARM®-processor architecture has become the most popular one for embedded and application processors, and it is widely adopted in embedded devices including smartphones. We used our experience of building the PC-encoding compiler for the Intel x86 architecture [21] [22] as the basis for our implementation of the PC-encoding compiler for the ARM® processor. Our implementation protects the return addresses without inserting a protection code for accessing the memory; therefore, the protection incurs a minimal performance overhead.

Regarding the implementation presented in this paper, the key utilized for the encoding process is the self-address, *i.e.*, the location of the instruction defining PC-bound data. This key value of the self-address allows a low overhead implementation; however, if the degree of ASLR randomization is weak or no re- randomization occurs after a crash, it is possible for attackers to determine the key value using replay attacks and a source-code analysis. For more-secure protection, it may be necessary to utilize cryptographic keys that are more difficult to guess [22].

The PC-encoding implementation presented in this paper does not provide protection for every type of attacks because it has focused only on the return addresses among the many types of PC-bound data. While compromising the return address is the most prevailing software attacks for compromising the control flow integrity, many software attacks that do not rely on the return address exist. To protect other PC-bound data, a few techniques have been proposed. For example, it is possible to insert decoding instructions into the PLT region to prevent GOT-overwrite attacks, whereby an encode instruction can be added to the *dl_resolve()* function [21]. Also, one may utilize the relocation table to find every indirect jump [18]. We are currently in the process of incorporating these techniques into our ARM®-processor PC encoding compiler.

ACKNOWLEDGEMENTS

This work was supported in part by the National Research Foundation of Korea (NRF 2015R1A2A2A01).

REFERENCES

1. Ahn, Y.-J., Lee, Y., Choi, J. and Lee, G. (2014) Countering Code Injection Attack at TLB Miss IEEE Computer, 47, 66-72. https://doi.org/10.1109/MC.2013.228
2. Microsoft. A Detailed Description of the Data Execution Prevention (DEP) Feature in Windows XP Service Pack 2,Windows XP Tablet PC Edition 2005, and Windows Server 2003. https://support.microsoft.com/en-us/kb/875352
3. Park, Y.J., Zhang, Z. and Lee, G. (2006) Micro-Architectural Protection against Buffer Overflow Attack. IEEE Micro, 26, 62-71. https://doi.org/10.1109/MM.2006.76
4. Red Hat. New Security Enhancements in Red Hat Enterprise Linux v.3, update3. http://h10032.www1.hp.com/ctg/Manual/c00387685.pdf
5. Roemer, R., Buchanan, E., Shacham, H. and Savage, S. (2012) Return-Oriented Programing: Systems, Languages, and Applications. ACM Transactions on Information and System Security, 15, 2:1-2:34.
6. Bletsch, T., Jiang, X., Freeh, V.W. and Liang, Z. (2011) Jump-Oriented Programming: A New Class of Codereuse Attack. Proceedings of the 6th ASIACCS, pp. 30-40, March. https://doi.org/10.1145/1966913.1966919
7. Buchanan, E., Roemer, R., Shacham, H. and Savage, S. (2008) When Good Instructions Go Bad: Generalizing Return-Oriented Programming to RISC. ACM Conference on Computer and Communications Security (CCS), Alexander, 27-31 October 2008, 27-38. https://doi.org/10.1145/1455770.1455776
8. Checkoway, S., Davi, L., Dmitrienko, A., Sadeghi, A.-R., Shacham, H. and Winandy, M. (2010) Return-Oriented Programming without Returns. ACM Conference on Computer and Communications Security (CCS), Chicago, 4-8 October 2010, 559-572.
9. Dai Zovi, D. (2010) Practical Return-Oriented Programming. SOURCE Boston.
10. Davi, L., Dmitrienko, A., Sadeghi, A.R. and Winandy, M. (2010) Return-Oriented Programming without Returns on ARM. Technical Report HGI-TR-2010-002, Ruhr-University Bochum, July 2010. http://www.trust.rub.de/home/ publications/ DaDmSaWi2010
11. Ahn, D. and Lee, G. (2015) A Memory Access Validation Scheme against Payload Injection Attacks. IEEE Transactions on Dependable and Secure Computing, 12, 387-399. https://doi.org/10.1109/TDSC.2014.2355844
12. Ruan, Y., Kalyanasundaram, S. and Zou, X. (2016) Survey of Return-Oriented Programming Defense Mechanisms. Security and Communication Networks, 9, 1247-1265. https://doi.org/10.1002/sec.1406

13. Forrest, S., Hofmeyr, S. and Somayaji, A. (2008) The Evolution of System-Call Monitoring. Annual Computer Security Applications Conference, Anaheim, 8-12 December 2008, 418-430. https://doi.org/10.1109/acsac.2008.54
14. Abadi, M., Budiu, M., Erlingsson, U. and Ligatti, J. (2009) Control-Flow Integrity: Principles, Implementations, and Applications. ACM Transactions on Information and System Security, 15, 1-40. https://doi.org/10.1145/2240276.2240279
15. Pewny, J. and Holz, T. (2013) Control-Flow Restrictor: Compiler-Based CFI for iOS. Proceedings of the 29th Annual Computer Security Applications Conference, New Orleans, 9-13 December 2013, 309-318. https://doi.org/10.1145/2523649.2523674
16. Zeng, B., Tan, G., and Morrisett, G. (2011) Combining Control-Flow Integrity and Static Analysis for Efficient and Validated Data Sandboxing. Proceedings of the 18th ACM conference on Computer and Communications Security, Chicago, 17-21 October 2011, 29-40. https://doi.org/10.1145/2046707.2046713
17. Zhang, M. and Sekar, R. (2013) Control Flow Integrity for COTS Binaries. 22nd USENIX Security Symposium, Washington DC, 14-16 August 2013, 337-352.
18. Zhang, C., Wei, T., Chen, Z., Duan, L., Szekeres, L., McCamant, S., Song, D. and Zou, W. (2013) Practical Control Flow Integrity and Randomization for Binary Executables. Proceedings of the IEEE Security and Privacy Symposium, San Francisco, 19-22 May 2013, 559-573.
19. Goktas, E., Athanasopoulos, E., Bos, H. and Portokalidis, G. (2014) Out of Control: Overcoming Control-Flow Integrity. Proceedings of the 2014 IEEE Symposium on Security and Privacy, San Jose, 18-21 May 2014, 575-589. https://doi.org/10.1109/SP.2014.43
20. Lee, G. and Tyagi, A. (2000) Encoded Program Counter: Self-Protection from Buffer Overflow Attacks. International Conference on Internet Computing, Las Vegas, 26-29 June 2000, 387-394.
21. Lee, G. and Pyo, C. (2013) Method and Apparatus for Securing Indirect Function Calls by Using Program Counter Encoding. US Patent No. US8583939 B2.
22. Pyo, C. and Lee, G. (2002) Encoding Function Pointers and Memory Arrangement Checking against Buffer Overflow Attack. 4th International Conference on Information and Communications Security, Lecture Notes in Computer Science 2513, Singapore, 9-12 December 2002, 25-36. https://doi.org/10.1007/3-540-36159-6_3
23. Barrantes, E.G., Ackley, D.H., Forrest, S. and Stefanovic, D. (2005) Randomized Instruction Set Emulation. ACM Transactions on Information and System Security, 8, 3-40. https://doi.org/10.1145/1053283.1053286
24. Gupta, A., Habibi, J., Kirkpatrick, M.S. and Bertino, E. (2015) Marlin: Mitigating Code Reuse Attacks Using Code Randomization. IEEE Transactions on Dependable and Secure Computing, 12, 326-337. https://doi.org/10.1109/TDSC.2014.2345384
25. Computer Science Department at the University of Illinois at Urbana-Champaign. The LLVM Compiler Infrastructure. http://llvm.org
26. Sinnadurai, S., Zhao, Q. and Wong, W. (2008) Transparent Runtime Shadow Stack: Protection against Malicious Return Address Modifications.
27. Nergal (2001) The Advanced Return-Into-Lib(C) Exploits: PaX Case Study. Phrack Magazine, 58, 54.
28. Shacham, H. (2007) The Geometry of Innocent Flesh on the Bone: Return-into-Libc without Function Calls (on the x86). 14th ACM Conference on Computer and Communications Security, Alexandria, 29 October-2 November 2007, 552-561. https://doi.org/10.1145/1315245.1315313
29. Tran, M., Etheridge, M., Bletsch, T., Jiang, X., Freeh, V. and Ning, P. (2011) On the Expressiveness of Return-Intolibc Attacks. 14th International Conference on Recent Advances in Intrusion Detection, Menlo Park, 20-21 September 2011, 121-141. https://doi.org/10.1007/978-3-642-23644-0_7
30. Black Hat USA Whitepaper (2010) Payload Already Inside: Data Reuse for ROP Exploits.
31. Pax Team. PaX Address Space Layout Randomization (ASLR). http://pax.grsecurity.net/docs/aslr.txt

32. Shacham, H., Page, M., Pfaff, B., Goh, E., Modadugu, N. and Boneh, D. (2004) On the Effectiveness of Addressspace Randomization. 11th ACM Conference on Computer and Communications Security, Washington DC, 25-29 October 2004, 298-307.
33. Cowan, C., Pu, C., Maier, D., Hintongif, H., Walpole, J., Bakke, P., Beattie, S., Grier, A., Wagle, P. and Zhang, Q. (1998) Stackguard: Automatic Adaptive Detection and Prevention of Buffer-Overflow Attacks. 7th USENIX Security Symposium, San Antonio, 26-29 January 1998, 63-78.
34. Gem5 Simulator. http://www.gem5.org

CHAPTER 5

Cyber Conflicts as a New Global Threat

Alexander Kosenkov

Information Society Research Center, Chernihiv 14000, Ukraine

ABSTRACT

In this paper, an attempt is made to analyze the potential threats and consequences of cyber conflicts and, in particular, the risks of a global cyber conflict. The material is based on a comprehensive analysis of the nature of cyber conflict and its elements from both technical and societal points of view. The approach used in the paper considers the societal component as an essential part of cyber conflicts, allowing basics of cyber conflicts often disregarded by researchers and the public to be highlighted. Finally, the conclusion offers an opportunity to consider cyber conflict as the most advanced form of modern warfare, which imposes the most serious threat and whose effect could be comparable to weapons of mass destruction.

Keywords: cyber conflict; information warfare; cyber warfare; information operations

1. INTRODUCTION

During the last decade, global social and political landscapes were changed by the revolutionary development of information and communications technologies (ICT). New ICT has also significantly influenced warfare, among other ways through the emergence of network-centric warfare doctrine and unconventional, hybrid, information, and asymmetric warfare. The most significant transformation brought by the ICT was the emergence of a totally new form of conflict—cyber conflict (in this paper, cyber conflict is defined as conflict with the application of cyberspace capabilities in order to achieve objectives in or through cyberspace)—the rise of which we are witnessing worldwide today. Despite this clear and evident threat, there are still ongoing debates about the existence of cyber warfare. It is obvious that cyber conflicts are the game changers in modern warfare. They brought unprecedented changes incomparable to any preceding them. For instance, cyberspace is the first fully artificial space (no matter within or outside of the information environment) which, alongside land, sea, air, and space is considered to be a domain pursued for military superiority [1].

However, the understanding of cyber conflicts and changes happening in the warfare remains rather superficial. Current research cannot offer a holistic approach to cyber conflict. Its nature is still largely unknown to us [2,3,4,5,6,7]. As a result, we cannot address the main question of pressing issue today: how dangerous cyber conflicts are and what consequences and threats they bring. The answer to this question will determine not only the further development of military strategies and the international legal regulation of warfare, but also further civil development (both technological and social).

The most dominant current approaches to cyber conflicts are insufficient. As such, this paper concentrates on an effort to provide an alternative and more societal perspective on what cyber conflict is and how dangerous it could be. For this reason, the paper does not pretend to give an exhaustive characterization of cyber conflicts in general, but instead will primarily focus on issues relevant to the under-researched societal aspects of cyber conflicts.

This paper will make an attempt to answer the question of how serious the threat of cyber conflict—particularly global cyber conflict—is, and if we could call it the next challenge for the whole of modern civilization, alongside nuclear warfare. To do this, we first need to understand why the current approach to cyber conflicts has not yet produced significant results. Secondly, it is important to understand the basic elements of cyber conflicts (CCs) (such as the means of cyber conflicts, MCCs), and also to understand how they are changing warfare. Subsequently, we should understand how warfare has changed in general.

2. RESULTS

2.1. Cyber Conflicts Research Problem

Apparently, and somewhat predictably, the primary problem with existing CCs research is the approach to the research object. While CCs and MCCs have become cutting edge and different from any conflict and weapon in the physical realm, researchers are trying to apply a narrow technical understanding of warfare that worked before CCs and are fastening an old fashioned paradigm when trying to understand the radically different means, methods, objectives, and impacts of cyber conflicts. The old-fashioned coercion-centric paradigm currently dominating in research is deeply insufficient to understand cyber conflicts, as tools have shifted from coercion in its classical form to more advanced means. It is hard to say that the current approach is even partially successful while: (1) there are no reliable mechanisms for cyber conflicts assessment (not on a case-by-case and fact-specific basis [8]); (2) it is still impossible to appropriately evaluate the effects of conflict that do not cause mass casualties and/or destruction [9]; (3) it is unclear how cyber conflicts are interrelated with conflicts conducted with conventional means; (4) it is ambiguous what the potential strategic implications of cyber conflicts could be [9]; (5) legal regulation is based on persistent efforts to interpret existing norms [10], rather than accept the need for special regulation of cyber conflicts like the one for other cyberspace-related issues such as e-commerce and cyber crime. Even information operations could address the use of old "tools", but not CCs. Therefore, the need to identify the basic features that make CCs unique in comparison to physical conflict and impede its research is of primary importance. These features include:

- Fast emergence. CCs have emerged very quickly and are rapidly changing together with ICT, seriously diminishing the application of the historical approach, which is the basic one for military studies. Historical methodology is still important, but only for the period relating to cyberspace. In addition, there are neither sufficient historical materials nor appropriate methodologies to understand the conflict's history, which spans less than 30 years. It is also important that, for this period, no single wide-scale CC has taken place, but only "local" ones (limited to few nations and/or a certain region).
- Insufficient social basis. During the relatively short period of CCs' existence, appropriate institutions and sufficient public knowledge to evaluate the potential of CCs and cope with its threats were not formed. Such a situation could lead to paradoxes, such as the idea that "malicious code has not, so far, generated sufficient harm or damage

to warrant serious human rights attention" [11], only because the human right for secure cyberspace had not yet been declared.

- Dependence on the social sphere. CCs' effects depend on the way and degree of integration of ICT into society.
- Complete mediation by cyberspace. This means that an operation is maintained in a totally new landscape existing without familiar time and space dimensions, instead having new "human" dimensions.
- CCs could almost be considered an "ideal conflict", having blurred lines between peace and war, military and civilians, war and crime, and even war and the right for protest. This is leading to the massive weaponization of previously peaceful spheres of life.
- High potential for the broad involvement of non-state actors. Currently, sources needed for participation in CCs or the creation of MCCs are not monopolized by the state or any other social institution, and are not extremely expensive, which could affect their availability to a wide range of persons. Some transnational companies already compete with states for control over information and ICT services. Occurring simultaneously, the absence of both physical and serious technical barriers gives anyone the ability to use MCCs. Private persons are becoming not only combatants in cyber conflict, but targets as well. Previously, private entities were not primary targets in the conflicts, as they were "unreachable" behind the defense lines created by the state. Now, however, when private organizations are global and each one is reachable through the Internet, private entities are becoming one of the primary targets. As the role of the state in the protection of private person's interests have significantly decreased, it is widely debated who should ensure the security of private information assets in cyberspace: private entities themselves, or the government. The state cannot ensure cyber security for all private persons, while still there is no reliable mechanism to ensure public interests exclusively through private actors. It makes the situation very uncertain. Who will be capable of coping and how will they cope with a serious cyber conflict or crisis in the future?
- Need for the provision of special resources. Unlike previous conflicts, in CCs, there is the need for intellectual, human, and computational resources which are hardly measurable and not yet well managed by the military.
- Complicated nature. Cyberspace as a battle domain does not only interact with physical battle spaces (such as physical battlefields interacting between each other). Cyberspace is deeply integrated with physical battlefields. Exactly for this reason, cyber commands

function within Army, Fleet, Air Force, and Marine Forces in the USA [12]. CCs are also tightly linked to cyber-security in general, which means that there is the need for deep private–military cooperation in the sphere of once exclusively military competence. The complicated nature of CCs can be illustrated by the fact that often researchers are hampered in the differentiation of contiguous to CC kinds of warfare (information, hybrid, electronic warfare, etc.).

- Covert nature. CCs are unobservable to the general public, as MCCs could be operated exclusively remotely, and there may be no tangible evidence to prove the involvement of certain adversaries. The general public can only directly observe the effects of CCs, not the conflict itself, which gives wide potential for information manipulation.

On the strength of the features of CCs and the fact that ICT and society are actively converging, we can conclude that CCs have two main elements that we need to consider: technological and social. The technological elements include the classical warfare paradigm dealing with the use of new technical tools and a new medium (cyberspace) to reach traditional military targets with the objective to destroy, disrupt, and/or incapacitate the enemy. As this field is comparatively known to the military doctrine, its main parameters are characteristics of technical means and technologies. The societal element appears in the sphere of military competence as the result of the "blurring of lines" in the cyberspace. It deals not with the infliction of damage or incapacitation, but with the "transformative" use of social means available in cyberspace. In order to go beyond the general characteristics given above, and in order to try to provide more complex evaluations, we need to consider technical and social elements of MCCs separately.

2.2. Technical Elements of Cyber Conflicts

As the technical element of CCs is the first known one, it has the best consideration. It constitutes the application of the technical means of cyber conflicts (technical MCCs), including malicious software and hardware, malicious activities (DDOS (Distributed Denial of Service), hacking, phishing, etc.) and devices controlled with cyberspace means (including those programmed for autonomous operation) to gain superiority in the conflict.

The following features make technical MCCs a weapon of the next generation of warfare:

- Dynamic and changeable nature [13]. Technical MCCs are being developed and changed very quickly. Unlike any kind of weapon, they have not any common form and are limited by minimal constraints.

- Single or limited use [13]. If a technical MCC was used to attack the target, it is highly likely that its characteristics and mechanisms of attack would become known and would be used to build countermeasures, remove vulnerabilities, etc. Only the technical MCCs that are the most innovative and unknown to the adversary will be the most efficient. The longer a technical MCC is used, the lower efficiency it has, and the fewer targets it can hit. It is impossible to develop a universal virus worth billions of US dollars that could be efficiently "deployed" for a few decades to hit different targets. Even the successful use of advanced persistent threat (APT) against a single target for a long time does not guarantee that APT would not be removed tomorrow and that it could be used to hit other targets of high priority.
- High scalability. Technical MCCs could be applied to a target of any scale, from individual pacemakers to critical infrastructures of global significance.
- Unpredictability. Technical MCCs have far more attack vectors and malicious mechanisms to harm the target than conventional weapons. For example, a technical MCC or vulnerability could be deployed in an enemy system covertly and activated at H-hour.
- Unobvious nature of technical MCCs' effect. Technical MCCs by nature do not inflict any direct damage to an object of an attack (e.g., destroy equipment, disrupt communication, etc.). They have their own interim target of influence: artificial data systems, the impact on which will cause damage to the target (whatever it is), information stored in the system or physical objects managed by the system.
- Exceptional nature of technical MCCs. At first glance, especially for the general public [14], the threats of technical MCCs are insignificant in comparison to previous generations of weapons, such as nuclear or space weapons. This makes technical MCCs almost an ideal instrument to use and an issue of serious concern.
- Further complications. Both technical MCCs and protection against them are actively evolving to become more resilient, mutable, adaptive, and smart. These trends also make technical MCCs more autonomous and potentially less controllable. Naturally, they could have only a limited scope of targets, like Stuxnet had. However, that does not exclude the potential application of broad-spectrum uncontrollable destructive technical MCCs, as such attacks have also shown their efficiency.
- Clandestine operation. Due to cyber battlespace peculiarities, the majority of technical MCCs are built to operate covertly. This means

that not only the operation itself, but also its consequences could be unnoticed for a long time. That makes the "fog of cyber conflict" even more dense.

- Recoverability of damage and time-limited effect. Technical MCCs could disrupt, incapacitate, or destroy critical infrastructure, but in the most cases "homefield advantage" gives a defending party an opportunity to repair the damage and rebuild technical protection in the short term.
- Offensive nature [15]. In the case of nuclear weapons, their immense destructive power makes them offensive. As for technical MCCs, we can say that their offensive nature is rooted in unpredictability and their broad, unmanageable effect.

Any of these features separately does not seem to be a radical game-changer for warfare, but when combined into a single means of warfare, they can lead to the transformation of the nature of modern conflict. In particular, these characteristics combined make the basic pillars and mechanisms of modern peace inapplicable in the case of CCs. Arms control and non-proliferation were basic for the reduction of escalation during the Cold War, but how can the means of cyber conflicts be controlled if they have no physical guise, if you cannot detect their deployment in most cases, if they do not demand significant resources to be built, and when intelligence gathering about them is hampered, even today? However, there are no alternative mechanisms that could be used to settle the application of technical MCCs. Uncertainty regarding technical MCCs rises even more if we take into account that the buildup of cyber capabilities is non-linear and quite unpredictable, due to the peculiarities of the required resources. These problems significantly reinforce mutual distrust among potential parties of the CCs.

As more progressive mechanisms of peace preservation are inoperative, we should try to get back to the doctrine of mutually-assured destruction and rational deterrence theory, which also appear to be obsolete. Adversaries could only assume that the defending party could retaliate against large-scale cyber attacks both with technical MCCs and military options to annihilate the attacker, but still they cannot be entirely sure. There may be no rational deterrent threat while reliable evaluation mechanisms for technical MCCs are absent. As Martin Libicki wrote: "The current paucity of attacks has nothing to do with the fear of retaliation and more to do with the inability of other states to generate a sufficiently interesting capability or a sufficiently pressing opportunity" [9]. So, what will make non-measurable capabilities "interesting" and "opportunity pressing"? The creation of a "cyber triad capability" equivalent to a nuclear triad [16] cannot help to achieve credibility of cyber deterrence for the same reason—absence of reliable evaluation of an enemy's capabilities. Deterrence theory also looks to be inapplicable for a few other reasons. Firstly, due to the inability to identify an attacker clearly, borderless cyberspace could allow the launch of distributed attacks from any part of the world, including the territory of the defending state; Secondly, it is unclear how this retaliation mechanism would work in the case of an attack being launched by a non-state actor; Thirdly, it is currently unclear when a retaliation mechanism should be launched, where the red line is defined, and even which attacks are considered to be large-scale.

All aforementioned factors certainly trigger further exponential build up of cyber capabilities and a "cyber arms race" that could be far more threatening and massive in comparison to a conventional "arms race". We could consider only a few factors that confirm that assumption. The number and variety of means potentially applicable in a "cyber arms race" is unprecedented. The process of weaponization is truly massive, starting from putting backdoors to any equipment, software, and any electronic device, and ending with the weaponization of the Internet. We can only imagine what effects this arsenal could have in case of its full-scale application. Low demand for the material resources necessary to build technical MCCs will mean that the number of constraints for the development of technical MCCs will also be maximally low. This does not mean that all of the actors will be able to develop highly efficient technical MCCs, but all of them could definitely try to create their own cyber arsenal. The creation of nuclear arsenals has been accompanied by public attention, non-proliferation education campaigns, and civic controls that hinder the arms race with social mechanisms. In the absence of an explicit and directly perceptible threat from cyber arsenals, it is doubtful that the growth of cyber arsenals will cause such social resonance in the future.

Finally, the high velocities of CCs and the large number of operated technical MCCs will demand the application of automated intelligent control systems that will be able not only to retaliate (like the Soviet/Russian "Dead Hand" system that is capable of automatically triggering the launch of intercontinental ballistic missiles under certain conditions), but possibly also to strike first under different scenarios. This significantly increases the unpredictability and threats of CCs.

To all of the above, the doctrine of military response to large-scale cyber attacks reanimates the threat of global conventional war triggered by unpredictable cyber conflict.

Technical MCCs potentially have a unique application strategy: the infliction of organizational damage in order to cause state failure, humanitarian crisis, or any other state of enemies' incapacitation. Unlike conventional military attack, the application of technical MCCs could become ideal to avoid large scale military conflict, while successfully neutralizing the enemy nation as a single social organism. However, such a strategy for the application of technical MCCs' could be successful against outsiders in the competition for superiority in cyberspace. At the same time, the infliction of organizational damage with social MCCs (considered in the next section) could be successfully applied against any adversary.

2.3. The Social Element of Cyber Conflict

As mentioned earlier, cyberspace has made the social sphere within it an accessible and therefore obligatory field of military operation. As military operations have shifted from exclusively hard power to a mix of hard and soft power application, soft power operations in the social sphere are an integral part of modern warfare. Simultaneously, it has made social mechanisms more applicable as means for achieving military goals, and it has also made society a more reachable target than ever before. For these reasons, we will determine social means of cyber conflicts (social MCCs) as any means available in or through cyberspace (informational, psychological, technical, etc.), those that use social mechanisms to inflict any societal influence (both in cyberspace and outside of it).

The application of social MCCs is already not an option, but rather a necessity, since the Internet creates a single borderless information space and simultaneously undermines state sovereignty [17]. While losing traditional mechanisms of social control, state actors are trying to regain it with newly available tools and try to compete for the single informational space, while experiencing political crisis due to the gradual erosion of sovereignty.

One of the basic and main directions of the application of social MCCs is anti-government: the disorganization of governance, organization of anti-government protests, delusion of the adversary's population, public opinion influence, and the reduction of an opponent's will to resist [18]. Nowadays, the application of social MCCs goes far beyond this anti-government vector. They are also targeting society in general to make it incapable of restoring and restructuring "damaged" governance.

The war of ideas was one of the key strategic elements that led to the end of the Cold War. Alongside the ideological battle, the main actors during the Cold War also applied subversion of any kind, ranging from informational to the support of armed groups, and often both of these notions converged deeply. The strategy of subversion in proxy wars in third world countries was especially successful: coups and revolutions were happening in different parts of the world. There were even well known, unsuccessful examples of (ideologically motivated) active armed subversion in countries belonging to one of the blocks, such as Red

Brigades, Red Army Faction, etc. Large-scale armed subversion has never broken up on the territory of the USSR or the USA due to strong social regulation (maintained by the official state institutions) and social self-regulation. The mechanism of social regulation inter alia is based on the ability of state institutions to fully control informational space and flows and determine social conditions. The social-self regulation is the ability of social institutions to remove, alter, or neutralize unwanted social elements through social pressure and other mechanisms.

Cyberspace has changed both of these mechanisms: information is no longer fully controllable by the state, social space is also gradually becoming global, and people interact through social institutions in cyberspace rather than offline. In the Internet era, fewer and fewer local factors have influence, but more and more social factors originating from the global cyberspace influence social behavior, and consequently, social structure. In a practical military sense, it means that there is great potential to influence the emergence and activity of different social groups on the adversary's territory. During the Cold War, even very scarce influence and resources allowed the initiation of armed subversion and terrorist activities, such as those mentioned before. Cyberspace enables wide informational, social, ideological, and even financial support for subversive groups, and simultaneously disables social regulation and self-regulation that make subversion ultra-efficient both in quantitative and qualitative aspects.

Despite this, the application of social MCCs is not widely considered; however, there is open source information that the main competitors in cyberspace already have corresponding systems at their disposal. Between February–March 2011, mass media published information that the United States Department of The Air Force in June 2010 placed an order for "persona management software" for 50 users, each of which will manage 10 personas. According to published information, each persona should have "background, history, supporting details, and cyber presence that are technically, culturally and geographically consistent. Personas must be able to appear to originate in nearly any part of the world and can interact through conventional online services and social media platforms. The service includes a user friendly application environment to maximize the user's situational awareness by displaying real-time local information" [19]. In August 2012, a Russian newspaper "Kommersant" published an article alleging that in January 2012 the Foreign Intelligence Service of the Russian Federation announced three "closed" tenders for the development of special software solutions with code designations "Dispute", "Monitor-3", and "Storm-12" [20]. The purpose of the "Dispute" system was described as "research processes of formation of communities of information dissemination internet-centers in social networks" so as to "determine factors of information popularity and distribution". System

"Monitor-3" should be created to ensure the "development of methods of organization and management of virtual internet community of involved experts, covering assignment of tasks, control of operation in social media and regular obtainment of information in specified fields from involved experts." Finally, system "Storm-12" would be "a special software package of automated dissemination of information in large social networks and organization of informational support of measures according to prepared scenarios of influence on specified mass audience of social networks".

Information regarding both the American and the Russian solutions is very basic, but nevertheless it is important as a declaration of interest to the application of such systems. Similar but maybe less-advanced systems are already used by large corporations (e.g., social media command centers) and owners of social bot networks for social media monitoring and "promotion" of information.

As recent studies show, even the manipulation of the functionality of a web service could inflict serious social effect (like how manipulations of the Facebook information feed caused "massive-scale emotional contagion" [21]). The fact that both solutions were ordered from private companies also confirms the threat of potential wide involvement of non-state actors to both technical and social elements of CCs.

The cases of the application of social MCCs are very rarely considered, because effects of their application are difficult to identify and measure. Nevertheless, there is open source information about such cases. One of them is "social cyber-attack" during the violent events in Assam (India) in July 2012 according to the research by Rebecca Goolsby [22].

Then-unknown persons exploited the high velocities and trusted nature of cyber communications to embed false information in message flows in order to foment strife and undermine stability. The author does not give any details on the mechanism of the attack, but the fact that those events were recognized as "social cyber attack" is very important.

It is apparent that social MCCs are dynamic, hardly traceable, clandestine, and offensive in their nature. Their worst threat is that unlike technical MCCs, their effect could have a strategic significance which is hardly predictable, unlikely scalable, and barely controllable—even in the case of insignificant (at first sight) application. For example, the spread of destructive ideologies or views with the purpose of subverting the enemy could cause global consequences in the long run. However, the social sphere of cyberspace and its interaction with society are still under-researched, and it is difficult to give any assessments regarding the application of social MCCs.

3. DISCUSSIONS

Both technical and social means of cyber conflicts absorb and advance features of weapons of previous generations, making cyber conflicts—and particularly global cyber conflict—a serious threat to modern society. Key features of cyber conflicts are profoundly different from the features of conventional conflicts (see Table 1), simultaneously making the face of war less brutal, but its essence even more dangerous.

Table 1. Summary table.

Feature	Conventional Conflict	Cyber Conflict
Primary means	Coercive, destructive	Non-coercive, transformative
Conflict structure	Centralized	Potentially ultra-decentralized
Form	Fixed	Mutable
Delimitation of war and peace	Present	Absent
Dynamics	Medium	High
Timeframe	Precise	Vague
Involvement of private interests	Medium	High
Participation of non-state actors	Medium	High
Capability for differentiation of targets	Medium	Low
Control of conflict means (in the case of massive strike)	High	Low
Intelligence, adversary's capabilities assessment	Efficient	Hampered
Military planning	Efficient	Hampered
Deterrence mechanisms	Present	Absent
Public perception of conflict	Direct	Mediated
Potential for deception regarding the conflict	Low	High
Existence of efficient social and legal mechanisms applicable to the conflict	Present	Absent
Infliction of direct social effect	Absent	Present

In the worst case scenario, the maximum application of cyber capabilities could supersede effects of all kinds of modern weapon, due to the potential impact on weapon systems and the strategic destructive influence on society. Further analysis of cyber conflicts goes far beyond mathematical models or classical analysis. It demands a more precise, comprehensive, applicable, and transdisciplinary approach. Beyond a brand new approach in the research of cyber conflicts, we also need an innovative and proactive approach in politics and an interaction between cyber conflict research and regulation. Cyberspace and cyber conflict are too dynamic to be regulated with the use of usual approaches. Apparently, in our modern Information Era, a return to the control of information on a national level would be obsolete. Still, the demand for new regulatory institutions is not met on any level, neither national, nor international. There is no other obvious solution to the problems linked with the threat of cyber conflicts and the means of cyber conflicts, demanding the active development of alternative solutions based on research results.

We definitely need to better understand what cyber conflict is and what its means are. For this, the development of a terminological apparatus is basic and crucial. The other important direction of further research is potential approaches to the analysis of cyber conflicts and their means, including the classification of the means of cyber conflicts. The classification of the means of cyber conflict into two groups offered in this paper is merely a starting point, but it is definitely one of the variants to better understanding the nature of cyber conflicts. In particular, the classification is important to assume that the most dangerous damage that could be inflicted through cyberspace is organizational and functional, and not a physical one. However, this assumption requires further evidence and more detailed study.

The concept of the social means of cyber conflict due to its newness also needs closer attention and rigorous approach. First of all, in order to prove its consistency, there is a need to understand how exactly the social means of cyber conflicts differ from information warfare maintained through cyberspace and the particular threats of such means of conflict.

The means of cyber conflicts are probably the first means of warfare in human history that humanity possesses and applies but still does not fully understand and control. It makes cyber conflict research not just an auxiliary part of warfare, but its essential component.

REFERENCES

1. U.S. Department of Defence. *Joint Publication 3-12 (R) Cyberspace Operations*; U.S. Department of Defence: Washington, DC, USA, 2013; pp. 1–2. Available online: http://www.dtic.mil/doctrine/new_pubs/jp3_12R.pdf(accessed on 1 May 2016).
2. Carr, J. *Inside Cyber Warfare: Mapping the Cyber Underworld*; O'Reilly Media Inc.: Sebastopol, CA, USA, 2011; pp. 1–14.
3. Rosenzweig, P. *Cyber Warfare: How Conflicts in Cyberspace Are Challenging America and Changing the World*; Praeger: Santa Barbara, CA, USA, 2013; pp. 15–73.
4. Sutherland, B. *Modern Warfare, Intelligence and Deterrence*; John Wiley & Sons Inc.: Hoboken, NJ, USA, 2011; p. 320.
5. Ducheine, P.A.L.; Schmitt, M.N.; Osinga, F.P.B. *Targeting: The Challenges of Modern Warfare*; T.M.C. Press: The Hague, The Netherlands, 2015; p. 293.
6. Zetter, K. *Countdown to Zero Day: Stuxnet and the Launch of the World's First Digital Weapon*; Crown Publishers: New York, NY, USA, 2014; p. 448.
7. Schmitt, M. Classification of Cyber Conflict. *J. Confl. Secur. Law* **2012**, *17*, 245–260.
8. U.S. Department of Defense. The Department of Defense Cyber Strategy. 2015. Available online: http://www.defense.gov/Portals/1/features/2015/0415_cyber-strategy/Final_2015_DoD_CYBER_STRATEGY_for_web.pdf (accessed on 1 May 2016).

9. Libicki, M. *Cyberdeterrence and Cyberwar*; RAND Corporation: Santa Monica, CA, USA, 2009.
10. Schmitt, M.N. *Tallinn Manual on the International Law Applicable to Cyber Warfare*; Schmitt, M.N., Ed.; Cambridge University Press: Cambridge, UK, 2013.
11. Casey-Maslen, S. *Weapons under International Human Rights Law*; Cambridge University Press: Cambridge, UK, 2014; pp. 305–307.
12. Stratcom.mil. U.S. Cyber Command—U.S. Strategic Command. 2016. Available online: https://www.stratcom.mil/factsheets/2/Cyber_Command/ (accessed on 1 May 2016).
13. Denning, D. Assessing Cyber War. In *Assessing War: The Challenge of Measuring Success and Failure*; Blanken, L., Ed.; Georgetown University Press: Washington, DC, USA, 2015; pp. 266–284.
14. Korwitts, K. Are Americans Worried about Their Cybersecurity? 2015. SurveyMonkey Blog. Available online: https://www.surveymonkey.com/blog/2015/02/05/americans-worried-cybersecurity/ (accessed on 1 May 2016).
15. Ongstad, M. Cyber-Warfare: Offensive vs. Defensive Balance, 2015. Security Zap. Available online: http://securityzap.com/cyber-warfare-bounded-chaos/ (accessed on 1 May 2016).
16. Sharma, A. Cyber Wars: A Paradigm Shift from Means to Ends. *Strateg. Anal.* **2010**, *34*, 70–71.
17. Taylor, S. Erosion of National Sovereignty by 21st Century Technology, 2003. International-Business-Center. Available online: http://international-business-center.com/international_business_resources/Sovereignty.pdf(accessed on 1 May 2016).
18. Jaitner, M. Russian Information Warfare: Lessons from Ukraine. In *Cyber War in Perspective: Russian Aggression against Ukraine*; Kenneth, G., Ed.; NATO CCD COE Publications: Tallinn, Estonia, 2015; p. 89.
19. Sherman, E. So, Why Does the Air Force Want Hundreds of Fake Online Identities on Social Media? [Update], 2011. Cbsnews. Available online: http://www.cbsnews.com/news/so-why-does-the-air-force-want-hundreds-of-fake-online-identities-on-social-media-update/ (accessed on 1 May 2016).
20. Barabanov, I.; Safronov, I.; Chernenko, E. Intelligence by The Bot, 2012. Kommersant. Available online: http://www.kommersant.ru/doc/2009256 (accessed on 1 May 2016).
21. Kramer, A.; Guillory, J.; Hancock, J. Experimental evidence of massive-scale emotional contagion through social networks. *Proc. Natl. Acad. Sci. USA* **2014**, *111*, 8788–8790.
22. Goolsby, R. On Cybersecurity, Crowdsourcing, and Social Cyber-Attack, 2013. Wilson Center. Available online: https://www.wilsoncenter.org/sites/default/files/127219170-On-Cybersecurity-Crowdsourcing-Cyber-Attack-Commons-Lab-Policy-Memo-Series-Vol-1.pdf (accessed on 1 May 2016).

CHAPTER 6

Cloud Computing Security: A Survey

Issa M. Khalil[1,*], Abdallah Khreishah[2] and Muhammad Azeem[3]

[1]*Qatar Computing Research Institute (QCRI), Qatar Foundation, Doha, Qatar*

[2]*Department of Electrical and Computer Engineering, Newark College of Engineering, New Jersey Institute of Technology, University Heights, Newark, NJ 07102, USA*

[3]*College of Information Technology, United Arab Emirates University, PO Box 15551, Al Ain, United Arab Emirates*

ABSTRACT

Cloud computing is an emerging technology paradigm that migrates current technological and computing concepts into utility-like solutions similar to electricity and water systems. Clouds bring out a wide range of benefits including configurable computing resources, economic savings, and service flexibility. However, security and privacy concerns are shown to be the primary obstacles to a wide adoption of clouds. The new concepts that clouds introduce, such as multi-tenancy, resource sharing and outsourcing, create new challenges to the security community. Addressing these challenges requires, in addition to the ability to cultivate and tune the security measures developed for traditional computing systems, proposing new security policies, models, and protocols to address the unique cloud security challenges. In this work, we provide a comprehensive study of cloud computing security and privacy concerns. We identify cloud vulnerabilities, classify known security threats and attacks, and present the state-of-the-art practices to control the vulnerabilities, neutralize the threats, and calibrate the attacks. Additionally, we investigate and identify the limitations of the current solutions and provide insights of the future security perspectives. Finally, we provide a cloud security framework in which we present the various lines of defense and identify the dependency levels among them. We identify 28 cloud security threats which we classify into five categories. We also present nine general cloud attacks along with various attack incidents, and provide effectiveness analysis of the proposed countermeasures.

Keywords: cloud computing; cloud security; security vulnerabilities; threats; attacks; insider attackers

1. INTRODUCTION

Cloud computing provides a centralized pool of configurable computing resources and computing outsourcing mechanisms that enable different computing services to different people in a way similar to utility-based systems such as electricity, water, and sewage. In electricity, for example, people started to connect with central grids, supported by power utilities rather than relying on their own electricity production capabilities. This migration is beneficial in reducing the cost and time of production and in providing better performance and reliability [1]. Similarly, clouds provide their customers with high performance and more reliable computing services such as e-mail, instant messaging, and web services at a lower cost.

Cloud computing does not have a common accepted definition yet [2]. The National Institute of Standards and Technology (NIST) [3] defined five essential characteristics of cloud computing, namely: on-demand self-service, broad network access, resource pooling, rapid elasticity or expansion, and measured service. Also, cloud computing is described as a dynamic and often easily extended platform to provide transparent virtualized resources to users through the Internet [4]. Cloud computing architecture consists of three layers: (i) Software as a service (SaaS); (ii) Platform as a service (PaaS) and (iii) Infrastructure as a service (IaaS) [5]. The clouds are also viewed as five component architectures that comprise clients, applications, platforms, infrastructure and servers [6]. The current clouds are deployed in one of four deployment models: (a) public clouds in which the physical infrastructure is owned and managed by the service provider; (b) community clouds in which the physical infrastructure is owned and managed by a consortium of organizations; (c) private clouds in which the infrastructure is owned and managed by a specific organization and (d) hybrid clouds which include combinations of the previous three models [7]. Figure 1 shows cloud deployment models together with their internal infrastructure (IaaS, PaaS and SaaS). Cloud deployment models have similar internal infrastructure, but vary in their policies and user-access levels.

Clouds bring out tremendous benefits for both individuals and enterprises. Clouds support economic savings, outsourcing mechanisms, resource sharing, any-where any-time accessibility, on-demand scalability, and service flexibility. Clouds minimize the need for user involvement by masking technical details such as software upgrades, licenses, and maintenance from its customers. Clouds could also offer better security advantages over individual server deployments. Since a cloud aggregates resources, cloud providers charter expert security personnel while typical companies could be limited with a network administrator who might not be well versed in cyber security issues. Similarly, clouds are more resilient to Distributed Denial of Service (DDoS) attacks due to the availability of resources and the elasticity of the architecture. The clouds support mobile computations where Virtual Machines (VMs) migrate from one physical machine to another. In addition to alleviating dedicated DDoS attacks, mobile computations help to avoid settings in which a single administrator has exclusive control over the computation.

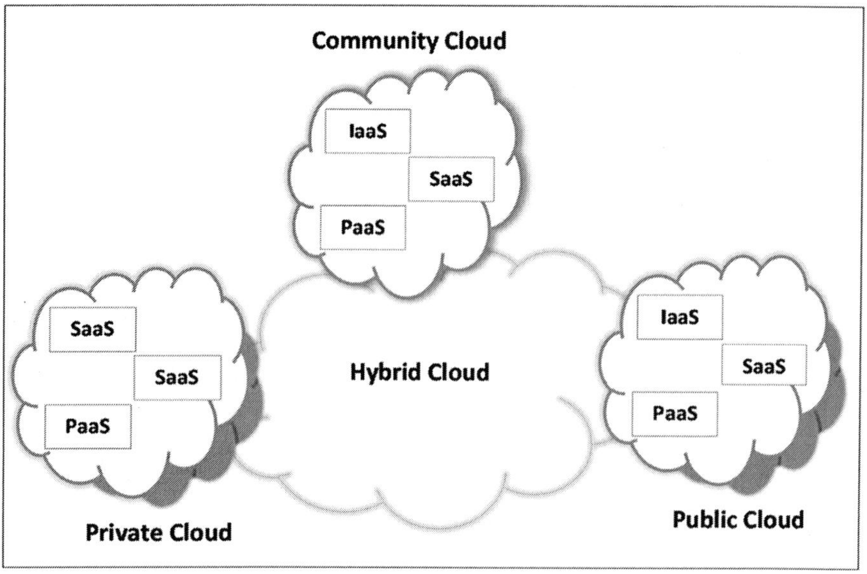

Figure 1. Cloud deployment models and infrastructure.

The new concepts introduced by the clouds, such as computation outsourcing, resource sharing, and external data warehousing, increase the security and privacy concerns and create new security challenges. Moreover, the large scale of the clouds, the proliferation of mobile access devices (e.g., smartphones and tablets), and the direct access to cloud infrastructure amplify cloud vulnerabilities and threats. As clouds become more and more popular, security concerns grow bigger and bigger as they become more attractive attack targets due to the concentration of digital assets.

Many researchers and practitioners work on identifying cloud threats, vulnerabilities, attacks, and other security and privacy issues, in addition to providing countermeasures in the form of frameworks, strategies, recommendations, and service oriented architectures (e.g., [2,8,9, 10,11,12,13]). Additionally, efforts in other domains such as ad hoc networks have been tuned to address the emerging security problems in the clouds (e.g., [14,15,16,17,18]). Many researchers (e.g., [1,19,20,21, 22,23,24,25]) have addressed single attributes of cloud computing security such as data integrity, authentication vulnerabilities, auditing, *etc.* Others (e.g., [3,22,23,24,25,26,27]) provide surveys that cover specific areas of cloud security concerns and proposed solutions. In [3,27], the authors briefly and broadly discuss cloud security issues involving data, applications and virtualization. The authors in [22] discuss similar cloud security issues but with deeper investigations. In [23,25], the authors present surveys on cloud security requirements such as confidentiality, integrity, transparency, availability, accountability, and assurance. In [24], the authors present a survey on the different security issues of the service delivery models of the clouds. In [26], the authors discuss the security challenges specific to the public clouds. In [28], Hashizume *et al.* classify the security issues in the cloud based on the SPI (SaaS, PaaS, IaaS) cloud infrastructure and services model. The authors provide deeper classification of the fourth category (C4) in our classification model (Section 2). Additionally, the authors explain fundamental security concepts including vulnerabilities, threats, and attacks and provide mapping among these concepts. Our work provides a higher classification level and assumes prior knowledge of the fundamental security concepts. In [29], Zissis *et al.* evaluate cloud security requirements. They propose a Trusted Third Party solution that calls upon cryptography to ensure the authentication, integrity and confidentiality of data and communications. In [30], Whaiduzzaman *et al.* present key management and broad aspects of privacy and security issues in the domain of vehicular cloud computing.

To successfully address the cloud security issues, we need to understand the compound security challenges in a holistic way. Specifically, we need to: (i) investigate various cloud security attributes including vulnerabilities, threats, risks, and attack models; (ii) identify the security requirements including confidentiality, integrity, availability, transparency, *etc.*; (iii) identify the involved parties (clients, service provides, outsiders, insiders) and the role of each party in the attack-defense cycle; and (iv) understand the impact of security on various cloud deployment models (public, community, private, hybrid). The main contribution of this paper is that it provides a holistic study of the security issues in the clouds that cover almost all the cloud components (data centers, computing infrastructure, interfacing and networking, *etc.*), network layers (application, transportation, IP, *etc.*), and cloud stakeholders (providers, consumers, third party contractors, *etc.*). In this paper, we provide a comprehensive survey on the cloud security and privacy concerns that includes: (i) cloud computing security issues (vulnerabilities, threats, and attacks); (ii) attack classifications; (iii) relations and dependencies among attacks; (iv) known attacks; (v) comparative analysis of some of well-known countermeasures; (vi) insights from the current security solutions to identify and address unattended security challenges.

This paper is organized as follows. In Section 2, we describe cloud security categories, issues and dependencies. We present some of the well-known attacks and countermeasures in Section 3. In Section 4, we present the findings of comparative evaluation of some well-known general cloud computing solutions. Further discussion on cloud security issues is presented in Section 5. In Section 6, we conclude the paper.

2. CLOUD SECURITY CATEGORIES, ISSUES AND DEPENDENCIES

As part of this work, we have conducted a survey on the current cloud security issues and the state-of-the-art security solutions. We identify 28 security issues (Table 2) that we categorize into five classes (Table 1). We have also provided a comparative analysis of the current security solutions and the state-of-the-art countermeasures.

2.1. Categories and Issues

We classify cloud computing security related issues into the following five categories, which are also summarized in Table 1. A similar approach to classify the issues is found in [19] but it is limited to small set of cloud security concerns and only partially covers four categories.

(C1) The Security Standards category deals with regulatory authorities and governing bodies that define cloud security policies to ensure secure working environment over the clouds. It includes service level agreements, auditing and other agreements among users, service provider and other stakeholders.

(C2) The Network category refers to the medium through which the users connect to cloud infrastructure to perform the desired computations. It includes browsers, network connections and information exchange through registration.

(C3) The Access Control category is a user-oriented category and includes identification, authentication and authorization issues.

(C4) The Cloud Infrastructure category includes security issues within SaaS, PaaS and IaaS and is particularly related with virtualization environment.

(C5) The Data category covers data integrity and confidentiality issues.

Table 1. Cloud Security Categories.

No.	Category	Description
C1	Security Standards	Describes the standards required to take precaution measures in cloud computing in order to prevent attacks. It governs the policies of cloud computing for security without compromising reliability and performance.
C2	Network	Involves network attacks such as Connection Availability, Denial of Service (DoS), DDoS, flooding attack, internet protocol vulnerabilities, *etc.*
C3	Access Control	Covers authentication and access control. It captures issues that affect privacy of user information and data storage.
C4	Cloud Infrastructure	Covers attacks that are specific to the cloud infrastructure (IaaS, PaaS and SaaS) such tampered binaries and privileged insiders.
C5	Data	Covers data related security issues including data migration, integrity, confidentiality, and data warehousing.

In Table 2, we map the identified cloud security issues into the suitable categories defined earlier (Table 1). We have labeled these issues with "I1, I2, ..., In" where Ix refers to cloud security issue number x. Special attention is required towards mutual security standards such as Secure Sockets Layer (SSL)/Transport Layer Security (TLS), XML signature, XML Encryption Syntax and Processing, and Key Management Interoperability Protocols. Currently, cloud computing lacks appropriate security standards (I1) [1]. Even if security standards are defined properly, many security issues are still associated with compliance risks (I2) due to lack of governess for audits and assessment of corporate standards [1]. Cloud customers do not have enough knowledge of procedures, processes and practices of the provider, especially in the areas of identity management and segregation of duties. Organizations that seek to obtain certifications may be put on risk by denying an audit by cloud customers. One of the most important aspect of cloud computing security is auditability (I3); however, we do not have an audit net for cloud service providers [13,31]. If a service provider outsources a service to a third party where functionality is not transparent, users must be able to inspect the whole process [12]. Security standards (C1) and governing bodies are part of service level agreements (SLA) (I4) and legal aspects, respectively which have not been taken into practices for cloud computing [32,33].

Table 2. Cloud Security Issues and Classifications.

Category	Label	Issues
Security Standards	I1	Lack of security standards
	I2	Compliance risks
	I3	Lack of auditing
	I4	Lack of legal aspects (Service level agreement)
	I5	Trust
Network	I6	Proper installation of network firewalls
	I7	Network security configurations
	I8	Internet protocol vulnerabilities
	I9	Internet Dependence
Access	I10	Account and service hijacking
	I11	Malicious insiders
	I12	Authentication mechanism
	I13	Privileged user access
	I14	Browser Security
Cloud Infrastructure	I15	Insecure interface of API
	I16	Quality of service
	I17	Sharing technical flaws
	I18	Reliability of Suppliers
	I19	Security Misconfiguration
	I20	Multi-tenancy
	I21	Server Location and Backup
Data	I22	Data redundancy
	I23	Data loss and leakage
	I24	Data location
	I25	Data recovery
	I26	Data privacy
	I27	Data protection
	I28	Data availability

SLA defines the relationship among parties (provider—recipient) and is extremely important for both parties [9]. It includes identifying/defining the customer's needs, simplifying complex issues, encouraging dialog in the event of disputes, providing a framework for understanding, reducing/removing areas of conflict, eliminating unrealistic expectations. The user may suffer, in case of data loss, if the above factors are not taken into consideration as he may not be able to put claims on service providers. These interactions shape the Trust (I5) relationship between the users and the different cloud stakeholders which is required when users transfer data on cloud infrastructure [34]. Strong justifications are required to gain customers' trust in that regard.

Network category (C2) related issues are deemed to be the biggest security challenges in clouds since cloud computing is more prone to network related attacks compared to the traditional computing paradigms [2]. In addition, cloud operations are tightly coupled and highly depend on networking. Therefore, cloud network security issues receive more attention in this work compared to the other security categories. The ratio of network attacks and fraud dramatically increases as people and organizations migrate their data into clouds. Security experts anticipate that clouds will be the focus of hackers in future due to the concentration of valuable "assets" (data and computation) within the clouds. The possible lack of proper installations of network firewalls (I6) and the overlooked security configurations (I7) within clouds and on networks, make it easier for hackers to access the cloud on behalf of legitimate users [35]. Hackers can occupy resources (hardware/application) by generating bogus data or they can run malicious code on the hijacked resources. Denial of service can be launched by first identifying vulnerabilities in Internet protocols (I8) such as SIP (Session Initiation Protocol) which could deem the Internet to be un-trusted [36]. Migrating to cloud will increase the Internet dependency (I9) as a main communication medium for cloud access. Therefore, if, due to some attacks, the Internet is disabled and the cloud services become unavailable, this may cause production to become severely crippled [37]. I9, therefore, implies all the network reliability issues.

Account and service hijacking (I10) involves phishing, fraud and software vulnerabilities where attackers steal credentials and gain unauthorized access to servers [1]. This unauthorized access is a threat to integrity, confidentiality and availability of data and services [1]. Unauthorized access can be launched from within or outside the organization. Malicious insiders (I11) such as dishonest administrators severely impact organizations' security. Given their level of access, they infiltrate corporate and cause brand damage, financial and productivity losses. Therefore, it is critical for cloud customers to clearly determine the guarantees that the cloud providers use to detect and defend against insider threats. The current authentication mechanisms (I12) may not be applicable in cloud environments as customers no longer belong to or are able to access a single tightly controlled system [4]. A single customer may access data and compose services from multiple cloud providers using a mobile application or a browser. This kind of access brings in an inherent level of risk and this risk has been called privileged user access (I13) [6]. Unauthorized access becomes possible through browser vulnerabilities. Therefore, Internet browser (I14) is the first stage where security measures should be considered because vulnerabilities in the browser open the door for many follow-on attacks.

The insecure interface of Application Programming Interface (API) (I15) issue covers the vulnerabilities in the set of APIs in the cloud portal (customers use these APIs to connect to a cloud) which can expose an organization to several threats such as unauthorized access, content transmission, reusable token and logging capabilities [1]. Quality of service (QoS) (I16) is an unattended issue [32] because many cloud service providers focus only on fast performance and low cost [31]. In this work, we consider QoS in the domain of any function or activity that directly or indirectly affect security. A simple error in the configuration of one or more of the cloud components may cause severe consequences because cloud configurations could be shared by many services [4]. Technical flaws (I17), also known as reputation fate sharing [38], in which errors transfer from a corrupted server to each virtual machine created on that server becomes worse when the corruption transfers through the infected mobile VM to other servers. Therefore, it is extremely important to identify and fix fate sharing incidents and implement the best practices to prevent them from reoccurring. Reliability of suppliers (I18) is an important factor that requires a background check on the staff to control data and hardware access [4]. It is highly recommended that companies should evaluate its staff in order to protect its assets and data and provide this information to public to gain customer's trust. Servers in the cloud are the backbone to its infrastructure that provides numerous services such as directory service, data storage and mail. Intruders can access the system if the security attributes of the servers are not configured properly (security misconfiguration—I19) [39]. This misconfiguration could happen in the application stack, the framework, the web server, the custom code as well as the platform. Note that this is different from inadequate network security configuration (I7), which includes network level security misconfigurations. Cloud serves serve multiple simultaneous users through virtualization, which allows the sharing of the same software and hardware resources by different users. This multi-tenancy (I20) capability could lead to information leakage from one tenant to other server mates [40]. Attacks such as VM-to-VM and compromised VM are becoming hub for future attacks. In terms of server location (I21) precautions, it is important to keep in mind that the floor should be anti-static, should have no window for security reasons, should have a rack with seismic bracings and should be properly grounded [41]. Cloud infrastructure cannot be completely trusted at this stage and it is critical to maintain backup offline.

Data redundancy (I22) [6], data loss and leakage (I23) [40], data location (I24) [6], data recovery (I25) [4], data privacy (I26) [42], data protection (I27) [43] and data availability (I28) [43] have been marked as major and important issues in different case studies which require data to be properly encrypted, transmitted, protected, controlled and available in the time of need.

Figure 2 shows the cloud components where security issues may be raised. Each component, such as policies, clients, cloud infrastructure, and network, is prone to certain security attacks and requires attack prevention/detection/response strategies.

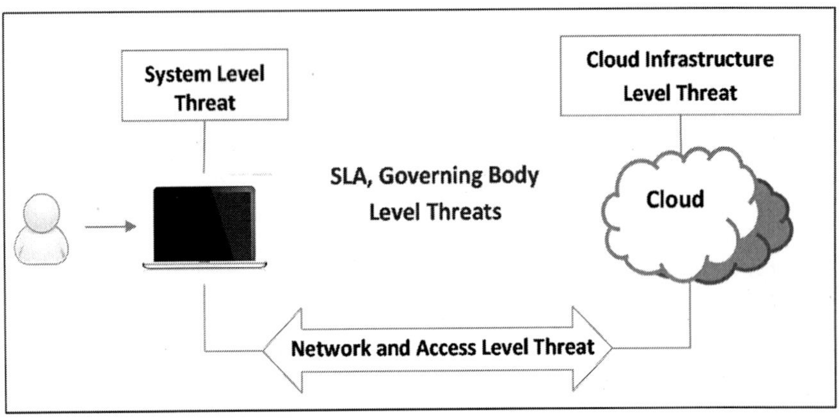

Figure 2. Cloud components that are prone to security threats.

2.2. Dependencies among Cloud Security Categories and Issues

In addition to identifying cloud security issues and classifying them into several categories, we have identified dependencies among these categories and the security issues they encompass. If one of the categories is prone to certain attacks, other categories may also become prone to these attacks. For example, issues I1–I4 (Table 2) fall under category C1 (Table 1). Security related issues under this category might be entry doors through which other threats infiltrate into the cloud. Suitable management and security precautions taken in one category (e.g., C1) may greatly minimize or even eliminate security issues in the other categories (C2, C3, *etc.*). If proper policies are implemented at one category, then fewer issues will arise in other categories (only those issues that are genuine to a particular category rather than issues that take advantage of vulnerabilities in other categories). We have covered many threats/vulnerabilities in this survey and will now investigate the dependency relationships among them. We follow thematic analysis ([31,43]) to extract the dependency relationships among the cloud security issues we surveyed. Initially, we extracted the appropriate text from the literature we surveyed (column 1 in Table 3). We then identified the security issues in the selected text and performed manual coding to identify the particular features of that selected text. This coding process is essential for organizing the data into meaningful groups. Table 3 presents an example, which contains textual description (text extraction), identified code, identified rule and the rule description. The symbol used in describing the rules is represented as "→". It simply means that the security issue on the left of the symbol leads to or increases in the probability of occurrence of the issue(s) on the right of symbol.

Table 3. Data Extraction Example.

Text Extraction (from Primary Studies)	Problems Coded	Identified Rule	Rule Description
Account and service hijacking involves phishing, fraud and software vulnerabilities where attackers steal credentials and gain an unauthorized access to server [1].	• Account and service hijacking (I10) • Data Loss and Leakage (I23)	Account and service hijacking → Data Loss and Leakage	Account and service hijacking increase the possibility of data loss and leakage
Insecure interface of API (customers use these APIs to connect to cloud) which can expose organization to several threats such as unauthorized access, content transmission [1]	• Insecure interface of API's (I15) • Weak authentication mechanisms (I13) • Data Loss and Leakage (I23)	Insecure interface of API's → authentication mechanism weakness, Data Loss and Leakage	Insecure interface of API's leads to increase in the probability of information leakage and the weakness of the authentication mechanism.

The same procedure has been followed in order to determine dependencies among other cloud security issues that we have identified in this survey. A sample of these dependencies has been presented in the form of rules in Table 4. These rules aim at providing practitioners with deep insights about cloud computing security issues to take suitable precaution measures. Practitioners can also trace the source of any security issue through these rules. For example, the main cause of wrapping attacks can be tailored to weak browser security as stated by Rule 7, whereas weak browser security can be linked to security misconfiguration as stated by Rule 11. These rules could be helpful in protecting a cloud computing environment against various attacks by providing a comprehensive view of the attacks' map rather than considering each attack in an isolated setup.

Table 4. Rules that Capture Dependencies among Cloud Security Issues.

No.	Rules	Sample References
1	Lack of security standard (I1) → compliance risks (I2), account and service hijacking (I10), internet protocol vulnerabilities (I8), malicious insider (I11), authentication mechanisms weakness (I12)	[1,4,7,41,42]
2	Lack of auditing (I3) → malicious insider (I11)	[7,37,39,41,44,45]
3	Lack of legal aspects (Service level agreement) (I4) → authentication mechanism weakness (I12)	[1,2,4,19,32,46]
4	Insecure interface of API (I15) → account and service hijacking (I10)	[1,4]
5	Compliance risk (I2) → account and service hijacking (I10)	[41]
6	Weak Browser security (I14) → account and service hijacking (I10)	[4,41]
7	Internet protocol vulnerabilities (I8) → authentication mechanism weakness (I12)	
8	Security misconfiguration (I19) → insecure interfaces of API (I15), account and service hijacking (I10)	[4,41–43]
9	Malicious insider (I11) → Data loss and Leakage (123)	[6,33]
10	Lack of quality of service (I16) → insecure interfaces of API (I15), Data loss and Leakage (I23)	[4,6,33,41,43]
11	Authentication mechanism weakness (I12) → Data loss and Leakage (123)	[6,33]

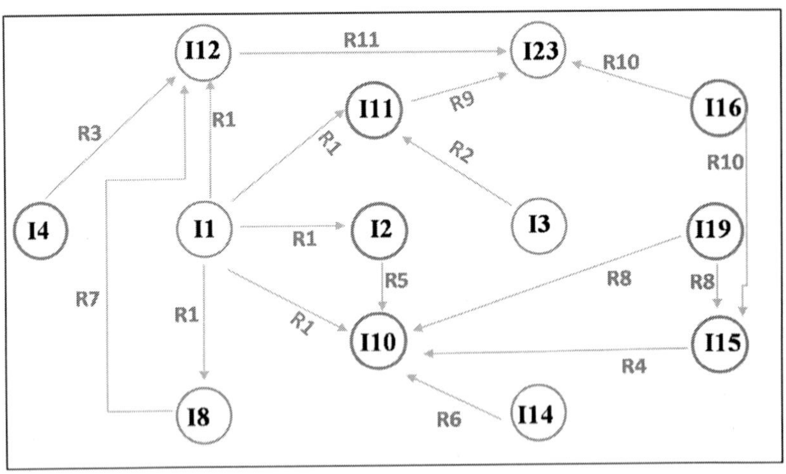

Figure 3. Dependencies among cloud security issues.

Figure 3 shows a directed graph representation of the dependencies among the surveyed cloud security issues. In the figure, nodes represent security issues, a directed edge from node X to node Y indicates that the occurrence of issue Y is facilitated by the occurrence of issue X. Finally, codes on edges refer to the rules in Table 4, where Rn refers to rule number n.

3. KNOWN ATTACKS AND COUNTERMEASURES: AN EVALUATION

"All the vulnerabilities and security issues that on-premise, non-virtualized and non-cloud deployments have still remain in the cloud", Lawrence Pingree, analyst for Gartner, said. "All that cloud and virtualization does is enhancing the potential risks by introducing virtualization software and potentially mass data breach issues, if an entire cloud provider's infrastructure is breached [105]." In this work, we classify cloud applicable attacks into nine groups; provide sample attack incidents from each group, and present comparative analysis of some of the famous security mitigation techniques. Table 5presents a summary of attack group names, known attack incidents in each group, attack consequences, attack category (from Table 1), exploited vulnerabilities (from Table 2), and references for further readings about each attack group. A description of each attack group along with evaluation of the state-of-the-art countermeasures are presented in the following subsections.

3.1. Theft of Service Attacks

The Theft of Service attack [37] utilizes vulnerabilities in the scheduler of some hypervisors. The attack is realized when the hypervisor uses a scheduling mechanism, which fails to detect and account of Central Processing Unit (CPU) usage by poorly behaved virtual machines. This failure may further allow malicious customers to obtain cloud services at the expense of others. This attack is more relevant in the public clouds where customers are charged by the amount of time their VM is running rather than by the amount of CPU time used. Since the Virtual Machine Manager (hypervisor) schedules and manages virtual machines, vulnerabilities in the hypervisor scheduler may result in inaccurate and unfair scheduling. These vulnerabilities mainly result from the use of periodic sampling or low-precision clock to measure CPU usage: like a train passenger hiding whenever ticket checkers come for tickets. In the Theft of Service attack, the hacker ensures that its process is never scheduled when a scheduling tick occurs. The common incidents of this attack include: (1) using cloud computing services (e.g., Human Resource, HR, systems) for long period of time while keeping it hidden from the vendor and (2) using cloud computing resources (e.g., storage system or OS platform) for a long period without representing it in a billing cycle.

A countermeasure to this attack has been provided by Zhou *et al.* in [37] by modifying the scheduler to prevent the attack without sacrificing efficiency, fairness or I/O responsiveness. These modifications do not affect the basic credit and priority boosting mechanisms. The modified schedulers are: (1) exact scheduler; (2) uniform scheduler; (3) passion scheduler and (4) Bernoulli scheduler. The main differences among these schedulers are in the scheduling and monitoring policies and in time-interval calculations. The experiment conducted by authors with the modified schedulers provides accurate and fair scheduling. The modifications in hypervisor are shown to be beneficial, as compared to Xen hypervisor (currently running in Amazon Elastic Compute Cloud—EC2).

Another theoretical countermeasure has been provided by Gruschka *et al.* in [44]. They suggest using a new instance of cloud-to-user surface in victim machine to monitor the scheduling of parallel instances. Then, the outputs of both the attacker and the legitimate instances are compared. A significant difference in results is reported to the responsible authorities as an attack.

Table 5. Known Attacks against Clouds.

Sr. #	Attack Name	Attack Incidents	Consequences	Category	Vulnerability/ Caused by	Sample References
1	Theft-of-service		• Cloud service usage without billing • Cloud resource stealing with less/no cost	Cloud Infrastructure	I1, I3, I6, I8, I11, I14, I19	[37,44]
2	Denial of service	DDoS Http-Based DDoS Xml-Based DDoS REST-Based-DDoS Shrew attack (light traffic) DoS)	• Service/hardware unavailability • Wrapping a malicious code in Xml signature to gain unauthorized access to information • Accessing a browser history or any other private information through unsecure Http browsing	Network, Cloud Infrastructure	I1, I3, I10, I14, I19	[34,49]

3	Cloud malware injection		• Credential information leakage • User data leakage • Cloud machine abnormal behavior	Cloud Infrastructure	I7, I11, I13, I15	[44,50–52]
4	Cross VM side channels	Timing side channels Energy-consumption side channels	• User data/information leakage • Cloud resources/infrastructure information leakage	Cloud Infrastructure	I15, I19	[53–55]
5	Targeted shared memory		• Cloud resource's information leakage • User information/data leakage • Provides open window for other attacks such as side channels and cloud malware injection	Cloud Infrastructure	I1, I3, I10, I15, I19,	[53,56,57]
6	Phishing		• Unauthorized access to personal information • Installing a malicious code into user computer • Force cloud computing structure to behave abnormally • Make server unavailable for end-user	Cloud Infrastructure, Network, Access	I1, I6, I8, I10, I12, I14	[58,59]
7	Botnets	Stepping stone attack	• Unauthorized access to cloud resources • Make cloud system work abnormally • Stealing sensitive information • Stealing user data	Network, Cloud Infrastructure, Access	I1, I6, I10, I12, I14	[60,61]
8	Audio Steganography		• Unavailability of cloud storage system • Accessing user data • User data deletion	Cloud infrastructure, Access,	I1, I3, I6, I10, I14, I19	[62,63]
9	VM rollback attack		• Launch brute force attack • Damage cloud infrastructure • Leakage of sensitive information	Cloud Infrastructure, Access	I1, I3, I6, I10, I14, I19	[64,65]

This solution has not been validated or verified by authors and does not provide any guarantee for a beneficial result. There are other solutions provided for hypervisor scheduling such as [45,47,48] but they are only limited to improving other aspects of virtualized I/O performance and VM security such as CPU-bound issues. These studies do not examine scheduling fairness and accuracy in presence of attackers, which is the backbone for the Theft-of-Service attack.

3.2. Denial of Service Attacks

Most of the serious attacks in cloud computing come from denial of service (DoS), particularly HTTP, XML and Representational State Transfer (REST)-based DoS attacks. The cloud users initiate requests in XML, then send requests over HTTP protocol and usually build their system-interface through REST protocols such as those used in Microsoft Azure and Amazon EC2. Due to vulnerabilities in the system-interface, DoS attacks are easier to implement and very difficult for security experts to countermeasure [49]. XML-based distributed denial of service (DDoS) and HTTP-based DDoS attacks are more destructive than traditional DDoS because these protocols are widely used in cloud computing with no strong deterrence mechanisms available to avoid them. HTTP and XML are critical and important elements of cloud computing, so security over these protocols becomes crucial to providing healthy development of a cloud platform.

Karnwal *et al.* in [49] provide a framework called "cloud defender" that is based on five stages: (1) sensor filter; (2) hop count filter; (3) IP frequency divergence filter; (4) puzzle resolver filter and (5) double signature filter. The first four filters detect HTTP-based DDoS attacks and the fifth filter detects XML-based attacks. REST-based attacks are mentioned without providing a framework to prevent it. One of the reasons could be that REST-based attacks are closely related with the user interface, which may vary from user-level to system-level applications. These applications are different in nature, based on different requirements, and there is no single hard and fast rule to implement the security measurements at the interface level. The solution provided in this article consists of the following modules:

- **Sensor:** It monitors the incoming request messages. If it identifies that there is hypothetical increase in number of messages coming from same or particular consumer, it marks it as suspicious.
- **HOP Count filter:** It will count the hop count value (how many nodes, does message traverse from source to destination) and compare it with pre-defined HOP count. If a difference is found, it means that the

header or the message has been modified on hacker machine and thus is marked suspicious.

- **IP Frequency Divergence:** Marks a message suspicious, if there is same frequency of IP messages.
- **Double Signature:** It doubles the XML signature: one in header and one in bottom. In case of attack, both XML signatures need to be verified.
- **Puzzle Solver:** It deals with some intelligent puzzles, where results should be imbedded in some Simple Object Access Protocol (SOAP) header. In case of attack (HTTP DDoS), the cloud defender will send back the puzzle to IP, from which it is receiving messages. If the cloud defender received back the solved puzzle then the request is deemed legitimate, otherwise it is marked as HTTP DDoS attack.

The problem in this framework is that it lacks practical validation and is based on the assumption that the number of modules in the system is directly proportional to the number of attacks expected. Moreover, exhaustive monitoring of messages on each node would considerably slow the network traffic. Finally, the framework lacks the proper mechanisms for node coordination in case of attack incidence detection.

Riquet *et al.* [34] claim that "there is no strong solution available to prevent the DDoS attacks". To validate the claim, the authors conduct the experiment to evaluate the effectiveness of the actual security solutions against distributed attacks. The security solutions involved in the experiment are SNORT and commercial firewall. The authors conclude that the failure of security systems lies within two aspects: either the security solution can be obsolete because it is not updated, or the solution can rely on unsuitable methods. They did not propose any solution that can prevent distributed security attacks. Other widely used DDoS countermeasures are firewalls. However, due to firewall location (at the border of a network), it would not be able to detect distributed attacks once they are in the network [50].

3.3. Malware Injection Attacks

Cloud malware injection attack refers to a manipulated copy of the victim's service instance, uploaded by attacker to cloud, so that some service requests to the victim's service are processed within that malicious instance. An attacker can get access to user data through this attack. The attacker actually exploits its privileged access capabilities in order to attack that service security domain. The incidents of this attack include credential information leakage, user private-data leakage and unauthorized access to cloud resources. The challenge does not only lie in the failure to detect the malware injection attack but also in the inability to determine the particular node on which the attacker has uploaded the malicious instance [44]. Retrospective detection (examination of hard-drive and memory) has been a widely used technique to detect the host of malware instances. Liu *et al.* in [50] propose a new retrospective detection approach based on portable executable (PE) format file relationship. This approach has been implemented and validated in HADOOP platform. This approach proves higher detection rate as well as lower false positive rate. The main drawback of this approach is that its success is based on three assumptions (pre-requisites): (1) most legitimate programs and malware files are in PE format and lie within a windows platform; (2) the number of legitimate files is greater than that of malware files in user's computer; and (3) creating/writing/reading PE format files seldom happen in a user's computer. However, an attacker could exploit any vulnerability in cloud to attack without following any of these pre-requisites. The authors fail to discuss the consequences of the absence of these pre-requisites such as (1) how efficient this approach would be if one or more of the assumptions are not fulfilled; (2) how much damage and attacker could cause to system or data in absence of these assumptions.

Another countermeasure to the attack called "CloudAV" is provided by Oberheide *et al.* in [51]. CloudAV provides two main features that make it more efficient, accurate and fast as a malware detection system:

- Antivirus as a network service: the detection capabilities by host-based antivirus can be more efficiently and effectively provided as cloud-network-service. Each host runs a light weight process to detect new files and then sends them to network service for quarantine and for further analysis rather than running complex analysis software on each end-host.
- N-version protection: malicious software identification is determined by multiple heterogonous detection engines in parallel similar to the idea of N-version programming. The notion of N-version protection has been provided in this solution so that the malware detection system should leverage detection capabilities of multiple heterogeneous detection engines to determine malicious and unwanted files more effectively. However, the number of false positives encountered during normal operations increase compared to 1-version engines. To manage the false positives, the administrator has to set a trade-off between coverage (a single detector is enough to mark a file as malicious) and false positives (a consensus of a number of detectors is required to mark a file as malicious).

The authors prove the efficiency of CloudAV through validation in a cloud environment. CloudAV also provides better detection of malicious software, enhanced forensics capabilities, new threat detection through retrospective detection approach and improved deployability and management. The validation experiment proves that CloudAV provides 35% better detection coverage against threats compared to single antivirus engines and 98% detection coverage of an entire data-set of a cloud. However, cloud-based security solutions generally suffer from three problems, namely—security coverage, scalability, and privacy. As malware can be embedded in a large number of file types, attackers may be able to bypass cloud solutions as they are limited to few file types and hence degrade the detection coverage. Additionally, exporting all binaries or PDF files to the cloud for investigation does not scale and may create a single point of failure by flooding the cloud with benign binaries. Finally, exporting the binaries and files into the cloud for inspection creates privacy issues since there is always a risk that a sensitive file could be exported to the cloud as well.

In [52], the authors provide a framework based on behavior analysis to detect suspicious programs in clouds. It allows end users to delegate security labs, the execution and the analysis of a potential malicious program and force the program to behave as if it were executed directly in real end-user environment. There are two advantages for this: (1) it allows security lab to monitor the execution of potential malicious programs in realistic end user environment and (2) it allows end-users to raise their level of protection by leveraging better computational resources [52].

3.4. Cross VM Side-Channel Attacks

VM side channel attack is an access-driven attack in which an attacker VM alternates execution with the victim VM and leverages the processor cashes to infer the behavior of the victim. It requires that the attacker resides on a different VM on the same physical hardware as that of the victim's VM. Ristenpart *et al.* in [57] discuss a comprehensive example on how to collect information from a target VM through cross VM side channel attack. One incident of side channel attacks is the timing side channel attack [54] which is based on measuring how much time various computations take to perform. Successful modulation of this measured time may lead to leakage of sensitive information about the owner of the computation or even the cloud provider. Timing channels are especially hard to control and pervasive on clouds due to massive parallelism. Moreover, timing side channel attacks are hard to detect since they do not leave trails or raise any alerts. Cloud customers may not have the authorization to check for possible side channels from other cloud mates obviously due to privacy concerns. On the other hand, cloud providers can thoroughly check and detect timing attack incidents but may not be willing to report such breaches due to many considerations such as protecting company reputation. Another incident of side channel attacks is the energy-consumption side channel attack [55]. Instead of directly attacking the software stack (virtualization layer), attackers can indirectly collect sensitive information about the cloud using energy consumption logs. This type of data (energy consumption log) is maintained to monitor the infrastructure status and to provide computer energy efficient workload mapping. In [55], authors investigate the potential of extracting valuable information from raw energy consumption logs which may affect user's privacy and security. Dozens of hypervisors could exist in a cloud computing environment, each of which could be the host of the targeted VM. Therefore, it may take a while for the attacker to determine which hypervisor is hosting the targeted VM. The more time it takes an attacker to determine the host machine, the higher is the probability of attack detection. However, if the attacker can somehow get the power consumption data, it may become possible for him to narrow the possible set of servers that could be running the targeted VM. This gives attackers better chances to determine the correct server before being detected. Currently, no efficient solutions have been provided against timing-side channel attacks and energy consumption side channel attacks.

3.5. Targeted Shared Memory Attacks

In this attack, attackers take advantage of shared memory (cache or main memory) of both physical and virtual machines. It is an initial level attack in cloud computing that can lead up to several different types of attacks such as side channel attacks and malware injection attacks [53]. For example, authors in [57] perform cross-virtual-machine-side-channels attack on Amazon EC2 and measure the cache activity of other users, which provides an example of activity-information leakage in cloud computing. Attackers can get unauthorized access to information that reveals the internal structure of the cloud such as the number of processes running, the number of users logged-in in a specific time and the temporary cookies residing in memory.

Another example of targeted shared memory attack is explored by Rochsa and Correia in [56]. The goal is to access the memory dumps in virtual machines through malicious insider attack. This access has led to the extraction of the current running processes in the system and users' private information.

Thus far, in the literature, no one has claimed to solve or prevent targeted shared memory attacks. Researchers and practitioners are working to get more information about the attack and no strong solution is available to prevent it except current anti-viruses or firewalls that limit users' access to the shared memory.

3.6. Phishing Attacks

Phishing is an attempt to access personal information from unsuspecting user through social engineering techniques. It is commonly achieved by sending links of webpages in emails or through instant messages. These links appear to be correct, leading to a legitimate site such as bank account login or credit card information verification but they practically take users to fake locations. Through this deception, the attacker can obtain sensitive information such as passwords and credit card information. Phishing attacks can be classified into two categories: (1) an abusive behavior in which an attacker hosts a phishing attack site on cloud by using one of the cloud services and (2) hijack accounts and services in the cloud through traditional social engineering techniques [58].

Cloud security alliances (CSA) mentioned that cloud service providers do not maintain sufficient control over systems in order to avoid being hacked or spammed. To prevent such attacks, CSA proposes a few precaution measurements such as strict registration process, secure identity check procedure and enhanced monitoring skills [58]. Privacy laws in cloud computing do not allow cloud service providers to look at what customers are doing, so if a malicious individual or organization is performing something nefarious (phishing attack or uploading malicious code) by using cloud services, it cannot be detected until or unless notified by some security software [59]. Researchers in [58,59] discuss the fact that the present cloud privacy laws restrict cloud providers to become the first to know about nefarious activities in their clouds, regardless of the enhanced monitoring and comprehensive inspection of network traffic.

3.7. Botnet Attacks (Stepping-Stone Attack)

In Stepping Stone, attackers try to achieve their goals (such as spying, DoS, damaging, *etc.*) while avoiding revealing their identities and locations to minimize the possibility of detection and trace-back. This is achieved by indirectly attacking the targeted victim through a sequence of other hosts (called stepping stones). Stepping stone hosts can be recruited through illegal botnets. A bot-master, through botnet attack, can setup command and control server and stepping-stones into clouds in order to steal sensitive information and to gain unauthorized access to cloud resources in a bid to make it behave abnormally. In recent years, botnet attacks have been reported in Amazon EC2, Google AppEngine and Raytheon UK. A Zeus command and control was hosted on Amazon EC2 cloud [66]. A computer was infected by using relay commands through Google AppEngine [67], which allowed attackers to steal sensitive information from the Raytheon cloud [68]. Cloud computing is an ideal environment for botnet attacks [60]. A cloud has rich and elastic computing resources (bandwidth, processing and storage), which are easy to access. The attacker can either compromise a cloud-based server as their command and control server or they can lease a high performance virtual machine with the help of fake or stolen credit cards.

Many researches worked to countermeasure botnets and steeping stone attacks by identifying whether a particular host is a stepping stone or not. Most of the detection work is based on the hypothesis of strong correlation between the incoming and outgoing traffic of a possible stepping stone host. Such correlation can be based on packet content, login behavior, frequency of network activity, timing properties, and periodicity of network traffic. However, many of these techniques are easy to fool by attackers using encrypted traffic and authentication forging or by introducing random delays (jitter), while others are shown to be inefficient due the huge traffic that need to be monitored and analyzed. One of the most notable detection techniques is presented by Lin *et al.* in [60]. They introduce what they call a "pebble" trace scheme to trace-back the bot master. It first identifies the cryptographic keys of the botnet communication in order to configure the botnet operations and then it traces back the bot master. It involves the design and implementation of a new key identification scheme and an approach for tracing-back bot master across stepping-stones beyond multiple clouds. The solution only considers symmetric key cryptography with no discussion about asymmetric cryptography.

A different mechanism, based on self-protection, has been present by Kourai *et al.* in [61]. The mechanism, dubbed xFilter, is a packet filter that runs in a virtual machine that monitors the underneath VM and achieves pinpoint active response by using VM introspection. xFilter inspects the memory of the VM being monitored, using VM introspection, and obtains information about guest operating systems without interacting with them. xFilter can deny packets, by using sender process's information, from particular sender or process. When xFilter detects an outgoing attack, it automatically identifies the attack source and generates a new filtering rule in order to stop the stepping-stone attack. This mechanism is proved to be efficient because even if cloud server is compromised, this mechanism will continue to provide other services as much as possible. For example, when the apache server is compromised, only the privileges of user www-data are taken over at worst, while other applications such as Postfix mail server will continue running legitimately. This solution has a limitation that can be dangerous for the business of cloud providers. For example, the attacker may intentionally use local SMTP server to mount SPAM attacks because other legitimate applications are also using SMPT server to send emails. If xFilter detects the SPAM attack, it will update the rule repository to deny all the traffic coming from the SMTP server including that from legitimate applications or users.

Srivastava *et al.* in [69] provide a detection mechanism that inspects the Internet traffic. This solution, named VMwall, is based on application-level firewall using VM introspection. One of the main differences of this solution compared to xFilter is that it degrades the network performance considerably when large number of packets and nodes are to be inspected. On the other hand, since xFilter inspects the server memory, the degradation would be minimized [69].

3.8. Audio Steganography Attacks

Audio Steganography attack has been regarded as one of the most serious attack to cloud storage systems. Audio Steganography helps users to hide their secret data within regular audio files. The steganography user can transmit secret information through sending media files, which appear to be normal sound files. Hackers utilize this feature to deceive the current security mechanisms or traditional countermeasures (e.g., steg-analysis) for protecting cloud storage systems by hiding their malicious code in sound files and sending it to victim servers [70]. Very little research has considered proposals to thwart Audio Steganography attacks against cloud storage systems, which make it an open area that requires practical solutions [71].

Liu *et al.* in [71] perform a careful analysis of Audio Steganography attack on cloud storage systems. They design and implement a scheme called StegAD (steganography Active defense) to tackle the threat of data leakage by using Audio Steganography attacks. The first step, in this solution, is to scan the hiding place of audio files under cloud storage system through famous RS image gray scale steg-analysis algorithm. After acquiring suspicious files, authors use SADI (Steganography Audio Dynamical Interference) technique to interfere in all the possible places in those suspicious files. Authors try to avoid damaging innocent files (which have been marked as suspicious during the scanning process) though adopting an approach where an interference has to be in multiple hiding places or most significant places. However, this solution does not provide any information about how to decide the significant hiding places. Authors first use random noise to replace information including the most significant one and then compare the previous unchanged information with the changed one. By doing so, steganography and innocent files will have different consequences. This difference will determine whether the audio file has appropriate content or some malicious code that can damage the cloud storage system. There are many questions that have not been answered in this solution such as: (1) How is the comparison between steganography and innocent file carried out? (2) What are the specific types of audio files considered in this experiment?

3.9. VM Rollback Attacks

The virtualization environment in cloud computing is the most vulnerable area to attack. The hypervisor can suspend a VM at any time during execution, take a snapshot of current CPU states, disk and memory and resume a snapshot later without guest VM awareness. This feature has been widely used for fault tolerance and VM maintenance; however, it also provides an open window to an attacker to launch VM rollback attacks. In a rollback attack, a user can take advantage of previous snapshots and run it without the user's awareness and then clean the history and again run the same or different snapshot. By cleaning the history, the attacker will not be caught for his suspicious activities. For example, an attacker can launch a brute force attack to guess a login password for VM, even if the guest OS has a restriction on the number of attempts such as blocking the user after three failed attempts or erasing all data after 10 times, the attacker can still rollback the VM to its initial state after each try. The attacker will clear the counter inside the VM and bypass the restriction and run the brute-force attack again [64].

Szefer *et al.* in [71] provide an architecture named "Hyperwall" in order to manage hypervisor vulnerabilities. The solution to prevent VM rollback attack is based on disabling the suspend/resume functionalities of the hypervisor. The suspend/resume feature is powerful for virtualization and disabling it will not provide a better solution. Another limitation of this solution is the excessive user interaction with the cloud system. It requires end users to get involved during VM booting, suspending and resuming. This means that the system needs to ask for permission every time it reboots, migrates or suspends a VM which makes it inconvenient and impractical [71]. Xia *et al.* in [64] provide a solution that works without disabling any basic functionalities of the hypervisor as compared to the Hyperwall. In this solution, only the end user can tell whether a rollback is malicious or not by auditing the log of VM activities. Although this solution has minimized the user involvement compared to the Hyperwall, the changing infrastructure of cloud computing still demands autonomous working of VM operation with some user involvement.

4. COMPARATIVE EVALUATION OF WELL-KNOWN GENERAL CLOUD SECURITY MECHANISMS

The European Union Agency for Network and Information Security (ENISA) has done significant work in addressing many security issues related to the cloud. It provides stakeholders with information that helps them to understand, assess, and manage the risks when migrating into the clouds. It also provides advisory services on setting and monitoring SLAs to optimize security gains. ENISA also provides cooperative studies with various stakeholders to identify the critical cloud services and analyze the impact of the cloud service failure in such circumstances. In the following subsections, we present the state-of-the-art general tools that are individually and collectively used to countermeasure cloud security attacks.

4.1. Intrusion Detection Systems (IDS)

Intruders, through impersonating legitimate users, can access cloud infrastructures causing it to be unavailable for legitimate users. It has been shown that attackers can easily get information regarding victim machines in the IaaS component of the cloud [70]. This information can help in attacking cloud users by co-locating the malicious virtual machine with the victim's virtual machine. These attacks include denial of service (DoS) and distributed denial of service (DDoS) attacks that mainly target data confidentiality, integrity, and availability [72]. Such attacks can be avoided by implementing IDS which offers additional security measures by investigating network traffic, log files and user behavior [73]. IDS is defined as a system that collects and analyzes information, from different key points, for security auditing and monitoring in order to check whether this is a violation of network policies or not. Intrusion detection can be classified into two categories (1) misuse detection (MD) and (2) anomaly detection (AD) [74]. MD deals with information characteristics of users input and making a comparison with database results (previous inputs by the same user). On the other hand, anomaly detection stores user behavior in feature database, which can be compared with current behavior. If there is a high rate of difference in comparison, then the invasion occurred. IDS have two types (1) host based IDS (HIDS) which monitors the behavior on a single host and (2) network based IDS (NIDS) which analyses traffic flowing through a network [75]. Roschke *et al.* in [76] discuss a third type called hybrid IDS also known as distributed IDS, which combines the functions of both NIDS and HIDS.

The authors in [73] propose an IDS system named Grid and Cloud Computing Intrusion Detection System (GCCIDS) which is based on NIDS and HIDS. It consists of an audit system that detects and covers attacks that have not been covered, previously, by other NIDS and HIDS systems. It works by integrating knowledge and behavior analysis in order to detect intrusions. The main components of GCCIDS include node, service, event auditor and storage system. The main limitations in GCCIDS include the high communication overhead and redundancy. Each node identifies the local event and alerts all other connected nodes. The overhead increases dramatically when the number of nodes increases due to the massive computations and communications involved. Additionally, GCCIDS does not provide any information as to whether a node should immediately alert other nodes as intrusion occurs or at a certain predefined periodic time interval. Let us consider the case of immediate sharing with a grid, for example, of 1000 nodes. Each time intrusion occurs, the detecting node will alert all the other 999 nodes generating high overhead of communication exchange. Attackers can utilize this 'alert sharing' as an open window to disrupt the network. Attackers behave as intruders in different intervals of time, triggering certain nodes to detect these intrusions and hence notifying other nodes, which considerably increases the communication overhead. If a node selects not to immediately alert other nodes, inconsistency arises. A node that identifies an attack contains the information about the attack, while other nodes are not aware of it. Each node, in this system, consists of a local database that has information related to intrusions occurred previously. The local repository leads to redundancy.

GCCIDS uses both knowledge-based and behavior–based techniques for attack incident detection. Knowledge-based techniques cannot detect new attacks because detection depends on pre-defined rules. However, this limitation can be alleviated through regularly updating local repositories with information about new attacks. For behavior-based technique, GCCIDS uses feed forward artificial neural network (FFANN). However, FFANN is not useful at the starting phase due to little or no data availability. However, as the time passes and more computations are done by FFANN, the results improve.

The redundancy of repository in GCCIDS has been removed in an IDS system called Distributed, Collaborative and Data driven Intrusion Detection and Prevention framework (DCDIDP) [77]. DCDIDP creates global database to be used for detection tasks by the ID prevention module. DCDIDP consists of three level architectures, namely: network, host and global infrastructure. Network and host architecture maintain local database of policy and rules and contribute to global database. The global database shares information regarding intrusions among different clouds. The main features of DCDIDP include being distributed (policies are distributed among hosts), collaborative (hosts collaborate with each other to stay synchronized for information sharing) and data driven (dynamic evaluation of rules and access list). DCDIDP can be implemented in IaaS, PaaS and SaaS and provides effective intrusion prevention. However, the collaboration among different clouds requires an extensive trust management, which does not exist in the current DCDIDP framework. It does not provide approaches to promote trust among cloud users beyond what is stated in SLA. Information sharing among different clouds is also dependent on the structure of each cloud. Finally, DCDIDP has not been evaluated and verified through practical implementations.

Dastjerdi *et al.* [78] propose a new IDS system by combining and extending the peer-to-peer IDS based on mobile agents [79] and the distributed intrusion detection using mobile agent (DIDMA) [80]. It consists of four main components namely IDS control center (IDS CC), agency, application specific static agent detector and specialized investigative mobile agent. IDS CC is central part of IDS component administration. Dastjerdi *et al.* claim that their proposal reduces network load and provides better trust management.

Figure 4 represents the overall view of IDS structure that consists of NIDS and HIDS. Each IDS (regardless of being deployed on distributed networks, grid or cloud) requires some basic components such as alert sharing, analyzer, technique to detect the suspicious behavior, *etc.* Researchers and practitioners are providing solutions, in the form of IDS, DIDS or HIDS, by reducing the number of components and by increasing the performance of IDS. Cloud infrastructure is changing so rapidly that current intrusion detection systems are not flexible enough to cope with these changes. One solution can be autonomous IDS that can update its policy as soon as cloud infrastructure changes. An unattended area here is to develop mechanisms for distributed IDS (Network or host based), which involve both inter and intra clouds considerations. Infrastructure heterogeneity, among clouds, and use of efficient communication protocols poses another challenge in cloud security.

4.2. Autonomous Systems

An autonomous system is an IDS that works with pre-specified basic rules. These rules configure, heal, optimize and protect themselves automatically, thereby reducing human efforts and involvement [81]. These rules are specified either by management or through artificial intelligence. It is impossible, without autonomic computing, to manage next generation distributed-systems such as clouds and grids effectively. Deolitzshcer *et al.* [82] present an intelligent autonomous agent for incident detection named Security audit as a Service (SaaS). This agent is assumed to be aware of the underlying business flow of instances of the deployed clouds. SaaS collects data directly at the source, analyses it, aggregates information and then distributes it. The central part of this system is based on data analysis that is performed through security service level agreement (SSLA). SaaS addresses three main problems of cloud computing namely: (1) abusing cloud resources; (2) missing security monitoring in cloud infrastructure and (3) defective isolation of shared resources. SaaS involves the use of large number of sensors that can capture many events. These sensors receive security policies from SSLA. Even though SaaS is based on autonomous agent, its security policy is still based on pre-defined rules, which limits the detection capabilities only to those attacks that are already known. Moreover, SaaS involves the use of large number of agents and functions such as initiating agent, moving agent, killing agent, *etc.*, which creates high communication among agents and increases the computational overhead.

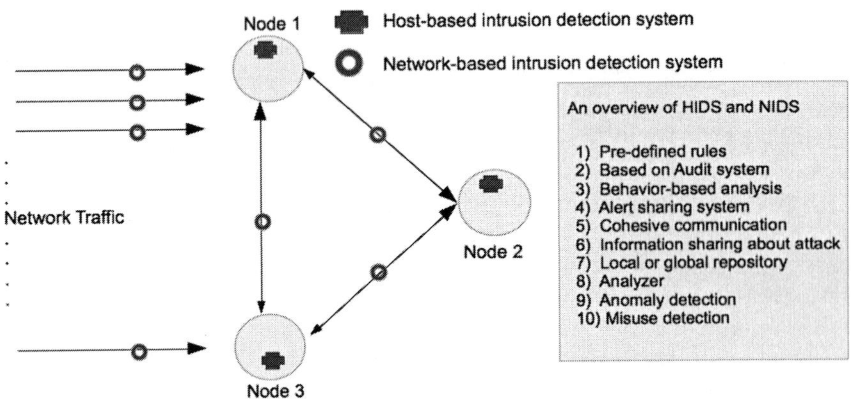

Figure 4. Basic architecture of Intrusion Detection Systems.

Balen *et al.* [83] provide a pure concept of autonomous system, as compared to SaaS [82], particularly autonomic manager in grid and cloud computing. It provides a feature of self-configuration, self-healing, self-optimization and self-protection. The autonomic system is one which includes the autonomic manager, which is able to build and execute plans for implementation, based on sent and received information. A pure autonomous system architecture is presented by Sodhi *et al.* in [84]. This architecture is based on IaaS, where control of cluster nodes is fully autonomous. This architecture uses real time information from cluster nodes and decentralizes the policy management from the master node to other working nodes. It has several main components, namely: (1) cloud controller—a gateway for clients into cloud which determines the suitable node to run VM that satisfies client needs; (2) cloud agent—an intelligent software component that responds to the queries of the cloud controller regarding the availability of VM configuration for a specific lease duration; (3) VM foundry—VM image repository interface dedicated to answer queries for particular VM configurations and it creates the one-time-URLs for the VM image. The cloud agent is further based on several components including request handler, VM manager, policy manager, capability manager and data store. The key point which differentiates this system from other IaaS based systems is that it consists of decentralized policy management rather than based on master–slave relationship architecture that provides a bottleneck issue. If a problem occurs in the master, it may cause the system to function abnormally or even to shut down. This issue has been avoided through decentralization of policies to other nodes. Workload distribution mechanisms for IaaS are static. Decentralization needs to be an autonomous, due to rapid change in cloud infrastructure. Decentralization of policy management among different nodes will increase reliability and security (e.g., if one node is compromised, information leakage from other nodes can still be controlled).

Non-functional requirements with respect to autonomous IaaS node structure is still not much explored. Yazir *et al.* in [85] discuss an approach for dynamic and autonomous resource management in cloud computing with respect to scalability, feasibility and flexibility. Similar to [84], Yazir *et al.* present an approach that deals with decentralization of autonomous tasks, carried out by independent agents. The authors' contributions are based on two steps (1) resource management is decomposed into independent tasks and each task is executed by autonomous node agent by adopting distributed architecture and (2) configuration is carried out by node agent through multiple criteria decision analysis (MCDA) using PROMETHEE method [86]. The simulation of this system proves to achieve scalability through distributed approach which reduces computational complexity. The approach used in the system is potentially feasible in large data centers as compared to centralized approaches. Dynamic resource allocation provides higher flexibility due to its ability to change/add configurations. The main purpose of introducing an autonomous system in a cloud is to avoid wasting time and to utilize resources efficiently. The authors conclude that the PROMETHEE approach is promising with respect to non-functional attributes such as scalability, feasibility and flexibility although there is no function for proper resource management among virtual machines [87]. For example, HDD volume and memory volume setting is done manually or by cost estimation. There is no flexible management system by number of user access, at a given time or by load averages.

4.3. Federated Identity Management System

The backbone of cloud computing security is tightly coupled with identities used to access cloud infrastructure. Management of identities (IDM) is about maintaining the integrity of identities, throughout their life cycle, to make it and its related data (e.g., authentication and authorization results) available to different services in secure and privacy-protected manner [88]. The concept of federated identity management (FIM) is about managing identities by allowing an identity subject to establish links between his/her identities, each of which can be used for a different service, across geographical and organizational borders [88]. Establishing a logical link between identities is called identity federation [88]. The federation is a group of organizations that establish trust among themselves in order to cooperate safely in business [89]. The process to repeat authentication of user (Single Sign-On) can be an example of federated identity [89]. The main issue with single Sign-On lies in the wider damage that it causes in case of compromise. If a user identity is compromised, the illegitimate user will not be verified again, which could create higher level of information leakage. Another issue is lacking dynamic federation and agile mechanism in FIM systems [90]. It is an architectural concern and requires further investigation.

Figure 5 represents the basic functionality of IDM that consists of eight steps: login, requesting application or data, requesting token for ID verification, generating token, verifying it and sending/accessing the data/application. The user logs in IDM through his login ID (step 1) and requests to access application/data from the cloud (step 2) simultaneously. The cloud asks the user for a suitable token to be generated by the IDM for further authentication (step 3). The user requests the token from the IDM (step 4). The IDM generates the token and shares it with the user and the cloud (step 5). The user sends the token to the cloud in order to complete the step for final authentication (step 6). The cloud compares the token sent by the user and that sent by the IDM (step 7). Finally, if the verification succeeds, the cloud grants access to the user. There are three major standards to generate tokens in IDM namely—SAML, OpenID and Information Card. SAML consists of different sets of technical standards in order to implement the FIM. The notable service designed by SAML is single sign-on. It has been deployed widely and follows the strict security/privacy requirements, e.g., enterprise, governments and telecom [91]. OpenID is similar to SAML except it provides a smaller set of functions together with simple expressions of identity related data [91]. In Information Card standard, identities are managed as a set of cards. In the real word, a person usually has a set of cards such as national ID and driving license in order to represent her and all these cards are used for different purposes. The same mechanism has been applied in Information Card standards.

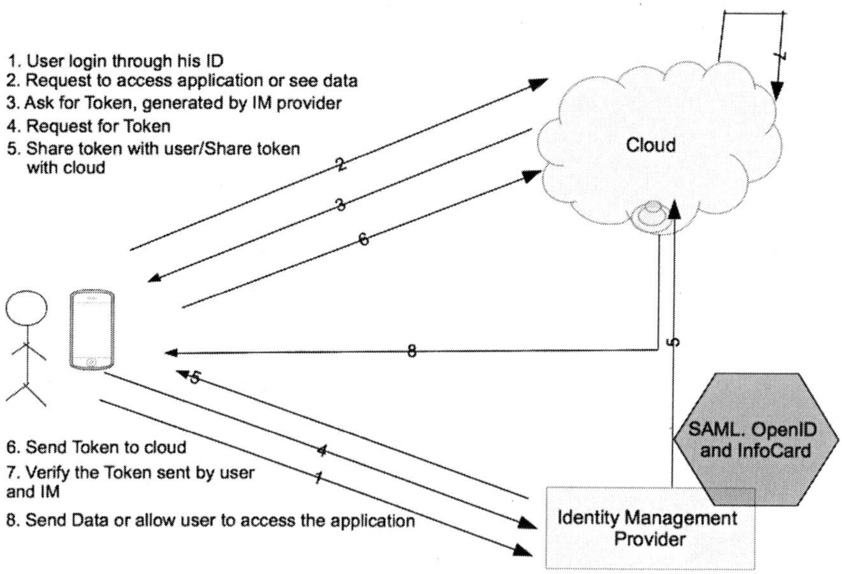

Figure 5. Federated Identity Management System.

Leandro *et al.* [89] propose multi-tenancy authorization system for cloud computing using SAML standards (Shibboleth [92]). They promote the use of Shibboleth as access control system without using a trusted third party [89]. Shibboleth consists of four components (1) handle service—designated to authenticate user and issue handle token to the user; (2) attribute authority—designated to handle requests for software product attributes and apply corresponding privacy policy; (3) directory service—attribute storage of local user and (4) authentication mechanism-designated for user authentication with central service through login/password. It provides strong authorization but not authentication. In other words, it is difficult to steal identity during the running session once the user is authenticated with Shibboleth. However, Shibboleth does not provide a mechanism to ensure the legitimacy of the person connected with the system. Illegitimate person with valid username and password can avail the services without being double-checked. With this argument, the use of shibboleth does not guarantee complete secure transactions. Moreover, the multi-tenancy authorization system generates separate identity provider for each user/organization where each identity provider is using same policies. This particular architecture design helps users to modify security policies according to their need. However, outsourcing identity providers few concerns [93] including: (1) how to make sure that there will be no shift of data and processes to another location; (2) how to delete data after expiration of contract and (3) how to avoid both accidental and deliberate interference across the domain of clouds. In principle, there is no scheme to match the access control requirements with those that are provided by cloud providers. Organizations have no control over their data even after signing a contract with a cloud provider because it is not an easy task to enforce that the cloud provider will always meet the enterprise's requirements.

Another concept of central approach in IDM systems is discussed in [94,95]. Angin *et al.* in [94] propose entity-centric approach called Active Bundle Scheme for IDM with comparison of application-centric approach. This approach allows the entity to (1) create/manage its digital identities in order to authenticate in such a way that it does not reveal its actual identity and relationship between identities to vendor/service providers and (2) to protect personally identifiable information from unauthorized access. The same concept has been discussed in [89] except that Angin *et al.* do not implement or validate the solution. Identity-centric IDM is rationale response for the need of trust and security, generated by business explosion and social transaction, facilitating the exploit of an ever-increasing amount of personal data. The work in [74] refers to a particular type of Internet where trust and security are native, by design. This concept can be achieved through (1) total separation of storage of personal data and their exploitation by organizations and (2) through disaggregating organization centric data systems to re-aggregation around identity-centric systems.

5. DISCUSSION

Cloud computing is an emerging paradigm that involves all the basic components of computing such as end-user machines (PCs), communication networks, access management systems and cloud infrastructures. To achieve comprehensive cloud security, the data and cloud infrastructure must be protected against known/unknown attacks across all cloud components. The number of browser based attacks in 2011 increased from 580,371,937 to 946,393,693 [96]. This notable increase is mainly due to the wide adoption of cloud computing which makes the platform very attractive for attackers due to the growing value of the data assets and resources available on the clouds. Unfortunately, we cannot protect the cloud-computing infrastructure from all the known/unknown attacks because it requires additional computational overhead and resources. Current security solutions like IDS, DIDS, firewalling, outsourcing the identity management systems, installing antivirus, *etc.*, [97,98,99,100,101,102] are expensive and degrade performance. Therefore, the major cloud security research challenge lies not only in providing high level security measures but also in doing so with minimum resources and reduced performance degradation.

Most of cloud vendors falsely claim to provide secure data and computational environments for cloud users. However, for such claims to be realistic, collective efforts are required at higher levels (e.g., governing bodies) instead of leaving it to individual organizations. Our current work helps in achieve that goal by providing a comprehensive study of the attacks against clouds, establishing dependencies among various attacks, and correlating attacks to vulnerabilities across various cloud components. This study can support the endeavors to provide preventive measures as well as proactive tools in defending the clouds. Using this study, we found that data and system security should be embedded in the design of cloud architecture to achieve better security. Moreover, security measures should be dynamic and autonomous. Cloud computing infrastructure is changing fast requiring security measures and policies to be updated regularly at the same pace to match the changing behavior of the clouds. Furthermore, licensing is crucial to the security of clouds. Standard policies should be strictly implemented in clouds and organizational/governing bodies should visit clouds' staff and infrastructure on regular bases to evaluate the efficiency of the security precautions adopted by the vendors. The statistics for attacks, occurring in any cloud, should be publically available to determine the reliability of cloud vendors. This type of sharing helps other cloud's security experts to guard against new attacks. Also, it is extremely important to holistically investigate the various cloud security related parameters including risks, threats, challenges, vulnerabilities, and attacks. The possibility of being attacked can be reduced by deeply understanding the dependencies among these parameters. Finally, note that virtualization is a backbone of cloud computing. However, the concept of using virtualization in cloud computing is not yet mature as there are numerous number of attacks that target the virtualization environment. Examples of these attacks include information leakage during VM migration, service theft by manipulating VMs, uploading malicious VMs on cloud server, and rolling back VMs. Therefore, it is extremely important to develop reliable schedulers that, by design, contain sufficient security mechanisms.

We have identified a few areas that are still unattended in cloud computing security such as auditing, and migration of data from one cloud to another. Emphasis in current research has always been on fast performance and low cost services, but the quality (e.g., availability, scalability, reliability, *etc.*) of service has not been seriously considered.

Non-functional requirements with respect to autonomous IaaS node structure is still not much explored. Another big concern is related with data. Data migration from one cloud to another is not achievable, at this moment, because of the heterogeneous nature of clouds. Moreover, clouds lack the tools that ensure that user data has been deleted from the cloud if the contract has expired. These data privacy threats require researchers' attention to provide some standards for permanent data deletion. We plan in the future to explore the possibility of providing suitable frameworks for DIDS for heterogeneous clouds together with scheduling algorithms for Green IT.

Other related research issues in the area of cloud infrastructure include mobile computing challenges [103,104]. In mobile platforms, limited memory, low processor speed and higher computational requirements create hurdles in the efforts to provide best performance on these platforms. In addition to this, mobile applications provide higher level of threat, as there is a weak or even no security "check and balance" on application's development. It has been claimed in [91], that 20% of the 48,000 applications, in android market, allow third party applications to access your sensitive data as well as allowing it to make calls and send texts without user consents. Apple Inc. has implemented a security framework in which each application should be submitted to Apple security team to determine the threat to user data or system before including it in the App Store.

6. CONCLUSIONS

The adoption of cloud computing paradigm is continuously growing. In 2010, the IT spending in America to migrate to cloud computing solutions was estimated at $20 billion. Analysts believe that the cost reduction factor in cloud computing will further accelerate the adoption of cloud computing in the public sectors. With the massive growth in cloud computing adoption, the security attracted the attention of researchers and practitioners but still has not received enough attention.

In this work, we conduct a survey on the current cloud security issues and the state-of-the-art security solutions. We identify 28 cloud security issues such as firewall misconfigurations, malicious insiders, tampered binaries, multi-tenancy, side channels, weak browser security, and mobility. Then, we classify these issues into five security categories, namely: security standards, network, access, cloud infrastructure, and data. We also identify nine attack classes that target the clouds and present variable incidents of each attack such phishing, fate sharing, botnet, and malware injection. For each attack class, we present the state-of-the-art countermeasures and provide a comparative analysis of the effectiveness and the shortcomings of the proposed solutions. Finally, we present and evaluate the effectiveness of the state-of-the-art general countermeasures for cloud security attacks including intrusion detection systems, autonomous systems, and federated identity management systems. We also highlight the shortcomings of these systems that include the high communication and computation overhead and the detection efficiency and coverage.

REFERENCES

1. Tripathi, A.; Mishra, A. Cloud computing security considerations. In Proceedings of the 2011 IEEE International Conference on Signal Processing, Communications and Computing (ICSPCC), Xi'an, China, 14–16 September 2011; pp. 1–5.
2. Wang, J.-J.; Mu, S. Security issues and countermeasures in cloud computing. In Proceedings of the 2011 IEEE International Conference on Grey Systems and Intelligent Services (GSIS), Nanjing, China, 15–18 September 2011; pp. 843–846.
3. Final Version of NIST Cloud Computing Definition Published. Available online: http://www.nist.gov/itl/csd/cloud-102511.cfm (accessed on 25 August 2013).
4. Lv, H.; Hu, Y. Analysis and research about cloud computing security protect policy. In Proceedings of the 2011 International Conference on Intelligence Science and Information Engineering (ISIE), Wuhan, China, 20–21 August 2011; pp. 214–216.
5. Mell, P.; Grance, T. *The NIST Definition of Cloud Computing*; NIST: USA USA. , 2009. available at: http://csrc.nist.gov/publications/nistpubs/800-145/SP800-145.pdf.
6. Jain, P.; Rane, D.; Patidar, S. A survey and analysis of cloud model-based security for computing secure cloud bursting and aggregation in renal environment. In Proceedings of the 2011 World Congress on Information and Communication Technologies (WICT), Mumbai, India, 11–14 December 2011; pp. 456–461.
7. Gowrigolla, B.; Sivaji, S.; Masillamani, M.R. Design and auditing of cloud computing security. In Proceedings of the 2010 5th International Conference on Information and Automation for Sustainability (ICIAFs), Colombo, Sri Lanka, 17–19 December 2010; pp. 292–297.
8. Houmansadr, A.; Zonouz, S.A.; Berthier, R. A cloud-based intrusion detection and response system for mobile phones. In Proceedings of the 2011 IEEE/IFIP 41st International Conference on Dependable Systems and Networks Workshops (DSN-W), Hong Kong, China, 27–30 June 2011; pp. 31–32.
9. Gu, C.-D.; Li, J.-X.; Wu, J.-P.; Fu, Y.-L.; Lu, K.; Si, M.-X. Wireless broadband application technology investigation of IPv6 optical network cloud computing. In Proceedings of the 2010 6th International Conference on Advanced Information Management and Service (IMS), Seoul, Korea, 30 November–2 December 2010; pp. 191–194.
10. Sabahi, F. Virtualization-level security in cloud computing. In Proceedings of the 2011 IEEE 3rd International Conference on Communication Software and Networks (ICCSN), Xi'an, China, 27–29 May 2011; pp. 250–254.
11. Wang, C.; Wang, Q.; Ren, K.; Lou, W. Towards secure and dependable storage services in cloud computing. *IEEE Trans. Serv. Comput.* **2012**, *5*, 220–232.
12. Lingfeng, C.; Hoang, D.B. Towards scalable, fine-grained, intrusion-tolerant data protection models for healthcare cloud. In Proceedings of the 2011 IEEE 10th International Conference on Trust, Security and Privacy in Computing and Communications (TrustCom), Changsha, China, 16–18 November 2011; pp. 126–133.

13. Morin, J.; Aubert, J.; Gateau, B. Towards cloud computing SLA risk management: Issues and challenges. In Proceedings of the 2012 45th Hawaii International Conference on System Science (HICSS), Maui, HI, USA, 4–7 January 2012; pp. 5509–5514.
14. Khalil, I.M. ELMO: Energy aware local monitoring in sensor networks. *IEEE Trans. Dependable Secur. Comput.* **2011**, *8*, 523–536.
15. Khalil, I.; Bagchi, S. MISPAR: Mitigating stealthy packet dropping in locally-monitored multi-hop wireless Ad Hoc networks. In Proceedings of the 4th International Conference on Security and Privacy in Communication Netowrks (SecureComm '08), Istanbul, Turkey, 22–25 September 2008; ACM: New York, NY, USA, 2008; article 28. 1–10.
16. Khalil, I. MCC: Mitigating colluding collision attacks in wireless sensor networks. In Proceedings of the 2010 IEEE Global Telecommunications Conference (GLOBECOM 2010), Miami, FL, USA, 6–10 December 2010; pp. 1–5.
17. Hayajneh, M.; Khalil, I.; Gadallah, Y. An OFDMA-based MAC protocol for under water acoustic wireless sensor network. In Proceedings of the 2009 ACM International Conference on Wireless Communications and Mobile Computing (IWCMC'09), Leipzig, Germany, June 21 – 24 2009; pp. 810–814.
18. Khalil, I.; Hayajneh, M.; Awad, M. SVNM: Secure verification of neighborhood membership in static multi-hop wireless networks. In Proceedings of the IEEE Symposium on Computers and Communications, 2009, ISCC 2009, Sousse, 5–8 July 2009; pp. 368–373.
19. Sengupta, S.; Kaulgud, V.; Sharma, V.S. Cloud computing security—Trends and research directions. In Proceedings of the 2011 IEEE World Congress on Services (SERVICES), Washington, DC, USA, 4–9 July 2011; pp. 524–531.
20. Chow, R.; Golle, P.; Jakobsson, M.; Shi, E.; Staddon, J.; Masuoka, R.; Molina, J. Controlling data in the cloud: Outsourcing computation without outsourcing control. In Proceedings of the 2009 ACM Workshop on Cloud Computing Security, Chicago, IL, USA, 13 November 2009; ACM Press: New York, NY, USA, 2009; pp. 85–90.
21. Samarati, P.; di Vimercati, S.D.C. Data protection in outsourcing scenarios: Issues and directions. In Proceedings of the 5th ACM Symposium on Information, Computer and Communications Security (ASIACCS '10), Chicago, IL, USA, 4–8 October 2010; ACM: New York, NY, USA, 2010; pp. 1–14.
22. Popovic, O.; Jovanovic, Z.; Jovanovic, N.; Popovic, R. A comparison and security analysis of the cloud computing software platforms. In Proceedings of the 2011 10th International Conference on Telecommunication in Modern Satellite Cable and Broadcasting Services (TELSIKS), Nis, Serbia, 5–8 October 2011; Volume 2, pp. 632–634.
23. Gul, I.; ur Rehman, A.; Islam, M.H. Cloud computing security auditing. In Proceedings of the 2011 The 2nd International Conference on Next Generation Information Technology (ICNIT), Gyeongju, Korea, 21–23 June 2011; pp. 143–148.
24. Kandukuri, B.R.; Paturi, V.R.; Rakshit, A. Cloud security issues. In Proceedings of the IEEE International Conference on Services Computing, 2009 (SCC '09), Bangalore, India, 21–25 September 2009; pp. 517–520.
25. Chen, Z.; Yoon, J. IT auditing to assure a secure cloud computing. In Proceedings of the 2010 6th World Congress on Services (SERVICES-1), Miami, FL, USA, 5–10 July 2010; pp. 253–259.
26. Ryan, G.W.; Bernard, H.R. Data Management and Analysis Methods. Available online: http://www.rand.org/pubs/external_publications/EP20000033.html (accessed on 25 August 2013).
27. Holloway, I.; Todres, L. The status of method: Flexibility, consistency and coherence. *Qual. Res.* **2003**, *3*, 345–357.
28. Hashizume, K.; Rosado, D.G.; Fernández-Medina, E.; Fernandez, E.B. An analysis of security issues for cloud computing. *J. Internet Serv. Appl.* **2013**, *4*, 5.
29. Zissis, D.; Lekkas, D. Addressing cloud computing security issues. *Future Gener. Comput. Syst.* **2012**, *28*, 583–592.
30. Md Whaiduzzaman, M.; Sookhak, M.; Gani, A.; Buyya, R. A survey on vehicular cloud computing. *J. Netw. Comput. Appl.* **2013**.
31. Braun, V.; Clarke, V. Using thematic analysis in psychology. *Qual. Res. Psychol.* **2006**, *3*, 77–101.

32. A Survey on Cloud Computing Security, Challenges and Threats|Whitepapers| TechRepublic. Available online: http://www.techrepublic.com/whitepapers/a-survey-on-cloud-computing-security-challenges-and-threats/3483757(accessed on 18 March 2012).
33. Thalmann, S.; Bachlechner, D.; Demetz, L.; Maier, R. Challenges in cross-organizational security management. In Proceedings of the 2012 45th Hawaii International Conference on System Science (HICSS), Maui, HI, USA, 4–7 January 2012; pp. 5480–5489.
34. Riquet, D.; Grimaud, G.; Hauspie, M. Large-scale coordinated attacks: Impact on the cloud security. In Proceedings of the 2012 Sixth International Conference on Innovative Mobile and Internet Services in Ubiquitous Computing (IMIS), Palermo, Italy, 4–6 July 2012; pp. 558–563.
35. Gonzalez, N.; Miers, C.; Redigolo, F.; Carvalho, T.; Simplicio, M.; Naslund, M.; Pourzandi, M. A quantitative analysis of current security concerns and solutions for cloud computing. In Proceedings of the 2011 IEEE Third International Conference on Cloud Computing Technology and Science (CloudCom), Athens, Greece, 29 November–1 December 2011; pp. 231–238.
36. Rachel Suresh, N.; Mathew, S.V. Security concerns for cloud computing in aircraft data networks. In Proceedings of the 2011 International Conference for Internet Technology and Secured Transactions (ICITST), Abu Dhabi, United Arab Emirates, 11–14 December 2011; pp. 132–136.
37. Fangfei, Z.; Goel, M.; Desnoyers, P.; Sundaram, R. Scheduler vulnerabilities and coordinated attacks in cloud computing. In Proceedings of the 2011 10th IEEE International Symposium on Network Computing and Applications (NCA), Cambridge, MA, USA, 25–27 August 2011; pp. 123–130.
38. Who Can You Trust in the Cloud? A Review of Security Issues within Cloud Computing. Available online: http://www.drjeffdaniels.com/1/post/2011/10/who-can-you-trust-in-the-cloud-a-review-of-security-issues-within-cloud-computing.html (accessed on 18 March 2012).
39. Mollet, N.G. Cloud Computing Security. Bachelor of Engineering Degree Information Technology Thesis, Helsinki Metropolia University of Applied Sciences, Helsinki, Finland, 11 April 2011.
40. Behl, A. Emerging security challenges in cloud computing: An insight to cloud security challenges and their mitigation. In Proceedings of the 2011 World Congress on Information and Communication Technologies (WICT), Mumbai, India, 11–14 December 2011; pp. 217–222.
41. Mathisen, E. Security challenges and solutions in cloud computing. In Proceedings of the 2011 5th IEEE International Conference on Digital Ecosystems and Technologies Conference (DEST), Daejeon, Korea, 31 May–3 June 2011; pp. 208–212.
42. Bhardwaj, A.; Kumar, V. Cloud security assessment and identity management. In Proceedings of the 2011 14th International Conference on Computer and Information Technology (ICCIT), Dhaka, Bangladesh, 22–24 December 2011; pp. 387–392.
43. Mahmood, Z. Data location and security issues in cloud computing. In Proceedings of the 2011 International Conference on Emerging Intelligent Data and Web Technologies (EIDWT), Tirana, Albania, 7–9 September 2011; pp. 49–54.
44. Gruschka, N.; Jensen, M. Attack surfaces: A taxonomy for attacks on cloud services. In Proceedings of the 2010 IEEE 3rd International Conference on Cloud Computing (CLOUD), Miami, FL, USA, 5–10 July 2010; pp. 276–279.
45. Cherkasova, L.; Gupta, D.; Vahdat, A. Comparison of the three CPU schedulers in Xen. *ACM SIGMETERICS Perform. Eval. Rev.* **2007**, *35*, 42–51.
46. Fu, W.; Li, X. The study on data security in cloud computing based on virtualization. In Proceedings of the 2011 International Symposium on IT in Medicine and Education (ITME), Cuangzhou, China, 9–11 December 2011; Volume 2, pp. 257–261.
47. Kim, H.; Lim, H.; Jeong, J.; Jo, H.; Lee, J. Task-aware virtual machine scheduling for I/O Performance. In Proceedings of the 2009 ACM SIGPLAN/SIGOPS International Conference on Virtual Execution Environments, Washington, DC, March 11-13, 2009; pp. 101–110.

48. Cherkasova, L.; Gupta, D.; Vahdat, A. When virtual is harder than real: Resource allocation challenges in virtual machine based IT environments. Technical Report HPL-2007-25. HP Laboratories, Palo. Alto, Feb 2007.
49. Karnwal, T.; Sivakumar, T.; Aghila, G. A comber approach to protect cloud computing against XML DDoS and HTTP DDoS attack. In Proceedings of the 2012 IEEE Students' Conference on Electrical, Electronics and Computer Science (SCEECS), Bhopal, India, 1–2 March 2012; pp. 1–5.
50. Liu, S.-T.; Chen, Y.-M. Retrospective detection of malware attacks by cloud computing. In Proceedings of the 2010 International Conference on Cyber-Enabled Distributed Computing and Knowledge Discovery (CyberC), Huangshan, China, 10–12 October 2010; pp. 510–517.
51. Oberheide, J.; Cooke, E.; Jahanian, F. CloudAV: N-version antivirus in the network cloud. In Proceedings of the 17th Conference on Security Symposium (SS '08); USENIX Association: Berkeley, CA, USA, 2008; pp. 91–106.
52. Martignoni, L.; Paleari, R.; Bruschi, D. A framework for behavior-based malware analysis in the cloud. In Proceedings of the 5th International Conference on Information Systems Security (ICISS '09), Kolkata, India, 14–18 December 2009; Springer-Verlag: Berlin, Heidelberg, 2009; pp. 178–192.
53. Khorshed, M.T.; Ali, A.B.M.S.; Wasimi, S.A. A survey on gaps, threat remediation challenges and some thoughts for proactive attack detection in cloud computing. *Future Gener. Comput. Syst.* **2012**, *28*, 833–851.
54. Aviram, A.; Hu, S.; Ford, B.; Gummadi, R. Determinating timing channels in compute clouds. In Proceedings of the 2010 ACM Workshop on Cloud Computing Security Workshop (CCSW '10); ACM: New York, NY, USA, 2010; pp. 103–108.
55. Hlavacs, H.; Treutner, T.; Gelas, J.; Lefevre, L.; Orgerie, A. Energy consumption side-channel attack at virtual machines in a cloud. In Proceedings of the 2011 IEEE Ninth International Conference on Dependable, Autonomic and Secure Computing (DASC), Sydney, NSW, Australia, 12–14 December 2011; pp. 605–612.
56. Rocha, F.; Correia, M. Lucy in the sky without diamonds: Stealing confidential data in the cloud. In Proceedings of the 2011 IEEE/IFIP 41st International Conference on Dependable Systems and Networks Workshops (DSNW '11), Hong Kong, China, 27–30 June 2011; IEEE Computer Society: Washington, DC, USA, 2011; pp. 129–134.
57. Ristenpart, T.; Tromer, E.; Shacham, H.; Savage, S. Hey, you, get off of my cloud: Exploring information leakage in third-party compute clouds. In Proceedings of the 16th ACM Conference on Computer and Communications Security (CCS '09), Chicago, IL, USA, 9–13 November 2009; ACM: New York, NY, USA, 2009; pp. 199–212.
58. Top Threats to Cloud Computing V1.0, Cloud Security Alliance, March 2010.
59. Grosse, E.; Howie, J.; Ransome, J.; Reavis, J.; Schmidt, S. Cloud computing roundtable. *IEEE Secur. Priv.* **2010**, *8*, 17–23.
60. Lin, W.; Lee, D. Traceback attacks in cloud—Pebbletrace botnet. In Proceedings of the 2012 32nd International Conference on Distributed Computing Systems Workshops (ICDCSW), Macau, China, 18–21 June 2012; pp. 417–426.
61. Kourai, K.; Azumi, T.; Chiba, S. A self-protection mechanism against stepping-stone attacks for IaaS clouds. In Proceedings of the UIC/ATC; 2012; pp. 539–546.
62. Liu, B.; Xu, E.; Wang, J.; Wei, Z.; Xu, L.; Zhao, B.; Su, J. Thwarting audio steganography attacks in cloud storage systems. In Proceedings of the 2011 International Conference on Cloud and Service Computing (CSC), Hong Kong, China, 12–14 December 2011; pp. 259–265.
63. Mazurczyk, W.; Szczypiorski, K. Is cloud computing steganography-proof? In Proceedings of the 2011 Third International Conference on Multimedia Information Networking and Security (MINES '11), Shanghai, China, 4–6 November 2011; IEEE Computer Society: Washington, DC, USA, 2011; pp. 441–442.
64. Antunes, N.; Vieira, M. Defending against web application vulnerabilities. *Computer* **2012**, *45*, 66–72.
65. Parno, B.; Lorch, J.R.; Douceur, J.R.; Mickens, J.; McCune, J.M. Memoir: Practical state continuity for protected modules. In Proceedings of the 2011 IEEE Symposium on

Security and Privacy (SP '11), Oakland, CA, USA, 22–25 May 2011; IEEE Computer Society: Washington, DC, USA, 2011; pp. 379–394.

66. Zeus Bot Found Using Amazon's EC2 as C&C Server. Available online: http:// www.theregister.co.uk/2009/12/09/amazon ec2 bot control channel/ (accessed on: Feb 1, 2014).
67. Google Cloud Platform Used for Botnet Control. Available online: http:// www. infosecurity-magazine.com/view/5115/google-cloud-platform-used-for-botnet-control/ (accessed on: Feb 1, 2014).
68. Raytheon UK Targeted in Cloud-Based Attack. Available online: http://www. zdnet.co.uk/news/security-threats/2011/10/12/raytheon-uk-targeted-in-cloud-based-attack-40094173/ (accessed on: Feb 1, 2014).
69. Srivastava, A.; Giffin, J. Tamper-resistant, application-aware blocking of malicious network connections. In Proceedings of the 11th International Symposium, RAID 2008, Cambridge, MA, USA, 15–17 September 2008; pp. 39–58.
70. Tupakula, U.; Varadharajan, V.; Akku, N. Intrusion detection techniques for infrastructure as a service cloud. In Proceedings of the 2011 IEEE Ninth International Conference on Dependable, Autonomic and Secure Computing (DASC), Sydney, Australia, 12–14 Dec. 2011; pp. 744–751.
71. Szefer, J.; Lee, R.B. Architectural support for hypervisor-secure virtualization. *SIGARCH Comput. Arch. News* **2012**, *40*, 437–450.
72. Lo, C.-C.; Huang, C.-C.; Ku, J. A cooperative intrusion detection system framework for cloud computing networks. In Proceedings of the 2010 39th International Conference on Parallel Processing Workshops (ICPPW), San Diego, CA, USA, 13–16 September 2010; pp. 280–284.
73. Vieira, K.; Schulter, A.; Westphall, C.B.; Westphall, C.M. Intrusion detection for grid and cloud computing. *IT Prof.* **2010**, *12*, 38–43.
74. Wang, D.; Zhou, Z. Application of cloud model in intrusion detection. In Proceedings of the 2010 2nd International Conference on e-Business and Information System Security (EBISS), Wuhan, China, 22–23 May 2010; pp. 1–4.
75. Van athi, R.; Gunasekaran, S. Comparison of network intrusion detection systems in cloud computing environment. In Proceedings of the 2012 International Conference on Computer Communication and Informatics (ICCCI), Coimbatore, India, 10–12 January 2012; pp. 1–6.
76. Roschke, S.; Cheng, F.; Meinel, C. Intrusion detection in the cloud. In Proceedings of the Eighth IEEE International Conference on Dependable, Autonomic and Secure Computing, 2009 (DASC '09), Chengdu, China, 12–14 December 2009; pp. 729–734.
77. Zargar, S.T.; Takabi, H.; Joshi, J.B.D. DCDIDP: A distributed, collaborative, and data-driven intrusion detection and prevention framework for cloud computing environments. In Proceedings of the 2011 7th International Conference on Collaborative Computing: Networking, Applications and Worksharing (CollaborateCom), Orlando, FL, USA, 15–18 October 2011; pp. 332–341.
78. Dastjerdi, A.V.; Bakar, K.A.; Tabatabaei, S.G.H. Distributed intrusion detection in clouds using mobile agents. In Proceedings of the Third International Conference on Advanced Engineering Computing and Applications in Sciences, 2009 (ADVCOMP '09), Sliema, Malta, 11–16 October 2009; pp. 175–180.
79. Ye, D.; Bai, Q.; Zhang, M.; Ye, Z. P2P distributed intrusion detections by using mobile agents. In Proceedings of the Seventh IEEE/ACIS International Conference on Computer and Information Science, 2008 (ICIS 08), Portland, OR, USA, 14–16 May 2008; pp. 259–265.
80. Kannadiga, P.; Zulkernine, M. DIDMA: A distributed intrusion detection system using mobile agents. In Proceedings of the Sixth International Conference on Software Engineering, Artificial Intelligence, Networking and Parallel/Distributed Computing, and First ACIS International Workshop on Self-Assembling Wireless Networks, 23–25 May 2005; pp. 238–245.
81. Erdil, D.C. Dependable autonomic cloud computing with information proxies. In Proceedings of the 2011 IEEE International Symposium on Parallel and Distributed

Processing Workshops and Phd Forum (IPDPSW), Shanghai, China, 16–20 May 2011; pp. 1518–1524.
82. Doelitzscher, F.; Reich, C.; Knahl, M.; Clarke, N. An autonomous agent based incident detection system for cloud environments. In Proceedings of the 2011 IEEE Third International Conference on Cloud Computing Technology and Science (CloudCom), Athens, Greece, 29 November–1 December 2011; pp. 197–204.
83. Balen, D.; Westphall, C.; Westphall, C. Experimental assessment of routing for grid and cloud. In Proceedings of the Tenth International Conference on Networks (ICN 2011), St. Maarten, The Netherlands Antilles, January 23-28, 2011; pp. 341–346.
84. Sodhi, B.; Prabhakar, T.V. A cloud architecture using smart nodes. In Proceedings of the 2011 IEEE Asia-Pacific Services Computing Conference (APSCC), Jeju Island, Korea, 12–15 December 2011; pp. 116–123.
85. Yazir, Y.O.; Matthews, C.; Farahbod, R.; Neville, S.; Guitouni, A.; Ganti, S.; Coady, Y. Dynamic resource allocation in computing clouds using distributed multiple criteria decision analysis. In Proceedings of the 2010 IEEE 3rd International Conference on Cloud Computing (CLOUD), Miami, FL, USA, 5–10 July 2010; pp. 91–98.
86. Mareschal, B. *Aide a la Decision Multicritere: Developpements Recents des Methodes PROMETHEE*; Cahiers du Centre d'Etudes en Recherche Operationelle: Bruxelles, Belgium, 1987; pp. 175–241.
87. Uchida, N.; Takahata, K.; Shibata, Y. Proposal of overlay cloud computing system by virtual autonomous network configuration. In Proceedings of the 2011 International Conference on P2P, Parallel, Grid, Cloud and Internet Computing (3PGCIC), Barcelona, Spain, 26–28 October 2011; pp. 307–310.
88. Bishop, M. *Computer Security: Art and Science*; Addison-Wesley Professional: Reading, MA, USA, 2002.
89. Leandro, M.A.P.; Nascimento, T.J.; dos Santos, D.R.; Westphall, C.M.; Westphall, C.B. Multitenancy authorization system with federated identity for cloud-based environments using shibboleth. In Proceedings of the Eleventh International Conference on Networks; 2012; pp. 88–93.
90. Sanchez, R.; Almenares, F.; Arias, P.; Diaz-Sanchez, D.; Marin, A. Enhancing privacy and dynamic federation in IdM for consumer cloud computing. *IEEE Trans. Consum. Electron.* **2012**, *58*, 95–103.
91. Revealed: Why Android Beats iPhone for Organized Crime. Available online: http://blogs.computerworld.com/16392/security_android_beats_iphone_for_crime (accessed on 13 January 2013).
92. *Oxford English Dictionary*; In Shibboleth; 1989.
93. Albeshri, A.; Caelli, W. Mutual protection in a cloud computing environment. In Proceedings of the 2010 12th IEEE International Conference on the High Performance Computing and Communications (HPCC), Melbourne, VIC, Australia, 1–3 September 2010; pp. 641–646.
94. Angin, P.; Bhargava, B.; Ranchal, R.; Singh, N.; Linderman, M.; Othmane, L.B.; Lilien, L. An entity-centric approach for privacy and identity management in cloud computing. In Proceedings of the 2010 29th IEEE Symposium on Reliable Distributed Systems, New Delhi, India, 31 October–3 November 2010; pp. 177–183.
95. Ates, M.; Ravet, S.; Ahmat, A.M.; Fayolle, J. An identity-centric internet: Identity in the cloud, identity as a service and other delights. In Proceedings of the 2011 Sixth International Conference on Availability, Reliability and Security (ARES), Vienna, Austria, 22–26 August 2011; pp. 555–560.
96. Kaspersky Security Bulletin. Statistics 2011. Available online: http://www. securelist. com/en/analysis/204792216/Kaspersky_Security_Bulletin_Statistics_2011 (accessed on 13 January 2013).
97. You, P.; Peng, Y.; Liu, W.; Xue, S. Security issues and solutions in cloud computing. In Proceedings of the 2012 32nd International Conference on Distributed Computing Systems Workshops (ICDCSW), Macau, China, 18–21 June 2012; pp. 573–577.

98. Bhadauria, R.; Chaki, R.; Chaki, N.; Sanyal, S. A Survey on Security Issues in Cloud Computing. Cornell University Library: USA, 2013. Available online: http://arxiv.org/abs/1109.5388 (Accessed on: Feb 1, 2014).
99. Kanday, R. A survey on cloud computing security. In Proceedings of the 2012 International Conference on Computing Sciences (ICCS), Phagwara, India, 14–15 September 2012; pp. 302–311.
100. Zhou, M.; Zhang, R.; Xie, W.; Qian, W.; Zhou, A. Security and privacy in cloud computing: A survey. In Proceedings of the 2010 Sixth International Conference on Semantics Knowledge and Grid (SKG), Beijing, China, 1–3 November 2010; pp. 105–112.
101. Verma, A.; Kaushal, S. Cloud Computing Security Issues and Challenges: A Survey. In *Advances in Computing and Communications*; Abraham, A., Mauri, J.L., Buford, J.F., Suzuki, J., Thampi, S.M., Eds.; Communications in Computer and Information Science; Springer Berlin Heidelberg: Berlin, Germany, 2011; pp. 445–454.
102. Ren, K.; Wang, C.; Wang, Q. Security challenges for the public cloud. *IEEE Internet Comput.* **2012**, *16*, 69–73.
103. Panta, R. K.; Bagchi, S.; Khalil, I. Efficient wireless reprogramming through reduced bandwidth usage and opportunistic sleeping. *Ad Hoc Networks (an Elsevier Journal)* **2009**, *Volume 7*(Issue 1), 42–62.
104. Khalil, I. MCC: Mitigating colluding collision attacks in wireless sensor networks. In Proceedings of the IEEE Global Communications Conference (IEEE GLOBECOM'10), Miami, Florida, USA, December 6 – 10, 2010; pp. 1–5.
105. http://blog.scalar.ca/Blog/bid/87248/Mitigating-common-cloud-computing-risks (Accessed on: Feb 1, 2014).

CHAPTER 7

Cybersecurity: A Stochastic Predictive Model to Determine Overall Network Security Risk Using Markovian Process

Nawa Raj Pokhrel, Chris P. Tsokos

Department of Mathematics and Statistics, University of South Florida, Tampa, USA

ABSTRACT

There are several security metrics developed to protect the computer networks. In general, common security metrics focus on qualitative and subjective aspects of networks lacking formal statistical models. In the present study, we propose a stochastic model to quantify the risk associated with the overall network using Markovian process in conjunction with Common Vulnerability Scoring System (CVSS) framework. The model we developed uses host access graph to represent the network environment. Utilizing the developed model, one can filter the large amount of information available by making a priority list of vulnerable nodes existing in the network. Once a priority list is prepared, network administrators can make software patch decisions. Gaining in depth understanding of the risk and priority level of each host helps individuals to implement decisions like deployment of security products and to design network topologies.

Keywords: Vulnerability, Attack Graph, Markov Model, Exploitability, CVSS, FIRST, NVD, IDS

1. INTRODUCTION

Computer networks are undoubtedly vulnerable no matter what level of hard ware, software or a combination of both types of security parameters are incorporated. As long as the network servers provide services on different host servers, they depend on the server software that may have security holes which makes them susceptible to malicious attacks. To detect and/or prevent the network accessible resources from suspicious attacks, various commercial Intrusion Detection Systems (IDSs) [1] /Prevention Systems are available in the market. These intrusion detection/prevention based tools provides some sort of a signal that alerts the network administrator and provides them a partial picture of the network [2]. One of the most important challenges on today's networks is to develop the mechanism to aggregate the security risk of all systems in a network to evaluate the overall security risk.

In order to evaluate the security risk of a large scale enterprise, an administrator must consider not only single vulnerability exploit but also the multi-stage and the multi-host vulnerability attack used by the attackers. To incorporate this fact, an attack graph is built to find out the logical relationship between multiple exploits. However, when size and complexity of the network increases, two major problems occur. First, the attack graph grows exponentially when the size of the network and algorithm complexity increase. Secondly, comprehending the information conveyed by the graph becomes difficult. Therefore, the attack graph that addresses the issues mentioned earlier were chosen and we will explain further in the next section.

Very little has been done in scientific and research community to develop statistical model that quantify the overall network security risk. Most of the work focuses on qualitative and subjective aspect of networks without having formal statistical model. To get rid of this problem, we introduce the statistical model that uses Markov chains in conjunction with CVSS framework metrics to analyze risks associated with structures of various networks. The model can be used to identify critical nodes in the host access graph where attackers may be most likely to focus. Based on that information, a network administrator can make appropriate, prioritized decisions for system patching. Further, a flexible risk ranking technique is described, where the decisions made by an attacker can be adjusted using a bias factor. The model can be generalized for use with complicated network environments.

In recent studies, S.M. Rajasooriya [3] and P.K. Kaluarachchi [4] have developed a very interesting and useful statistical model that predicts the expected path length and evaluation of the security risk under different vulnerabilities by utilizing CVSS framework with Markovian process.

In the present study, we are proposing a stochastic model for the security risk evaluation for the entire network based on the Exploitability sub-score and Impact sub-score. We are considering a realistic network topology having three host servers and each host consists of one vulnerability. Based on the network architecture and given firewall rules, a host access graph is constructed. From the host access graph one state transition probability matrix is computed by utilizing Exploitability sub-score and Impact sub-score. By using the Markovian random walk, we can prioritize the risk associated with each node via ranking.

Finally, summing up the risk associated with all the nodes presents in the network, we determine the overall network security risk. This quantitative value can be taken as a security metric to determine the risk of an entire network. Finally, the schematic network topology in our study represents a typical security system that is in operation. Thus, our proposed statistical model and methodology can be applied to a specific security system that is in place for a given company.

2. BACKGROUND AND TERMINOLOGIES OF CYBERSECURITY

In this section, we have defined some of the basic terminology related with cyber security. We also explain the basic idea of the Markov chain process that is implemented to develop the stochastic model to achieve our objective. Figure 1 provides the schematic presentation of the CVSS framework, [5] and vividly reveals the holistic idea to compute the base score along with Exploitability sub- score and Impact sub-score.

2.1. Vulnerabilities

A vulnerability is a flaw that exists in computer resources or control that can be exploited by one or more threats. A software vulnerability [6] is an instance of an error in the specification, development, or configuration of software such that its execution can violate the security policy. Attackers normally use the known vulnerabilities which are listed publicly on National Vulnerability Database (NVD) [7] to penetrate the system. Sometimes attackers may use a vulnerability that has not been disclosed publicly which is called zero day vulnerability. There is almost no defense against a zero day attack [8]. Zero day vulnerability remains unknown to vendors; thus information about the new vulnerabilities gives the attackers a free pass to attack any target host. The zero day attack has not been used in this study.

2.2. Attack Graphs

Attackers usually penetrate any type of computer network via a chain of exploits where each exploit in the chain creates the foundation for upcoming exploits. A combination of such exploits make the chain called attack path; a collection of such attack paths develop the attack graph. An attack graph is a succinct representation of all paths through a system that ends in a state where an intruder has successfully achieved its goal [9] [10]. There are many algorithms that have been developed in the scientific and research community to construct the attack graphs. However, it is very difficult to analyze the network via attack graph when a number of nodes and complexity of the network increase. As the scalability and complexity of the network increase exponentially, the computation cost to create the attack graph increases. As a result, it is difficult to interpret the attack graph precisely. On the other hand, most of the attack graphs are designed for a single target, and cannot be used to evaluate the overall security of the networks with several targets. To address these striking problems Anming Xie, Zhuhua Cai, Cong Tang, Jianbin Hu, and Zhong Chen [11] developed a novel approach to generate and describe the attack graph.

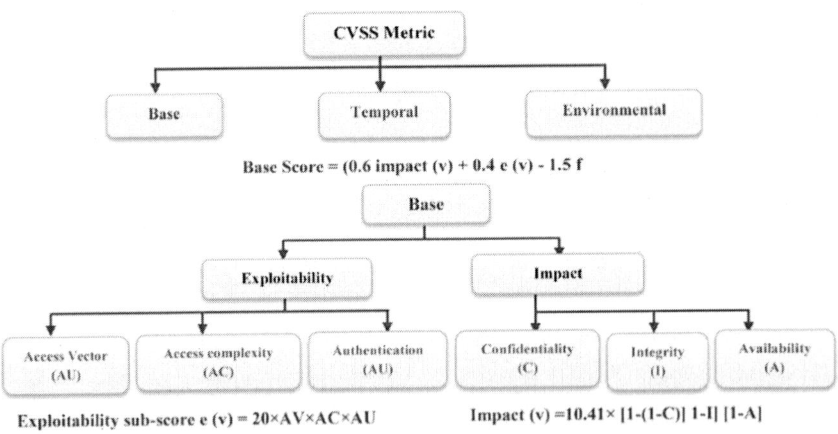

Figure 1. Common vulnerability system for base metric calculation model.

They developed a two layer attack graph, where the upper layer is a host access graph and the lower layer is composed of some host pair attack graphs. The lower level describes all the detailed attack scenarios between each host pair, and the upper level shows the direct network access relationship between each host pair by ignoring detailed information. In this study our stochastic model is based on upper layer attack graphs; that is, host access graphs have been utilized.

2.3. Common Vulnerability Scoring System (CVSS)

CVSS [12] is the open framework that provides the quantitative scores repre- senting the overall severity and risk of the known vulnerabilities. It is maintained by the Forum of Incident Response Team (FIRST) [13]. A CVSS score is on the scale of 0 to 10 and consists of three major metrics group: base, temporal and environmental as mentioned in Figure 1. Vulnerabilities with the base score range from 0 - 3.9 is considered Low vulnerability, 4.0 - 6.9 as Medium, and 7.0 - 10 as High. The base score is computed using two sub-scores; Exploitability sub-score and Impact sub-score using standard expression mentioned in Figure 1. These two sub-scores are the fundamental quantitative value for our analysis.

2.4. Markov Chain

A Markov chain is regarded as one of the best modeling techniques that has been used effectively in various fields such as reliability analysis [14] , performance analysis, dependability analysis [15] [16] , and cybersecurity analysis [17] , among others. We will model the host access attack graph described in the previous subsection using a Markov chain with the real behavior of the attacker in conjunction with the Markovian properties.

Mathematically, a Markov chain can be defined as a discrete stochastic process [18]. More specifically let S be a set of states (in the present study S is finite, we can think of it as nodes in host access graph). A Markov chain is a sequence of random variables $X_0, X_1, X_2, \cdots, X_n \in S$that satisfies the "Markovian property", that is,

$$P\left[X_{n+1} = y \middle| X_0 = x_0, X_1 = x_1, \cdots, X_n = x_n\right] = P\left[X_{n+1} = y \middle| X_n = x_n\right]$$

The Markovian properties reveal the fact that the transitions between states are memoryless; transitioning to the next step depends only on the current state and not on any of the other previous states. We can correlate this property with the attacker's behavior in a sense that an attacker needs to exploit several nodes before reaching the goal node. When the attacker starts attacking an immediate node to reach the goal node, there are many nodes available before reaching the goal node called intermediate node. When an attacker reaches any intermediate node, there is no memory of previous node. The attacker launches further attacks until the goal node is found. To advance the attack, the attacker should move from one intermediate node to another/several intermediate node/s. In the present study, we have assumed that selection of the best intermediate node depends on three parameters, namely Exploitability sub-score, Impact sub-score, and an individual skill of the attacker called Bias factor.

Without loss of generality, transition states are independent of time. Mathematically, there exists some transition probability matrix, $P(x, y)$ such that

$$P(x,y) = P\left[X_{n+1} = y \mid X_n = x\right], \text{ for all } n.$$

We can create a new set of states S ′ [n], having a different set of states associated with each timestep. In the present study, $P(x,y)$ represents the transition probability matrix. To simulate the Markov chain, a stochastic transition probability matrix P and the initial probability distribution is required. In the present study, initial risk associated with each nodes in the host access graph is considered as initial probability distribution which will be explained further in Section 4. Once we have the stochastic matrix P and the initial risk, then utilizing the basic properties of Markovian process, we can determine the risk of the entire network.

3. CYBER SECURITY ANALYTICAL FRAMEWORK

The schematic network given below, Figure 2, shows a bird's eye view of our proposed cyber security model. The most important component of our model is the attack graph. It is constructed by considering the input as network topology, services running on each host, attack rules defined on firewalls, and vulnerabilities associated with each host running different services.

For simplicity limited numbers of nodes are present in our network illustration and we have developed a host access graph manually. However, as the size and complexity of the network increase, we can use any kind of attack graph generation tools [19] to construct the intended attack graph of interest. Nodes present on the attack graph represent the host. Each host runs different kinds of services and there may exist various vulnerabilities. CVSS assigns severity scores for each vulnerability. The score is computed based on the standard expressions. The standard expression depends on several matrices that provide a quantitative score to approximate ease and impact of exploit. In the present study, we have applied both scores to determine whether it is beneficial to move from one node to another node from the attacker's perspective. These two scores, that is, Exploitability sub-score and Impact sub-score, are combined to provide the basis of assigning the edges of attack graphs to represent the values of the probability distribution. This probability represents the possibility of a vulnerability to be exploited by an attacker. While implementing our stochastic model, the behavior of the attacker is another concern. In this study, we assume that the attacker will choose the vulnerability that maximizes the chances of succeeding in compromising the goal state. Due to any reason, if the attacker terminates attacking, then the attacker will move to the initial state. Finally, utilizing the properties of Markov chain, the risk of the individual node is computed. Nodes are prioritized based on computed risk. Then, we sum the risks of all the nodes that will give us the total security risk present in the network.

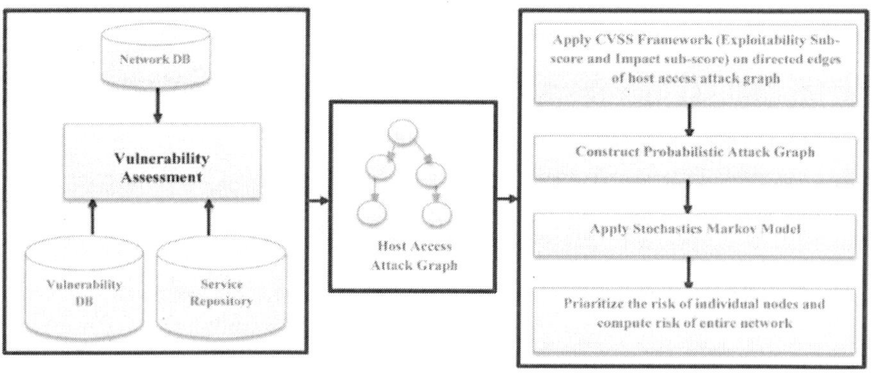

Figure 2. Cyber security analytical framework.

4. MODEL REPRESENTATION

The central component of the proposed stochastic model exclusively depends on the host access graph mentioned in the previous section. Before delving into the modeling approach, let us formally explain the host access graph as shown below by Figure 3.

In Figure 3 below, $S_i, i=1,2,3,\ldots,g$ are host nodes and S_g is a goal node. A node represents a host in the host access graph; thus, the number of nodes is equal to the number of hosts in the network. Similarly, directed edges between two nodes represent the access relationship between the corresponding two hosts so that there is only one directed edge from one node to another at most. Hence, there are no multiple edges in the graph, and our proposed model retains only the highest access achieved between the hosts, since higher levels of access to the destination host means more powerful attacks are achieved. A directed solid edge lines from host S_1 to host S_2 in Figure 3 represents the access available on S_2 from S_1. Similarly, dashed lines from host S_2 to host S_g illustrate that there are other intermediate nodes present in between these nodes and the same explanation is applicable to other hosts.

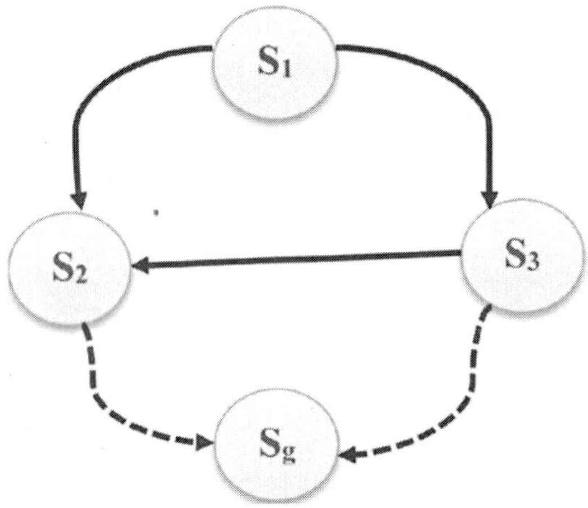

Figure 3. An example of host access graph.

Once the host access graph is constructed, then our basic foundation is developed for further analysis. To make this graph more applicable and realistic, we have modified it by adding one additional dummy node to represent the attacker. The attacker starts exploiting the immediate node by gaining a high level of privileges. In reality, even if an attacker is equipped with sophisticated tools and a high level of experience, there is no guarantee that he/she will reach the goal node. This may happen due to reaching a level of difficulty or being discovered by an intrusion response team or any type of unusual circumstance. Whenever the attacker stops launching attacks at any point due to any reason, then he/she goes back to the initial state from where the attacking began. To incorporate this attack scenario, a dummy node A is introduced. For any node S_i, we define the edge(S_i=A). This is demonstrated by Figure 4 below, where a node A represents an attacker. There is a directed solid edge from every node to the attacker node A, this implies that when the attacker gives up exploiting the node further due to any reason, again he/she goes back to the initial state and proceeds to search for alternative options. Similarly, the meaning of dashed lines are similar to Figure 3 as mentioned before.

In our proposed model, the attacker starts attacking the immediate node and keeps on launching attacks until it reaches the goal node. One big question that arises here is "**what happens if the attacker is encountered with the multiple nodes to reach the goal node and on what basis the attacker decides to select the best node from the available alternatives**." We have assumed that the attacker's decision solely depends on two parameters. The first parameter is Exploitability; it is all about the level of complexity involved to attack the vulnerable node. The second parameter deals with Impact factor, which means how much impact can an attacker make when a vulnerable node is exploited. CVSS provides numerical scores scale of (0,10) where 0 signifies the most secure and 10 signifies the least secure of the mentioned parameters. These two parameters are conceptually expressed by,

$$\textbf{ExploitabilityBenefit} = f(\textbf{Exploitability}, \textbf{Impact}) \quad (1)$$

In Equation (1), we have coined the new term ExploitabilityBenefit. It is defined as the function of Exploitability and Impact factor. Using these values an attacker determines the level of benefit to change from one to another node. To clarify this idea, let us take any two nodes from the host access graph as shown below, by Figure 5, where S_j and S_k are node j and node k, respectively with V_j and V_k being the corresponding vulnerabilities.

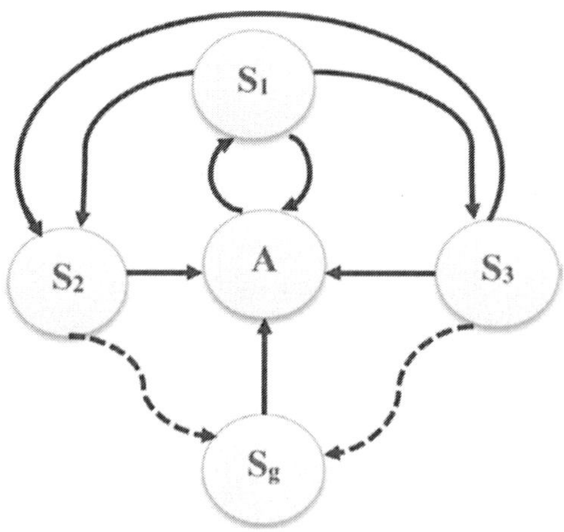

Figure 4. Modified host access graph.

In Figure 5 below, there is a directed edge from node j to node k. An attacker makes the decision whether to move from node j to node k based on the ExploitabilityBenefit value. Moreover, making a final decision to move from one node to another node not only depends on Exploitability and Impact factor but also depends on the skills and expertise of the attacker. This is the subjective factor and varies from individual to individual. In reality, it is an indispensable factor to make the attacking decision. We have represented this parameter in our model and is termed a Bias factor, Bias in a sense that its value varies from attacker to attacker. Incorporating all three mentioned parameters (Exploitability, Impact, and Bias), Equation 1 is further extended mathematically to,

$$a_{jk} = \boldsymbol{\beta}\,\mathrm{Exp}(v_k) + (1-\boldsymbol{\beta})\,\mathbf{Impact}(v_k) \qquad 0 < \boldsymbol{\beta} < 1 \tag{2}$$

In the above Equation (2), a_{jk} is the ExploitabilityBenefit score to move from the node j to node k. Similarly, **Exp(V$_k$)** is a function that measures the level of difficulty in exploiting the node k. The quantitative value that determines the level of difficulty scale of 0 to 10 is provided by CVSS. On the other hand, **Impact(V$_k$)** is a function that measures the potential damages or losses that occur due to a successful exploitation of node *k* and its quantitative score is provided by CVSS.

The possibility that a successful exploitation and damages/ losses occur depends on experience and skills of the attacker. To incorporate this fact, we introduce a Bias factor $\boldsymbol{\beta}$; its value ranges from 0 to 1 to indicate the level of experience and skills that the attacker possesses. When we combine Exploitability and Impact score with their corresponding Bias factor, a final weighted value is obtained to move from the node *j* to node *k*. To move the attacker from the initial node to the goal node, he/she needs to penetrate several intermediate nodes. Let us assume *j* is the initial node and g is the goal node and consists of three intermediate nodes namely *k*, *l*, and m. One possibility is that the attacker reaches the goal node by exploiting node *j* to node *k*, node *k* to node *l*, node *l* to node *m*, and finally node *m* to node *g*. To materialize this idea in mathematical notion, we need to construct the weighted adjacency matrix *A* as shown below.

$$A = \begin{bmatrix} a_{00} & a_{01} & \cdots & a_{0g} & \cdots & a_{0n} \\ a_{10} & 0 & \cdots & a_{1g} & \cdots & a_{1n} \\ \vdots & \vdots & \ddots & \vdots & \ddots & \vdots \\ \vdots & \vdots & \ddots & \vdots & \ddots & \vdots \\ a_{n0} & a_{n1} & \cdots & a_{ng} & \cdots & 0 \end{bmatrix}$$

Each element of the adjacency matrix is computed using Equation (2).

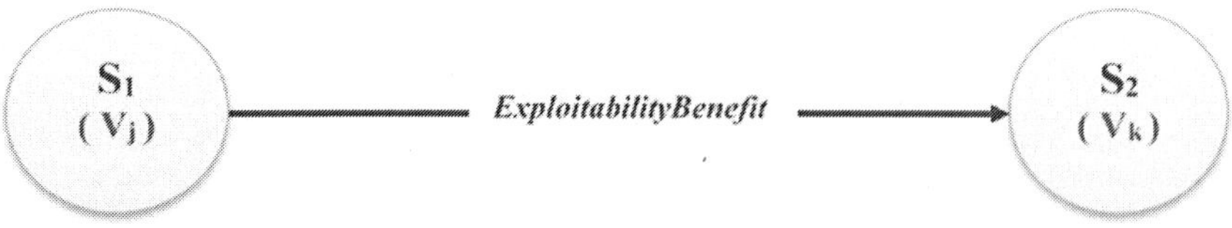

Figure 5. A couple of nodes in host access graph.

Diagonal values of the adjacency matrix are all zero because no cost is involved to move from the current node to the node itself. Elements of the matrix *A* are not normalized, thus, the non normalized values are converted into probabilities using Equation (3). This equation reveals the fact that in each step the attacker goes from node *j* to k with probability given by

$$p_{jk} = \frac{A(j,k)}{\sum_i A(j,i)} \tag{3}$$

Writing Equation (3) in matrix form we have,

$$P = DA \tag{4}$$

where, *A* is the weighted adjacency matrix. *P* is the transition matrix that provides the transition probability that the attacker moves from one state to another state and *D* is the diagonal matrix computed using Equation (5) below,

$$D_{jk} = \begin{cases} \frac{1}{\sum_i A(j,i)} & \text{if } j = k \\ 0 & \text{Otherwise} \end{cases} \tag{5}$$

Finally, we have constructed the transition matrix (using Equation (4)) representing transitions probability that an attacker moves from one state to another state, that is, from state *j* to state *k*.

5. THE RISK BASED ON RANKING

Consider an attacker starts attacking from the initial node to the goal node. The attacker must obtain a user level or root level of privilege on the intermediate node to advance the attack further to reach to the goal node.

In reality the attacker should try to obtain the highest level of privilege. Host access graphs are created based on the philosophy of gaining high level of privilege. Nodes of the host access graph are treated as OR nodes, which can be satisfied if any of the child node is true. The risk analysis is based on the relative rank value for every node of the host access graph. *R* is the risk vector and its initial risk value is computed based on the number of hosts present in the host access graph. Suppose there exist *N* nodes in the host access graph; then simply set all the node ranks equal to $1/N$. This initial risk is first injected by the starting node of an attacker. This risk value flows level by level until convergence. The complete risk ranking algorithm is described by the schematic diagram given below by Figure 6.

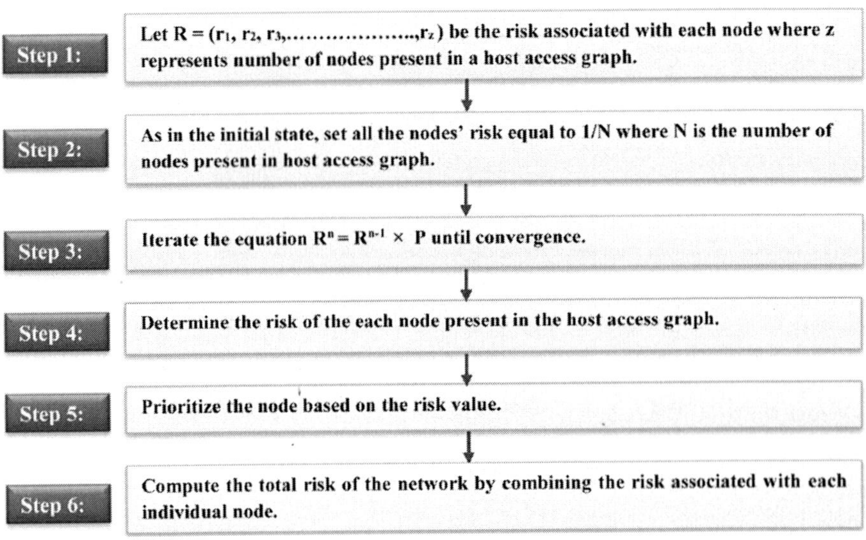

Figure 6. Flow chart to compute risk of overall network.

The risk value of r_k for a node k depends upon the rank of its parents. The risk value of the node set by the initial node represents the starting node of the attacker. When the ranking process is started then intermediate risk value is computed via iteration. The intermediate value will flow level by level until a steady state is achieved. Mathematically, suppose r_k is the risk of node k given in the host access graph; then the risk of node k is computed using Equation 6, given by,

$$r_k = \sum r_k p_{jk} \tag{6}$$

Suppose, $R=(r_1,r_2,r_3,\cdots,r_z)$ is the risk vector, where r_j is the rank of node

j. Equation (6) is further extended to Equation (7) as shown below. The risk values are normalized, where $0 \le r_k \le 1$, for all j, and $\sum r_k = 1$. Thus, written in matrix form the risk vector R is given by R times the probability transition matrix P, that is,

$$R = RP \tag{7}$$

The value of R in Equation (7) is recursive and must be iteratively calculated until convergence, which is expressed by Equation 8, that is,

$$R^t = R^{t-1}P \tag{8}$$

The attacking process is based on the Markovian random walk, that is, an essential condition for the iterative computation to converge [10]. The probability distribution of risk analysis of the host access graph after the attacker follows one link is $\boldsymbol{R_1=RP}$, where R is the risk vector and P is the one step transition probability matrix identified by Equation (4). Similarly, after two links the probability distribution is $\boldsymbol{R_2=R_1P}$. Assuming this iteration converges to a steady state probability, then we have $\boldsymbol{R^t=R^{t-1}}$, where $\boldsymbol{R^t}$ is an eigenvector of P.

6. NETWORK ENVIRONMENT: ILLUSTRATION

To validate our proposed stochastic model, we have modified the network scenario [20] [21] to make it more realistic and practical as shown below by Figure 7. In this network, there are three target hosts. These are publicly accessible Web Server (denoted by WS), a publicly accessible File Server (denoted by FS), and Backend Database Server (denoted by BEDS). An attacker is located outside of the network. The packet transmission to the target host is controlled via two firewalls: External Firewall (EF) and Internal Firewall (IF). EF allows any packet to be transmitted to WS and FS from outside of the network but no one can access the resources of BEDS from outside of the network directly. IF manages the transmission of the packet within the internal network.

The firewall rules are created to filter inbound and outbound traffic. A summary of firewall rules of the network scenario are shown in Table 1 below.

We have assumed that each of the target hosts consists of a single vulnerability. The attacker utilizes the vulnerability score to compromise the host. These are shown below by Table 2 along with its Exploitability sub-score and Impact sub-score taken from NVD.

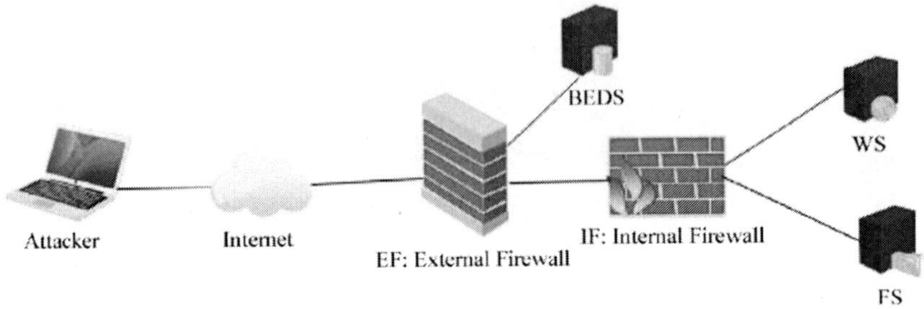

Figure 7. Experimental topology.

Table 1. Firewall rules.

Source	Destination	Service	Action
All	WS	http	Allow
All	WS	ftp	Allow
All	FS	ftp	Allow
WS	BEDS	oracle	Allow
FS	BEDS	ftp	Allow
All	All	All	Deny

Based on the experimental topology with its firewall rules and vulnerability associated with a respective host, we have generated a host access graph as shown below by Figure 8. To simplify the explanation, we have denoted the attacker, Web Server, File Server, and Backend Database Server as $\boldsymbol{M_0}$,$\boldsymbol{M_1}$,$\boldsymbol{M_2}$ and $\boldsymbol{M_3}$ respectively. The edges from all the nodes to the attacker node $\boldsymbol{M_0}$ are omitted to view the graph more clearly. When the process illustrated by Equation (2) is applied on the host access graph of the experimental topology in the below Figure 8, we can obtain the weighted adjacency matrix as given by.

$$A = \begin{bmatrix} 0 & 8.2 & 9.3 & 0 \\ 1 & 0 & 9.3 & 8.2 \\ 1 & 8.2 & 0 & 8.2 \\ 1 & 0 & 0 & 0 \end{bmatrix}$$

Note that the diagonal elements of the above weighted adjacency matrix are all zero in a sense that practically no cost is involved to move from the current node to the same node. For the sake of simplicity, we have assumed the value of $\boldsymbol{\beta}$, the Biased factor to be 0.5. When the attacker stops attacking further due to any unusual circumstances, then it is certain that he/she will return to the initial node. Hence, elements of the first column of the weighted adjacency matrix is 1, that is, weights of the edges from all host nodes to the attacker's node($\boldsymbol{M_0}$) is considered as 1, a sure event. The rest of all the elements of the weighted adjacency matrix are calculated using Equation (2). For example, the entry of the first row and second column is (0.5 ´ 10 + 0.5 ´ 6.4) = 8.2. This is the weighted value that the attacker uses to move from the node $\boldsymbol{M_0}$ to node $\boldsymbol{M_1}$. The same explanation is applicable for the rest of the elements of the weighted adjacency matrix. We have used the application software package "R" for all required calculations.

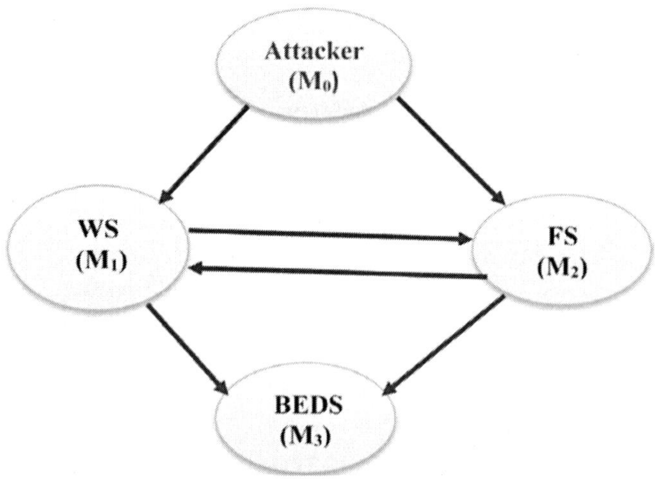

Figure 8. Host access graph for experimental topology.

Table 2. Host vulnerabilities.

Host	Vulnerability	CVE-ID	Score	Impact Sub-score	Exploitability Sub-score
WS	Apache Chunked Code	CVE-2002-0392	7.5	6.4	10
FS	Wuftpd Sockprintf	CVE-2003-1327	9.3	10	8.6
BEDS	Oracle Tns listener	CVE-2012-1675	7.5	6.4	10

Table 3. Risk association with each node.

Node	Risk
M_0	0.261
M_1	0.245
M_2	0.262
M_3	0.231

Once we have the weighted adjacency matrix A, then we need to convert its elements into respective probabilities; thus, it requires constructing a diagonal matrix. The entries of the main diagonal are obtained by using Equation (5) as shown below.

$$D = \begin{bmatrix} 0.05714 & 0 & 0 & 0 \\ 0 & 0.05405 & 0 & 0 \\ 0 & 0 & 0.05747 & 0 \\ 0 & 0 & 0 & 1 \end{bmatrix}$$

An element of the first row and the first column of the diagonal matrix is 1/(8.2 + 9.3) = 0.05714. The same idea is used to compute the rest of all the elements. Utilizing weighted adjacency matrix and the diagonal matrix computed as shown above, we have obtained a transition matrix P via Equation (4), that is,

$$P = \begin{bmatrix} 0 & 0.46857 & 0.5314 & 0 \\ 0.0540 & 0 & 0.5027 & 0.4432 \\ 0.0575 & 0.4712 & 0 & 0.4713 \\ 1 & 0 & 0 & 0 \end{bmatrix}$$

Note that the extents of the first row second column is, 0.46857. It is the transition probability of the attacker moving from node $\boldsymbol{M_0}$ to node $\boldsymbol{M_1}$. As similar explanation is applicable to the rest of the entries of the transition matrix P as shown above. Now, the host access graph as shown by Figure 8, consists of four nodes including the attacker's node. Based on our risk ranking algorithm explained in Figure 6, if we have four nodes then 1/4 = 0.25 is the initial risk of each node, hence the initial risk vector, R = (0.25, 0.25, 0.25, 0.25). Finally, when the initial risk(R) and transition probability(P) are iteratively multiplied using Equation (8), convergence is achieved by using the following values as listed in Table 3.

In Table 3, four nodes M_0,M_1,M_2 and M_3 are listed with their respective risk in terms of numerical value. $M_0$is the dummy node added to the host access graph to represent the attacker and is connected to every other nodes in the graph. An assumption of our ranking algorithm, initial risk of the all nodes are equal. Once the node is added to the graph and assigned the initial risk then it's final risk value is computed. As long as dummy node is considered we can ignore it's value from our analysis. Except M_0, rest of the nodes are actual nodes present in our network.

From the numerical value, we can conclude that node M_2 is more risky than M_1 and M_3, so the vulnerability of the file server needs to be patched first before other nodes. The total sum of the risk associated with the node M_1, M_2, and M_3 becomes 0.74. This value can be used as a security metric revealing the fact that this network is not very secure with respect to the given vulnerabilities and access relationship among the servers, and hence appropriate action must be implemented.

7. CONCLUSIONS

In this study, we have developed a stochastic model for cybersecurity using host access graph to determine the overall network security risk. Our model uses Markov chains in conjunction with CVSS framework to comprehend and analyze the risk associated with the structure of the network. This developed model determines the critical nodes existing in the host access attack graph where the attacker is most likely to visit. Based on this information, a network administrator can make the appropriate decision about system patching with priorities. The risk ranking algorithm that we implemented is very flexible in a sense that we can model the attacker in terms of skills and expertise by changing the Bias factor β in ExploitabilityBenefit computation. The proposed model can be generalized to complicated network environment, however, the calculations are more complex but tractable. The proposed findings are based on a typical security system, however, the modeling aspect and scientific methodology is applicable to a specific security system that is in existence or it is required by a given enterprise.

For future study, we plan to extend the model by incorporating other factors such as zero day vulnerability, propagation distance between the nodes and topological information in order to create a more comprehensive and integrated approach to evaluate overall security risk.

REFERENCES

1. Jha, S., Sheyner, O. and Wing, J.M. (2002) Minimization and Reliability Analyses of Attack Graphs (No. CMU-CS-02-109). Technical Report, School of Computer Science Carnegie-Mellon University, Pittsburgh.
2. Kemmerer, R.A. and Vigna, G. (2002) Intrusion Detection: A Brief History and Overview. IEEE Journals and Magazines, 35, 27-30.
3. Rajasooriya, S.M., Tsokos, C.P. and Kaluarachchi, P.K. (2016) Stochastic Modelling of Vulnerability Life Cycle and Security Risk Evaluation. Journal of Information Security, 7, 269-279. https://doi.org/10.4236/jis.2016.74022
4. Kaluarachchi, P.K., Tsokos, C.P. and Rajasooriya, S.M. (2016) Cybersecurity: A Statistical Predictive Model for the Expected Path Length. Journal of Information Security, 7, 112-128. https://doi.org/10.4236/jis.2016.73008
5. Mell, P., Scarfone, K. and Romanosky, S. (2007) A Complete Guide to the Common Vulnerability Scoring System Version 2.0. FIRST-Forum of Incident Response and Security Teams, 1-23. https://www.first.org/cvss/cvss-v2-guide.pdf
6. Krsul, I.V. (1998) Software Vulnerability Analysis. Doctoral Dissertation, Purude University, Indiana.
7. National Vulnerability Database (NVD). https://nvd.nist.gov/
8. Bilge, L. and Dumitras, T. (2012) Before We Knew It: An Empirical Study of Zero-Day Attacks in the Real World. Proceedings of the 2012 ACM Conference on Computer and Communications Security, Raleigh, 16-18 October 2012, 833-844. https://doi.org/10.1145/2382196.2382284
9. Jha, S., Sheyner, O. and Wing, J. (2002) Two Formal Analyses of Attack Graphs. Proceedings of 15th IEEE Computer Security Foundations Workshop, Cape Breton, 24-26 June 2002, 49-63. https://doi.org/10.1109/CSFW.2002.1021806
10. Mehta, V., Bartzis, C., Zhu, H., Clarke, E. and Wing, J. (2006) Ranking Attack Graphs. International Workshop on Recent Advances in Intrusion Detection, Hamburg, 20-22 September 2006, 127-144. https://doi.org/10.1007/11856214_7
11. Xie, A., Cai, Z., Tang, C., Hu, J. and Chen, Z. (2009) Evaluating Network Security with Two-Layer Attack Graphs. Annual Computer Security Applications Conference, Honolulu, 7-11 December 2009, 127-136. https://doi.org/10.1109/acsac.2009.22
12. Houmb, S.H. and Nunes Leal Franqueira, V. (2009) Estimating ToE Risk Level Using CVSS. Proceeding of the 4th International Conference on Availability, Reliability and Security, Fukuoka, 16-19 March 2009, 718-725.
13. Forum of Incident Response and Security Teams (FIRST). https://www.first.org/about
14. Bolch, G., Greiner, S., de Meer, H. and Trivedi, K.S. (2006) Queueing Networks and Markov Chains: Modeling and Performance Evaluation with Computer Science Applications. John Wiley & Sons, Somerset.
15. Trivedi, K.S. (2002) Probability & Statistics with Reliability, Queuing and Computer Science Applications. John Wiley & Sons, New Work.
16. Sahner, R.A., Trivedi, K. and Puliafito, A. (2012) Performance and Reliability Analysis of Computer Systems: An Example-Based Approach Using the SHARPE Software Package. Springer Science & Business Media, Berlin.
17. Abraham, S. and Nair, S. (2014) Cyber Security Analytics: A Stochastic Model for Security Quantification Using Absorbing Markov Chains. Journal of Communications, 9, 899-907. https://doi.org/10.12720/jcm.9.12.899-907
18. Lawler, G.F. (2006) Introduction to Stochastic Processes. CRC Press, Boca Raton.
19. Sheyner, O. and Wing, J. (2003) Tools for Generating and Analyzing Attack Graphs. International Symposium on Formal Methods for Components and Objects, Leiden, 4-7 November 2003, 344-371.

20. Hewett, R. and Kijsanayothin, P. (2008) Host-Centric Model Checking for Network Vulnerability Analysis. Computer Security Applications Conference, Washington DC, 8-12 December 2008, 225-234. https://doi.org/10.1109/acsac.2008.15
21. Ammann, P., Pamula, J., Ritchey, R. and Street, J.D. (2005) A Host-Based Approach to Network Attack Chaining Analysis. Computer Security Applications Conference, Tucson, 5-9 December 2005, 72-84.

CHAPTER 8

Cyber Security: Nonlinear Stochastic Models for Predicting the Exploitability

Sasith M. Rajasooriya*, Chris. P. Tsokos,
Pubudu Kalpani Kaluarachchi

Department of Mathematics and Statistics, University Of South Florida, Tampa, Florida, USA

ABSTRACT

Obtaining complete information regarding discovered vulnerabilities looks extremely difficult. Yet, developing statistical models requires a great deal of such complete information about the vulnerabilities. In our previous studies, we introduced a new concept of "Risk Factor" of vulnerability which was calculated as a function of time. We introduced the use of Markovian approach to estimate the probability of a particular vulnerability being at a particular "state" of the vulnerability life cycle. In this study, we further develop our models, use available data sources in a probabilistic foundation to enhance the reliability and also introduce some useful new modeling strategies for vulnerability risk estimation. Finally, we present a new set of Non-Linear Statistical Models that can be used in estimating the probability of being exploited as a function of time. Our study is based on the typical security system and vulnerability data that are available. However, our methodology and system structure can be applied to a specific security system by any software engineer and using their own vulnerabilities to obtain their probability of being exploited as a function of time. This information is very important to a company's security system in its strategic plan to monitor and improve its process for not being exploited.

Keywords: Vulnerability Lifecycle, Stochastic Modeling, Security Risk Factor, Markov Process, Risk Evaluation

1. INTRODUCTION

"Risk" is an unavoidable phenomenon in the Cyber world. Information systems ranging from very small and personal level apps to massive corporate and government applications and system platforms are facing the threat from Cyber-at- tacks [1] in various dimensions. The number of such attacks and the magnitude of the hazards have been heavily increasing throughout recent years. Hackers are getting more active and effective. The risk is getting higher. System administrators and defending professionals are working hard to understand attackers, attacking strategies and effectively defend attacking attempts. To establish successful defending platforms, a proper understanding of the "risk" associated with a given vulnerability [2] [3] is required. If we have effective models that enable the defenders and system administrators to successfully predict the risk of a given vulnerability being exploited as a function of time, it will be helpful to plan and implement security measures, allocate relevant resources and defend the systems accordingly. We, in this study, improve the Markovian approach of Vulnerability Life Cycle Analysis [2] to come up with better modelling techniques to evaluate the "risk factor" using probability and statistical methods.

The objective of this study is to propose and present a rational set of methods to identify the probabilities for each different state in the vulnerability life cycle [2] [4] [5] and use this information to develop three different statistical models to evaluate the "Risk Factor" [2] [5] of a particular vulnerability at time "t". In our recent study "Stochastic Modelling of Vulnerability Life Cycle and Security Risk Evaluation" (Journal of Information Security, 7, 269-279) [2] , we introduced the strategy of using Markov processes to obtain the "transition probability matrix" of all the states of a particular vulnerability as a function of time. We iterated the Markov process and determined that it reached the "steady state" with probabilities of reaching the "absorbing states" [1] [2]. The two absorbing states were identified as "exploited" and "patched" states. We proceeded to introduce the "Risk Factor" that could be used as an index of the risk of the vulnerability being exploited [1] - [7]. Finally, we presented successful statistical models that could calculate the "Risk Factor" more conveniently without going through the Markovian process [1] [2] [6].

However, in this process, we used a logical and realistic approach to assign initial probabilities for each state of the vulnerability. In this study, we introduce more relevant and sophisticated sets of methods to assign the initial probabilities for each state of Vulnerability Life Cycle based on several logical assumptions. We use the CVSS score [3] [8] as we did earlier, but here we calculate and introduce initial probabilities taking the entire CVE Data Base (http://www.cvedetails.com/) into consideration.

Finally, using our new methods, we develop three new statistical models for vulnerabilities that differ based on their vulnerability score ranging from 0 to 10 as low risk (0 - 3.9), medium risk (4 - 6.9) and high risk (7 - 10). Using these models the user will be able to estimate the "Risk" of a particular vulnerability being exploited at time "t" and to observe the expected behavior of the vulnerability throughout its life cycle.

1.1. Vulnerability Life Cycle Analysis Method

In our previous study [2] , we introduced the use of Markov chain process to develop the transition probability matrix including all the important states of Vulnerability Life Cycle. The Vulnerability Life Cycle Graph that we discussed is presented below by "Figure 1". When we draw a Life Cycle Graph for a given vulnerability, it has several nodes which represent the stages of the Vulnerability Life Cycle. Earlier we assigned logical probabilities for a hacker to reach each state by examining the properties of a specific vulnerability. Life Cycle Graph has two absorbing states [2] [4] [5] [6] that are named "Patched" state [2] [4] [5] [6] [7] and "Exploited" state [1] [2] [4] [5] [6] [7]. Therefore, this allowed us to model the Life Cycle Graph as an absorbing Markov chain. It should be noted that in the figure below the states three and five are absorbing states of this Life Cycle Graph as there are no out flaws from those states.

We define, ⍰$_i$ to be the probability of transferring from state i to state j.

Where, i, j= 1,2,3,4,5. $i, j = 1,2,3,4,5.$

In actual situations the probability of discovering a vulnerability can be assumed very small. Therefore, for ⍰$_1$ we had assigned a small value. Then probabilities for ⍰$_2$,⍰⍰$_3$,⍰⍰$_4$,⍰⍰$_5$,, were also assigned accordingly. Then we checked several random values for ⍰$_i$s and observed the behavior of each different state to be a function of time.

Using these transition probabilities we could derive the absorbing transition probability matrix for a Life Cycle of a particular Vulnerability, which follows the properties defined under Markov Chain Transformation Probability Method [2].

However, in our present study, instead of randomly assigning transition probabilities for each of the state presented in the Life Cycle, we use a new set of methods that are probabilistically more reliable. It is challenging to acquire a complete set of information relevant to Vulnerabilities in a manner that we can calculate the required probabilities conveniently. Therefore, we use available and reliable data resources about Vulnerabilities to develop our methodology that we discuss in the section that follows.

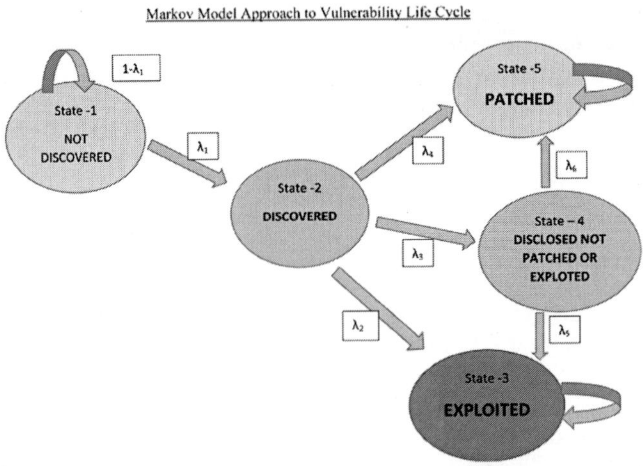

Figure 1. Markov Model Approach to Vulnerability Life Cycle with Five States.

1.2. Common Vulnerability Scoring System (CVSS) and Common Vulnerabilities and Exposures (CVE)

It is important to discuss here the usage of Common Vulnerability Scoring System (CVSS) [8] and CVE Details [9] , as we gather data from those resources. Common Vulnerability Scoring System (CVSS) is the commonly used and freely available standard for assessing the magnitude of Information System Vulnerabilities. CVSS gives a score for each vulnerability scaling from 0 to 10 based on several factors. National Vulnerability Database (NVD) [3] provides CVSS score and updates continuously as new vulnerabilities are discovered. CVSS score is calculated using three main matrices named, Base Matric, Temporal Metric and Environmental Metric. However, NVD data base provides us with the Base Metric Scores for the Vulnerability only because the Temporal and Environmental Scores are varied on other factors related to the organization that uses the computer system. The Base score for more than 75,000 different vulnerabilities are calculated using 6 different Matrices. It is managed by the Forum of Incident Response and Security Teams (FIRST).

CVSS establishes a standard measure of how much concern vulnerability warrants, compared to other vulnerabilities, so that efforts can be prioritized. The scores range from 0 to 10. Vulnerabilities with a base score in the range 7.0 - 10.0 are High, those in the ranges 4.0 - 6.9 are Medium, and 0 - 3.9 are Low. Hence, the three transition probability matrices and statistical models that we develop in this study are based on this classification of the CVSS score.

Common Vulnerabilities and Exposures (CVE) is a dictionary resource and CVE Detail website [9] provides us with the data base in the basic categories with different CVSS scores. CVE Details provide us with quantities of vulnerabilities in different levels of magnitudes ranging from 0 to 10. Instead of randomly assigning a reasonable probability for each different states ($\square_i$ s), we now use these data resources as per their availability in estimating probabilistically reliable values for each state. Our approach in assigning initial probabilities into each state of the Life Cycle is discussed in the subsection 2.2 below.

2. METHODOLOGY

2.1. Methodology of Assigning Initial Probabilities

Our objective now is focused on assigning initial probabilities for different states in the Life Cycle. In Table 1, below we present these initial probabilities that are required in our present study. Estimating them requires a great deal of data resources. To estimate $\square_1$ as an example, requires the total number of vulnerabilities in each category ranging from 0 to 10 in magnitudes, and information on their discovery with respect to time. Similarly for other states, we need the num- ber of vulnerabilities discovered, exploited before disclosed, exploited after discovery but before patched, patched before the disclosure, patched after the disclosure, under each CVSS score level.

We start with the CVSS scores available for each vulnerability and categorize them and take the counts for the three different levels of vulnerabilities for possible states. However, it should be noted that, there are no data resources available providing all the data requirements here we have. Therefore, when the CVSS classifications available in the CVE detail website satisfy our requirements, we use those data and when they are not sufficient to make a reliable estimate we use information given by “Stefan Frei” in his thesis [4] and “Secunia Vulnerability information report” [10].

Table 1. States Represented by the Transition Probabilities in the Vulnerability Life Cycle.

Probability- λ_i	State Represented
λ_1	Discovered
λ_2	Exploited before patched or disclosed
λ_3	Disclosed but not yet patched or exploited
λ_4	Patched before disclosed
λ_5	Exploited after disclosed
λ_6	Patched after disclosed

We categorized 75,705 vulnerabilities according to their CVSS score and under each of the three categories to find out number of total vulnerabilities and number of exploitations. We shall use this information to assign probabilities of discovery (λ_1) and exploitability (λ_2) for each CVSS score level.

To assign probabilities for Disclosed but not yet patched or exploited (λ_3), Patched before disclosed (λ_4), exploited after disclosed (λ_5) and patched after disclosed (λ_6) we used Secunia vulnerability report information [10] and Frei's results given in his study [4].

2.2. Estimating λ_1

To calculate an estimate for λ_1, "the probability of a vulnerability is being discovered" [11] [12] for three categories of CVSS score, it is ideal to have an estimate for the population of "total number of (known and unknown) vulnerabilities at a particular time" so that we can get the proportion of discovered vulnerability out of the total. But, at a given time, it is impossible to know the total number of vulnerabilities in the cyber world as the number of vendors, application software, system software and other apps are uncountable, so are the number of vulnerabilities that could be existing. Therefore, to have a logical estimate for the total number of vulnerabilities for each year, we first calculated the cumulative number of vulnerabilities, and then calculated the number of vulnerabilities discovered in a particular year as a proportion of cumulative number of vulnerabilities in the next calendar year. Once we have taken these proportions considering all the years from 1999 till 2015, we took the average of those proportions to be our estimate for λ_1.

2.3. Assumptions Made for λ_1

When calculating λ_1, it was assumed that, the number of unknown vulnerabilities in a particular year are discovered in the next year and the accumulated number of vulnerabilities in a particular year is an estimate for the population size of the vulnerabilities in the previous year.

2.4. Estimating λ_2

Estimate for λ_2, "the probability of a particular vulnerability being exploited [13] [14] before patched or disclosed" was calculated using the data provided in the CVE Detail website. The entire set of exploited vulnerabilities were calculated for 10 different categories (or CVSS score levels) of interest.

2.5. Estimating λ_3, λ_4, λ_5 and λ_6

λ_3, "the probability of a vulnerability being disclosed but not yet patched or exploited" is calculated using the equation, $\lambda_3 = 1 - (\lambda_2 + \lambda_4)$.

For λ_4, "the probability of a vulnerability being patched before disclosed", we used information available in "Secunia Report on Vulnerability".

To estimate λ_5, "probability of a vulnerability being exploited after disclosed" and λ_6, "probability of a vulnerability being patched after disclosed" we used information given by "Stefan Frei" in his doctoral thesis [4].

Frei, estimates that the probability of a vulnerability being exploited after it is disclosed is greater than the probability of it being patched. He estimates that there is a probability around 0.6, for a disclosed vulnerability being exploited. Therefore, we, in developing our model used, fix values of 0.6 and 0.4 respectively for λ_5 and λ_6.

"Table 2" below presents our results on probabilities for each state with respect to each category/level of vulnerability.

Using these transition probabilities for each level we can now derive the absorbing transition probability matrix for a Vulnerability Life Cycle, which follows the properties defined under Markov Chain Transformation Probability Method [15] [16] [17] [18] [19].

2.6. Transition Matrix for Vulnerability Life Cycle

2.6.1. Executing the Markov Process to Transition Probability matrix

Now that we have the Vulnerability Life Cycle Graph with two absorbing states and initial probability estimates for each state, we can write the general form of the transition probability matrix [15] [16] [19] for vulnerability life cycle as follows.

$$P = \begin{bmatrix} 1-\lambda_1 & \lambda_1 & 0 & 0 & 0 \\ 0 & 0 & \lambda_2 & \lambda_3 & \lambda_4 \\ 0 & 0 & 1 & 0 & 0 \\ 0 & 0 & \lambda_5 & 0 & \lambda_6 \\ 0 & 0 & 0 & 0 & 1 \end{bmatrix}$$

where,

$Pi\ (t)$-Probability that the system is in state i at time t.

For $t = 0$ we have:

$P_1\ (0) = 1$, Probability that the system is in State 1 at the beginning ($t = 0$).

$P_2\ (0) = 0$, $P_3\ (0) = 0$, $P_4\ (0) = 0$, $P_5\ (0) = 0$.

Table 2. Estimates of Transition Probabilities for each Category of Vulnerabilities.

Vulnerability level	λ_1	λ_2	λ_3	λ_4	λ_5	λ_6
Low	0.1777	0.016303	0.183696615	0.8	0.6	0.4
Medium	0.1888	0.08104	0.118960089	0.8	0.6	0.4
High	0.1804	0.147552	0.052448328	0.8	0.6	0.4

Therefore, the initial probability can be given as [1 0 0 0 0], that is, the probabilities of each state of the Vulnerability Life Cycle initially. It is clear that, the "State 1" (Not Discovered) with probability of one represents that at the initial time (for $t = 0$), where the Vulnerability has not yet been discovered and therefore the probabilities for all others stages are zero.

Now, for three different categories of Vulnerabilities, we can iterate the transition probability matrix using Markovian process [15] until the matrix reaches its "steady state". The iteration algorithm is explained below.

For $t = 0$, we have

$$\overrightarrow{P^{(0)}} = \begin{bmatrix} 1 & 0 & 0 & 0 & 0 \end{bmatrix}.$$

For $t = 1$, results in

$$\overrightarrow{P^{(1)}} = \overrightarrow{P^{(0)}} P.$$

For $t = 2$, we can write

$$\overrightarrow{P^{(2)}} = \overrightarrow{P^{(0)}} P^{(2)}$$

And thus, for $= n$, we have

$$\overrightarrow{P^{(n)}} = \overrightarrow{P^{(0)}} P^{(n)}.$$

Using this method, we can now find the probability that is changing with time and is related to each "state" and then proceed to find the statistical model that can fit the vulnerability life cycle.

As an example, for the vulnerabilities in Category one, where ⍰$_1$ = 0.1777, ⍰$_2$ = 0.0163, ⍰$_3$ = 0.1837, ⍰$_4$ = 0.8, ⍰$_5$ = 0.6, ⍰$_6$ = 0.4the transition probability matrix is written as follows:

$$P = \begin{bmatrix} 0.8223 & 0.1777 & 0 & 0 & 0 \\ 0 & 0 & 0.0163 & 0.1837 & 0.8 \\ 0 & 0 & 1 & 0 & 0 \\ 0 & 0 & 0.6 & 0 & 0.4 \\ 0 & 0 & 0 & 0 & 1 \end{bmatrix}$$

As we execute this algorithm, for the vulnerabilities of category one, the stationarity (steady state) was reached (considering to 4 decimal digits) at $t = 86$, that is, the minimum number of steps so that the vulnerability reaches its absorbing states is 86 and the resulting vector of probabilities for each of the absorbing states is obtained as the output of the calculation process. As shown below, the transition probabilities are completely absorbed into the two absorbing states which gives the "probability of the vulnerability being exploited" and the "probability of the vulnerability will be patched". All other states have reached the probability of zero. That is,

$$P = \begin{bmatrix} 0.8223 & 0.1777 & 0 & 0 & 0 \\ 0 & 0 & 0.0163 & 0.1837 & 0.8 \\ 0 & 0 & 1 & 0 & 0 \\ 0 & 0 & 0.6 & 0 & 0.4 \\ 0 & 0 & 0 & 0 & 1 \end{bmatrix}$$

$$\Rightarrow P^{(86)} = \begin{bmatrix} 0 & 0 & 0.1524 & 0 & 0.8476 \\ 0 & 0 & 0.1524 & 0 & 0.8476 \\ 0 & 0 & 1 & 0 & 0 \\ 0 & 0 & 0.6 & 0 & 0.4 \\ 0 & 0 & 0 & 0 & 1 \end{bmatrix},$$

$$\overrightarrow{P^{(86)}} = \overrightarrow{P^{(0)}} P^{(86)} = \begin{bmatrix} 0 & 0 & 0.1265 & 0 & 0.8735 \end{bmatrix}.$$

That is, it will take the hacker 86 steps and a 12.7% chance to exploit the security system and 87.3% probability to reach the patched state. Thus we are sure that after $t = 86$, one of the two states will be reached.

Initially, we defined the 3rd state as "the state of being exploited" and the 5th state as "the state of being patched" in the vulnerability life cycle. Based on the current data resources available relevant to the vulnerabilities of category one we can use these results as estimates for the probabilities of being exploited and being patched. The results from this Markovian model [15] for the vulnerability life cycle show that the sum of the resulting probabilities equals to one (0.1265 + 0.8735 = 1).

This in other words indicates that our model estimates that one of these results are expected after $t = 86$ (ex: after 86 days) for a vulnerability in category one. Hence, it is clear that once the "steady state" is achieved, for a vulnerability of category one, estimates of the probability of being exploited is 12.65% and the probability of being patched is 87.35%.

Similarly, for vulnerabilities of categories two and three, the transition probability matrices can be obtained. Transition probability matrices and resulting steady state vectors for those categories are given below.

For vulnerabilities of Category 2;

$$P = \begin{bmatrix} 0.8112 & 0.1888 & 0 & 0 & 0 \\ 0 & 0 & 0.081 & 0.119 & 0.8 \\ 0 & 0 & 1 & 0 & 0 \\ 0 & 0 & 0.6 & 0 & 0.4 \\ 0 & 0 & 0 & 0 & 1 \end{bmatrix}$$

$$\Rightarrow P^{(80)} = \begin{bmatrix} 0 & 0 & 0.1524 & 0 & 0.8476 \\ 0 & 0 & 0.1524 & 0 & 0.8476 \\ 0 & 0 & 1 & 0 & 0 \\ 0 & 0 & 0.6 & 0 & 0.4 \\ 0 & 0 & 0 & 0 & 1 \end{bmatrix}$$

$$\overrightarrow{P^{(80)}} = \overrightarrow{P^{(0)}} P^{(80)} = \begin{bmatrix} 0 & 0 & 0.1524 & 0 & 0.8476 \end{bmatrix}.$$

For vulnerabilities of Category 3;

$$P = \begin{bmatrix} 0.8196 & 0.1804 & 0 & 0 & 0 \\ 0 & 0 & 0.1476 & 0.0524 & 0.8 \\ 0 & 0 & 1 & 0 & 0 \\ 0 & 0 & 0.6 & 0 & 0.4 \\ 0 & 0 & 0 & 0 & 1 \end{bmatrix}$$

$$\Rightarrow P^{(84)} = \begin{bmatrix} 0 & 0 & 0.1790 & 0 & 0.821 \\ 0 & 0 & 0.1790 & 0 & 0.821 \\ 0 & 0 & 1 & 0 & 0 \\ 0 & 0 & 0.6 & 0 & 0.4 \\ 0 & 0 & 0 & 0 & 1 \end{bmatrix}$$

$$\overrightarrow{P^{(84)}} = \overrightarrow{P^{(0)}} P^{(84)} = \begin{bmatrix} 0 & 0 & 0.1790 & 0 & 0.821 \end{bmatrix}.$$

"Table 3" below summarizes our results. Number of iterations (steps) that it takes to reach the "steady states" and resulting row vectors of probabilities for each three categories of vulnerabilities are given in this table.

2.6.2. "Risk Factor"—Calculating the Risk as a Function of Time

Now that we have the steady state vector with the probabilities for patching and getting exploited, we can calculate the risk of a particular vulnerability using the"risk factor". In our previous study [2] we have introduced this risk factor as follows.

$$\text{Risk } v_i(t) = \Pr(v_i \text{ is in state 3 at time } t) \times \text{Exploitability score}(v_i)$$

Exploitability score [3] for the vulnerability can be taken from the CVSS score as we mentioned earlier. With our results for three different levels of vulnerabilities, now we have a better index for the risk factor since our initial probabilities were not just chosen randomly, but were estimated using the available and reliable data sources. As an example, let's consider a vulnerability in the lower level with an exploitability score of 2.4. Assume that we need to find the Risk factor of that vulnerability at t = 50. Then, using the Markov process we can come up with the resulting vector of the vulnerability that gives us the probabilities of being in each different state at that particular time. However, iterating Markov process for each time would not be a very efficient process due to the analytical calculations. Therefore, we proceed to move on to develop three different nonlinear statistical models that make it much more convenient for the designed calculation.

Table 3. Number of iterations (steps) to reach the steady state and Steady State Vector for each category of Vulnerability.

Category	Number of iterations	Steady state	Probability of being exploited	Probability of being patched	Sum
Low	86	[0.0000 0.0000 0.1265 0.0000 0.8735]	0.1265	0.8735	1
Medium	80	[0.0000 0.0000 0.1524 0.0000 0.8476]	0.1523	0.8476	1
High	84	[0.0000 0.0000 0.1790 0.0000 0.8210]	0.179	0.821	1

To further explain the usage of the Risk Factor let's take an example. Consider a vulnerability given in Table 4. With the published date and the exploitability score known for that vulnerability, we can now calculate the risk of being exploited at a particular date from the published date. For the first vulnerability V_1 (CVE 2016-0911) which is a low risk vulnerability the risk factor is 0.2474 and for the other two categories of medium and high risk levels, vulnerabilities V_2(CVE 2016-2832) and V_3(CVE 2016-3230), risk factors are 0.3667 and 1.17702 respectively.

The risk factor can be graphed as a function of time. The figure below shows the behavior of the risk factor of the middle level vulnerability V_2(CVE 2016-2832) over a time period of 101 days starting from 6/13/2016. We notice that the risk factor increases rapidly within around first 10 days indicating that once a vulnerability is published, the risk of being exploited rapidly increases. Even after this rapid increase, the risk does not show a decreasing behavior. This specific behavior is due to our model structure of the vulnerability life cycle. That is, consisting with two absorbing states (being exploited and being patched), we assume that either one of two outcomes are possible for a given vulnerability. Therefore, considering state of being exploited as an absorbing state the life cycle does not move to any other state beyond being exploited which explains why this graph stay increased without decreasing over the time.

Figure 2 above illustrates the behavior of the Risk Factor as a function of time. The curve shows a rapid increase in the risk factor initially as expectable since the vulnerability immediately create a risk with its discovery and disclosure. Based on the graph, we can conclude that over the time with a life cycle consisting two absorbing states, the Risk Factor of a given vulnerability increases rapidly and become stable at a higher level of risk without decreasing back. This behavior exemplifies the threat any vulnerability would impose on an information system. As far as a proper patch is released and installed a probable harm from a given vulnerability increases monotonously. However, it should not be misinterpreted in the view point that the risk from a given vulnerability never reduces. Our Absorbing Markovian Model does not consider some of the interactions that might take place in the real world situations. Our intention here is to show the impact of a vulnerability until it is not patched. Outcomes from the situations where patching attempts and exploit attempts after and before disclose should be explained in much border modeling aspect of the vulnerability life cycle.

Table 4. Three vulnerabilities in each categories with their details and the calculated risk factors.

Vulnerability	Published date	CVSS score	Exploitability score	Age of the Vulnerability to the date 6/24/2016 (t_j)	Risk factor $R(v_i(t_j))$
V_1(CVE 2016-0911)	6/19/2016	1.9 (Low)	3.4	5	0.2474
V_2(CVE 2016-2832)	6/13/2016	4.3 (Medium)	2.8	11	0.3667
V_3(CVE 2016-3230)	6/15/2016	9 (High)	8	9	1.1702

3. NONLINEAR STATISTICAL MODELS FOR EXPLOITABILITY

3.1. Model Building

In the previous section we developed an analytical algorithm that identifies the number of steps (time) that the transition probability matrix of the vulnerability life cycle will reach a steady state. Thus, for a given vulnerability in the categories of Low, Medium and High risk levels, we can include with the probability of being exploited (having hacked) and the probability of being patched as a function of time. However, this process is time consuming and the Markovian iteration process [1] [2] [15] [16] would be quite difficult to perform every time. Using this approach to find the minimum number of steps for each category we obtained t = 86 steps for category one vulnerabilities, t = 80 steps for category two vulnerabilities and t = 84 steps for category three vulnerabilities. Then, we rec- orded the probability of being exploited at the each step. Thus, we have for each category a 2 ´ 86, 2 ´ 80 and 2 ´ 84, matrices of information, respectively. Our goal is to utilize this information and develop a statistical model for each category to be able to predict the probability of being exploited as a function of time and thus bypassing the analytical difficulties.

A sample of the data for each category is shown in Appendix A. All these of the data sets exhibit nonlinear behavior and thus multiple regression is not applicable. After very exhaustive research, we were able to identify two sets of nonlinear statistical models for each category.

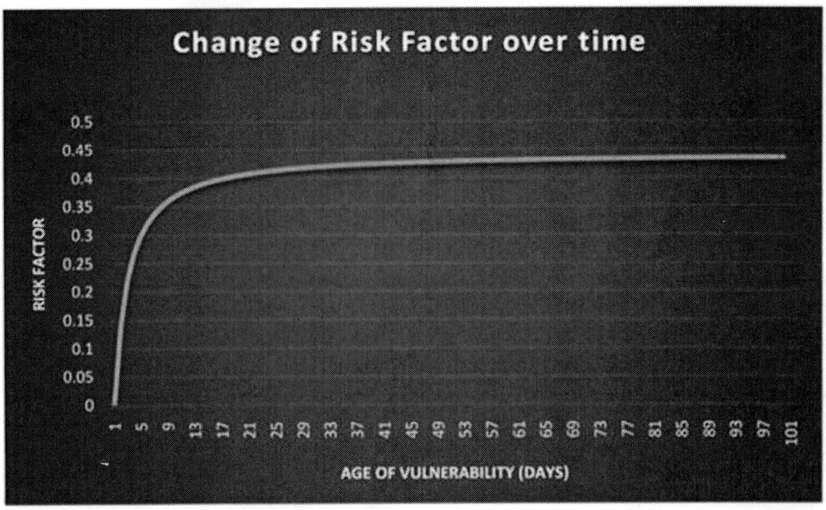

Figure 2. Behavior of the Risk Factor as a function of time.

The general analytical focus of the statistical models that we found is of the forms:

Model 1: Y (exploitation probability) = $\alpha_0 + \alpha_1 \frac{1}{t} + \alpha_2 \ln t + \varepsilon$ and

Model 2: Y (exploitation probability) = $\beta_0 + \beta_1 \frac{1}{t} + \beta_2 \ln(\ln t) + \varepsilon$, where, Y is the probability of being exploited, ⍰and ⍰ are the vector of coefficients or weights, t being the time given in steps and ⍰ is the modelling error. We used the method of maximum Likelihood estimation to obtain the estimates of the coefficients that drives these models.

Model-1

The best nonlinear statistical model that we developed for Low, Medium and High Vulnerability categories are given below along with their R^2 (coefficient of determination), R^2_{adj} (R^2 adjusted).

Low (Category one) risk vulnerabilities:

$$Y = 0.084197 - 0.116756\left(\frac{1}{t}\right) + 0.011321\ln(t),$$

with $R^2 = 0.8684, \quad R^2_{adj} = 0.8653.$

Medium (Category two) risk vulnerabilities:

$$Y = 0.111073 - 0.143992\left(\frac{1}{t}\right) + 0.011461\ln(t),$$

with $R^2 = 0.8888, \quad R^2_{adj} = 0.8859.$

High (Category three) risk vulnerabilities:

$$Y = 0.133927 - 0.169314\left(\frac{1}{t}\right) + 0.012375\ln(t),$$

with $R^2 = 0.8988, \quad R^2_{adj} = 0.8963.$

As we will discuss R^2 reflects on the quality of the proposed model.

Model-2

In investigating to see if we can improve the precision of the Model 1, we have found that by implementing another logarithmic filter to our initial model to further homogenizing the variance of our data.

We obtained a set of models that gives us better results increasing the accuracy of our prediction approximately by 9% compared to the Model 1. New model equations for each of the categories are given below.

Low (Category one) risk vulnerabilities:

$$Y = 0.135441 - 0.308532\left(\frac{1}{t}\right) + 0.002030\ln\left(\ln(t)\right)$$

with $R^2 = 0.9576,\quad R^2_{adj} = 0.9566.$

Medium (Category two) risk vulnerabilities:

$$Y = 0.169518 - 0.356821\left(\frac{1}{t}\right) + 0.007011\ln\left(\ln(t)\right)$$

with $R^2 = 0.962,\quad R^2_{adj} = 0.961.$

High (Category three) risk vulnerabilities:

$$Y = 0.135441 - 0.308532\left(\frac{1}{t}\right) + 0.002030\ln\left(\ln(t)\right)$$

with $R^2 = 0.9588,\quad R^2_{adj} = 0.9577.$

Thus, Model 2 is a significant improvement in the R^2 over model 1.

Both models give very good predictions of the probability of exploitation as a function of time. However, "Model-2" seems to give better predictions because of the additional logarithmic filtering that we applied to homogenize the variance further. Table 5 summarizes the 6 model equations with respective R^2 (coefficient of determination), R^2_{adj} (R^2 adjusted) values for convenient comparison.

3.2. Evaluation of the Models

We used R^2 (coefficient of determination), R^2_{adj} (R^2 adjusted) and residual analysis using actual data that we did not use in the model building to validate the accuracy and the quality of these models. R^2 is commonly used to measure the goodness of a statistical model and is defined as,

$$R^2 = \frac{SS_{Reg}}{SS_{Total}} = 1 - \frac{SS_{Res}}{SS_{Total}},$$

where SS_{Res} or SSE is the Sum of Squares of Residual and SS_{Total} is the Total

Sum of Squares. It is also referred to as the Coefficient of Determination. In our case the R^2 = 0.96 states that the model is an excellent fit such that the 96% of the behavior in the response variable (probability of being exploited) is explained and predicted by the attributable variable (time-t) and only a 4% of the change in the response variable is not explained due to the variance.

In order to be more confident in interpreting the value of R^2 we also calculate the R^2_{adj} (R^2adjusted) to address the issue of bias.

R^2_{adj} (R^2 adjusted) is defined by

$$R^2_{adj} = 1 - \frac{(n-1)SS_{Res}}{(n-p)SS_{Total}},$$

where, n is the sample size and, p is the number of risk factors (attributable variables) in our models. The closer the R^2 and R^2_{adj} to one, the higher the quality of our models.

Table 5. New Nonlinear Statistical Models to estimate the probability of being exploited as a function of time.

	Model 1		
Category	Model Equation	R^2	R^2_{adj}
Low	$Y = 0.084197 - 0.116756(1/t) + 0.011321\ln(t)$	0.8684	0.8653
Medium	$Y = 0.111073 - 0.143992(1/t) + 0.011461\ln(t)$	0.8888	0.8859
High	$Y = 0.133927 - 0.169314(1/t) + 0.012375\ln(t)$	0.8988	0.8963
	Model 2		
Category	Model Equation	R^2	R^2_{adj}
Low	$Y = 0.135441 - 0.308532(1/t) - 0.002030\ln(\ln t)$	0.9576	0.9566
Medium	$Y = 0.169518 - 0.356821(1/t) - 0.007011\ln(\ln t)$	0.962	0.961
High	$Y = 0.191701 - 0.383521(1/t) - 0.00358\ln(\ln t)$	0.9588	0.9577

We also performed residual analysis of all the models to determine if the error factor has significantly contributed to the accuracy of our models. In all cases, the residual error was not significant. Finally we tested all our models with the actual data that we did not include in developing the models and the results were exceptional.

As mentioned, we needed a best fitting three Statistical models to calculate the "risk factor" conveniently. In other words, we expected to obtain a best fitting model that can replace the Markovian iteration and hence to avoid the difficulty in estimating of the probabilities for time "t" earlier to the "steady state". With these new models we have achieved our goal.

4. CONCLUSION

In this study, we continue to improve the models we build up in our previous study [2]. We have improved the calculation methods of initial probabilities and created the Transition Probability Matrix in using of the Markovian process that we introduced in our previous studies. We used CVSS data presented in CVE details website and calculated initial probabilities for discovering and exploiting a vulnerability based on the records on last 17 years data. Finally, we created two sets of three models for predicting the risk of a particular vulnerability being exploited as a function of time. The models we presented are proven to have an excellent fit with the Markovian process probabilities. Therefore, we can replace the Markovian process using these models since these models enable us to get rid of analytical requirement to execute the Markovian iteration process of identifying the steady states of being exploited or being patched for each vulnerability.

REFERENCES

1. Kaluarachchi, P.K., Tsokos, C.P. and Rajasooriya, S.M. (2016) Cybersecurity: A Statistical Predictive Model for the Expected Path Length. Journal of Information Security, 7, 112-128. https://doi.org/10.4236/jis.2016.73008
2. Rajasooriya, S.M., Tsokos, C.P. and Kaluarachchi, P.K. (2016) Stochastic Modelling of Vulnerability Life Cycle and Security Risk Evaluation. Journal of information Security, 7, 269-279. https://doi.org/10.4236/jis.2016.74022
3. NVD. National Vulnerability Database. http://nvd.nist.gov/
4. Frei, S. (2009) Security Econometrics: The Dynamics of (IN) Security. PhD Dissertation, ETH, Zurich.
5. Joh, H. and Malaiya, Y.K. (2010) A Framework for Software Security Risk Evaluation Using the Vulnerability Lifecycle and CVSS Metrics. Proceedings of the International Workshop on Risk and Trust in Extended Enterprises, November 2010, 430-434.
6. Kijsanayothin, P. (2010) Network Security Modeling with Intelligent and Complexity Analysis. PhD Dissertation, Texas Tech University, Lubbock, TX.
7. Alhazmi, O.H., Malaiya, Y.K. and Ray, I. (2007) Measuring, Analyzing and Predicting Security Vulnerabilities in Software Systems. Computers & Security, 26, 219-228. https://doi.org/10.1016/j.cose.2006.10.002
8. Schiffman, M. Common Vulnerability Scoring System (CVSS).http://www.first. org/cvss/CVE Details. http://www.cvedetails.com/

9. Secunia Vulnerability Review 2015: Key Figures and Facts from a Global Information Security Perspective. March 2015. https://secunia.com/?action= fetch&filename= secunia_vulnerability_review_2015_pdf.pdf
10. Alhazmi, O.H. and Malaiya, Y.K. (2008) Application of Vulnerability Discovery Models to Major Operating Systems. IEEE Transactions on Reliability, 57, 14-22. https://doi.org/10.1109/TR.2008.916872
11. Alhazmi, O.H. and Malaiya, Y.K. (2005) Modeling the Vulnerability Discovery Process. Proceedings of 16th International Symposium on Software Reliability Engineering, Chicago, 8-11 November 2005, 129-138. https://doi.org/10.1109/ISSRE.2005.30
12. Noel, S., Jacobs, M., Kalapa, P. and Jajodia, S. (2005) Multiple Coordinated Views for Network Attack Graphs. VIZSEC'05: Proceedings of the IEEE Workshops on Visualization for Computer Security, Minneapolis, MN, 26 October 2005, 99-106. https://doi.org/10.1109/vizsec.2005.1532071
13. Mehta, V., Bartzis, C., Zhu, H., Clarke, E.M. and Wing, J.M. (2006) Ranking Attack Graphs. In: Zamboni, D. and Krügel, C., Eds., Recent Advances in Intrusion Detection, Vol. 4219 of Lecture Notes in Computer Science, Springer, Berlin, 127-144.
14. Lawler, G.F. (2006) Introduction to Stochastic Processes. 2nd Edition, Chapman and Hall/CRC, Taylor and Francis Group, London, New York.
15. Abraham, S. and Nair, S. (2014) Cyber Security Analytics: A Stochastic Model for Security Quantification Using Absorbing Markov Chains. Journal of Communications, 9, 899-907.https://doi.org/10.12720/jcm.9.12.899-907
16. Jajodia, S. and Noel, S. (2005) Advanced Cyber Attack Modeling, Analysis, and Visualization. 14th USENIX Security Symposium, Technical Report 2010, George Mason University, Fairfax, VA.
17. Wang, L., Singhal, A. and Jajodia, S. (2007) Measuring Overall Security of Network Configurations Using Attack Graphs. In: Barker, S. and Ahn, G.J., Eds., Data and Applications Security XXI. DBSec 2007. Lecture Notes in Computer Science, Vol. 4602, Springer, Berlin, Heidelberg, 98-112. https://doi.org/10.1007/978-3-540-73538-0_9
18. Wang, L., Islam, T., Long, T., Singhal, A. and Jajodia, S. (2008) An Attack Graph-Based Probabilistic Security Metric. DAS 2008, LNCS 5094, 283-296.

APPENDIX A

Matrix values used for model building under each category.

Low Vulnerability (0 - 3.9)		Medium Vulnerability (4 - 6.9)			
Y_i	t_i	Y_i	t_i	Y_i	t_i
0.002897	1	0.0153	1	0.026618	1
0.024865	2	0.041188	2	0.054112	2
0.042929	3	0.062188	3	0.076645	3
0.057784	4	0.079223	4	0.095114	4
0.069998	5	0.093042	5	0.110251	5
0.080042	6	0.104252	6	0.122657	6
0.088302	7	0.113345	7	0.132825	7
0.095093	8	0.120722	8	0.141159	8
⋮	⋮	⋮	⋮	⋮	⋮
0.126521	77	0.152416	71	0.179021	75
0.126521	78	0.152416	72	0.179021	76
0.126521	79	0.152416	73	0.179021	77
0.126521	80	0.152416	74	0.179021	78
0.126521	81	0.152416	75	0.179021	79
0.126521	82	0.152416	76	0.179021	80
0.126521	83	0.152416	77	0.179021	81
0.126521	84	0.152416	78	0.179021	82
0.126521	85	0.152416	79	0.179021	83
0.126521	86	0.152416	80	0.179021	84

CHAPTER 9

Security Policy Scheme for an Efficient Security Architecture in Software-Defined Networking

Woosik Lee and Namgi Kim *

Department of Computer Science, Kyonggi University, Suwon 16227, Korea

ABSTRACT

In order to build an efficient security architecture, previous studies have attempted to understand complex system architectures and message flows to detect various attack packets. However, the existing hardware-based single security architecture cannot efficiently handle a complex system structure. To solve this problem, we propose a software-defined networking (SDN) policy-based scheme for an efficient security architecture. The proposed scheme considers four policy functions: separating, chaining, merging, and reordering. If SDN network functions virtualization (NFV) system managers use these policy functions to deploy a security architecture, they only submit some of the requirement documents to the SDN policy-based architecture. After that, the entire security network can be easily built. This paper presents information about the design of a new policy functions model, and it discusses the performance of this model using theoretical analysis.

Keywords: SDN; NFV; security architecture; security policy

1. INTRODUCTION

Nowadays, hardware (H/W)-based security architectures are moving toward software (S/W)-based security architectures. Software-defined networking (SDN) [1] makes it possible to implement an S/W security architecture, which consists of a control plane and a data plane. The control plane sends a message about the requirement specifications to the data plane using OpenFlow application program interfaces (APIs). When the data plane receives the requirement message from the control plane, the data plane builds the virtual network topology. Then, the network functions virtualization (NFV) technique [2] is used to deploy virtual security devices on the switches or routers with OpenFlow functions.

Recently, a number of global companies have tried to integrate SDN into their architectures. Cisco proposed using the open networking environment (ONE) technique instead of SDN. The SDN market was expected to reach sales of about $2 billion in 2016 [3]. Moreover, researchers at a number of universities and companies have studied security topics related to SDN. Currently, about 90 companies, including HP, IBM, NEC, and NICIRA, have taken part in open networking foundation (ONF) industry standard institutes, and they have commercialized the controllers and the network virtualization functions [4,5,6].

However, previous SDN systems have some disadvantages, such as a lack of scalability, performance degradation, difficult network management, and vulnerable security. In order to solve these problems, it is necessary to consider a security SDN-based architecture, which contains solution functions such as efficient security paths, the rearrangement of security topology, and management policies for switches and routers. In this paper, we propose a security policy scheme for an efficient security architecture in SDN. The proposed security policy scheme has four policy configuration functions: separating, chaining, merging, and reordering. If we use these functions, we can easily manage entire security systems.

This paper makes several contributions to the existing literature. First, the proposed SDN policy-based architecture solves the existing network management problem of insufficient scalability, and the meta-model, the pseudocode, and the logic layer related to it are demonstrated. Second, we analyzed the cost of the physical devices using mathematical analysis techniques. Finally, we constructed a simulation to demonstrate the effectiveness of the proposed policy-based SDN technique. For the policy functions of separating, chaining, merging, and reordering, we also demonstrated the utility of policy-based SDN techniques.

This paper has the following structure. In Section 2, we discuss works related to security SDN. Section 3 describes the background of security

SDN. Section 4 defines four policy functions: separating, chaining, merging, and reordering. Section 5 explains the security policy meta-model, and Section 6 explains the pseudocode and examples for the four policy functions. In Section 7, we analyze the proposed system theoretically. In Section 8, we analyze experimental results to show that the proposed security policy scheme is superior. Lastly, we summarize this paper and describe the direction of future work.

2. RELATED WORK

Some previous studies have investigated the ability of SDN/NFV systems to defend against DDoS attacks [7,8,9,10,11]. Wan et al. proposed a global system architecture to defend against distributed denial-of-service (DDoS) attacks [7]. This system has two steps: detection and response. In the detection step, the suspicious attack flows are extracted from the received flows based on diverse security-role-mapping. After that, the global system generates alert messages, and sends them to the system's security managers. Khatua et al. proposed the Monitoring and Optimizing Virtual Resources (MOVR) architecture [8]. The MOVR architecture consists of a provisioner, a deployer, a controller, a monitor, a policy-arbitration-Quality of Service (QoS) module, and an application repository. Furthermore, MOVR manages and optimizes the resource use of cloud applications. Aicherry et al. proposed optimal algorithms to solve the problem of optimized virtual machine (VM) placement when the location of the data sets is given [9]. The proposed algorithms try to capture the best tradeoff point between minimizing latencies and incurring bandwidth costs. These algorithms were evaluated and proven using a simulation study. Fischer presented a survey of virtual network embedding (VNE) algorithms [10]. In general, VNE algorithms deal with the main resource allocation challenge in network virtualization. This causes two sub-problems: Virtual Node Mapping (VNoM), where the virtual nodes should be allocated in the physical nodes; and Virtual Link Mapping (VLiM), where the virtual links that connect these nodes should be mapped to paths connecting the corresponding nodes in the substrate network. Chowdhury et al. introduced new VNE algorithms that provided better coordination between the two phases [11]. The proposed algorithms, D-ViNE and R-ViNE, use deterministic and randomized rounding techniques, respectively [11]. That study used a simulation to prove the performance of the proposed algorithms in terms of the acceptance ratio and the revenue of the cost incurred by the substrate network in the long run [11]. Unlike the previously mentioned studies, Chowdhury et al. [12] and Jo et al. [13] focused on security policy based on SDN/NFV architectures. Chowdhury et al. proposed a policy-based inter-domain virtual network (PolyViNE) embedding framework that embeds end-to-end virtual networks in a decentralized manner [12]. They also proposed a forwarding mechanism for the location aware virtual network, based on a hierarchical addressing scheme (COST) and a location awareness protocol (LAP), to rapidly embed virtual networks. Jo et al. proposed a centralized network policy controller to efficiently handle packet flows in a multi-provider network environment [13], and discussed the construction and characteristics of the proposed controller. Moreover, they also provided various examples of virtual scenarios [13]. However, the results of the studies mentioned above are lacking in scalability, because many security vendors adopt different types of security architectures. In order to solve these problems, we propose an SDN policy-based scheme for an efficient security architecture.

There are many more recent studies related to SDN [14,15,16, 17,18,19,20,21,22,23,24,25,26,27,28,29,30,31,32,33,34].

According to Saxena [14], the latest SDN-based trends can be classified as a programming protocol, or as a ClickOS-based or generic SDN security system. We have also analyzed representative elements, such as distributed SDN controllers, Kandoo, DevoFlow, AVANT-GUARD, and FRESCO, as OpenFlow security systems. Satasiya et al. [15] demonstrated SDN security enhancements using firewalls in a distributed scenario environment. In particular, OpenFlow switches efficiently adjusted the firewall policy, changed the policy, and applied the security policy; that study demonstrated the performance through an experiment in the comment window [15]. Shin et al. [16] approached the question of how to use SDN to enhance security. In our study, we analyzed the definition and advantages of each field by classifying them into four SDN features: dynamic flow control, network-wide visibility with centralized control, network programmability, and a simplified data plane. In [18], an example of normal network flow using a simple data flow was shown; it provided an example of a man in the middle of a security attack, and an example of a denial-of-service (DoS). Ranjbar et al. [19] applied the policy-box concept to the Secure Sockets Layer (SSL) protocol to authenticate a hello message using the handshake message technique, thereby enhancing the safety of data transmission and reception. In [21], a security policy checking technique was applied to a flow table by including a conflict detection module and a conflict resolution module to check the security policy efficiently. Similarly, in [22], we discovered and responded to external attacks through a security architecture. Using experiments, [24] showed that throughput can be increased by applying OpenFlow to e-mail transmissions and receptions efficiently. In [25], a new framework was proposed, in which a security agent manages attack detection and monitors topology information, while the application generates blocking flows and reads and filters syslogs in a new type of security framework.

Liu et al. [26] presented a very simple form of firewall network address translation (FW-NAT) connection and cache-FW-NAT for security service chaining. In [27], a scenario was presented in which the security of multiple devices is efficiently achieved by applying SDN to various devices in an Internet of Things (IoT) environment. Rawat and Reddy [32] described the basic SDN architecture, and explained intrusion and anomalous attack definitions for DDoS, the architecture's applications, and other energy efficient SDN techniques. In [33], the possibility of SDN was proposed, and various SDN-related topics were addressed.

3. BACKGROUND

A distributed denial-of-service (DDoS) attack is one type of security attack. There are many cases of this type of security breach, such as the attack on the official residence of the Korean president in 2009, as well as the attack on banks and broadcast websites in 2013. Consequently, the need to construct a security architecture has increased quickly in order to deal with various hacking attacks, including advanced persistent threats (APTs) [35]. In this paper, we consider a target system to be a system that protects against attacks including DDoS attacks.

An SDN/NFV security architecture consists of a control plane and a data plane (Figure 1). The control plane contains the orchestration system and the SDN/NFV controller system, which exchanges control messages with legacy systems. More specifically, the control plane can perform a series of steps to set the path of a data packet flowing into the data plane, and it utilizes the data collected before setting the path. In particular, the control plane includes service chaining. Service chaining can logically apply route changes and ensure security using various types of security policies that exist in the service chaining pool in the data plane.

The data plane builds the security system from the service chaining pool, which has virtual security machines based on the control messages received by the control plane. More specifically, the data plane includes an open flow. The data flowing in the open flow receives a configuration message from the control plane's service chaining, which then creates the network; the configured network then transmits the attack packets sent from the malicious user. It has a security function for processing. Security features can vary for each open switch, and the throughput for attack packets can also vary from switch to switch. Moreover, the self-defense SDN security system of the data plane, which uses legacy detailed analysis/detection devices, detects anomalous traffic through the sFlow.

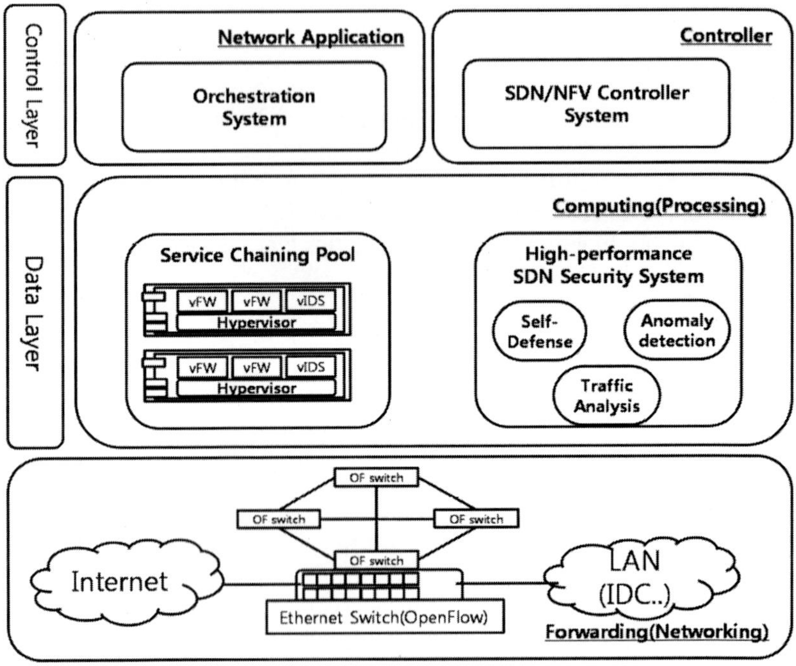

Figure 1. Software-defined networking (SDN)/ network functions virtualization (NFV) System Architecture.

For example, suppose computer company A is preparing to release a new product. At this time, computer company A places DDoS attacks on computer companies B and C so that B and C cannot transmit bad content to A's products on the same day. At this time, due to the DDoS attack of A, the systems of companies B and C become paralyzed, and company A can release its new product safely. In this scenario, when the SDN security system is applied, the DDoS attack is detected efficiently, and the attack data is efficiently solved by distributing the paths of the attacked companies B and C. All of the other network attacks can be efficiently solved using the SDN security system.

4. SECURITY POLICY SCHEME SECURITY ARCHITECTURE

We propose a novel security architecture using various policies based on SDN (Figure 1). This architecture consists of four layers: the presentation layer, the application layer, the control layer, and the infrastructure layer. In the presentation layer, system managers can approach diverse services through the web or the console terminals. In the application layer, we deploy our proposed policy configurable methods to easily manage security systems. In this layer, a variety of commands can be given to the control layer through service channels in order to configure the system. The control layer contains several functions, such as the OpenFlow APIs, service chaining, self-defense, and legacy devices. Lastly, the infrastructure layer builds the security networks based on the information received by the control layer.

The policy configurable schemes are deployed on the application layer of the policy security architecture. This architecture lays the foundation for utilizing four policy functions by applying a virtualized network function (VNF) like Figure 2. It provides four policy configurable functions, as follows:

- Separating: this divides the virtual services and decreases the size of the attack flows using the load balancer.
- Chaining: this links many VNFs to prevent various attack flows and constructs big security systems.
- Merging: this combines unnecessary VNFs to optimize the security system and the system's resources.
- Reordering: this reorders current VNFs depending on the type and strength of the current attack flows.

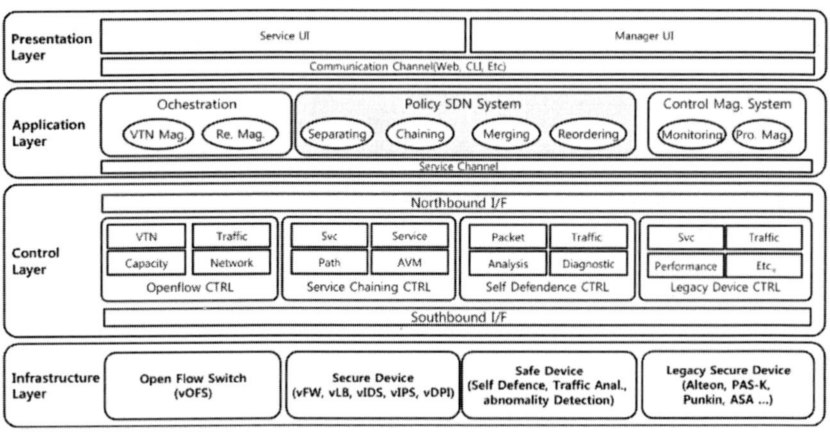

Figure 2. Policy security architecture.

We can easily manage the virtual security network system using SDN-based, security configurable policy functions. Therefore, if SDN system managers use an SDN policy-based security architecture, they do not need to spend time trying to understand the complex system's structure. Moreover, they can easily prepare security methods based on different types of attack flows.

5. SECURITY POLICY META-MODEL

If system managers want to use the policy configurable methods of an SDN-based architecture, they should consider various configurable uses based on the type of attack flows. Then, the security policy meta-model is required for setting up an SDN policy-based architecture. In Figure 3, the security policy meta-model consists of an SDN management policy, SDN management policy conditions, and the entities of the SDN management policy actions.

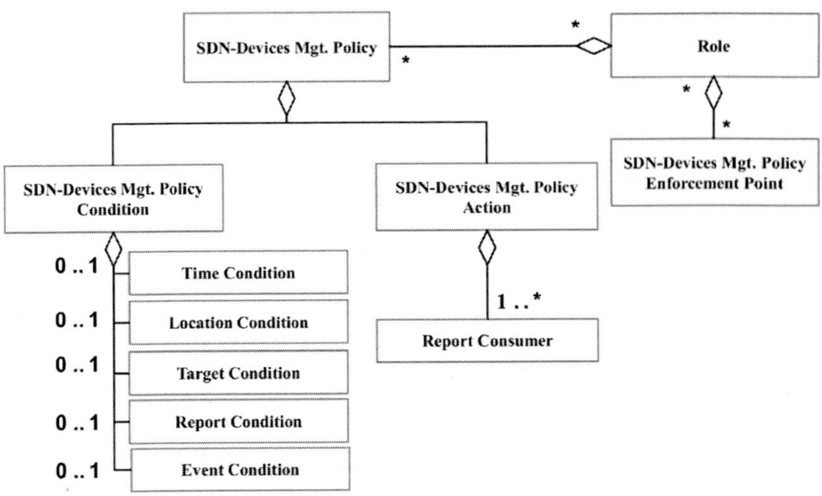

Figure 3. Security Policy Scheme security architecture.

In the entities of the SDN management policy actions, the SDN management policy entity contains actions for mapping particular conditions related to various attack flows. The subordinate entities of the SDN manage five conditions: the time, the location, the target, the report, and the event. The time condition configures the data collection time—the gap between the communication times—to obtain the security state information. Here, the security state information means a type of network attack, a pattern of a network attack time, an attack position, and an attack amount, in order to select a security policy. For example, if a data packet arrives every five seconds and the data packet suddenly flows in the same pattern every second, the network management device determines the packet as being abnormal, and it informs the network security manager about the security state information.

The location condition configures the information about including or excluding areas to restrict the security location. The target condition has a role that is similar to the location condition. It configures the including or excluding devices of the security targets. The report condition configures the type of virtual security status information. The event condition configures the event occurrence conditions based on the current security states. Then, the SDN management policy actions send the resulting, refined information about the policy conditions to the action destinations.

Depending on the policy, the role is given individually, and the role of the action that takes an action against the corresponding attack flow is given according to the role. The role is given a Policy Enforcement Point (PEP) based on when the attack comes in. Also, when a real-time data packet is checked, and the policy is changed and the processing for the attack is not necessary, the PEP is lost and the corresponding role is not performed. When a new attack comes in again, the PEP is given. This type of iteration takes advantage of Role-Based Access Control (RBAC), which provides a new role without redundant privileges.

6. SECURITY POLICY SCHEMES

This section presents a discussion of the pseudocodes, and provides examples of four security policies—separating, chaining, merging, and reordering—in order to demonstrate how to use the policy configurable methods in a real security infrastructure.

Definition 1 defines a data packet. A data packet is a combination of a normal packet and an attack packet. If a malicious attacker is not present in the network environment, only normal packets flow. However, if a malicious attacker is present in the network environment, and if an attack packet exists, a normal packet and an attack packet flow together. In this case, the normal packet is represented in the form of a normal packet. For example, 50 is a normal packet, based on a total of 100 packets. Similarly, if there is an attack packet, it is expressed as (normal packet)/(attack packet). In a network environment where 30 attack packets and 60 normal packets are transmitted based on 100 packets, the data packets are expressed as 60/30 (60 normal packets/30 attack packets).

In this paper, a data packet is regarded as being a combination of a normal flow and an attack flow. A data packet is expressed as a normal flow using a mathematical expression method. It is expressed as (normal flow)/(attack flow) when an attack flow is also included in the data packet.

Definition 2 defines the network as containing a physical layer and a virtual layer. A device without a security function is placed in the physical layer, and represented by using the symbol N (number). For example, if there are three devices in the physical layer, N1, N2, and N3 are placed in that layer. The virtual layer is a device with security functions, and it is expressed as S (number). The security processing capability of the devices placed in the virtual layer is expressed in the form of Process: (number). The virtual device may be temporarily stripped of its physical layer; in that case, the SN (number) symbol is used. A device belonging to a physical layer does not have the ability to process an attack flow, whereas a device belonging to a virtual layer does have that capability. Attack flow processing capability is expressed in the form of Process: (number). In the case of an SN node, it is used in the same form as a virtual layer device.

The basic resource of the device placed in the physical layer of the system discussed in this paper is set to 100. The cost of processing based on the data packet flowing to each device is calculated using Formula (1). Then, according to the calculation's result, the cost that is consumed by matching the information presented in Table 1 is calculated.

Table 1. Experimental parameters.

Min.	Max.	Cost
0	1/3	1
3/1	2/3	3
2/3	9/10	10
9/10	1	70
1	11/10	500
11/10	∞	5000

Definition 3 further defines the physical layer. In the case of a device belonging to the device, it is assumed that it, basically, has 100 resources, and the amount of data added to each device is calculated by using Formula (1). The costs are calculated based on the values obtained from that formula, as shown in Table 1.

Formula (1) shows the formula for calculating the cost. The input data x of Formula (1) means the size of the data packet flowing to the security equipment. x is placed in the molecule of the formula. Moreover, the denominator of the formula is the amount of device capacity that the security device can handle. Using the output data from Formula (1), we can get the cost value from Table 1.

Formula (1) yields a value based on the amount of data flowing into the device versus the resources the device can accommodate. In the proposed architecture discussed in this paper, since the device capacity is limited to 100, the denominator value is always fixed at 100. For example, if 50 data packets are flowing through the device, the value of 50/100 = 0.5 is given by Formula (1).

$$\phi(x) = \frac{x}{device\ capacity} \tag{1}$$

The values obtained from Formula (1) are calculated based on the information presented in Table 1. The cost calculation is based on [36], which shows that the value increases sharply on the basis of 1.

Figure 4 shows the pseudocode of the separating configurable method. As seen in the discussion of the relationship between the available resources and the loads of attack flows presented in Section 6, the separating method adds a new security device if the size of the attack flow exceeds 1. If that occurs, it reconfigures the previous network paths to stop massive attack flows. More specifically, the Separating () function gets input data which is an attack flow. After that, the Separating () function uses Formula (1) to obtain the cost. If the cost is 1 or more, the Separating () function creates a new virtual device through vDevice (). Then, it places the newly created vDevice by calling the devices () function in the virtual network topology. Then, the path () function is called to rearrange the path so that packets can flow efficiently to the newly arranged vDevice.

Figure 5 shows an example of the separating configurable method. As seen in Figure 5a, 100 data packets flow to N2, which belongs to the physical layer. Therefore, based on Formula (1), the cost imposed on N2 is calculated as follows: (100) = 100/100 = 1. If the value is 1, the cost is 500 (Table 1). If the cost is 500, and if the amount of data packets flowing in N2 is effectively reduced, the cost can be drastically reduced. If the SN node is placed in the physical layer, the cost can be reduced. Figure 5b shows how the SN nodes are deployed to distribute the data packets. At this time, N2 and SN1 have a value of φ (50) = 50/100 = 0.5, based on Formula (1). According to the information presented in Table 1, the cost is 3; thus, the cost has decreased dramatically.

```
Function Separating()
Input: attack flow: a, target: d
If φ_device(a) > 1 then
newDevice ← new vDevice();
vNetwork.devices(newDevice);
vNetwork.path(d, newDevice);
end if
```

Figure 4. The pseudocode of the separating configurable method.

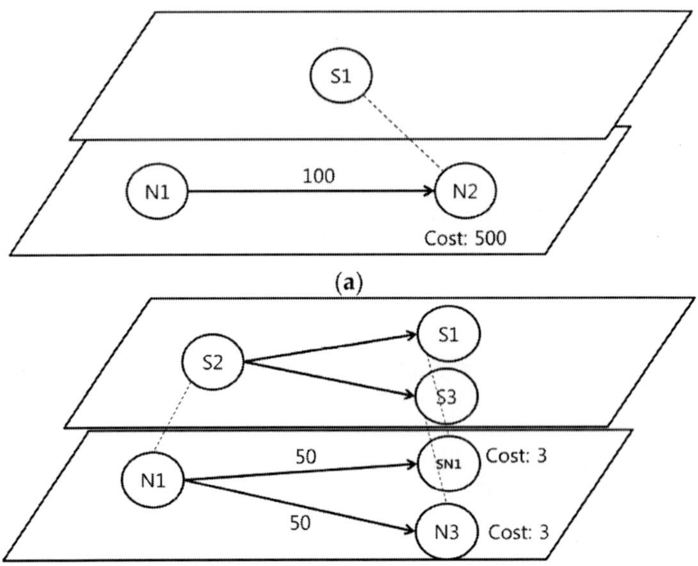

Figure 5. The example of the separating configurable method. (**a**) Network cost problem; (**b**) Solved network cost using separating method.

Figure 6 shows the pseudocode of the chaining configurable method. This method chains virtual security devices to detect and reduce the number of attack flows. If the SDN-based security network of a particular attack flow is already built, the chaining configurable method just passes the received attack flows to previous security systems. If not, it adds a new virtual security device and chains it to other security devices. More specifically, the Chaining () function receives an attack flow as input data. The Chaining () function determines whether the attack flow attack type is included in the current vNetwork. If there is no device capable of handling the attack type, the vDevice () function creates new security equipment of the corresponding type. It puts the created device into the vNetwork to process the attack flow. Otherwise, the Chaining () function will call the corresponding security device and chain it with the existing device, so that the attack flow can be processed.

```
Function Chaining()
Input: attack flow: a, target: d
If vNetwork.check(Type(φ_device(a))) != True then
    newDevice ← new vDevice(Type(φ_device(a));
    vNetwork.chain(newDevice);
else
    chainD ← vNetwork.find(Type(φ_a(x)))
    vNetwork.chain(chainD);
end if
```

Figure 6. The pseudocode of the chaining configurable method.

Figure 7 shows the use of the chaining rule to cope with an unexpected network attack flow. First, a 50/30 data packet flows through N2 placed in the physical layer. Here, 30 is an attack flow, but since S1, which is placed in the virtual layer, does not have a security policy corresponding to 30, a new type of security node is needed. At this time, of course, a new node may be placed in N1 to distribute the data packet or to reduce the amount of data, but it is not easy for the Start node to detect or handle the attack pattern. Therefore, it is efficient to arrange a new node that can process an attack flow between N1 and N2. If a new SN1 node is deployed using the chaining method, the attack packet can be efficiently processed. Therefore, 80 data packets are transmitted through SN1, 50 data packets eliminate the attack packets, and the cost of N3 is reduced to 3.

Figure 8 shows the pseudocode of the merging configurable method. This method removes some of the previous security network to increase network resource utilization. This algorithm first checks the gap between the size of the existing security network and the current attack flows. If the size of the virtual network is larger than the attack flows, the algorithm removes useless virtual security devices. More specifically, the Merging () function receives a value of attack flow as input data. If the value is smaller than the current capacity of the vNetwork, we know that a large amount of resources are used unnecessarily. At this time, the Merging () function automatically finds unnecessary devices and merges unnecessary processing devices. After that, it relocates the resources through the rearrange () function.

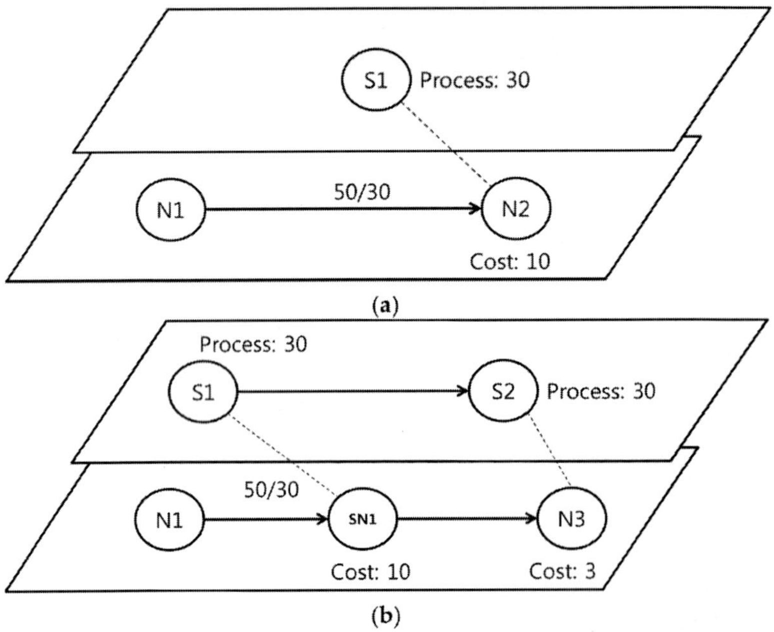

Figure 7. The example of the chaining configurable method. (**a**) Network attack flow problem; (**b**) Solved network cost using chaining configurable method.

```
Function Merging()
Input: attack flow: a, target: d
If a < vNetwork.resource() then
rest ← vNetwork.resource() − φ_device(a)
vNetwork.remove(rest);
vNetwork.rearrange(rest)
end if
```

Figure 8. The pseudocode of the merging configurable method.

Figure 9 provides an example of the merging configurable method. If all of the nodes process the attack flows, the security nodes are not needed. Unnecessary nodes increase the resource consumption of the hardware. The merging configurable method automatically removes the unnecessary network nodes. As seen in Figure 9b, S1 is removed. Therefore, the proposed SDN policy-based architecture reduces resource consumption.

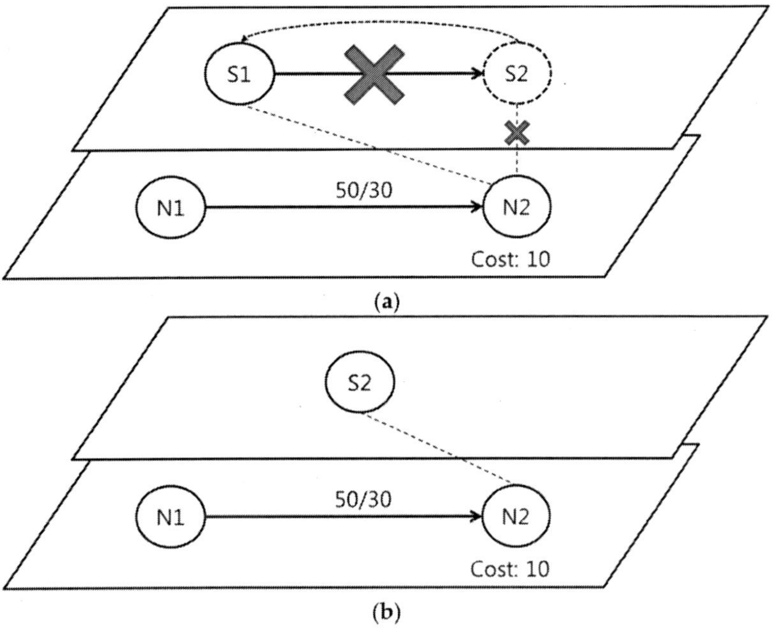

Figure 9. The example of the merging configurable method. (**a**) Unusable network usage; (**b**) Removing unusable node using merging configurable method.

Figure 10 shows the pseudocode of the reordering configurable method. This algorithm deploys virtual security devices close to the entrance of the attack flows to create efficient security networks. Actually, the location close to the attacking sources includes a number of normal packets [37]. Moreover, the location can largely reduce the damage done to the entire network system, because the ultimate goal of DDoS defense is to rapidly catch and remove anomalous flows. To be more specific about the code, the Reordering () function is called automatically when the current network needs to relocate. The Reordering () function calculates the total weight value using the weight () function. If the current weight value is higher than the preset optimal weight value α, a rearrangement process is performed. The optimal weight α value is calculated based on one hop between the node and the node according to the network topology configuration. We get α that weight bounding value multiplying the number of virtual equipment by half of the number of physical equipment links. For example, if there are four links of physical equipment and three pieces of virtual equipment, 2 × 4 = 6 is α. The weight value in Figure 11 becomes 3 + 4 × 2 and becomes 11. In this case, since the value of 6 is exceeded, it becomes a reordering target.

```
Function Reordering()
Input: attack flow: vNetwork
If vNetwork.weight (vNetwork) < α then
  vNetwork.reordering ()
end if
```

Figure 10. The pseudocode of the reordering configurable method.

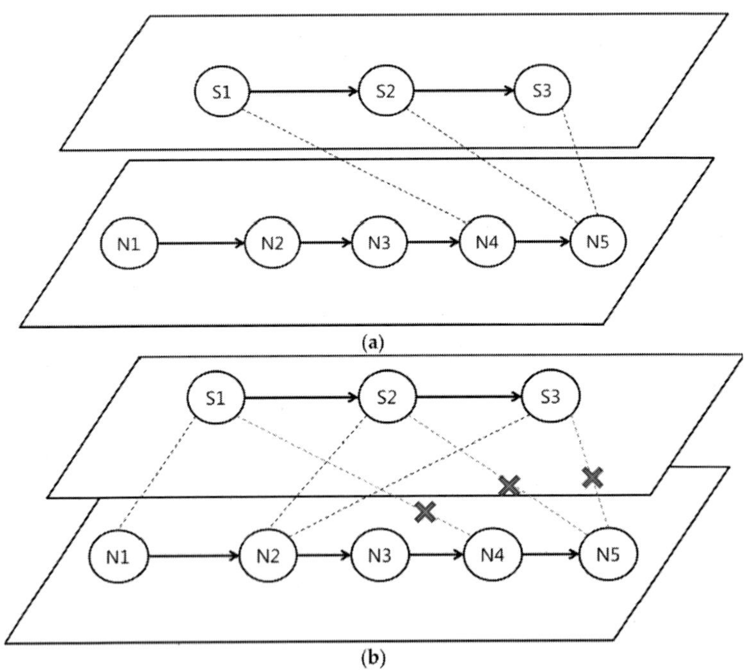

Figure 11. The example of the reordering configurable m. (**a**) Inefficient network flow path; (**b**) Rearranged network path.

Figure 11 presents a path reordering example, in which an inefficient path becomes an efficient path. As seen in Figure 11a, S1–S3 are deployed on the end of the network path. However, this is not a good way to detect attack flows because most attack flows attack the front network nodes. If the front network nodes are broken, the back nodes can become obsolete. As seen in Figure 11b, the reordering configurable method changes the back paths to front paths to increase network security.

7. THEORETICAL ANALYSIS

This section describes a network environment with a physical layer that does not have security processing capability, and a virtual layer that can efficiently process attack flows using a security policy scheme. Two networks with an existing environment are analyzed. For this analysis, it is assumed that half of the data packets are flowing through the attack flow. For example, in the case of 100 data packets, the flow is 50/50, 50 normal packets and 50 attack packets.

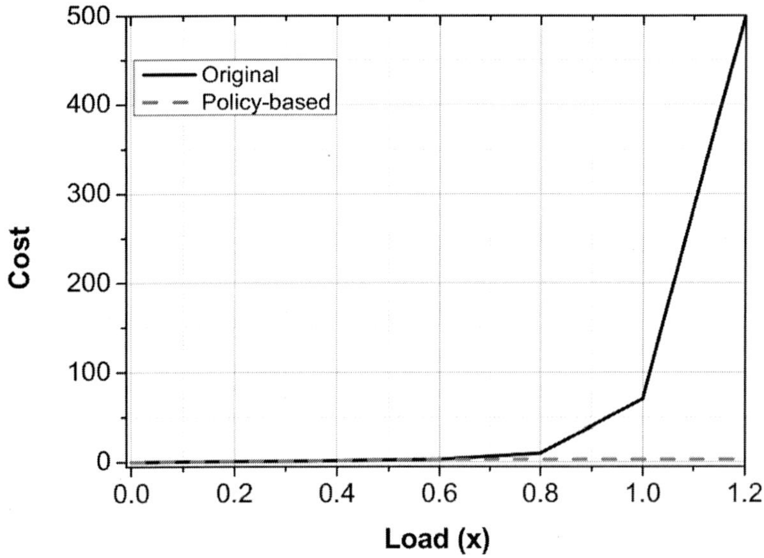

Figure 12. The relationship between the costs and loads.

The theoretical analysis results are presented in Figure 12. The black line shows the cost of the data packet, in which the device is placed in a simple physical layer in which no security policy is applied. The red line is added to the virtual layer, and the security policy is applied. In that scenario, the security policy is applied and 50 attack flows are processed. Then, the cost is recalculated, so that the cost to the simple physical layer can be reduced.

The graph shows that the overall physical layer results in an excessively high cost based on 0.8. Thus, the cost increases sharply based on the value 1 (Table 1). However, if a device with a security policy is deployed in the virtual layer, the cost is uniformly lower than 70 in all cases. This is because no matter how large the data size, the overall cost is reduced due to the security policy. For example, in the case of the load for the last 1.2, the value of 1.2 is 120/100, but when the virtual security policy is applied, the cost is 3, because 60/100 is 0.6.

8. EXPERIMENTAL RESULT THROUGH SIMULATION

This section compares and analyzes the simulation results to demonstrate the performance of the proposed method. For the simulation, we developed a virtual network configuration module. For the performance evaluation, we calculated the current cost by calculating the cost based on 100 data packets. The experiments were performed based on four hypothetical scenarios, and the experimental results were analyzed. The four scenarios are:

1) A network with only physical equipment that does not have any security policy;
2) A network environment where the attack flow is cleaned based on the security policy;
3) A network environment that processes attack packets through a security chain based on the number of attack flows divided by 5;
4) A comparison of a network with and without a security policy, in an environment where the normal packet/attack packet changes randomly over time.

First, Figure 13 shows the resulting graph for Scenario 1, in which the security policy is not applied. The x-axis of the graph represents the number of sensors, and the y-axis represents the cost. As shown in Figure 13, the cost increases proportionally as the number of sensors in the graph increases. This is because as the number of devices increases, the number of attack packets does not decrease; only the cumulative cost of the network device increases.

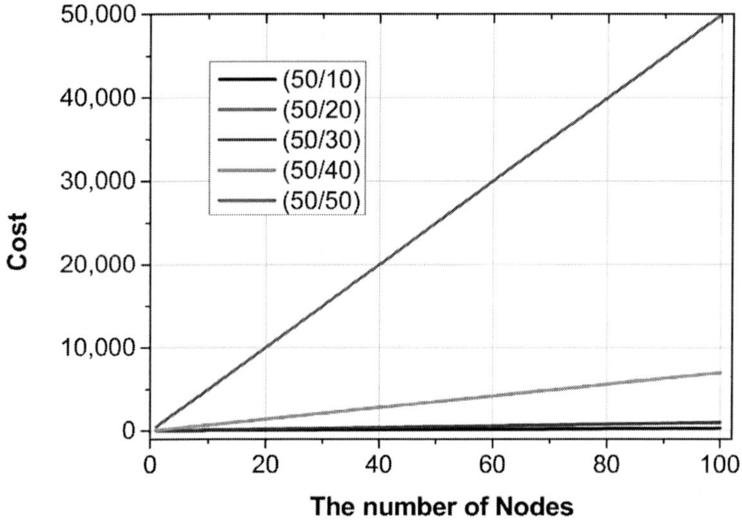

Figure 13. The cost of physical layer devices without security policy.

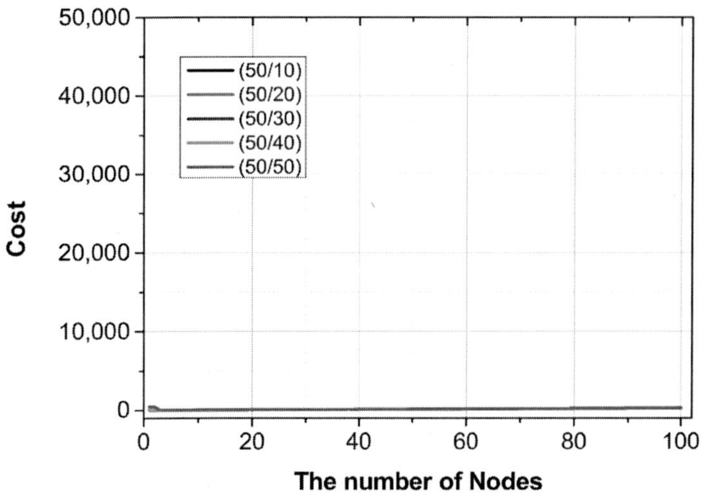

Figure 14. The cost of physical layer devices with a security policy scheme at the first node.

Figure 14 shows the resulting graph for Scenario 2. Unlike Scenario 1, the cost remains almost at 300 or less, regardless of the number of attack and normal packets, with little increase in cost. This occurs because, when a security device is encountered, the security policy processes all the attack flows.

Figure 15 shows the results for Scenario 3. Unlike Scenario 2, a device with a security policy does not process the attack flow all at once; rather, it processes it while decreasing it by −5. The cost is not fixed as a whole because of the scenarios in which the security devices process according to the security chaining policy. Since the devices to which the security policy applies are randomly applied as attack packet/5 and (attack packet/5)/number nodes, they are shaken because they are not applicable devices.

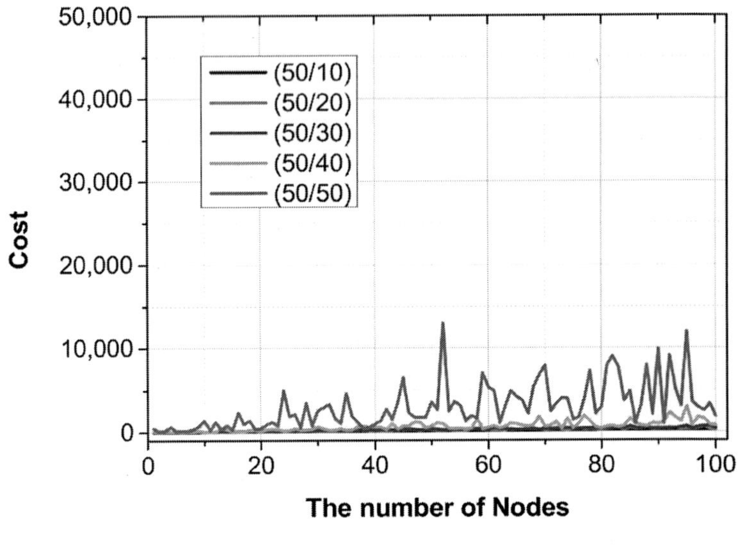

Figure 15. The cost of physical layer devices with a security policy scheme at a random device.

Finally, Figure 16 shows a graph in which the normal and attack packets are randomly changed from 0 to 50 in a network environment where 100 devices are scattered, and the cost is accumulated over time. If the security layer is not applied over time, and only the physical layer is present, this type of network environment is always worse than an environment where security is applied. However, if the cost of the security policy is reduced in the virtual network environment, the cost is effectively reduced and decreased.

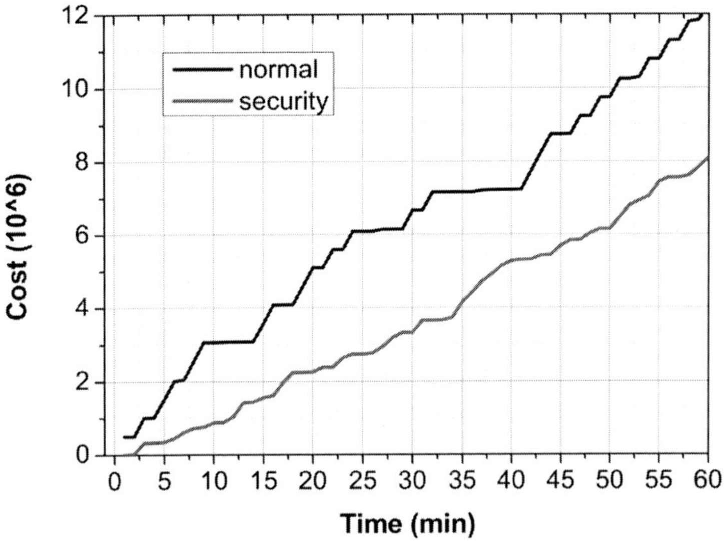

Figure 16. Normal scheme vs. policy security scheme.

9. CONCLUSIONS

In this paper, we proposed a policy-based path resetting method in an SDN environment. The specification and the mathematical analysis of the proposed numerical code and logic hierarchy were presented, and the simulation results were analyzed.

We then compared the proposed policy configurable methods with the previous system in terms of costs. The results show that the proposed policy configurable methods are better than the previous system that exists in the physical layer that cannot efficiently process attack flows. The reason is that policy configurable methods efficiently process the attack flows by reflecting the policy according to the attack types, whereas the previous system has only the fixed path, and when a new type of attack flow comes, it cannot process it due to the various attack types.

Especially, if the load is 1, the gap between the systems is high. The proposed SDN policy-based security architecture provides four policy configurable methods: separating, chaining, merging, and reordering. Security system managers can easily manage the entire security system using these methods. Moreover, the security policy configurable methods are not dependent on vendors due to independent policies because, in the proposed SDN policy-based security architecture, all vendors have the same policies.

In future work, we will consider whether the proposed SDN policy-based security architecture with the policy configurable methods can be deployed in real commercial devices to create an efficient security system.

ACKNOWLEDGMENTS

This research was supported by Basic Science Research Program through the National Research Foundation of Korea (NRF) funded by the Ministry of Education (2017R1C1B5016444).

REFERENCES

1. Bradai, A.; Singh, K.; Ahmed, T.; Rasheed, T. Cellular software defined networking: A framework. *IEEE Commun. Mag.* **2015**, *53*, 36–43.
2. Bo, H.; Gopalakrishnan, V.; Lusheng, J.; Seungjoon, L. Network function virtualization: Challenges and opportunities for innovations. *IEEE Commun. Mag.* **2015**, *53*, 90–97.
3. Lee, W.; Choi, Y.; Kim, N. Study on virtual service chain for secure software-defined networking. *Adv. Sci. Technol. Lett.* **2013**, *29*, 177–180.
4. Cisco. Cisco Nexus 1000V Switch and Cisco vPath 2.5 Virtual Services Ecosystem. *White Pap.* 2014. Available online: http://www.cisco.com/c/en/us/ products/collateral/ switches/nexus-7000-series-switches/white-paper-c11-730475.html(accessed on 13 June 2017).
5. Quinn, P. Service Function Chaining Creating a Service Plane Using Network Service Header. *Computer* **2014**, *47*, 38–44.
6. Jiang, Y.; Li, H.; Wei, H. An architecture of service chaining. *Internet-Draft.* 2013. Available online: https://tools.ietf.org/html/draft-jiang-service-chaining-arch-00 (accessed on 13 June 2017).
7. Wan, K.; Chang, R. Engineering of a global defense infrastructure for DDoS attacks. In Proceedings of the 10th IEEE International Conference on Networks, Singapore, Singapore, 27–30 August 2002; pp. 419–427.
8. Khatua, S.; Ghosh, A.; Mukherjee, N. Optimizing the utilization of virtual resources in Cloud environment. In Proceedings of the 2010 IEEE International Conference on Virtual Environments Human-Computer Interfaces and Measurement Systems (VECIMS), Taranto, Italy, 6–8 September 2010; pp. 82–87.
9. Alicherry, M.; Lakshman, T.V. Optimizing data access latencies in cloud systems by intelligent virtual machine placement. In Proceedings of the IEEE INFOCOM, Turin, Italy, 14–19 April 2013; pp. 647–655.
10. Fischer, A.; Botero, J.F.; Beck, M.T.; Meer, H.; Hesselbach, X. Virtual network embedding: A survey. *IEEE Commun. Surv. Tutor.* **2013**, *15*, 1888–1906.

11. Chowdhury, N.M.M.K.; Rahman, M.R.; Boutaba, R. Virtual network embedding with coordinated node and link mapping. In Proceedings of the IEEE INFOCOM, Rio de Janeiro, Brazil, 19–25 April 2009; pp. 783–791.
12. Chowdhury, M.; Samuel, F.; Boutaba, R. PolyViNE: Policy-based virtual network embedding across multiple domains. *J. Internet Serv. Appl.* **2010**, *4*, 49–56.
13. Jo, J.Y.; Lee, S.Y.; Kong, J.U.; Kim, J.W. A centralized network policy controller for SDN-based service overlay networking. *J. Korea Inf. Commun. Soc.* **2013**, *38*, 266–278.
14. Sazena, M.; Kumar, R. A recent trends in software defined networking (SDN) security. In Proceedings of the Computing for Sustainable Global Development, New Delhi, India, 16–18 March 2016; pp. 16–18.
15. Satasiya, D.; Raviya, R.; Kumar, H. Enhanced SDN security using firewall in a distributed scenario. In Proceedings of the Advanced Communication Control and Computing Technologies, Ramanathapuram, India, 25–27 May 2016; pp. 25–27.
16. Shin, S.; Xu, L.; Hong, S.; Gu, G. Enhancing network security through software defined networking (SDN). In Proceedings of the International Conference on Computer Communication and Networks, Waikoloa, HI, USA, 1–4 August 2016; pp. 1–4.
17. Husssein, A.; Elhajj, I.H.; Chehab, A.; Kayssi, A. SDN security plane: An architecture for resilient security services. In Proceedings of the IEEE International Conference on Cloud Engineering Workshop, Luxembourg, Luxembourg, 12–15 December 2016; pp. 4–8.
18. Cox, J.H.; Clark, R.J.; Owen, H.L. Leveraging SDN for ARP security. In Proceedings of the SoutheastCon, Norfolk, VA, USA, 30 March–3 April 2016; pp. 1–8.
19. Ranjbar, A.; Komu, M.; Salmela, P.; Aura, T. An SDN-based approach to enhance the end-to-end security: SSL/TLS case study. In Proceedings of the IEEE/IFIP Network Operations and Management Symposium, Istanbul, Turkey, 25–29 April 2016; pp. 25–29.
20. Yao, L.; Dong, P.; Zheng, T.; Zhang, H.; Du, X.; Guizani, M. Network security analyzing and modeling based on petri net and attack tree for SDN. In Proceedings of the International Conference on Computing Networking and Communications, Kauai, HI, USA, 15–18 February 2016; pp. 15–18.
21. Pisharody, S.; Chowdhary, A.; Huang, D. Security policy checking in distributed SDN based clouds. In Proceedings of the IEEE Communications and Network Security, Philadelphia, PA, USA, 17–19 October 2016; pp. 17–19.
22. Martins, J.S.B.; Cmpos, M.B. A security architecture proposal for detection and response to threats in SDN networks. In Proceedings of the IEEE ANDESCON, Arequipa, Peru, 19–21 October 2016; pp. 19–21.
23. Patel, P.; Tiwari, V.; Abhishek, M.K. SDN and NFV integration in openstack cloud to improve network services and security. In Proceedings of the International Conference on Advanced Communication Control and Computing Technologies, Ramanathapuram, India, 25–27 May 2016; pp. 25–27.
24. Rupasinghe, P.L.; Kulatunga, K.M.D.S.B.; Murry, L.; Keseva, K. SDN based security solution for legislative email communications: Safe guarding communication. In Proceedings of the International Conference on Computing, Communication and Automation, Greater Noida, India, 29–30 April 2016; pp. 29–30.
25. Ammar, M.; Rizk, M.; Hamid, A.A.; Seoud, A.K.A. A framework for security enhancement in SDN-based datacenters. In Proceedings of the IFIP International Conference on New Technologies Mobility and Security, Larnaca, Cyprus, 21–23 November 2016; pp. 21–23.
26. Liu, Y.; Guo, Z.; Shou, G.; Hu, Y. To achieve a security service chain by integration of NFV and SDN. In Proceedings of the International Conference on Instrumentation and Measurement, Computer, Communication and Control, Harbin, China, 21–23 July 2016; pp. 21–23.
27. Wilczewski, D. Security considerations for equipment controllers and SDN. In Proceedings of the IEEE International Telecommunications Energy Conference, Austin, TX, USA, 23–27 October 2016; pp. 23–27.
28. Bull, P.; Austin, R.; Popov, E.; Sharma, M.; Watson, R. Flow based security for IoT Devices using an SDN gateway. In Proceedings of the IEEE 4th International Conference on Future Internet of Things and Cloud, Vienna, Austria, 22–24 August 2016; pp. 22–24.

29. Gonzaiez, C.; Charfadine, S.M.; Flauzac, O.; Nolot, F. SDN-based security framework for the IoT in distributed grid. In Proceedings of the International Multidisciplinary Conference on Computer and Energy Science, Split, Croatia, 13–15 July 2016; pp. 13–15.
30. Huq, S. Hardening the SDN optical transport network security—Is it a pleonasm or oxymoron? In Proceedings of the Optical Fiber Communications Conference and Exhibition, Anaheim, CA, USA, 20–24 March 2016; pp. 20–24.
31. Basit, A.; Ahmed, N. Path diversity for inter-domain routing security. In Proceedings of the International Bhurban Conference on Applied Sciences and Technology, Islamabad, Pakistan, 10–14 January 2017; pp. 10–14.
32. Rawat, D.B.; Reddy, S.R. Software defined networking architecture, security and energy efficiency: A survey. *IEEE Commun. Surv. Tutor.* **2017**, *19*, 325–346.
33. Dacier, M.C.; Konig, H.; Cwalinski, R.; Kargi, F.; Dietrich, S. Security challenges and opportunities of software-defined networking. *IEEE Secur. Priv.* **2017**, *15*, 96–100.
34. Li, C.; Qin, Z.; Novak, E.; Li, Q. Securing SDN infrastructure of IoT-Fog network from MitM Attacks. *IEEE Internet Things J.* **2017**. Available online: http://ieeexplore.ieee.org/document/7883928/ (accessed 13 June 2017)
35. Koo, S.K. Cyber security in South Korea: The threat within. *The Diplomat.* 2013. Available online: http://thediplomat.com/2013/08/cyber-security-in-south-korea-the-threat-within/ (accessed on 13 June 2017).
36. Fortz, B.; Thorup, M. Internet traffic engineering by optimizing OSPF weights. *INFOCOM* **2000**, *2*, 519–528.
37. Zargar, S.T.; Joshi, J.; Tipper, D. A survey of defense mechanisms against distributed denial of service (DDoS) flooding attacks. *IEEE Commun. Surv. Tutor.* **2013**, *15*, 2046–2069.

CHAPTER 10

A Review of Security Concerns in Internet of Things

Engin Leloglu

R&D Department, Vestel Electronic Inc., Manisa, Turkey

ABSTRACT

The Internet of Things (IoT) represents a technologically optimistic future where objects will be connected to the internet and make intelligent collaborations with other objects anywhere, anytime. Although it makes appreciable development, there are still uncertainties about security concepts of its usage that is usually considered as a major concern in the design of IoT architectures. This paper presents a general survey of all the security issues in IoT along with an analysis of IoT architectures. The study defines security requirements and challenges that are common in IoT implementations and discusses security threats and related solutions on each layer of IoT architecture to make this technology secure and more widespread accordingly.

Keywords: Internet of Things, IoT, Security Requirements, Security Challenges, Security Threats, Security Solutions

1. INTRODUCTION

Although Internet of Things (IoT) is a well-known term and a rising trend in IT arena, there has been no agreed definition by the world community of users until now. In fact, there are many different groups in industry and standardization organizations that formulate similar ideas but in different forms and based on different components or aspects of an IoT system.

The best definition for the Internet of Things would be defined by ITU-T Y.2060:

"Global infrastructure for the society, enabling advanced services by interconnecting (physical and virtual) things based on existing and evolving interoperable information and communication technologies."

IoT is such a system that supplies connectivity and interactive communication for anything. Even though "being connected" is usually used in term of electronic devices in our daily life, physical objects that have hardware such as sensors or actuators, connect to the Internet with unique addresses. Data of physical object are transmitted continuously through wired/wireless networks to platforms where it will be interpreted. Physical objects are capable of understanding complexity of the environment and reacting due to their feature of sense and communication. The revolutionary advance in this case is that physical objects begin to be deployed and adopted widely. In addition, most of them begin to work properly without human intervention [1].

In future, every object in our daily life will be connected to Internet. Mobile phones will be used as the center point or the remote control for all objects in the physical world commonly called as IoT [2]. According to Gartner [3] , it is expected that the number of Internet-connected devices will increase from around 25 billion to 50 billion by 2020. Prevalence of such a big network induces new security risks that can allow attackers to steal even more personal information about the users or the organizations that are connected to such an IoT system.

Emphasizing security issues surrounding IoT is the main goal of this paper. Security is an important concern for IoT technology because of following reasons [4] :

- IoT is accepted as an extended version of some different technologies such as Wireless Sensor Networks, Mobile Broadband and 2G/3G Communications Networks which are already under threat because of various security flaws.
- Every device is connected to Internet in IoT technologies and Internet is an unsecured environment naturally. There are many evil-minded

people who are on the lookout for various system breaches and remote code executions.

- Objects in IoT communicate with each other; hence, there is a possibility that privacy and security can be hindered.

This study presents a general survey of all the security issues in IoT along with an analysis of IoT architectures. The paper describes security requirements and challenges that are usually faced in IoT implementations and mentions security threats and related solutions on each layer of IoT architecture to make this technology secure and more widespread.

The paper is organized as follows. In Section 2, IoT scope and recommended architecture are described. Section 3 studies security requirements and challenges for IoT implementations. In Section 4, security threats plaguing the Internet of Things are surveyed in such a way that all these threats are categorized based on layers of IoT architecture. Section 5 discusses security solutions and research directions on each layer and finally Section 6 concludes this study.

2. IOT SCOPE AND ARCHITECTURE

IoT purposes to enable things to be connected anyplace and anytime using any service/network [5]. Having this purpose of IoT in mind, it is stated that a correct and easy implementation of an IoT system mainly depends on identifying the right principles regarding the proper discovery, identification, configuration and manipulation of interconnected devices and sensors [6].

In the study of Uma Mahesh et al. [7] , a classification is proposed that helps in defining the various elements of IoT from a higher level perspective;

a) Hardware: Sensors, central units and built-in communication hardware are included in this level. Since a sensor has limited hardware, it is usually utilized in sensor networks that multiple sensors are linked together. A central unit that is a source of centralized services in IoTs, has a capable of storing, processing, and delivering data to users.

b) Middleware: It consists of storage and calculation tools for data analytics. Cloud computing is given as an example in this section.

Cloud computing is the integrity of several traditional technologies such as hardware virtualization, service-oriented architecture, load-balancing, distributed computing, grid computing, utility computing and autonomic computing. It can be considered as a natural step forward from the grid-utility model [8]. This style of computing relies on sharing of resources are provided as a service over the Internet to achieve coherence and economy of scale.

c) Presentation: There are visualization and interpretation tools in presentation level. These tools are designed for various applications and can be accessed from any platform.

From the network point of view, the opportunity of accessing information through tagged object by browsing on Internet primarily inspired the idea of IoT. Bringing objects into the digital world and identifying them by using their Internet addresses are supplied with different tagging technologies such as RFID, NFC and QR Codes [9]. RFID, intelligence embedded technology, sensor technology and nano-technology are pioneer technologies for the development of IoT. Radio frequency identification (RFID) is the foundation and networking core of the construction of IoT among them [10]. Kevin Ashton who was a pioneer of IoT underlines this issue in his article that RFID and the sensor technology strengthen traditional computers and gain them some significant features such as observation, identification and understanding the world of sensor data [11].

Wireless sensor network (WSN) is another type of data collection technology of the IoT that has some features to maintain the control over many nodes through wireless communication such as multi-hopping and self-organization. A WSN system contains a central unit that provides wireless connectivity back to the wired world and distributed nodes [12]. Each node is equipped with a sensor to detect physical phenomena such as light, heat, pressure, etc. [13]. Cooperative sensing, collecting and processing sensor information are purposes of this network model. The system can execute data collection and quantification, pro- cessing fusion and transmission application [14].

According to Jian An *et al.* [15] , the architecture of IoT should be an open architecture, using open protocols to support a variety of existing network applications. Likewise, it should additionally incorporate security, adaptability and semantic representation middleware to promote data world integration with Internet. In consideration of these ideas and some related studies [1] [16] [17] [18] [19] [20] , the architecture in Figure 1 is proposed to guide theoretical research.

1) Perception Layer: The sensor technology, intelligence embedded technology, nano technology and tagging technology are located in this layer. Main purpose of the layer is the identification of unique objects and the collection of information from the physical world with the help of its sensors [21].

2) Network Layer: It contains WSN, optical fiber communication networks, broad television networks, 2G/3G communications networks, fixed telephone networks and closed IP data networks for

each carrier. Transfer of collected information from sensors, devices, etc., to an information processing system is under the responsibility of this layer.

3) Support Layer: The layer involves information processing systems which takes information in one form and processes (transforms) it into another form. This processed data is stored in a database and will be available when there is a demand. This layer works very closely with applications. Therefore, researchers prefer to place it in application layer [22].

4) Application Layer: In this layer, there are practical and useful applications which are developed based on user requirements or industry specifications such as smart traffic, precise agriculture, smart home, mining monitor, etc.

3. SECURITY OF IOT

3.1. Existing Requirements and Challenges of Security

Hui Suo *et al.* [18] refer that IoT extends the term of 'internet' through corresponding technologies such as traditional Internet, mobile networks, sensor networks and so on. Every "thing" is connected to this "Internet" and these "things" communicates with each other. According to Rolf H. Weber [23] , these kinds of systems imply great potential for flexibility and scalability, but they have the risk of having security problems too. There are many issues about its wide adoption and without offering relevant solutions for the newly posed threats; it looks like it cannot be a practically applicable technology in close future.

Security requirements are examined in studies [21] [16] [18] [24] [19] [25] [26] in different dimensions. The requirements addressed in many studies can be summarized under five headings in Table 1.

In order to fulfill these requirements in Table 1, there are several challenges [21] [6] [16] [17] [27] [19] [26] [28] that must be handled in Table 2.

3.2. Existing Security Threats in IoT Systems

In this section, existing threats in IoT systems are examined in four categories based on IoT architecture which have been addressed in Section 2. The examination is summarized in Figure 2.

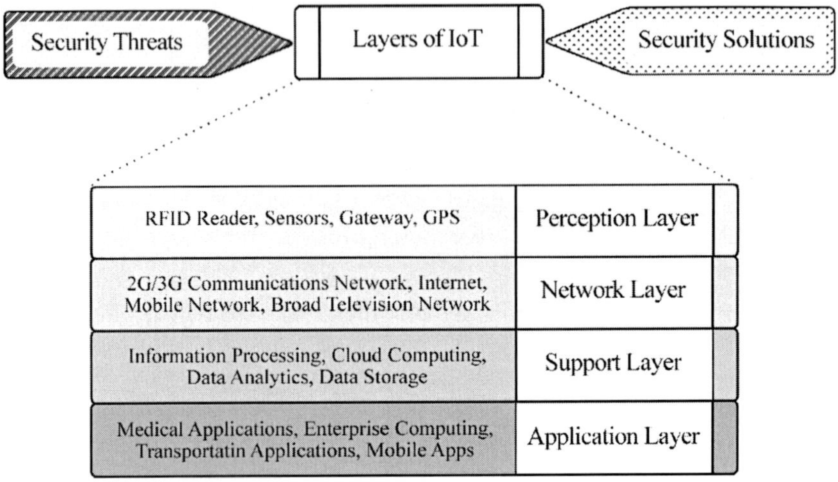

Figure 1. IoT Architecture.

Table 1. Security requirements.

Authenticity:	Only legal users should be allowed to access the system or sensitive information [16].
Authorization:	The privileges of device components and applications should be limited as so they are able to access only the resources they need to do their addressed tasks [25].
Confidentiality:	Information transmission between the nodes should be protected from intruders [18].
Integrity:	Related information should not be tampered [19].
Availability and Continuity:	In order to avoid any potential operational failures and interruptions, availability and continuity in the provision of security services should be ensured [26].

3.2.1. Threats of Perception Layer

Sensor and intelligence embedded technologies including RFID readers, sensors or GPS are under threat because of various security flaws. Main threats are discussed below:

Spoofing: It is initiated with a fake broadcast message sent to sensor network by the attackers. It makes it to assume its originality falsely which makes it appearing from the original source [29]. It is quite often that this scenario is results in the attacker obtaining full access to the system making it vulnerable.

Table 2. Security challenges.

Interoperability:	Relevant security solutions should not prevent the functionality of interconnected heterogeneous devices in IoT network system [27].
Resource constraints:	In IoT architecture, most of nodes lack of storage capacity, power and CPU. They generally use low-bandwidth communication channels. Hence, it is unable to apply some security techniques such as frequency hopping communication and public key encryption algorithm. Setup of security system is very difficult under these circumstances [6].
Data volumes:	Although some IoT applications use brief and infrequent communication channels, there are considerable number of IoT system such as sensor-based, logistics and large scale system that have potentials to entail huge volume of data on central network or servers [28].
Privacy protection:	Since a great number of RFID systems are short of suitable authentication mechanism, anyone can tracks tags and find the identity of the objects carrying them. Intruders can not only read the data, but can also modify or even delete data as well [21].
Scalability:	The IoT network consists of a large number of nodes. The proposed security mechanism on IoT should be scalable [19].
Autonomic control:	Traditional computers need users to configure and adapt them to different application domains and different communication environments. However, objects in IoT network should establish connections spontaneously, and organize/configure themselves for adapting to the platform they are operating in. This kind of control also involves some techniques and mechanisms such as self-configuring, self-optimizing, self-management, self-healing and self-protecting [27].

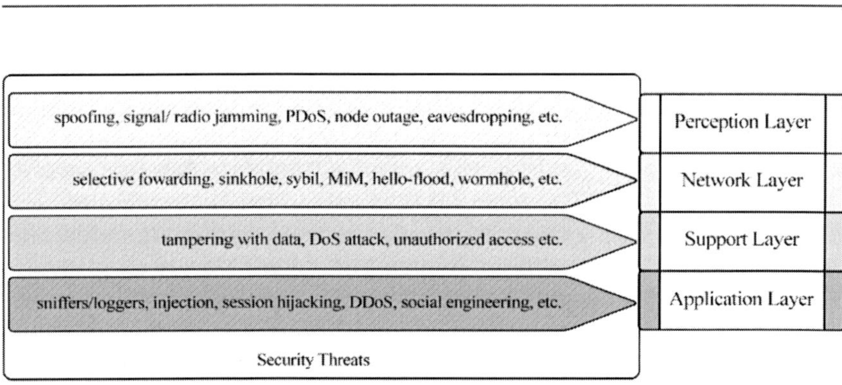

Figure 2. Threats on layers of IoT.

Signal/Radio Jamming: It is a type of DoS attack that it occupies the communication channel between the nodes and hinders them from communicating with each other [30].

Device-tampering/Node-capturing: The attacker captures the sensor node physically replaces the node with their malicious node. This type of attack usually results in the attacker gaining total control over the captured node and harms the network [31].

Path-based DoS Attack (PDoS): In this type of DoS attack, the attacker overpowers sensor nodes a long distance away by flooding a multihop end-to-end communication path with either replayed packets or injected spurious packets [32]. Diminished system availability and exhaustion in batteries of nodes are impacts of this physical attack.

Node Outage: The attack is applied logically or physically to the network and it stops the functionality of network components. Node services such as reading, collecting and initiating operations are stopped because of this attack [31].

Eavesdropping: Wireless characteristics of RFID system make it possible that attacker sniffs out the confidential information such as password or any other data flowing from tag-to-reader or reader-to-tag making the system vulnerable [21] [33].

Various kinds of perception layer attacks are listed below with related risks on security mechanisms of IoT in Table 3.

3.2.2. Threats of Network Layer

Network layer which is known as the next-generation network are exposed to many kinds of threats. Related threats that come from this layer are listed below:

Selective Forwarding: In such attacks, malicious nodes do not forward some messages and selectively drop them, ensuring that they cannot propagate later on. The attacker who is responsible for suppression or modification of packets originating from a select few nodes can sometimes forward the remaining traffic not to reveal her wrongdoing. There are different types of selective forwarding attacks. In one type, the malicious node can selectively drop the packets coming from a particular node or a group of nodes. This situation poses a risk of DoS attack for that node or a group of nodes. Another type of selective forwarding attack is called Neglect and Greed. In this type of attack, the subverted node arbitrarily skips routing some messages [34].

Table 3. Attacks and related risks on security mechanisms of IoT.

Attacks	Risks
Spoofing	Authenticity, integrity and confidentiality.
Signal/Radio Jamming	Availability and integrity.
Device-tampering/Node-capturing	Availability, integrity, authenticity and confidentiality.
Path-based DoSAttack	Availability and authenticity.
Node Outage	Availability and authenticity.
Eavesdropping	Confidentiality.

Sybil Attack: It is clarified as a malicious device illegitimately taking on multiple identities [35]. Sybil attack [36] , an attacker can "be in more than one place at once" as a single malicious node. It presents multiple identities to other nodes in the network reducing the effectiveness of fault tolerant schemes.

Sinkhole Attack (Blackhole): The sink hole is defined in [37] by intense resource contention among neighboring nodes of the malicious node for the limited bandwidth and channel access. It results in congestion and can accelerate the energy consumption of the nodes involved. With sink holes forming in a sensor network, it is vulnerable to several other types of denial of service attacks [38] [37] [39].

Wormhole: This form of DoS attack induces relocation of bits of data from its original position in the network. This relocation of data packet is carried out through tunneling of bits of data over a link of low latency [39].

Man-in-the-Middle Attack: This attack is described as a form of eavesdropping in which the unauthorized party can monitor or control all the private communications between the two parties hideously. The unauthorized party can even fake the identity of the victim and communicate normally to gain more information [21].

Hello-flood Attack: High traffic in channels is the main disrupting effect of this attack which congests the channel with an unusually high number of useless messages. Basically, a single malicious node sends a useless message which is then replied by the attacker to create a high traffic [30].

Acknowledgement Flooding: Routing algorithms in sensor-based systems need acknowledgements from time to time. In this type of DoS attack, a malicious node sends false information to destined neighboring nodes by the help of these acknowledgements [30].

3.2.3. Threats of Support Layer

Target of threats in support layer are mainly data storage technologies. These threats are discussed below:

Tampering with Data: The attack appears when a person from the inside tampers the data for personal benefits or commercial benefits of any 3rd party companies. The data can be extracted and modified easily on purpose from the inside [17].

DoS Attack: Similar effects of DoS attacks that are discussed in previous layers are seen in this layer, too; e.g. it shuts down the system which results in unavailability of the services.

Unauthorized Access: The attacker can easily infiltrate into the system and damage the system by preventing the access to the related services of IoT or deleting sensitive data. Hence, an unauthorized access can be fatal for the system [21].

3.2.4. Threats of Application Layer

The personalized services based on the needs of the users are included in the application layer; e.g. the interface that user can control devices in IoT [4]. Threats in this layer mainly target these services as mentioned below:

Sniffer/Loggers: Attackers can introduce sniffer/logger programs into the system that take important information from the network traffic. The main goal of the sniffer is to steal passwords, files (FTP files, E-mail files), and E-mail text. Many protocols are prone to sniffing [40].

Injection: Attackers may enter code directly into the application that is executed on the server. This is a very common attack, easy to exploit, and can cause some bad results such as data loss, data corruption and lack of accountability [41].

Session Hijacking: This attack reveals personal identities by exploiting security flaws in authentication and session management. This type of attack is very common and effects of attack are really important. With the identity of someone else, attacker can do anything the real user can do [41].

DDoS (Distributed Denial of Service): Its working principle is the same as the traditional Denial of Service attack. However, it is executed by multiple attackers at the same time [21] [30] [41].

Social Engineering: A serious threat for application layer where attackers can obtain information from users via chats, knowing each other etc. [4].

3.3. Recommended Solutions and Research Directions with Respect to Security in IoT

Recommended solutions and research directions with respect to security in IoT are examined in three categories: security of perception layer, security of network layer and security of support and application layers. The examination is summarized in Figure 3.

3.3.1. Security of Perception Layer

Taking security measures for the perception layer dates back times before IoT.

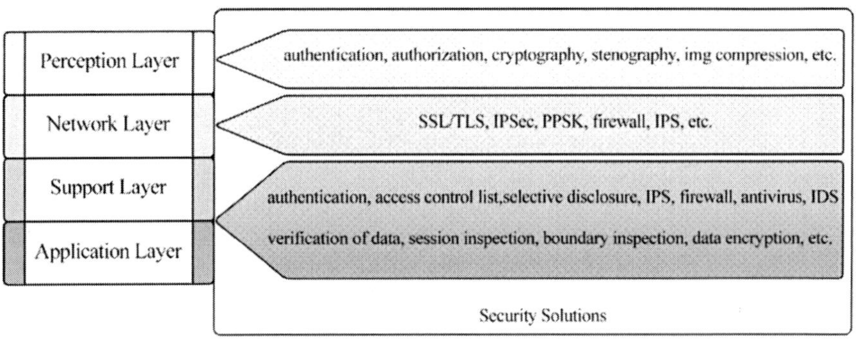

Figure 3. Security solutions on layers of IoT.

Table 4. Cryptograhic algorithms.

Type	Algorithm	Purpose
Symmetric Encryption	Advanced encryption standard (AES)	Confidentiality
Asymmetric Encryption	Rivestshamir Adelman (RSA)/Elliptic curve cryptography (ECC)	Digital Signatures, Key Transport
Asymmetric Key Agreement	Diffie-hellman (DH)	Key Agreement
Hashing	SHA-1/SHA-256	Integrality

Equipments such as RFID readers, sensors, gateways, GPS and other devices require to be secured efficiently. OWASP has identified poor physical security in the top 10 IoT vulnerabilities [42]. The first step is to ensure that only authorized people can have access to sensitive data produced by physical objects, that's why a physical identity and access management policy need to be defined [43]. Authentication and authorization requirements from IoT are satisfied in this similar fashion.

Data collection is an important issue for this layer. In [44] , this issue is examined in two separate headings. In one heading which is presented as multimedia data collection, there are some recommended security techniques such as multimedia compression, stenography, water marking, encryption, time session and intellectual property. The second heading is image data collection, to use security in images as image compression, and CRC.

Cryptographic processing is one of the main tasks in security mechanisms for sensor data on IoT. These operations that are often used in order to guarantee privacy of data include encryption and decryption, key and hash generation, and sign and verify hashes. Table 4 gives some frequently used cryptographic algorithms and their use purposes in Internet security protocols based on studies [18] and [45].

Wander et al. [46] compare two asymmetric algorithms in Table 4, RSA and Elliptic Curve Cryptography (ECC) [47] , on sensor nodes and prove that ECC is more efficient than RSA, and asymmetric cryptography is applicable for resource-constrained hardware. Hence, researchers focus on reducing complexity of asymmetric cryptographic algorithms and key distribution protocols. Wood et al. [48] and Hu *et al.* [49] present hardware cryptographic solutions for smart objects in their study. Key distribution mechanism of Liu *et al.* [50] and Chung *et al.* [51] are demonstrated in order to use in lightweight communication channels in resource-constrained networks. These improvements make cryptographic mechanisms in the context of WSNs more applicable. However, unique customized solutions are created and still there has been no standardized way of implementing services [52].

Risk Assessment is a fundamental of IoT security which determines the extent of the potential threat and the risk associated with an IoT system. The output of this process helps to identify appropriate controls for reducing or eliminating risk during the risk mitigation process. A number of organizations have developed guidelines for conducting risk assessment such as the U.S. National Institute of Standards and Technology (NIST) [53] [54] ; the International Standards Organization (ISO) and the International Electrotechnical Commission (IEC) [55].

3.3.2. Security of Network Layer

The security of network layer can be examined in two main sub-layers; wireless and wired. One of the initial actions in wireless security sub-layer is the development of protocols for authentication and key management

[56]. For example; SSL/TLS is developed to encrypt the link in the transport layer, and IP security protocol (IPSec) is developed to keep the network layer secure. They can provide authenticity, confidentiality and integrity in the each layer [18]. Also, using PPSK (Private Pre-Shared Key) for each sensor or device connected to the network provides another security measure for IoT system. By providing different unique keys, the access domain for each type of device can be defined easily. Moreover, disabling guest and default passwords in network devices such as routers and gateways should be done immediately upon installing a new network device. This includes strong password policies, password management and periodic change of passwords [43].

The wired security sub-layer is concerned with devices, which communicate with other devices on the IoT system using wired channels. Common security techniques are applied in wired type networks are firewalls and Intrusion Prevention System (IPS). If the network has firewall or IPS, it can inspect network packets deeply that are destined towards the destination. However, existing IoT has no ability in terms of packet inspection and packet filtering. There is an ongoing research on this issue where security researchers try to design a low resource-hungry firewall for IoT to provide the ability of packet inspection [4].

All information about the security of network layer that is discussed above is summarized in Table 5.

3.3.3. Security of Support and Application Layers

Devipriya *et al.* [44] claims that this topic contains two sub-layers. In one sub- layer, there are local applications and related middleware functions which should be secured with various techniques. For example, intelligent transportation systems can use encryption techniques, while smart home/smart metering systems uses steganography techniques. The second sublayer corresponds to national applications and their security systems, ensuring that sent and received data are secure. Therefore, various security techniques are applied in these systems based on the scope of each system such as authentication, authorization, access control list, selective disclosure, intrusion detection, firewall, and antivirus.

According to Farooq *et al.* [21] , authentication mechanism preventing the access of intruders is applied in support and application layer by integrated identity identifications. This identity security mechanism is exactly similar to that in the network layer. The difference is that these layers focus on authentications by some certain cooperating services which means users can even choose the associated information to be shared with the services.

Table 5. Security of Network Layer on IoT.

Sub-layers	Security Techniques	Purposes
Wireless	TLS/SSL	Authenticity, Confidentiality, Integrity
	IPSec	
	PPSK	
Wired	Firewall	
	IPS	

Data security is another issue on these layers [57]. There are various precautions taken by security system on IoT such as:

- Safe programming and anti-virus software testing against malicious code injections and service loopholes,
- Verification of data and developing temporary cache against malicious operations,
- Session inspection mechanism to stop attacks of hijacking and redo sessions,
- Boundary inspection, data encryption mechanism and resource access control to avoid leakage of privacy.

The IoT is vulnerable to a number of attacks that are mentioned in previous sections to disrupt the whole system, thus intrusion detection is a crucial concept for IoT deployments in real world such as industrial automation, building automation, smart metering and smart grids [58]. Attacks against a system are detected during analysis of actions in the system by a security mechanism broadly termed as Intrusion Detection System (IDS). When an attack is detected, IDS may log information about it and/or report an alarm. There are different existing intrusion detection techniques such as anomaly detection [59] , data mining techniques [60] [61] , statistical analysis [62] etc.

4. CONCLUSIONS

IoT is an emerging technology that has attracted a considerable number of researchers from all around the world. There have been major contributions making this technology adapted into our daily life. However, there are lots of key issues addressing security concerns of IoT and they need more research effort to be solved.

In this paper, security concepts of IoT were reviewed substantially. Requirements and challenges of security measures in IoT were analyzed and collected under different headings. All kinds of security threats that may be critical in the development and implementation of IoT in different fields have been discussed and classified with respect to layers of IoT architecture: perception layer, network layer, support layer and application layer. Finally, the recent solutions have been provided for these threats and research directions with respect to security concerns have been introduced such as cryptographic mechanisms and firewalls.

REFERENCES

1. Madakam, S., Ramaswamy, R. and Tripathi, S. (2015) Internet of Things (IoT): A Literature Review. Journal of Computer and Communications, 3, 164-173. https://doi.org/10.4236/jcc.2015.35021
2. Tyagi, S., Darwish, A. and Khan, M.Y. (2014) Managing Computing Infrastructure for IoT Data. Advances in Internet of Things, 4, 29-35. https://doi.org/10.4236/ait.2014.43005
3. Gartner Inc. Press Release (2014) http://www.gartner.com/newsroom/id/2905717
4. Gupta, J., Nayyar, A. and Gupta, P. (2015) Security and Privacy Issues in Internet of Things (IoT). International Journal of Research in Computer Science, 2, 18-22.
5. Yehia, L., Khedr, A. and Darwish, A. (2015) Hybrid Security Techniques for Internet of Things Healthcare Applications. Advances in Internet of Things, 5, 21-25. https://doi.org/10.4236/ait.2015.53004
6. Arseni, S.C., Halunga, S., Fratu, O., Vulpe, A. and Suciu, G. (2015) Analysis of the Security Solutions Implemented in Current Internet of Things Platforms. IEEE Grid, Cloud & High Performance Computing in Science, Romania, 28-30 October 2015, 1-4. https://doi.org/10.1109/ROLCG.2015.7367416
7. Chandrakanth, S., Venkatesh, K. and Mahesh, J.U. (2014) Internet of Things. International Journal of Innovations & Advancement in Computer Science, 3, 8.
8. Shawish, A. and Salama, M. (2014) Cloud Computing: Paradigms. Inter-Cooperative Collective Intelligence: Techniques and Applications, Studies in Computational Intelligence 495, Springer-Verlag, Berlin, Heidelberg. https://doi.org/10.1007/978-3-642-35016-0_2
9. Briseno, M.V., Hirata, F.I., Lopez, J.D.S., Garcia, E.J., Cota, J.N. and Hipolito, J.I.N. (2012) Using RFID/NFC and QR-Code in Mobile Phones to Link the Physical and the Digital World. InTech. https://doi.org/10.5772/37447
10. Li, B.A. and Yu, J.J. (2011) Research and Application on the Smart Home Based on Component Technologies and Internet of Things. Procedia Engineering, 15, 2087-2092. https://doi.org/10.1016/j.proeng.2011.08.390
11. Ashton, K. (2009) That "Internet of Things" Thing. RFID Journal. http://www.rfidjournal.com/articles/pdf?4986
12. National Instruments (2016) What Is a Wireless Sensor Network? http:// www.ni.com/white-paper/7142/en/
13. IEC Market Strategy Board (2014) Internet of Things: Wireless Sensor Networks. http://www.iec.ch/whitepaper/pdf/iecWP-internetofthings-LR-en.pdf
14. Wang, R., Wang, J. and Wang, N. (2015) Analysis of Key Technologies in the Internet of Things. 3rd International Conference on Material, Mechanical and Manufacturing Engineering, Guangzhou, 27-28 June 2015, 938-941. https://doi.org/10.2991/ic3me-15.2015.180
15. An, J., Gui, X.L. and He, X. (2012) Study on the Architecture and Key Technologies for Internet of Things. Advances in Biomedical Engineering, 11, 329-335.

16. Huang, X., Craig, P., Lin, H. and Yan, Z. (2015) SecIoT: A Security Framework for the Internet of Things. Security and Communication Networks, 9, 3083-3094. https://doi.org/10.1002/sec.1259
17. Cloud Security Alliance (2015) Security Guidance for Early Adopters of the Internet of Things (IoT). https://downloads.cloudsecurityalliance.org/ whitepapers/Security_Guidance_for _Early_Adopters_of_the_Internet_of_Things.pdf
18. Suo, H., Wan, J., Zou, C. and Liu, J. (2012) Security in the Internet of Things: A Review. IEEE International Conference on Computer Science and Electronics Engineering, Hangzhou, 23-25 March 2012, 648-651. https://doi.org/10.1109/ICCSEE.2012.373
19. Nguyen, K.T., Laurent, M. and Oualha, N. (2015) Survey on Secure Communication Protocols for the Internet of Things. Ad Hoc Networks, 32, 17-31. https://doi.org/10.1016/j.adhoc.2015.01.006
20. Yang, X., Li, Z., Geng, Z. and Zhang, H. (2012) A Multi-Layer Security Model for Internet of Things. Springer International Workshop on Internet of Things, Vol. 312, Changsha, 17-19 August 2012, 388-393. https://doi.org/10.1007/978-3-642-32427-7_54
21. Farooq, M.U., Waseem, M., Khairi, A. and Mazhar, S. (2015) A Critical Analysis on the Security Concerns of Internet of Things (IoT). International Journal of Computer Applications, 111, 1-6. https://doi.org/10.5120/19547-1280
22. Qian, X. and Zhang, J. (2010) Study on the Structure of "Internet of Things (IOT)" Business Operation Support Platform. IEEE International Conference on Communication Technology, Nanjing, 11-14 November 2010, 1068-1071. https://doi.org/10.1109/ICCT.2010.5688537
23. Weber, R.H. (2010) Internet of Things—New Security and Privacy Challenges. Computer Law and Security Review, 26, 23-30. https://doi.org/10.1016/j.clsr.2009.11.008
24. Chen, M., Wan, J.F. and Li, F. (2012) Machine-to-Machine Communications: Architectures, Standards and Applications. KSII Transactions on Internet and Information Systems, 6, 480-497.
25. Wind River Systems (2015) Security in the Internet of Things. http://www.windriver.com/whitepapers/security-in-the-internet-of-things/wr_security-in-the-internet-of-things.pdf
26. European Commission. IoT Privacy, Data Protection, Information Security. http://ec.europa.eu/information_society/newsroom/cf/dae/document.cfm?doc_id=1753
27. ITU-T. Y.2060: Overview of the Internet of Things. http://www.itu.int/rec/T-REC-Y.2060-201206-I
28. Mattern, F. and Floerkemeier, C. (2010) From the Internet of Computers to the Internet of Things. In: Sachs, K., Petrov, I. and Guerrero, P., Eds., From Active Data Management to Event-Based Systems and More, Springer, Berlin Heidelberg, 242-259. https://doi.org/10.1007/978-3-642-17226-7_15
29. Mitrokotsa, A., Rieback, M.R. and Tanenbaum, A.S. (2009) Classifying RFID Attacks and Defenses. Information Systems Frontiers, 12, 491-505. https://doi.org/10.1007/s10796-009-9210-z
30. Borgohain, T., Kumar, U. and Sanyal, S. (2015) Survey of Security and Privacy Issues of Internet of Things. International Journal of Advanced Networking Applications, 6, 2372-2378.
31. Anwar, R.W., Bakhtiari, M., Zainal, A., Hanan, A.A. and Qureshi, K.N. (2014) Security Issues and Attacks in Wireless Sensor Network. World Applied Sciences Journal, 30, 1224-1227.
32. Deng, J., Han, R. and Mishra, S. (2005) Defending against Path-Based DoS Attacks in Wireless Sensor Networks. ACM Workshop/Security of Ad Hoc and Sensor Networks, Alexandria, 7 November 2005, 89-96. https://doi.org/10.1145/1102219.1102235
33. Khoo, B. (2011) RFID as an Enabler of the Internet of Things: Issues of Security and Privacy. IEEE International Conferences on Internet of Things, and Cyber, Physical and Social Computing, Dalian, 19-22 October 2011, 709-712. https://doi.org/10. 1109/iThings/CPSCom.2011.83
34. Sharma, P., Saluja, M. and Saluja, K.K. (2012) A Review of Selective Forwarding Attacks in Wireless Sensor Networks. International Journal of Advanced Smart Sensor Network Systems, 2, 37. https://doi.org/10.5121/ijassn.2012.2304

35. Pooja, M. and Singh, Y. (2013) Security Issues and Sybil Attack in Wireless Sensor Networks. International Journal of P2P Network Trends and Technology, 3, 7-13.
36. Douceur, J.R. (2002) The Sybil Attack. Springer International Workshop on Peer-to-Peer Systems, Cambridge, 7-8 March 2002, 251-260. https://doi.org/10.1007/3-540-45748-8_24
37. Ahmed, N., Kanhere, S.S. and Jha, S. (2005) The Holes Problem in Wireless Sensor Network: A Survey. ACM SIGMOBILE Mobile Computing and Communications Review, 9, 4-18. https://doi.org/10.1145/1072989.1072992
38. Kalita, H.K. and Kar, A. (2009) Wireless Sensor Network Security Analysis. International Journal of Next-Generation Networks, 1, 1-10.
39. Karlof, C. and Wagner, D. (2003) Secure Routing in Wireless Sensor Networks: Attacks and Countermeasures. Ad Hoc Networks, 1, 293-315. https://doi.org/10.1109/snpa.2003.1203362
40. Kulshrestha, A. and Dubey, S.K. (2014) A Literature Review on Sniffing Attacks in Computer Network. International Journal of Advanced Engineering Research and Science, 1, 2.
41. Hermes Engineering. Security in Web Applications. http://www.hermes-ecs.com/en/page/59/documents
42. OWASP, Internet of Things Project. https://www.owasp.org/index.php/OWASP_Internet_of_Things_Top_Ten_Project
43. Zolanvari, M. and Jain, R. (2015) IoT Security: A Survey. http://www.cse. wustl.edu/~jain/cse570-15/ftp/iot_sec/index.html
44. Sujitha, R., Raghavan, N.V., Suganya, K.S. and Devipriya, A. (2014) A Novel Survey on Internet of Things, Security and Its Application. International Journal of Advanced Information and Communication Technology, 1, 8.
45. Polk, T. and Turner, S. (2011) Security Challenges for the Internet of Things. http://www.iab.org/wp-content/IAB-uploads/2011/03/Turner.pdf
46. Wander, A.S., Gura, N., Eberle, H., Gupta, V. and Shantz, S.C. (2005) Energy Analysis of Public-Key Cryptography for Wireless Sensor Networks. IEEE International Conference on Pervasive Computing and Communications, Kauai Island, 8-12 March 2005, 324-328. https://doi.org/10.1109/PERCOM.2005.18
47. Miller, S.D. and Venkatesan, R. (2009) Expander Graphs Based on GRH with an Application to Elliptic Curve Cryptography. Journal of Number Theory, 129, 1491-1504. https://doi.org/10.1016/j.jnt.2008.11.006
48. Wood, A. and Stankovic, J. (2006) AMSecure: Secure Link-Layer Communication in TinyOS for IEEE 802.15.4-Based Wireless Sensor Networks. ACM Conference on Networked Embedded Sensor Systems, Boulder, 31 October-3 November 2006, 395-396. https://doi.org/10.1145/1182807.1182873
49. Hu, W., Corke, P., Shih, W.C. and Overs, L. (2009) SecFleck: A Public Key Technology Platform for Wireless Sensor Networks. Springer European Conference on Wireless Sensor Networks, Cork, 11-13 February 2009, 296-311. https://doi.org/10.1007/978-3-642-00224-3_19
50. Liu, D., Ning, P. and Li, R. (2003) Establishing Pairwise Keys in Distributed Sensor Networks. ACM Conference on Computer and Communications Security, Washington DC, 27-30 October 2003, 52-61. https://doi.org/10.1145/948109.948119
51. Chung, A. and Roedig, U. (2008) DHB-KEY: An Efficient Key Distribution Scheme for Wireless Sensor Networks. IEEE International Workshop on Wireless and Sensor Networks Security, Atlanta, 29 September-2 October 2008, 840-846. https://doi.org/10.1109/MAHSS.2008.4660127
52. Raza, S. (2013) Lightweight Security Solutions for the Internet of Things. No. 139, Malardalen University Press Dissertations. http://www.diva-portal.org/smash/get/diva2:619066/FULLTEXT02.pdf
53. The U.S. National Institute of Standards and Technology (NIST) (2012) Guide for Conducting Risk Assessments. http://nvlpubs.nist.gov/nistpubs/Legacy/ SP/nistspecialpublication800-30r1.pdf

54. The U.S. National Institute of Standards and Technology (NIST) (2002) Risk Management Guide for Information Technology Systems. http://csrc.nist.gov/publications/ nistpubs/ 800-30/sp800-30.pdf
55. The International Standards Organization (ISO) (2009) The International Electrotechnical Commission (IEC). ISO/IEC 31010:2009 Risk management—Risk Assessment Techniques. http://www.iso.org/iso/catalogue_detail?csnumber=51073
56. Jara, A.J., Ladid, L. and Skarmeta, A. (2013) The Internet of Everything through IPv6: An Analysis of Challenges, Solutions and Opportunities. Journal of Wireless Mobile Networks, Ubiquitous Computing, and Dependable Applications, 4, 97-118.
57. Zhang, W. and Baosheng, Q. (2013) Security Architecture of the Internet of Things Oriented to Perceptual Layer. International Journal on Computer, Consumer and Control, 2, 2.
58. Raza, S., Wallgren, L. and Voigt, T. (2013) SVELTE: Real-Time Intrusion Detection in the Internet of Things. Ad Hoc Networks, 11, 2661-2674. https://doi.org/10.1016/ j.adhoc.2013.04.014
59. Verwoerd, T. and Hunt, R. (2002) Intrusion Detection Techniques and Approaches. Computer Communications, 25, 1356-1365. https://doi.org/10.1016/S0140-3664(02)00037-3
60. Patel, J. and Panchal, K. (2015) Effective Intrusion Detection System Using Data Mining Technique. International Journal of Emerging Technologies and Innovative Research, 2, 6.
61. Nguyen, H.A. and Choi, D. (2008) Application of Data Mining to Network Intrusion Detection: Classifier Selection Model. Springer Asia-Pacific Symposium on Network Operations and Management: Challenges for Next Generation Network Operations and Service Management, Beijing, 22-24 October 2008, 399-408. https://doi.org/ 10.1007/978-3-540-88623-5_41
62. Waskita, A.A., Suhartanto, H., Persadha, P.D. and Handoko, L.T. (2013) A Simple Statistical Analysis Approach for Intrusion Detection System. IEEE Conference on Systems, Process & Control, Kuala Lumpur, 13-15 December 2013, 193-197. https://doi.org/ 10.1109/SPC.2013.6735130

CHAPTER 11

A Comparison of Malware Detection Techniques Based on Hidden Markov Model

Saja Alqurashi, Omar Batarfi

Information Technology Department, King Abdul Aziz University, Jeddah, Saudi Arabia

ABSTRACT

Malware is a software which is designed with an intent to damage a network or computer resources. Today, the emergence of malware is on boom letting the researchers develop novel techniques to protect computers and networks. The three major techniques used for malware detection are heuristic, signature-based, and behavior based. Among these, the most prevalent is the heuristic based malware detection. Hidden Markov Model is the most efficient technique for malware detection. In this paper, we present the Hidden Markov Model as a cutting edge malware detection tool and a comprehensive review of different studies that employ HMM as a detection tool.

Keywords: Malware, HMM, Detection Tool, Obfuscation Techniques, Metamorphic

1. INTRODUCTION

Malware is a software which is developed for malicious intent [1]. Malware can steal sensitive data from a computer or it can infect files one after the other, and spreads the infection throughout the computer. Malware needs to be caught and removed from the infected computer promptly to avoid the leakage of sensitive data or any other malicious activity in the computer. Malwares can be classified into viruses, worms, Trojans, spywares, adwares, Rootkits, etc. [2].

To escape detection tools, malware developers evolve new techniques [3] [4]. They write malware in a fashion that it changes its appearance and alters its code on each infection—thus changes its appearance on each infection. Therefore, the signature-based detection schemes cannot detect them. The various techniques employed by malware developers are discussed below.

2. OBFUSCATION TECHNIQUES

Obfuscation techniques that change the syntax of program without change the semantic that make the malicious code more difficult to be analyzed and understand while preserving its semantics and functionality [5]. Obfuscation can be achieved by register exchange where registers and variables within the file are switched but the code remains the same; instruction swap, which substitutes instructions with equivalent instructions; instruction permutation; transposition that reorders the independent instructions; dead code insertion where "do nothing" instructions are inserted in the code [6].

2.1. Code Encryption

Refers to hiding the malicious code. Encrypted malware comprises of decryption/encryption engine, decryption key and encrypted malicious code [2]. Encrypted malwares can be classified.

2.2. Oligomorphic

The malware developers encrypt the code in a manner that it can change its decryptors lightly [2]. However, this malware has some limitations and can be detected by signature-based detection tools [7].

2.3. Polymorphic

The polymorphic malware encrypts itself with a different encryption algorithm/key in every infection. It can use a large number of encryption algorithms/keys and thus makes its detection very difficult and time consuming [3].

2.4. Metamorphic

The metamorphic malware is capable of changing itself to a completely new instance that does not have anything common to its original [2]. This behavior makes it the most complicated malware to detect.

3. MALWARE DETECTION TECHNIQUES

Malwares are worldwide epidemic and malware detection techniques (MDTs) serve as first line of defense against them. The effectiveness of a malware detection tool is based on the techniques it uses. Malware detection techniques can be primarily divided into the following three classes.

3.1. Signature-Based Techniques

Signature-based detection is widely used to detect known malware. Although it is very effective, but becomes ineffective if there is even a very small change in the code, which in turn changes its signature. Furthermore, this scheme requires the signature database to be updated on regular basis to detect new malware [6].

3.2. Behavior-Based Techniques

These techniques constantly observe program behavior to determine whether it is harmful or not. Thus, these techniques can also detect unknown malware. However, the effectiveness of these techniques is not yet proven. The experiments show that these techniques have high false positive ratio [3]. Moreover, these techniques take more time in detection process.

3.3. Heuristic Techniques

These techniques mainly use machine learning and data mining methods to identify the behavior of the running program. The major methods that have been used so far include Naive Bayesian, Neural Network and Hidden Markov Model [1] [3] [4] [8].

In recent work [1] [3] [4] [9] , Hidden Markov Model (HMM) has been shown as an efficient machine learning model to detect malware. HMM is based on statistical analysis of different states of a code, where each state has an associated probability of transition to other states.

HMM is a process modeling technique where each state of the process is defined in terms of its input data and its corresponding probability of occurrence. HMM is initially trained for different states of a malicious code along with its statistical properties. Based on this learning, HMM can detect, with high probability, the malicious codes of the same family. Thus, the more the training of HMM with different variants, the higher the chances of detection.

The following section gives us more details how HMM work.

4. HIDDEN MARKOV MODEL

4.1. Hidden Markov Model Overview

Hidden Markov models (HMMs) are generally used for statistical pattern analysis. Also can be used in speech recognition [10] , malicious code detection [11] and biological sequence analysis [12].

Hidden Markov model is a statistical model that has states and known probabilities of the state transitions is called a Markov model [13]. In such a Markov model, the states are visible to the observer. But a hidden Markov model (HMM) has states that are not directly observable [10]. HMM is a machine learning technique. HMM acts as a state machine. Every state is associated with a probability distribution for observing a set of observation symbols. The transition between the states has fixed probabilities. We train an HMM using the observation sequences to represent a set of data [13]. We can match an observation sequence against a trained HMM to determine the probability of seeing such a sequence. If the probability is high, the observation sequence is similar to the training sequences. HMMs are used in protein modeling, also can be used for software piracy detection [14]. As mentioned in [13] , the notations used in the hidden Markov models as following (Figure 1):

T = length of the observation sequence

N = number of states in the model

M = number of distinct observation symbols

Q = distinct states of the Markov Model

V = set of possible observations

A = state transition probability matrix

B = observation probability matrix

π = initial state distribution

O = observation sequence

A hidden Markov model is defined by the matrices A, B and π. An HMM is denoted as ⍰⍰⍰⍰⍰⍰⍰⍰⍰⍰⍰⍰⍰π⍰⍰.

The following three problems can be solved efficiently using HMM algorithms:

Problem 1: Given a model ⍰⍰⍰⍰⍰⍰⍰⍰⍰⍰⍰⍰⍰π⍰⍰ and an observation sequence O, we need to find $P(O|\lambda)$. That is, an observation sequence that can be scored to see how well it fits a given model.

Problem 2: Given a model ⍰⍰⍰⍰⍰⍰⍰⍰⍰⍰⍰⍰⍰π⍰⍰ and an observation sequence O, we can determine an optimal state sequence for the Markov model. That is, the most likely hidden state sequence can be uncovered.

Problem 3: Given O, N, M, we can find a model λ that maximizes probability of O. This is the training of a model in order to best fit an observation sequence.

These three problems can be efficiently solved by the following three algorithms:

- The Forward algorithm
- The Backward algorithm
- The Baum-Welch re-estimation algorithm

The forward-backward algorithm is for calculating the probability of being in a state qi at time t given an observation sequence O [13]. The forward algorithm, or α pass, determines $P(O|\lambda)$ The algorithm can be stated as follows.

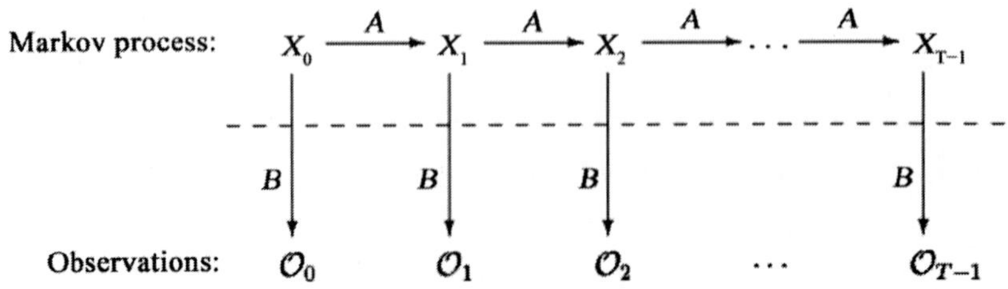

Figure 1. Represents a generic view of a hidden Markov model [13].

1) For t = 0, 1,..., T-1 and i = 0,1,..., N-1

2) ⍰$_i(i) = P(O_0, O_1,..., O_t, x_t = q_i|$⍰$)$

The probability of the partial observation sequence up to time t is ⍰$_i(i)$. Using the forward algorithm, $P(O|\lambda)$ can be computed as follows:

1) Let ⍰$_0(i)$ = ⍰$_1 b_i(O_0)$, for i = 0,1,..., N-1

2) For t = 1,2,...,T-1 and i = 0,1,..., N-1 compute

$$\alpha_t(i) = \sum_{j=1}^{n-1} \alpha_{t-1}(j) a_{ij} b_i(O_t)$$

3) Then $P(O|\lambda) = \sum_{j=0}^{n-1} \alpha_{t-1}(i)$

The backward algorithm helps to find a most likely optimal state sequence. This algorithm can be stated as follows:

1) For t = 1,2,...,T-1 and i = 0,1,..., N-1 define

2) ⍰$(i) = P(O_{t+1}, O_{t+2},..., O_{T-1}, x_t = q_i,$ ⍰$)$

Then ⍰$_t(i)$ can be calculated in following steps:

3) Let ⍰$_{T-1}(i)$ = 1, for i = 0,1,..., N-1

4) For t = T-2, T-3,..., 0 and i = 0,1,..., N-1, compute

$$\beta_t(i) = \sum_{j=1}^{n-1} a_{ij} b_j(O_{t+1}) \beta_{t+1}(j)$$

For t = 0,1,..., T-2 and i = 0,1,..., N-1 define

$$\gamma_t(i) = P(x_t = q_i | O, X)$$

The relevant probability up to time t is given by:

$$\gamma_t(i) = \frac{\alpha_t(i)\beta_t(i)}{P(O \mid X)}$$

The most likely state at any time t is the state for which □$_t$ (*i*) is maximum. The Baum-Welch algorithm helps in iteratively re-estimating the parameters *A*, *B*, *π* [13].

It provides efficient way to best fit the observations. The number of states N and number of unique observation symbols M are constant. However, other parameters like A, B and π are changeable with row stochastic condition. This process of re-estimating the model is explained as follows:

1) Initialize □□□□□ *A*, *B*, *π*□□ with an appropriate guess or random values. For example

$$\pi = 1/N, A_{ij} = 1/N, B_{ij} = 1/M.$$

2) Compute □$_t$ (*i*), □$_t$ (*i*), □$_t$ (*i*) and □$_t$ (*i*, *j*). where □$_t$ (*i*, *j*) is a digamma. The digammas can be defined as:

$$\gamma_t(i) = \alpha_t a_{ij} b_j \frac{O_{t+1}\beta_{t+1}(j)}{P(O \mid \lambda)}$$

□$_t$ (*i*) and □$_t$ (*i*, *j*) are related by:

$$\gamma_t(i) = (x+a)^n = \sum_{j=0}^{n-1} \gamma_t(i,j)$$

3) Re-estimate model parameters as: For *i* = 0,1,..., *N*-1 let

$$\pi_i = \gamma_0(i)$$

For *i* = 0,1,..., *N*-1 and *j* = 0,1,..., *N*-1, compute:

$$a_{ij} = \sum_{t=0}^{T-2} \gamma_t(i,j) \bigg/ \sum_{t=0}^{T-2} \gamma_t(i)$$

For *j* = 0,1,..., *N*-1 and *k* = 0,1,..., *N*-1, compute:

$$b_j(k) = \sum_{\substack{t \in \{0,1,\cdots,T-2\} \\ O_t = k}} \gamma_t(j) \Big/ \sum_{t=0}^{T-2} \gamma_t(i)$$

4) If $P(O|\lambda)$ increases go to Step 3.

Considering the potential and effectiveness of HMM-based MDTs, we have studied their strengths and weaknesses. In this paper, we examined 10 HMM-based MDTs and compared them to facilitate their selection for designing and developing secure systems. In addition, we also present a comprehensive literature review of MDT.

4.2. HMM as Malware Detection Tool

4.2.1. Traditional HMM Detector

Wong and Stamp in [3] [4] proposed a detection tool based on HMM to detect metamorphic virus. In their work, the authors compared their tool with commercial anti-virus tools for the morphed viruses generated by four virus engines: Next Generation Virus Creation Kit (NGVCK), Second Generation virus generator (G2), Virus Creation Lab for Win32 (VCL32), and Mass Code Generator (MCGEN). The commercial anti-virus could not detect morphed virus generated by NGVCK, whereas HMM based detector not only classified each virus to a particular family but showed a detection rate of 97% with only 3% false positive detections [3] [4]. Figure 2 show the HMM score used to classify the family virus, non-family virus and normal file.

The authors in [6] developed a code obfuscation engine that creates metamorphic viruses, which cannot be detected by any signature based technique, and validate detection based on HMM. The authors created 120 different variants of seed viruses. The code morphing engine randomly shuffles the virus assembly code by dividing it into different blocks and also inserts some blocks of dead code in the original code. These metamorphic viruses were scanned using commercial anti-virus (McAfee), which failed to detect any of these viruses. Then, these metamorphic viruses were tested using the proposed HMM detector. For all of the viruses, the score significantly varied from that for normal files. Thus, the HMM-based detector identified viruses from their similarity score only [6].

Another work in [15] developed metamorphic engine to produce highly diverse morphed copies of base viruses. The code obfuscation techniques used to develop engine are dead code insertion, equivalent instruction substitute and transposition. These metamorphic viruses were tested against a commercial anti-virus and HMM detector. The results showed that

HMM detector is effective to identify metamorphic viruses with high accuracy [15].

Authors in [8] proposed a code emulator designed to detect dead code in metamorphic virus. This emulator enhanced the effectiveness of HMM detector. The following graph shows us the architecture of the Code Emulator Process Flow. This emulator has capability to emulate all important CPU registers and can filter out changes in the instructions/subroutines caused by code obfuscation. The proposed emulator effectively identified 15%, 25% and 35% morphed viruses [8].

Shabana et al. [14] used HMM to detect software piracy (Figure 3). In their work, the authors [14] used a metamorphic generator to create morphed copies of a basic code. The authors extracted opcode sequences from these copies and trained HMM on these sequences. Based on this learning, HMM computed similarity score of the suspicious program to the basiccode. The higher the similarity score, the more likely it is that the suspicious program is an altered version of the basiccode, and vice versa. This approach proved to be highly effective for detecting morphed viruses.

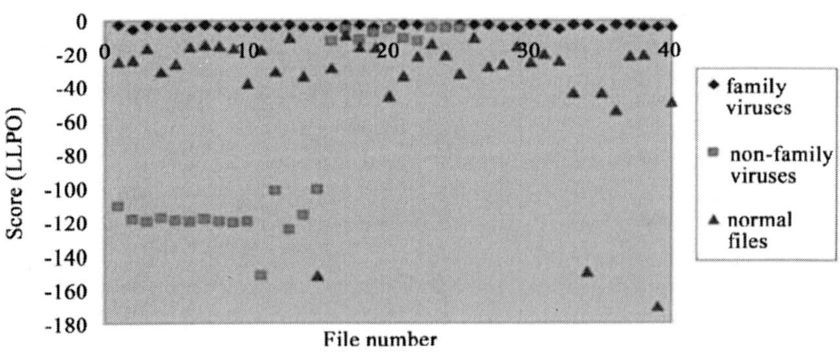

Figure 2. HMM score (LLPO).

4.2.2. Dueling HMM Detector

As mentioned in [3] [4] , HMM detector is effective for detecting metamorphic viruses. The work in [16] explored HMM in more depth. The authors built models for different compilers, extracted salient features of those models and used them in their proposed model to detect metamorphic viruses. In its classical implementation, HMM has been used to mark a file as infected if its virus code similarity exceeds a given threshold [4] [5]. However, authors' proposed approach marks the suspect file as a virus only if the HMM estimates a high probability by comparing the suspect file with several developed HMMs. This approach proved to be highly effective in detecting the malware that even used advanced metamorphic techniques. On the other hand, this approach is deficient in balancing false negative and false positive results. In addition, this approach suffers from high performance overheads as compared with the work in [4] and [5]. To overcome this problem of high overheads, the work in [13] brings forth a hybrid approach of dueling HMM and traditional HMM.

Thunga and Neelisetti [17] proposed an intelligent classification approach based on HMM to identify viruses of metamorphic family. In the proposed approach, the authors train multiple HMMs, one for each virus family. They represent "n" opcodes sequences in an executable file as "n-gram". The selection of n-gram affects the overall accuracy of the proposed approach. The n-gram sequence in the metamorphic virus is analyzed by comparing with the trained HMMs one by one using a "log-likelihood similarity measure". A virus is considered to be a part of the family for which the "log-likelihood similarity measure" is the highest. The authors observed 90% accuracy for each family of viruses. The proposed method is easily scalable for a higher number of virus families. In addition, parallel implementation of the comparison phase makes the method very efficient [17] (Figure 4).

4.2.3. Hyper HMM Detector

Researchers are still working to enhance the HMM detector. The authors in [18] proposed to use genetic algorithm with HMM. In HMM based techniques Baum-Welch method is used for solving one of the three problems [15] , i.e. estimating the parameters of the corresponding HMM given an output sequence. In this work the authors used genetic algorithm to solve the problem. The Baum-Welch algorithm is linear in nature and suffers from the local optima problem. The selection of genetic algorithm over traditional Baum-Welch method lies in the non-linearity of genetic algorithm.

There are two reasons to choose genetic algorithm over Baum-Welch algorithm [18] :

- Genetic algorithm is a part of random and evolutionary algorithms and does not suffer from the local optima problem but Baum-Welch algorithm suffers from this problem.
- Genetic algorithm works on set of populations (comprising of numbers of chromosomes at time, while the Baum-Welch algorithm works on individuals, so the time required to train the model increases and set of opcodes remains shallow.

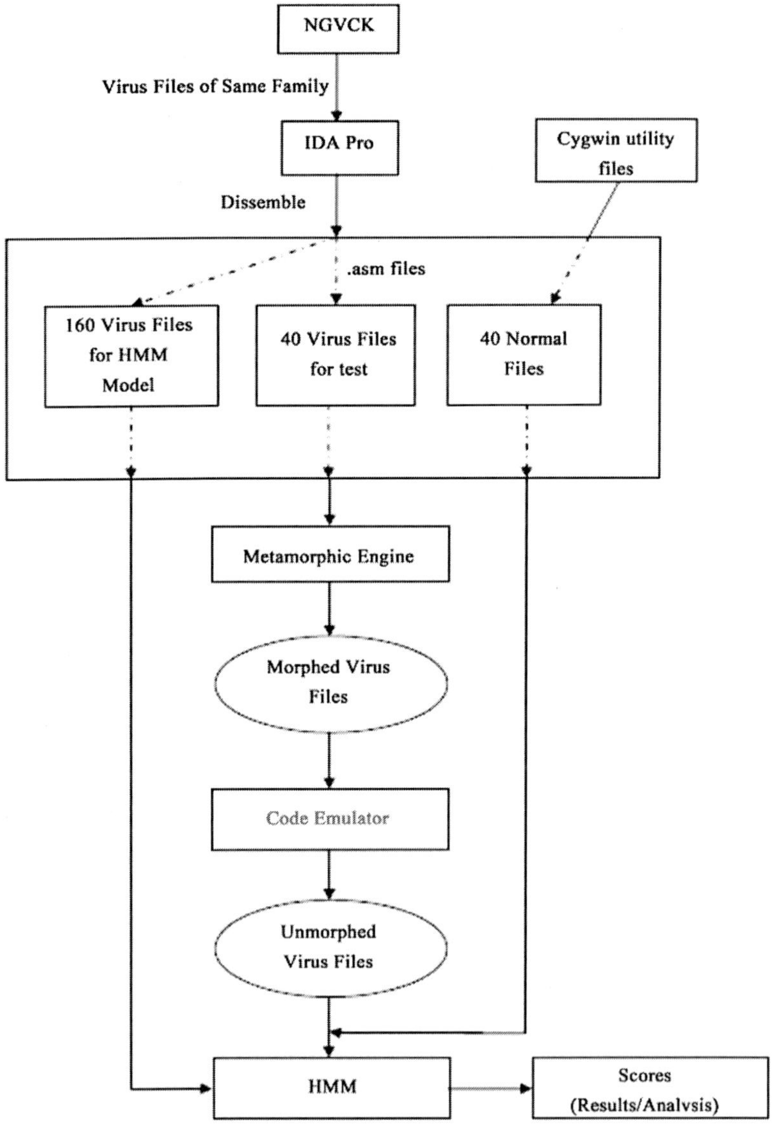

Figure 3. Code emulator process flow [8].

This proposed work [18] enhances HMM and results in higher accuracy in detecting metamorphic viruses.

Annachatre et al. [1] proposed new approach using HMM to detect metamorphic viruses based on classifier algorithm. In previous works like

[3] [4] and [16] , the authors used HMM alone to detect metamorphic viruses. In contrast to these studies, Annachatre et al. used a classifier algorithm to enhance the effectiveness of HMM detector. The authors trained HMMs on a collection of malware. Then these models were evaluated and based on the resulting score the malware samples were separated into clusters using k-means clustering algorithm as a classifier. This work showed the highest accuracy as compared to previous works such as [3] [4] and [16].

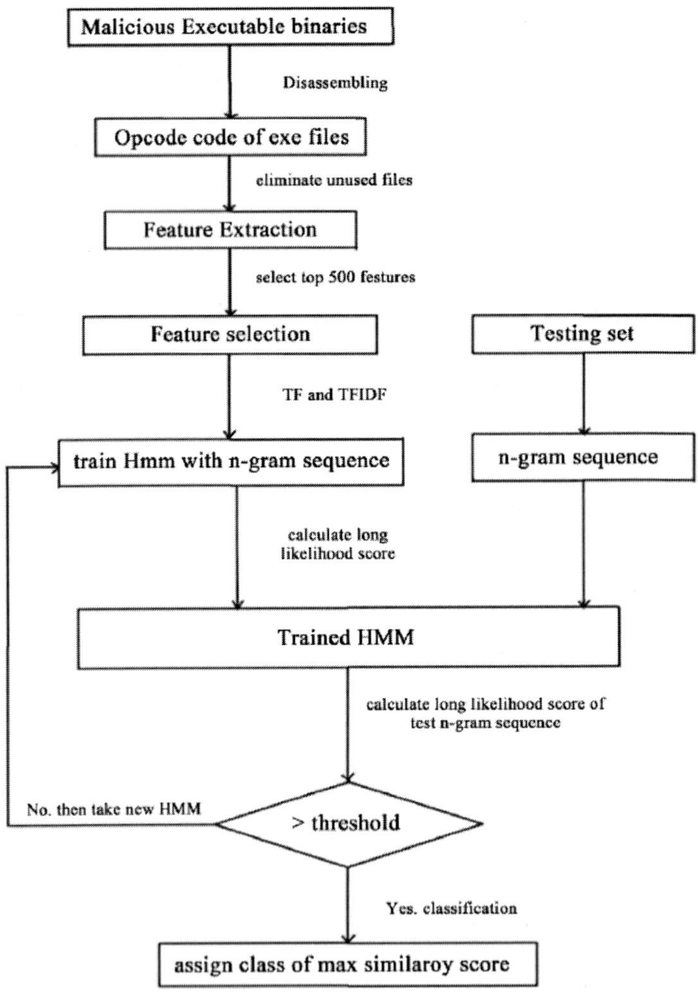

Figure 4. Work flow of the proposed HMM based classifier [17].

Payandeh et al. proposed a HMM based detection circle in [18] , where he characterized a virus family using three parameters: 1) the amount of virus similarities; 2) specifically-located character occurrence probability; 3) string occurrence probability. The proposed virus detection circle is developed on x, y coordinate axis, where x and y represent probabilities of the factors considered in the study. To evaluate the proposed approach, the authors used NGVCK kit to create morphed malware. Next, they calculated similarity scores of these viruses using Mishra's algorithm after making using Mishra method samples in each family are compared two by tow. The least, the most and the average quantity of samples comparison in each virus creation kit can be seen in the following Table 1. The proposed approach detected these malware with 91% accuracy. This work shows good result in malware detection but need to improve the detection speed.

Table 1. Min, Max and average kits similarities percentage.

	NGVCK	G2	VCL	PSMPC
Min	0.00000	0.12858	0.19909	0.00000
MAX	0.23099	1.00000	0.97642	0.96875
Average	0.04835	0.470112	0.650315	0.32857

5. COMPARISON

Article	Pros strengths	Cons/limitations
Analysis and Detection of Metamorphic Computer Viruses [3] [4]	Used HMM as detection and has ability to identify all malware.	Cannot classify malware to their family (HMM binary classification).
Code Obfuscation and Virus Detection [6]	HMM has ability to identify metamorphic viruses better than commercial AV.	-
Metamorphic Detection via Emulation [8]	Improved HMM detection using emulator to detect dead code in metamorphic malware.	-
Towards an Undetectable Computer Virus [15]	Proves how HMM detector is effective to identify metamorphic viruses with high accuracy.	Still HMM binary classification (classify malware to family and non-family).
Hidden Markov Models for Software Piracy Detection [14]	HMM detected piracy software with high accuracy.	Still HMM binary classification (classify malware to family and non-family).
Dueling Hidden Markov Models for Virus Analysis [16]	Achieved good result in detecting malware developed using advanced metamorphic techniques.	No balance between false positive and false negative. High performance overheads.
Identifying Metamorphic Virus Using n-grams and HMM [17]	Scalable for a number of HMMs (directly proportional to number of virus families).	-
Detecting Metamorphic Virus Using Hidden Markov Model and Genetic Algorithm [7]	Enhanced HMM using genetic algorithm to detect metamorphic viruses.	Still HMM binary classification (classify malware to family and nonfamily).
Hidden Markov Models for Malware Classification [1]	Improved malware detection by HMM using k-means clustering algorithm as a classifier.	Need to enhance the classifier.
Detecting Encrypted Metamorphic Viruses by Hidden Markov Models [18]	Characterized each family of malware in terms of three parameters: 1) string occurrence probability; 2) specifically-located character occurrence probability; 3) the amount of virus similarities. These parameters improved accuracy of malware detection using HMM.	The detection speed of was slower than traditional HMM. Also sample data is small to test the proposed solution.

6. RESEARCH DIRECTIONS

- To detect malware based on clustering algorithms such as K-means, decision Tree etc. based on learning models such as HMM and Neural Network.
- To study how different detection approaches performs against each obfuscation techniques like dead code technique.

7. CONCLUSION

Malware is any code that is developed for malicious intent. The malware has rapidly become a major security threat for computing community and is the basic reason for the most of the security problems on internet. Recent malware can easily deceive the signature-based detection approaches by altering their code while keeping its function intact. To solve this problem, some machine learning techniques such as, HMM and Neural Network are used. In current study, we have compared several HMM based malware detection approaches. From this survey, we conclude that HMM is an efficient model to detect malware and further studies may focus on how to improve the classification of malware based on HMM as malware detection tool.

REFERENCES

1. Annachhatre, C., Austin, T.H. and Stamp, M. (2015) Hidden Markov Models for Malware Classification. Journal in Computer Virology and Hacking Techniques, 11, 59-73. http://dx.doi.org/10.1007/s11416-014-0215-x
2. Bazrafshan, Z., Hashemi, H., Fard, S.M.H. and Hamzeh, A. (2013) A Survey on Heuristic Malware Detection Techniques. The 5th Conference on Information and Knowledge Technology (IKT 2013), Shiraz, 28-30 May 2013, 113-120. http://dx.doi.org/10.1109/ikt.2013.6620049
3. Wong, W. (2006) Analysis and Detection of Metamorphic Computer Viruses. MSc, San Jose State University.
4. Wong, W. and Stamp, M. (2006) Hunting for Metamorphic Engines. Journal in Computer Virology, 2, 211-229. http://dx.doi.org/10.1007/s11416-006-0028-7
5. Bayer, U., Moser, A., Kruegel, C. and Kirda, E. (2006) Dynamic Analysis of Malicious Code. Journal in Computer Virology, 2, 67-77. http://dx.doi.org/10.1007/s11416-006-0012-2
6. Venkatesan, A. (2008) Code Obfuscation and Virus Detection. MSc, San Jose State University.
7. Dastidar, S.G., Mandal, S. and Barbhuiya, F.A. (2012) Detecting Metamorphic Virus Using Hidden Markov Model and Genetic Algorithm. Proceedings of the International Conference on Soft Computing for Problem Solving (SocProS 2011). India, 20-22 December 2011.

8. Priyadarshi, S. (2011) Metamorphic Detection via Emulation Metamorphic Detection via Emulation. San Jose State University.
9. Austin, T.H., Filiol, E., Josse, S. and Stamp, M. (2013) Exploring Hidden Markov Models for Virus Analysis: A Semantic Approach. 46th Hawaii International Conference on System Sciences, Wailea, 7-10 January 2013, 5039-5048. http://dx.doi.org/10.1109/ hicss. 2013.217
10. Rabiner, L.R. (1989) A Tutorial on Hidden Markov Models and Selected Applications in Speech Recognition. Proc. IEEE, 77, 257-286. http://dx.doi.org/10.1109/5.18626
11. Annachhatre, C. (2013) Hidden Markov Models for Malware Classification. San Jose State University.
12. Krogh, A. (1998) An Introduction to Hidden Markov Models for Biological Sequences. Computational Methods in Molecular Biology, 32, 45-63. http://dx.doi.org/10. 1016/s0167-7306(08)60461-5
13. Stamp, M. (2004) A Revealing Introduction to Hidden Markov Models. Dep. Comput. Sci. San Jose State, 1-20.
14. Kazi, S. (2012) Hidden Markov Models for Software Piracy Detection. San Jose State University,
15. Desai, P. (2008) Towards an Undetectable Computer Virus. Intelligence, 1, 402-427.
16. Kalbhor, A., Austin, T.H., Filiol, E., Josse, S. and Stamp, M. (2014) Dueling Hidden Markov Models for Virus Analysis. Journal in Computer Virology and Hacking Techniques, 11, 103-118.
17. Thunga, S.P. and Neelisetti, R.K. (2016) Identifying Metamorphic Virus Using N-Grams and Hidden Markov Model. 2015 International Conference on Advances in Computing, Communications and Informatics (ICACCI), Kochi, 2015, 2016-2022.
18. Payandeh, A. (2014) Detecting Encrypted Metamorphic Viruses by Hidden Markov Models. 2014 11th International Conference on Fuzzy Systems and Knowledge Discovery (FSKD), Xiamen, 2014, 973-977.

CHAPTER 12

Batch Attribute-Based Encryption for Secure Clouds

Chen Yang[1], Yang Sun[2,†] and Qianhong Wu[2,†,*]

[1]*China Information Security Research Institute, No. 11 ShangDi Xinxi Road, Beijing 100085, China*

[2]*School of Electronics and Information Engineering, Beihang University, XueYuan Road No.37, Haidian District, Beijing 100191, China*

ABSTRACT

Cloud storage is widely used by organizations due to its advantage of allowing universal access with low cost. Attribute-based encryption (ABE) is a kind of public key encryption suitable for cloud storage. The secret key of each user and the ciphertext are associated with an access policy and an attribute set, respectively; in addition to holding a secret key, one can decrypt a ciphertext only if the associated attributes match the predetermined access policy, which allows one to enforce fine-grained access control on outsourced files. One issue in existing ABE schemes is that they are designed for the users of a single organization. When one wants to share the data with the users of different organizations, the owner needs to encrypt the messages to the receivers of one organization and then repeats this process for another organization. This situation is deteriorated with more and more mobile devices using cloud services, as the ABE encryption process is time consuming and may exhaust the power supplies of the mobile devices quickly. In this paper, we propose a batch attribute-based encryption (BABE) approach to address this problem in a provably-secure way. With our approach, the data owner can outsource data in batches to the users of different organizations simultaneously. The data owner is allowed to decide the receiving organizations and the attributes required for decryption. Theoretical and experimental analyses show that our approach is more efficient than traditional encryption implementations in computation and communication.

Keywords: data privacy; access control; cloud storage; batch attribute-based encryption

1. INTRODUCTION

In cloud computing, if a file owner would like to share his file with others, he just stores his data on a cloud server, then his friends/colleagues, including himself, can access the data by visiting the server from any place where there is an Internet connection. In this way, cloud storage makes it possible for people to exploit almost unlimited computation, storage space and information services anytime and anywhere without suffering from complicated local maintenance and management. Due to these advantages, cloud computing is becoming an indispensable part of organizations and individuals.

The security concern of the data owner is believed to be the main obstacle for wide adoption of cloud storage. Especially, the user who do not have access right may collude with the server for illegal access. Encryption is a standard way to protect data security. Public encryption is preferable in organization-oriented applications. In this scenario, one organization can have a cloud account associated with a public key, and anyone can securely upload files to this account by encrypting the files under the public key. Only the one who owes the corresponding secret key of the public key can decrypt the encrypted file, which prevents illegal access from the cloud server or other non-authorized ones. However, the traditional public key cryptosystems suffer from complicated key management in this scenario, since it is unknown who will be allowed to access a specific encrypted file when the system is set up or the file is encrypted. Attribute-based encryption (ABE) [1] is the up-to-date cryptographic concept to address this problem. In this case, the encryptor can specify the attributes required for decryption, and the access policy can be made for the secret key of each requestor. A requestor can decrypt a ciphertext only if the labeled attributes meet the access policy associated with the secret key of the requestor.

An issue in deploying ABE is that all known ABE encryption/decryption operations are time and resource consuming. Furthermore, the existing ABE schemes only allow encryption for the receivers of a single organization. Consider a scenario where the scientists from different universities jointly work on a project. In this case, if a scientist wants to share his or her research progress with the scientists of other universities, then he or she needs to encrypt the files to these organizations repetitively. In [2], an approach is proposed to speed up the decryption with the help of a semi-honest third party. However, to the best of our knowledge, no known work in the public literature has been done to speed up the ABE encryption in our motivating scenario. This situation inspires our work in this paper.

1.1. Our Contribution

In this paper, we investigate the acceleration of ABE encryption where one encrypts for the requestors of different organizations. Our contributions are summarized as follows.

We propose a batch attribute-based encryption (BABE) framework. In this framework, when the different ABE systems are set up, the users of different systems get their keys from the authority of the corresponding system, and these keys are associated with the access policies of the corresponding organizations. One data owner can simultaneously encrypt his or her data for the receivers from different systems in a batch way. The data owner can freely choose the receiving organizations and define separate attributes for the receivers of different organizations. One can decrypt only if his/her organization has been chosen and his/her attributes meet the access policy for his organization.

Following the BABE framework, we propose a concrete BABE scheme. The security of the scheme is formally proven under a well-established computational assumption. Even if an adversary colludes with the cloud server and all non-authorized users, he or she cannot get any useful information of the encrypted message. We conduct experiments in typical system parameters. The experimental results show that our BABE scheme is more efficient than existing ABE implementations. These features render our BABE an efficient solution to securing one-to-many organization-oriented sensitive data sharing in clouds.

1.2. Related Work

Due to its versatility, ABE has attracted extensive research [1,3,4,5]. The ABE concept was introduced by Sahai and Waters [1]. There are two types of ABE systems, *i.e.*, ciphertext-policy ABE (CP-ABE) and key-policy ABE (KP-ABE). In CP-ABE, the secret key of each user is associated with his/her attributes. When one encrypts for the users of the system, he or she specifies an access policy, which is a collection of attribute sets. Only the user whose attributes match the policy can decrypt. Similarly, in KP-ABE, the secret key of a user is associated with an access policy, and each ciphertext is labeled with a set of attributes. One can decrypt a ciphertext only if the labeled attributes meet the policy associated with the user's secret key. Yu *et al.* [6] proposed a KP-ABE scheme to achieve flexible access control over outsourced data.

In a regular ABE system, a single authority generates the secrets of all of the users in the system. This incurs the so-called single-point problem, that is all of the parties have to fully trust the single authority, who can read all of the messages encrypted for any users. Furthermore, no new user can join the system if the authority is occasionally unavailable. To mitigate this drawback, the notion of multi-authority ABE (MA-ABE) has been proposed. In this notion, multiple authorities jointly generate the secret keys for the users in the system. No single authority can read the messages encrypted for the users. New users can still be enrolled if some of the authorities are available. An encryptor can choose, for each authority, a number d_k and a set of attributes; he or she can then encrypt a message, such that a user can decrypt only if he or she has at least d_k of the given attributes from each authority k [7]. Chase and Chow improved the MA-ABE in [8] by exchanging a shared secret among the authorities during the system setup process. Their scheme is time consuming and needs heavy communication and computation. Yang *et al.* [9] designed an access control framework for multi-authority systems and proposed a secure multi-authority access control scheme for cloud storage. Li *et al.* [10] proposed an MA-ABE scheme for mobile cloud computing by introducing a cloud-based semi-trusted-authority between the mobile user and the attribute authorities.

ABE schemes require time-consuming computations in encryption and decryption, which prevent them from being widely deployed in cloud computing applications for enforcing fine-grained access control. Several works have been proposed to speed up ABE. Attrapadung *et al.* proposed ABE schemes [11,12] that only need a constant number of bilinear maps in decryption, albeit with the constraint of a bound on the maximum number of attributes. Hohenberger and Waters [2] introduced a method that needs a constant number of bilinear maps in decryption without the bound constraint on the attribute number. In contrast, no public work has been reported to accelerate the encryption process in ABE.

Fiat proposed the first batch signature scheme [13]. Since then, a large body of references has focused on the batch verification of signatures [14,15,16,17]. It is unclear whether these technologies can be employed to accelerate ABE encryption in our motivating scenario. Still in a single system-oriented setting, multi-receiver encryption and signcryption [18] have been proposed to reduce the encryption complexity. Baek, Safavi-Naini and Susilo proposed an efficient multi-receiver identity-based encryption scheme [19] in multi-cast encryption applications. All of these schemes are considered in a single organization-oriented scenario. A trivial application of these schemes to multiple organizations needs to repeat the basic encryption operation for each organization, which implies growing overheads linear with the number of organizations. In this paper, we propose to encrypt for the different organizations in a batch way and to provide a more efficient solution to the motivating applications.

1.3. Paper Organization

The rest of this paper is organized as follows. Section 2 presents a BABE framework and the adversary model. We propose a concrete BABE scheme in Section 3, together with detailed security and efficiency analyses. Section 4 concludes the paper.

2. MODELING BABE

2.1. The System Framework

We propose a BABE framework for cloud storage, as illustrated in Figure 1. The framework consists of four types of parties: the data owner, the cloud server, the data requestor/consumer and the authority. The data owner would like to share his or her data with the data requestors managed by different authorities. Each authority generates a secret key for the data requestor in its management domain according to the consumer's attributes (or the corresponding access policies). The data owner encrypts his or her file for the data requestors of different organizations, *i.e.*, the users managed by different authorities, by specifying the intended authorities and the attributes that the data requestors should have in the according authorities' management domains. Then, the data owner uploads the encrypted data to the cloud storage server. When a data requestor requests for the cloud server, the server responds with the corresponding ciphertext. The requestor can decrypt if the attributes labeled with the ciphertext meet the access policy associated with the secret key of the requestor; else, the requestor should get no useful information of the original data.

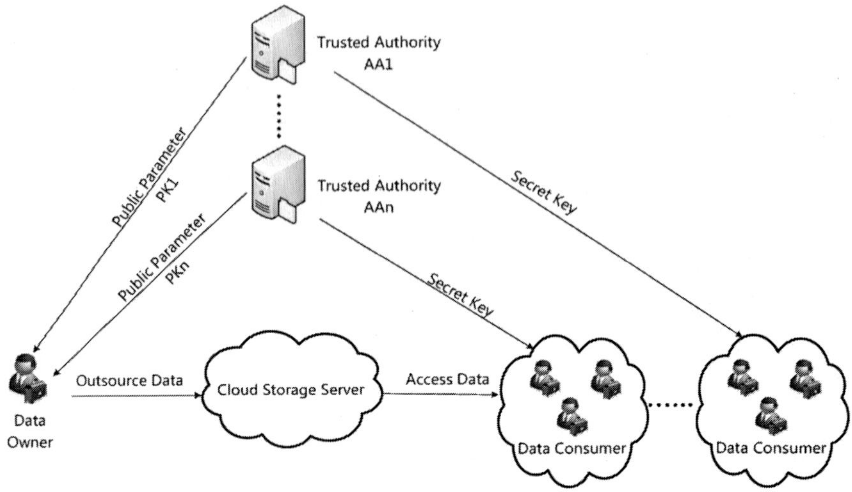

Figure 1. Batch attribute-based encryption (BABE) framework.

2.2. Defining BABE

A BABE scheme consists of four polynomial-time algorithms: *Setup, Encrypt, KeyGeneration* and *Decrypt*. Let I represent the collection of underlying ABE subsystems indexed from one to |I|. Denote that the *i*-th underlying ABE subsystem has master public key PKi and master secret key MKi for i∈I. The algorithms work as follows.

- $Setup(\lambda,U_i)\rightarrow(PK_i,MK_i)$. This is a randomized algorithm run by an authority AA_i. It takes as inputs the security parameter λ and an attribute universe U_i, which defines the set of allowed attributes in different underlying ABE subsystems. The authority AA_i outputs the public parameters PK_i and the mater keys MK_i.
- *Encrypt* $(\vec{PK},\vec{M},\vec{S})\longrightarrow\vec{CT}$. Assume that the data owner wants to share data M_i with the data requestors of the systems $i\in\psi\subseteq I$. This is a randomized algorithm that takes as inputs the public parameters vector $\vec{PK}$, a message vector $\vec{M}$, which contain different messages M_i, and a series of attribute sets $\vec{S}$, which contains attribute sets $S_i,i\in\psi$. It outputs $|\psi|$ ciphertext $CT_i,i\in\psi$ associated with the attribute sets $S_i,i\in\psi$.
- $KeyGen(MK_i,A_i)\rightarrow SK$. Assume that a data requestor belongs to the *i*-th subsystem. Then, MK_i is used to generate the secret key *SK*. This is a randomized algorithm that takes as inputs the master secret key MK_i and an access structure A_i and outputs a secret key *SK*.

- *Decrypt* $(SK,CT_i)\rightarrow$Mi. The decryption algorithm takes as inputs a secret key *SK* associated with the access structure A_i and a ciphertext CT_i associated with attribute set S_i. It outputs the message M_i if S_i satisfies A_i or the error message $\perp$ otherwise.

2.3. The Adversary Model

For sensitive files stored on the cloud, we mainly consider the secrecy of the files. In this scenario, both the cloud server and users may be potential attackers. Specifically, the cloud server (or the staff who manages the cloud server) may be curious and access the private files of the users without being known by the users. Furthermore, some unauthorized users may collude, even with the cloud server, to illegally access the files. However, we have to make a minimum trust assumption that the cloud server will honestly follow the scheme to execute the procedures and return the service to the users. Else, the scheme will not work and makes no sense in practice. We require that the attacker in such a situation cannot get any useful information of the outsourced data.

Now we formally define the security model of a BABE scheme. Let U_i be the attribute universe of the *i*-th underlying ABE scheme. All of the underlying ABE schemes share the security parameter λ. Each underlying ABE scheme is managed by an authority AA_i. I is the index set of the underlying ABE schemes. Formally, we define the security model for BABE via a game between a challenger and an adversary.

Initialize. The adversary declares the different underlying ABE schemes upon which he or she wants to be challenged, indexed by $\psi\subseteq$I. The adversary also declares the attribute set $S_i^*, i\in\psi$ of different ABE schemes upon which he or she wished to be challenged upon.

Setup. The challenger runs the *Setup* algorithm to set up the BABE system and sends the public parameters, $PK_i, i\in \mathbb{I}$, to the adversary.

Phase 1. For the *i*-th underlying ABE subsystem, the challenger initializes for $i\in$I an empty table T_i, an empty set D_i and an integer counter j_i=0. The adversary can repeatedly make the following queries:

***Create(A_i)*:** The challenger sets $j_i=j_i+1$. It runs the key generation algorithm on A_i to obtain the secret key *SK* and stores it in table T_i, forming the entry (j_i,A_i,SK).

***Corrupt(κ,i)*:** The adversary queries for the secret key corresponding to the κ-th entry in Table *i*. If there exists such an entry in table T_i, the challenger obtains the entry (κ,A_i,SK), sets $D_i= D_i \cup\{A_i\}$ and returns the secret key *SK* to the adversary. Else, it returns $\perp$.

Challenge. The adversary submits two equal-length messages, vector $\vec{M}_0$ and $\vec{M}_1$, with each vector having $|\psi|$ message $M_{0,i}, i \in \psi$ and $M_{1,i}, i \in \psi$. In addition, the adversary gives a set of attributes $S_i^*, i \in \psi$, such that for all $A_i \in D_i, i \in \psi$, the set $S_i^*, i \in \psi$ does not satisfy the access structure $A_i, i \in \psi$. The challenger chooses $b \in \{0,1\}$randomly and encrypts $\vec{M}_b$ under $S_i^*, i \in \psi$. The resulting ciphertext $CT_i^*, i \in \psi$ is given to the adversary.

Phase 2. Phase 1 is repeated with the restriction that the adversary cannot obtain any secret key that can be used to decrypt the challenge ciphertext. This means that it cannot issue a *Corrupt* query that would result in an access structure A_i that S_i^* satisfies being added to $D_i \in \psi$. Of course, the adversary cannot issue a decryption query on the challenge ciphertext $CT_i^*, i \in \psi$.

Guess. The adversary outputs a guess bit b' of b. The output of the experiment is one if and only if $b=b'$.

The advantage of the adversary A in this game is defined as $Pr[b'=b]-12$.

Definition 1. A BABE scheme is secure if all polynomial time adversaries have at most a negligible advantage in the above game.

3. THE PROPOSED BABE SCHEME

3.1. Mathematical Background

We briefly review the basic mathematical concepts used in our schemes.

Definition 2. (Access structure [20]). Consider a set of parties $P=\{P_1, P_2, ..., P_n\}$. A collection $A \subseteq 2\{P_1, P_2, ..., P_n\}$ is said to be monotone if for $\forall B, C$, we have that $B \in A$ and $B \subseteq C$, then $C \in A$. An access structure (respectively, monotone access structure) is a collection (respectively, monotone collection) A of non-empty subsets of $\{P_1, P_2, ..., P_n\}$, *i.e.*, $A \subseteq 2P \backslash \emptyset$. The authorized sets represent the sets in A, and the sets not in A are called the unauthorized sets.

Definition 3. (Linear secret sharing scheme [20]). Let P be a set of parties. Let W be an $l \times m$ matrix. Let f be a function that maps a row to a party. A secret sharing scheme Π for access structure A over a set of parties P is a linear secret-sharing scheme (LSSS) in Zpand is represented by (W,f) if it consists of two efficient algorithms:

Share(W,f): This takes as input $s \in Zp$, which is to be shared. It chooses $r_2, r_3, \cdots, r_n$, and let $\vec{v} = (s, r_2, \cdots, r_n)$. It outputs $W\vec{v}$ as the vector of the shares. The share $\omega_i = W_i\vec{v}$ belongs to party $f(i)$, where W_i is the i-th row of W.

Recon(W,f):

This takes as input an access set $S \in A$. Let $I=\{i|f(i)\in S\}$. It outputs a set of constants $(i,\mu i)i\in I$, such that $\sum i\in I\mu i\cdot\omega_i=s$.

In a KP-ABE scheme, a ciphertext is associated with a set of attributes S, and each secret key corresponds to an access structure A. One can decrypt if the attribute set S is authorized in the access structure $A(i.e.,S\in A)$.

Our scheme is built on bilinear groups briefly defined as follows.

Definition 4. (Bilinear group). Let G and GT be two multiplicative cyclic groups of prime order p. Let g be a generator of G and e be a bilinear map, e:$G\times G\rightarrow GT$. The bilinear map e has the following properties:

(1) Bilinearity: for all $g,h\in G$ and $a,b\in\mathbb{Z}_p$, we have $e(g^a,h^b)=e(g,h)^{ab}$.

(2) Non-degeneracy: $e(g,g)\neq 1$.

We say that G is a bilinear group if the group operation in G and the bilinear map e:$G\times G\rightarrow GT$ are both efficiently computable. Notice that the map e is symmetric since $e(g^a,h^b)=e(g,h)^{ab}=e(g^b,h^a)$.

3.2. The Proposal

We first give an outline of our BABE scheme. The scheme is proposed to accelerate the encryption process when one needs to encrypt for the users from different organizations in a cloud storage setting where ABE is used to enforce fine-grained access control. The data owner chooses the data he or she wants to share with the data requestors of the different systems. Then, he or she encrypts the data and sends the encrypted data to the cloud server. Authorized data requestors will be able to decrypt the encrypted data by using the secret key given by the corresponding authority. Using the traditional approach, the owner needs to encrypt each data item for the receivers of the different organizations repetitively, which is inefficient in practice. We suggest to encrypt in a batch way and propose a BABE scheme managing to solve this problem.

For $i\in\mathbb{I}$, we describe different subsystems with different universes U_i of different attributes. The attributes are indexed by integers $1, \cdots,|U_i|$. We use $|U_i|$ to represent the number of the attribute universe U_i. The number of the attributes may be different in distinct subsystems.

Setup. This algorithm, run by the authority AA_i, takes as inputs a system parameter λ and an attribute universe U_i. It generates a bilinear group G of prime order p, with generator $g\in G$. It selects random values $h_i,1, \cdots h_i,| U_i |\in G$. It further chooses a distinct $\alpha_i\in Z_p$ for each i. Finally, for each i, it outputs the public key and master secret key as:

$PK_i=(G,p,g,e(g,g)\alpha_i,h_i,1,\cdots,h_{i,|U|}),MK_i=(PK_i,\alpha_i)$

Encrypt. The data owner chooses the organizations that he or she wants to communicate with, denoted by $\psi\subseteq I$. Then, he or she asks the authority $AA_i,i\in\psi$ for the public key PK_i and chooses a series of attributes $\vec{S}$, where $S_i,i\in\psi$, a series of messages $\vec{M}\in GT$. The data owner chooses a random $s\in Z_p$. The ciphertext component used by i-th subsystem is $CT_i=(S_i,C_i,C',C_i,x)$ where:

$$C_i = M_i \cdot e(g,g)^{\alpha_i s}, C' = g^s, \{C_x = h^s_{i,x}\}_{x \in S_i}$$

After the encryption, the data owner sends the encrypted data to the cloud server.

KeyGen. For each i, the authority AA_i takes as inputs the master secret key MK_i and an LSSS access structure A_i represented by (W,f). Let W be an $l\times m$ matrix. The function f is associated with the rows of W. Let β denote the set of distinct attributes appearing in the access structure matrix W, *i.e.*, $\beta=\{d:\exists\tau\in[1,l],f(\tau)=d\}$. This algorithm chooses a random vector $\vec{v}=(\alpha_i,y_2,\cdots,y_m)\in Z_n$. Here, these values will be used to share the master secret α_i, and y_2, $\cdots$,y mare random numbers. For τ=1 to l, it calculates $\lambda\tau=\vec{v}\cdot W_\tau$, where W_τ is the vector corresponding to the τ-th row of W. The algorithm chooses random integers $r_1,\cdots r_l\in\mathbb{Z}_p$.It outputs the secret key SK as:

$$(D_1 = g^{\lambda_1} \cdot h^{r_1}_{i,f(1)}, R_1 = g^{r_1}, \forall d \in \beta \setminus f(1), Q_{1,d} = h^{r_1}_{i,d})$$

$$(D_l = g^{\lambda_l} \cdot h^{r_l}_{i,f(l)}, R_l = g^{r_l}, \forall d \in \beta \setminus f(l), Q_{l,d} = h^{r_l}_{i,d})$$

In the above, $\beta\backslash x$ means the set β excluding x.

Decrypt. The data requestor requests the encrypted data from the cloud server. The requestor runs the decryption algorithm with his/her secret key $(SK=PK_i,(D_1,R_1,Q_1,d),\cdots,(D_1,R_1,Q_1,d))$ for access structure (W,f) and the ciphertext $CT_i=(S_i,C_i,C',\{C_x\}_{x\in Si})$ for set S_i. Let W be an $l\times m$ matrix. The function f is associated with some rows of W. If Si does not satisfy the access structure, the decryption algorithm outputs $\perp$.

If S_i satisfies the access structure, we let $I\subseteq\{1,2,\cdots l\}$ be a set of indices and $\{\omega_\tau\}_{\tau\in I}\in\mathbb{Z}_p$ be a set of constants, such that $f(\tau)\in S_i$ and $\Sigma_{\tau\in I}\omega_\tau\cdot W_\tau=(1,0,0\cdots0)$ for all $\tau\in I$. Note that ω_τ can be found in polynomial time.

We represent the attributes satisfying the access structure as $\gamma=\{x:\exists\tau\in I,f(\tau)=x\}$. I is the set of indices corresponding to the rows used to decrypt the ciphertext, and γ is the set of distinct attributes associated with these rows. In fact, there are multiple I's that satisfy the constraints above. Typically, the smaller the size of I, the better. Observe that $\gamma \subseteq S_i$, where S_i is the attribute set used to encrypt the ciphertext M_i and $\gamma \subseteq \beta$, the set of attributes used to create the secret key.

To recover the value e(g,g)αis, we define a function v, which transforms a set of attributes into an element of G in the way $v(\gamma)=\prod_{x\in\gamma} h_{i,x}$. For each $\tau \in I$, the data requestor computes the value $D'_\tau = D_\tau \cdot \prod_{x\in\gamma/f(\tau)} Q_{\tau,x} = g^{\lambda\tau} f(\gamma)^{r\tau}$. For the ciphertext, the data requestor computes the value $L = \prod_{x\in\gamma} C_x = \prod_{x\in\gamma} h_{i,x}^s = f(\gamma)^s$.

Finally, the data requestor recovers the value $e(g,g)^{\alpha is}$ by computing:

$$\begin{aligned} & e(C', \prod_{\tau\in I} D'^{\omega_\tau}_\tau)/e(\prod_{\tau\in I} R_\tau^{\omega_\tau}, L) \\ &= e(g^s, \prod_{\tau\in I} g^{\lambda_\tau \omega_\tau} v(\gamma)^{r_\tau \omega_\tau})/e(\prod_{\tau\in I} g^{r_\tau \omega_\tau}, v(\gamma)^s) \\ &= e(g,g)^{\alpha_i s} \cdot e(g, v(\gamma))^{s\sum_{\tau\in I} r_\tau \omega_\tau}/e(g, v(\gamma))^{s\sum_{\tau\in I} r_\tau \omega_\tau} \\ &= e(g,g)^{\alpha_i s} \end{aligned}$$

Note that $C_i = M_i \cdot e(g,g)^{\alpha is}$. Hence, the data requestor can obtain M_i from C_i. From the computation process, it can be seen that the decryption algorithm requires only two pairing operations.

3.3. Security Analysis

The security of the proposal is based on the hardness of the q-decision bilinear Diffie–Hellman exponent (q-DBDHE) problem defined below.

Definition 5 (q-Decision bilinear Diffie–Hellman exponent [21]). In (G, G_T), the q-DBDHE problem states that, given:

$$(g, g^x, g^{(x^2)}, \cdots g^{(x^q)}, g^{(x^{q+2})}, \cdots g^{(x^{2q})}, h, T)$$

where $x \in \mathbb{Z}_p, g, h \in G$ and $T \in G_T$, decide whether $T = e(g,h)^{x^{(q+1)}}$ or T is a random element of G_T.

The q-DBDHE assumption states that any probabilistic polynomial time (PPT) algorithm has only negligible advantage in solving the above q-DBDHE problem, where the advantage is defined as $|Pr[T = e(g,h)^{x^{(q+1)}}] - Pr[T = R]|$.

The security of the proposed BABE scheme is guaranteed by the following claim.

Theorem 1. *(Security). The BABE scheme is selectively secure against chosen plaintext attacks under the* $|U|$–DBDHE *assumption in G.*

Proof. Let $|U|$ be the maximum of all of the $|U_i|$'s for security parameter λ. Assume that each attribute is indexed by a unique integer between one and $|U_i|$. Suppose there exists a PPT adversary *A* who can distinguish the encrypted message vectors with non-negligible probability under the selective security experiment [22]. Then, we show that there exists a PPT adversary *B* that can break the $|U|$–DBDHE assumption in *G*, which contradicts the hardness of the $|U|$–DBDHE problem.

Init: A chooses the underlying ABE schemes on which he or she wants to be challenged. For each sub-system, *A* outputs the attribute set $S_i^*, i \in [1,n]$ for the challenge ciphertext.

Setup: The challenger *B* is given the tuple:

$$(G, p, g, g^s, g^a, g^{(a^2)}, \cdots g^{(a^{|U|})}, g^{(a^{|U|+2})}, \cdots g^{(a^{2|U|})}, T)$$

for security parameter λ. The challenger is required to solve the $|U|$–*DBDHE* challenge, *i.e.*, to answer whether $T = e(g,g)^{a^{|U|+1}s}$ or a random element in G_T. The challenger randomly chooses $\alpha_i', z_{i,1}, \cdots, z_{i,|U_i|} \in \mathbb{Z}_p, i \in [1,n]$ and sets $e(g,g)^{\alpha_i} = e(g,g)^{\alpha_i'} \cdot e(g^a, g^{a^{|U|}})$, which means that $\alpha_i = \alpha_i' + a^{|U|+1}$. For $x \in [1,|U|]$, compute:

$$h_{i,x} = g^{z_{i,x}}, x \in S_i^*$$
$$h_{i,x} = g^{z_{i,x}} g^{a^x}, x \notin S_i^*$$

The public parameter PK_i for the *i*-th subsystem is $(G,p,g,e(g,g)^{\alpha i},h_{i,1}, \cdots, h_{i,}|U_i|)$ and is sent to the adversary *A*.

Phase 1: For system *i*, the challenger *B* initializes an empty table T_i, an empty set D_i and a counter $ji = 0$. The adversary *A* can query the challenger *B*, and the challenger *B* responds as follows:

(1). *Create*(A_i): The challenger *B* sets $j_i=j_i+1$. The access structure A_i is represented by (W,f), where *W* is an $l \times m$ matrix. Let K_i be the set of the rows in which the attributes are in S_i^* and K_i' be the rows in which the attributes are not in S_i^* (i.e., $K_i'=[1,l]/K_i$). Define an *m*-element vector $\vec{v}$ over Zp with the first element of $\vec{v}$ being one, for all $\tau \in K_i$, $\vec{v}\ W_\tau = 0$. W_τ is the vector row τ of the matrix *W*. Note that when S_i does not satisfy *W*, it must be the case that $(1, 0, \cdots, 0)$ is not in the span of rows W_τ for $\tau \in K_i$. With the property of LSSS, the vector $\vec{v}$ can be found in polynomial time. In addition, in order to share the secret α_i, *B* generates a secret key with the vector $\alpha_i \vec{v}$ by noting $v_1 = 1$. B computes ($\alpha_i \vec{v}$) W_τ regarding share λ_τ for $\tau \in [1, l]$.

The challenger B randomly chooses $r'_1, \cdots, r'_l \in Z_q$ and $y_2, \cdots, y_m \in Z_p$ to construct a new vector v n e w → = (0 , y 2 , y 3 ,··· , y m) . Then, it computes λ τ ′ = v n e w → W τ for τ ∈ [1 , l].

For $\tau \in K_i$, compute $D'_\tau = g^{\lambda'_\tau} \cdot h_{i,f(\tau)}^{r'_\tau}, R'_\tau = g^{r'_\tau}, Q'_{\tau,x} = h_{i,x}^{r'_\tau}, \forall x \in \beta \setminus f(\tau)$. .

For $\tau \in K'_i$, compute $c_\tau = \vec{v}W_\tau$. Set that $\lambda_\tau = c_\tau \cdot \alpha_i = c_\tau(\alpha'_i + a^{|U|+1})$. Set $R_\tau = g^{-c_\tau a^{|U|+1-f(\tau)}}$, which means $r_\tau = -c_\tau a^{|U|+1-f(\tau)}$. Then, set $R'_\tau = g^{-c_\tau a^{|U|+1-f(\tau)}} g^{r'_\tau}$, and compute:

$$
\begin{aligned}
D'_\tau &= g^{c_\tau \alpha'_i} \cdot R_\tau^{z_{i,\tau}} \cdot g^{\lambda'_\tau} \cdot h_{i,f(\tau)}^{r'_\tau} \\
&= g^{c_\tau \alpha'_i} \cdot g^{-z_{i,\tau} c_\tau a^{|U|+1-f(\tau)}} \cdot g^{\lambda'_\tau} \cdot h_{i,f(\tau)}^{r'_\tau} \\
&= g^{c_\tau \alpha'_i} \cdot g^{-z_{i,\tau} c_\tau a^{|U|+1-f(\tau)}} \cdot g^{\lambda'_\tau} \cdot h_{i,f(\tau)}^{r'_\tau} \cdot g^{c_\tau a^{|U|+1}} \cdot g^{-c_\tau a^{|U|+1}} \\
&= g^{c_\tau \alpha_i} \cdot (g^{z_\tau})^{r_\tau} \cdot (g^{a^{f(\tau)}}) \cdot g^{\lambda'_\tau} \cdot h_{i,f(\tau)}^{r'_\tau} \\
&= g^{c_\tau \alpha_i} \cdot h_{i,f(\tau)}^{r_\tau} \cdot g^{\lambda'_\tau} \cdot h_{i,f(\tau)}^{r'_\tau}
\end{aligned}
$$

Next, for all $x \in \beta \setminus f(\tau), Q'_{\tau,x} = h_{i,x}^{r_\tau + r'_\tau}$ is computed as follows:

$$
\begin{aligned}
h_{i,x}^{r_\tau + r'_\tau} &= g^{z_{i,x}(r_\tau + r'_\tau)} = g^{-z_{i,x} c_\tau a(|U|+1)-f(\tau)} g^{z_{i,x} r'_\tau}, x \in S_i^* \\
h_{i,x}^{r_\tau + r'_\tau} &= g^{z_{i,x}(r_\tau + r'_\tau)} (g^{a^x})^{(r_\tau + r'_\tau)} = g^{-z_{i,x} c_\tau a(|U|+1)-f(\tau)} g^{-c_\tau a(|U|+1)-f(\tau)+x} \cdot (g^{z_{i,x}} g^{a^x})^{r'_\tau}, x \notin S_i^*
\end{aligned}
$$

After the process above, the keys are valid with access policy (W , f). From the view of A , their distribution is identical to that of the keys generated by the *KeyGen* algorithm. Hence, the secret keys requested by the adversary is perfectly simulated.

(2). *Corrupt*(κ , i): The challenger B obtains the entry (κ ; A_i ; $S K$) if the κ-th entry appears in table T_i . Set $D_i = D_i \cup \{ A_i \}$. It then sends $S K$ to adversary A . If no such entry exists, then return $\perp$.

Challenge: A outputs two equal-length message vectors $\vec{M}_0, \vec{M}_1$, each of which contains n messages in the message space of the corresponding subsystem. The challenger B chooses a random bit b. It constructs and sends to A the challenge ciphertext:

$$CT_i^* = (C_i^* = M_b \cdot T \cdot e(g^{\alpha_i'}, g^s), C' = g^s, \forall x \in S^*, C_{i,x}^* = (g^s)^{z_{i,x}})$$

Phase 2: B responds to A 's queries in the same manner as in Phase 1, except that it refuses to answer any *Corrupt* query that would result in an access structure A_i , which S_i satisfies.

Guess: Finally, A outputs a bit b' . If $b = b'$, then B outputs that $T = e(g, g)^{a^{|U|+1}s}$, else it outputs that T is a random element.

3.4. Efficiency Analysis

In this section, we analyze the performance of our BABE scheme. It can be seen that our approach is more efficient than encrypting data for different organizations one by one using the underlying Hohenberger-Waters ABE (HW-ABE) [2] scheme. In the encryption process, the number of exponentiations grows with the number of attributes. Comparing to the plain implementation of the HW-ABE scheme, our approach is more efficient because C' is the same for all of the ciphertexts. Hence, it can be calculated once and then be reused. Assume that the data owner wants to share data with the users of n organizations simultaneously, and the average number of the attributes used in encryption is m. Our scheme needs (m + 1) n + 1 exponentiations, while the HW-ABE scheme needs (m + 2) n exponentiations. From the comparison, the improved efficiency is dominated by the average number of the attributes used by the data owner. We can save n- 1 exponentiations in the encryption process. The computation overhead for the data requestors is also very small. They need only two pairings and a number of multiplications. This is the same as the HW-ABE scheme [2].

We encoded our BABE and performed experiments on a PC with a 2.80 GHz CPU and 3 GB RAM, using the C programming language in the GMP (https://gmplib.org/) and PBC (https://crypto.stanford.edu/pbc/) library. For the encryption algorithms: (1) we generated n different 1024 bit-long random numbers as exponents; (2) we implemented the batch algorithm and normal algorithm, respectively. We executed Steps 1 and 2 100 times to eliminate experimental noise. We set the values of n ranging from 10 to 100 to see the performance improvement due to the batch algorithms.

Figure 2 show the time to compute n ciphertext in the HW-ABE and BABE with the average attribute number m = 4 or m = 8 . It can be seen that the time consumed in both BABE and HW-ABE grows linearly with the number of messages to be encrypted. However, the batch encryption takes about 15% less time for m = 4 or 10 % less time for m = 8 than the normal encryption, which confirms the theoretical analysis.

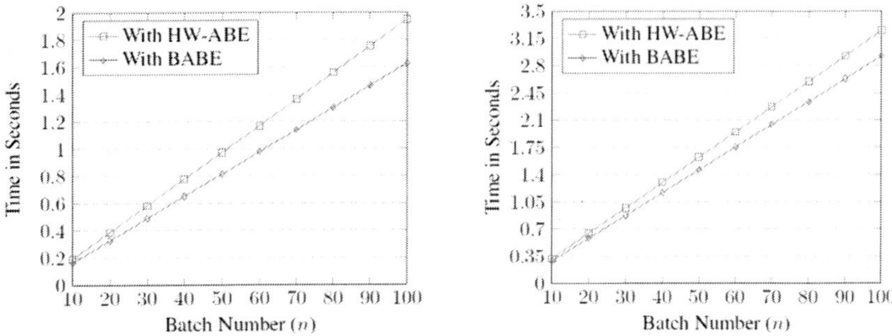

Figure 2. The encryption performance comparison for producing multiple ciphertexts with BABE/HW-ABE ($m = 4$, $m = 8$).

4. CONCLUSIONS

In this paper, we proposed BABE to accelerate the ABE encryption for the users of multiple organizations. Our approach makes the data owner able to share his or her data with the data requestors of different systems simultaneously. We formally proved the security of our scheme and compared it to previous work. The analyses and comparisons show that our scheme has desirable high performance. It is efficient to secure data to be outsourced to clouds.

ACKNOWLEDGMENTS

This paper is partially supported by the National Key Basic Research Program (973 Program) under Project 2012CB315905, by the Natural Science Foundation under Projects 61370190, 61272501, 61173154, 61402029 and 61003214, by the Beijing Natural Science Foundation through Projects 4132056 and 4122041, by the Natural Science Foundation of Guangdong Province through Projects 2014A030313517 and S2012020011071, the Fundamental Research Funds for the Central Universities, the Research Funds (No. 14XNLF02) of Renmin University of China, the Open Research Fund of the State Key Laboratory of Information Security (Institute of Information Engineering), the Chinese Academy of Sciences and the Open Research Fund of Beijing Key Laboratory of Trusted Computing.

REFERENCES

1. Sahai, A.; Waters, B. Fuzzy identity-based encryption. In Advances in Cryptology—EUROCRYPT 2005, Proceedings of the 24th Annual International Conference on the Theory and Applications of Cryptographic Techniques, Aarhus, Denmark, 22–26 May 2005; Springer: Berlin/Heidelberg, Germany, 2005; Lecture Notes in Computer Science. Volume 3494, pp. 457–473.
2. Hohenberger, S.; Waters, B. Attribute-based encryption with fast decryption. In Public-Key Cryptography–PKC 2013, Proceedings of the 16th International Conference on Practice and Theory in Public-Key Cryptography, Nara, Japan, 26 February–1 March 2013; Springer: Berlin/Heidelberg, Germany, 2013; Lecture Notes in Computer Science. Volume 7778, pp. 162–179.
3. Goyal, V.; Pandey, O.; Sahai, A.; Waters, B. Attribute-based encryption for fine-grained access control of encrypted data. In Proceedings of the 13th ACM Conference on Computer and Communications Security, Alexandri, VA, USA, 30 October–3 November 2006; pp. 89–98.
4. Bethencourt, J.; Sahai, A.; Waters, B. Ciphertext-policy attribute-based encryption. In Proceedings of the SP'07 IEEE Symposium on Security and Privacy, Berkeley, CA, USA, 20–23 May 2007; pp. 321–334.
5. Waters, B. Ciphertext-policy attribute-based encryption: An expressive, efficient, and provably secure realization. In Public Key Cryptography (PKC) 2011, Proceedings of the 14th International Conference on Practice and Theory in Public Key Cryptography, Taormina, Italy, 6–9 March 2011; Springer: Berlin/Heidelberg, Germany, 2011; Lecture Notes in Computer Science. Volume 6571, pp. 53–70.
6. Yu, S.; Wang, C.; Ren, K.; Lou, W. Achieving secure, scalable, and fine-grained data access control in cloud computing. In Proceedings of the IEEE INFOCOM, San Diego, CA, USA, 14–19 March 2010; pp. 1–9.
7. Chase, M. Multi-authority attribute based encryption. In Theory of Cryptography, Proceedings of the 4th Theory of Cryptography Conference, TCC 2007, Amsterdam, The Netherlands, 21–24 February 2007; Springer: Berlin/Heidelberg, Germany, 2007; Lecture Notes in Computer Science. Volume 4392, pp. 515–534.
8. Chase, M.; Chow, S.S. Improving privacy and security in multi-authority attribute-based encryption. In Proceedings of the 16th ACM Conference on Computer and Communications Security, Chicago, IL, USA, 9–13 November 2009; pp. 121–130.
9. Yang, K.; Jia, X. Attributed-based access control for multi-authority systems in cloud storage. In Proceedings of the 2012 IEEE 32nd International Conference on Distributed Computing Systems (ICDCS), Macau, China, 18–21 June 2012; pp. 536–545.
10. Li, J.; Huang, Q.; Chen, X.; Chow, S.S.; Wong, D.S.; Xie, D. Multi-authority ciphertext-policy attribute-based encryption with accountability. In Proceedings of the 6th ACM Symposium on Information, Computer and Communications Security, Hong Kong, China, 22–24 March 2011; pp. 386–390.
11. Attrapadung, N.; Libert, B.; de Panafieu, E. Expressive key-policy attribute-based encryption with constant-size ciphertexts. In Public Key Cryptography–PKC 2011, Proceedings of the 14th International Conference on Practice and Theory in Public Key Cryptography, Taormina, Italy, 6–9 March 2011; Springer: Berlin/Heidelberg, Germany, 2011; Lecture Notes in Computer Science. Volume 6571, pp. 90–108.
12. Attrapadung, N.; Herranz, J.; Laguillaumie, F.; Libert, B.; de Panafieu, E.; Ràfols, C. Attribute-based encryption schemes with constant-size ciphertexts. *Theor. Comput. Sci.* **2012**, *422*, 15–38.
13. Fiat, A. Batch rsa. In *Advances in Cryptology CRYPTO 89 Proceedings*; Springer: Berlin/Heidelberg, Germany, 1990; Lecture Notes in Computer Science; Volume 435, pp. 175–185.
14. Bellare, M.; Garay, J.A.; Rabin, T. Fast batch verification for modular exponentiation and digital signatures. In Advances in Cryptology EUROCRYPT 98, Proceedings of the

International Conference on the Theory and Application of Cryptographic Techniques Espoo, Finland, 31 May–4 June 1998; Springer: Berlin/Heidelberg, Germany, 1998; Lecture Notes in Computer Science. Volume 1403, pp. 236–250.
15. Zhang, C.; Lu, R.; Lin, X.; Ho, P.H.; Shen, X. An efficient identity-based batch verification scheme for vehicular sensor networks. In Proceedings of the IEEE INFOCOM 2008, the 27th Conference on Computer Communications, Phoenix, AZ, USA, 13–18 April 2008.
16. Ferrara, A.L.; Green, M.; Hohenberger, S.; Pedersen, M.Ø. Practical short signature batch verification. In Topics in Cryptology—CT-RSA 2009, Proceedings of the The Cryptographers' Track at the RSA Conference 2009, San Francisco, CA, USA, 20–24 April 2009; Springer: Berlin/Heidelberg, Germany, 2009; Lecture Notes in Computer Science. Volume 5473, pp. 309–324.
17. Camenisch, J.; Hohenberger, S.; Pedersen, M.Ø. Batch verification of short signatures. In Advances in Cryptology—EUROCRYPT 2007, Proceedings of the 26th Annual International Conference on the Theory and Applications of Cryptographic Techniques, Barcelona, Spain, 20–24 May 2007; Springer: Berlin/Heidelberg, Germany, 2007; Lecture Notes in Computer Science. Volume 4515, pp. 246–263.
18. Duan, S.; Cao, Z. Efficient and provably secure multi-receiver identity-based signcryption. In Information Security and Privacy, Proceedings of the 11th Australasian Conference, ACISP 2006, Melbourne, Australia, 3–5 July 2006; Springer: Berlin/Heidelberg, Germany, 2006; Lecture Notes in Computer Science. Volume 4058, pp. 195–206.
19. Baek, J.; Safavi-Naini, R.; Susilo, W. Efficient multi-receiver identity-based encryption and its application to broadcast encryption. In Public Key Cryptography-PKC 2005, Proceedings of the 8th International Workshop on Theory and Practice in Public Key Cryptography, Les Diablerets, Switzerland, 23–26 January 2005; Springer: Berlin/Heidelberg, Germany, 2005; Lecture Notes in Computer Science. Volume 3386, pp. 380–397.
20. Beimel, A. Secure Schemes for Secret Sharing and Key Distribution. Ph.D. Thesis, Technion-Israel Institute of Technology, Haifa, Israel, 1996.
21. Boneh, D.; Boyen, X.; Goh, E.J. Hierarchical identity based encryption with constant size ciphertext. In Advances in Cryptology–EUROCRYPT 2005, Proceedings of the 24th Annual International Conference on the Theory and Applications of Cryptographic Techniques, Aarhus, Denmark, 22–26 May 2005; Springer: Berlin/Heidelberg, Germany, 2005; Lecture Notes in Computer Science. Volume 3494, pp. 440–456.
22. Boneh, D.; Gentry, C.; Waters, B. Collusion resistant broadcast encryption with short ciphertexts and private keys. In Advances in Cryptology–CRYPTO 2005, Proceedings of the 25th Annual International Cryptology Conference, Santa Barbara, CA, USA, 14–18 August 2005; Springer: Berlin/Heidelberg, Germany, 2005; Lecture Notes in Computer Science. Volume 3621, pp. 258–275.

CHAPTER 13

Analyzing Security Threats to Virtual Machines Monitor in Cloud Computing Environment

Ahmad Fayez S. Althobaiti

Department of Computer and Information Sciences, Al-Imam Muhammad Ibn Saudi Islamic University, Riyadh, Saudi Arabia

ABSTRACT

The data and applications in cloud computing reside in cyberspace, that allowing to users access data through any connection device, when you need to transfer information over the cloud, you will lose control of it. There are multi types of security challenge must be understood and countermeasures. One of the major security challenges is resources of the cloud computing infrastructures are provided as services over the Internet, and entire data in the cloud computing are reside over network resources, that enables the data to be access through VMs. In this work, we describe security techniques for securing a VCCI, VMMs such *as Encryption and Key Management (EKM), Access Control Mechanisms (ACMs), Virtual Trusted Platform Module (vTPM), Virtual Firewall (VF), and Trusted Virtual Domains (TVDs)*. In this paper we focus on security of virtual resources in Virtualized Cloud Computing Infrastructure (VCCI), Virtual Machine Monitor (VMM) by describing types of attacks on VCCI, and vulnerabilities of VMMs and we describe the techniques for securing a VCCI.

Keywords: Cloud Computing, Security Threats, Virtual Machine Monitors, Cloud Security

1. INTRODUCTION

Deploying cloud computing in an enterprise infrastructure brings significant security concerns. Monitoring of the virtual machines with high security and minimal overhead is always very important, especially in those environments where hundreds of Virtual Machines VMs are running on dozens of physicals servers. In this paper we focus on security of virtual resources in Virtualized Cloud Computing Infrastructure (VCCI), Virtual Machine Monitor (VMM) by describing types of attacks on VCCI, and vulnerabilities of VMMs and we describe the techniques for securing a VCCI. Also it is identified that either monitoring hypervisor only will be enough to collect detailed resources consumptions or VMMs will also be required. To complete the experiment of resource monitoring, techniques for securing a VCCI, VMMs such as Encryption and Key Management (EKM), Access Control Mechanisms (ACMs), Virtual Trusted Platform Module (vTPM), Virtual Firewall (VF), and Trusted Virtual Domains (TVDs) is required [1] [2] [3].

2. FIVESAAS SECURITY CHALLENGES

Top security concerns in cloud computing: Insecure Application Program Interface (APIs) or programming interfaces, Data protection, Access management inside employee threats, and Share technology issues:

1) Hypervisor security.

2) Cross-side channel attacks between VMs.

In this paper we discuss attacks between Virtual Machines, and how we protected and isolation from attackers. In his case, Virtual Machines share the physical memory, Central Processing Unit (CPU) cycles, network buffers, DRAM of the physical Machines. So Attacks takes place in two steps:

1) Placement of attacker virtual machine on the same physical machine.

2) Exploiting the shared resources.

CPU cache leakage attack:

Measure load of the other virtual web server.

Extract AES and RSA keys.

Keystrokes timing analysis.

Extract user passwords from SSH terminal.

3. SECURITY ISSUES IN CLOUD ENVIRONMENT

Infrastructure-as-a-service (IaaS) security issues:

The resources such as servers, storage, networks, and other computing resources are provided by IaaS in the form of virtualized systems, which are accessed through the Internet. Access to cloud resources over the network takes essentially three distinct forms: Admin command to the cloud provider, admin command to Virtual Machine, and user interaction with the virtual machine using network services [4].

4. SECURITY THREATS TO CLOUD COMPUTING INFRASTRUCTURES

Application of clients running on Virtual Machine residing on Virtual Cloud Computing Infrastructure (VCCI), VMs aren't deal directly with physical hardware, VMs are manage by Virtual Machine Monitor, which is running in physical infrastructure. The VMM or hypervisor is software layer that allows several Virtual Machines to run on a physical machine. We have two types of hypervisors: type1 run directly upon HW. Type 2 run together with host OS. Type 2 includes Xen, and Kernel Virtual Machine (KVM), as shown in Figure 1.

4.1 Cross VM Side Channel Attacks

Attackers can use security gaps to attack on any component of VCCI that may effect on the others. In this paper we describe technique to overcome attackers on VCCI, and vulnerabilities of VMMs, the infrastructure needs to be secured by implementing security techniques that isolates the VMM, guest/host OS and physical hardware from the side effects of each other [2]. Identified two major attacks on VCCI (VM to VM and VM to Hypervisor) as shown in the Figure 2.

From above figure, attacks can take place through the major vulnerabilities (VM hopping, VM escape and VM mobility) identified in hypervisors.*VM hopping*: this attack can effect on denial of service, which make resources unavailable to user.*VM Escape*: this vulnerability allows a guest-level VM to attack its host.*VM Mobility*: under a VCCI, VMs can move from one physical host to another is called as VM mobility [5] [6].

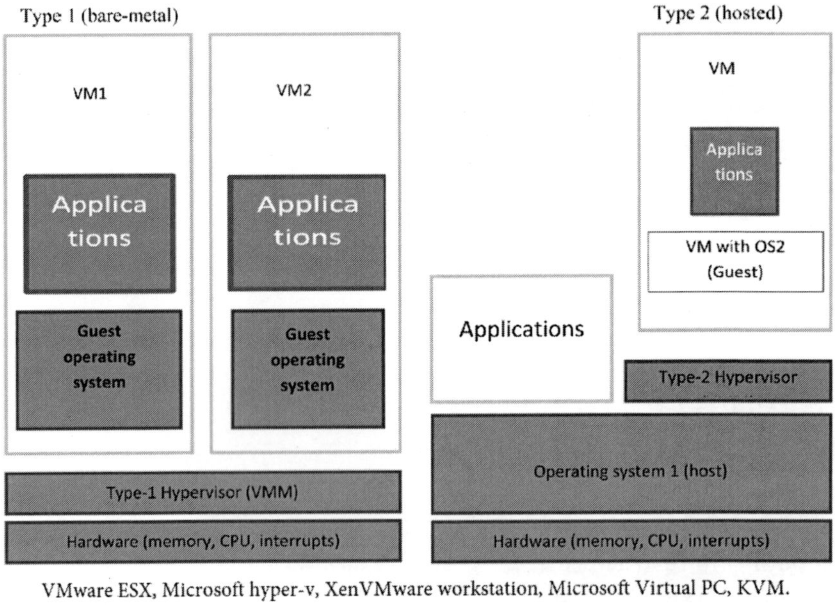

Figure 1.Types of hypervisors [5].

5. SOME OF THE SECURITY TECHNIQUES FOR SECURING THE VCCI

In this work we identified and analyzed some major approaches for securing a VCCI; these include EKM, ACMs, vTPM, VFs, and TVDs.

Describe Security Threats to Virtualized Cloud Computing Infrastructures A multi-tenant Cloud Computing Infrastructure(CCI) consists of several Virtual Machines (VMs) running on same physical platform by using virtualization techniques. The VMs are monitored and managed by kernel based software i.e. Virtual Machine Monitor (VMM) or hypervisor which is main component of Virtualized Cloud Computing Infrastructure (VCCI). Due to software based vulnerabilities, VMMs are compromised to security attacks that may take place from inside or outside attackers. In order to formulate a secure VCCI, VMM must be protected by implementing strong security techniques such as Encryption and Key Management (EKM), Access Control Mechanisms (ACMs), Intrusion Detection Tools (IDTs), Virtual

Trusted Platform Module (vTPM), Virtual Firewalls (VFs) and Trusted Virtual Domains (TVDs). In this work we describe the techniques of virtualizing a CCI, types of attacks on VCCI, vulnerabilities of VMMs and we describe the significance of security techniques for securing a VCCI.

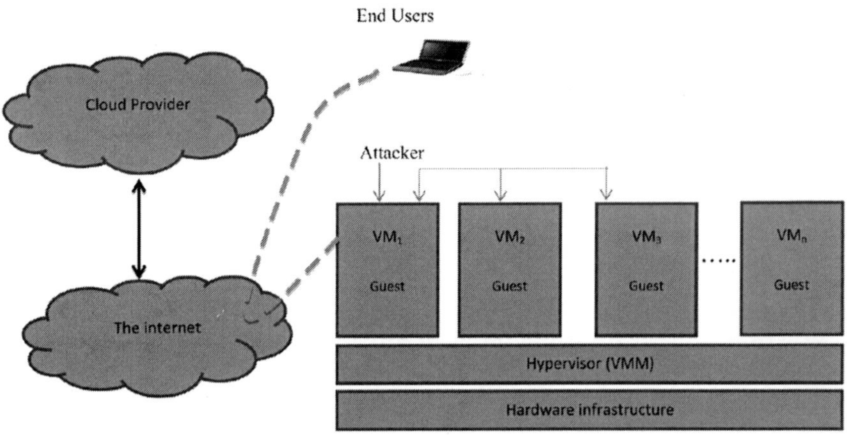

Figure 2. Attack on Virtual Cloud Computing Infrastructure (VCCI).

5.1. Encryption and Key Management (EKM)

Encryption and Key Management (EKM) is the common encryption methods that can be used on VCCI include symmetric and asymmetric algorithms. In this method, we protected data against the loss and theft is a shared responsibility of cloud customer and CSP. The common strongly encryption technique is Service Level Agreements (SLAs) [6]. Three different stages for protect confidential data for consumer:

a. Encryption of data-at-rest (encrypting the data on desk storage that protects data from illegal used and malicious CSP).

b. Encryption of data-at-transit (encrypting the confidential information such as credit cards while transmitting over the internet).

c. Encryption of data on backup media (external or internal storages), this protect from misuse of lost or stolen media.

5.2. Access Control Mechanisms (ACMs)

ACMs are responsible of protecting of a VCCI by restricting access, denying, limiting or to a system or an entity such as processes, VM and VMMs according to the well-defined security policies. Most common ACMs used in VCCI include Mandatory Access Control (MAC), Discretionary Access Control (DAC) and Role Based Access Control (RBAC). All these techniques are known as identity based ACMs as user subjects and resources objects are identified by unique names. Identification may be done directly or through roles assigned to the subjects [7]. ACMs guarantees integrity and confidentiality of the resources.

5.3. Virtual Trusted Platform Module (vTPM)

It's proposed by IBM researchers, is based on certificate chain linking vTPMs to the physical TPM in order to provide its capabilities and make it available to all VMs running on a platform. vTPMs can be located in a specific layer over the hypervisor. A vTPM instance is created for each VM by vTPM Manager which is built in a specific VM and may invoke its own vTPM through the hypervisor [8]. Each VM has its associated vTPM instance that emulates the TPM functionality to extend the chain of trust from the physical TPM to each vTPM via careful management of signing keys and certificates. A vTPM has its own virtual Endorsement Key (EK) and virtual Storage Root Key (SRK) beside some software on the host. In multi-tenant VCCI the system of vTPM virtualizes a physical TPM to be used by a number of VM on a single hardware platform.

5.4. Virtual Firewall (VF)

It is a firewall service running in a virtualized environment which provides usual packet filtering and monitoring services that a physical firewall provides [9]. VFs can execute in hypervisor-mode (hypervisor resident) and bride-mode. In order to protect the VMs and VMM, hypervisor-resident VFs must be implemented on the VMM where it is responsible to capture malicious VM activities including packet injections. These VFs require a modification to the physical host hypervisor kernel to install process hooks or modules allowing the VF system access to VM information and direct access to the virtual networks witches as well as virtualized network interfaces moving packet traffic between VMs. The hypervisor-resident VF can use the same hooks to then perform all firewall functions like packet inspection, dropping, and forwarding but without actually touching the virtual network at any point. Hypervisor resident VFs can be faster as compared to bridge-mode VFs because they are not performing packet inspection in VFs, but rather from within the kernel at native hardware speeds.

5.5. Trusted Virtual Domains (TVDs)

It is security technique formed at VCCI by grouping the related VMs running on separate physical machine into a single network domain with a unified security policy. The multiple instances of TVDs co-exist on a single platform under a shared resource policy. The use of TVD provides strong isolation among un-related VMs as the communication among TVDs takes places only according to the security policies defamed by administrator configured in the VMM. A malicious VM cannot join any TVD because in order to join TVD, a VM should fulfill the requirements of the policy so no malicious VM can affect the VMs of trusted users on cloud [10]. Normally the VMs residing in a TVD are labeled with a unique identifier. For instance the VMs of one customer will be labeled differently from the other customer. The labeling is used to identify the assigned VMs to a particular customer and to allow the same labeled VMs to run on inside the same TVD that must be designed by following a proper security guidelines and policies that doesn't exhibit any loop holes [11].

6. CONCLUSION AND FUTURE WORK

Many security challenges are facing the cloud computing, and it will be difficult to achieve end to end security. According to the above analysis, we can see that, each client assigned with one or multiple Virtual Machines, VMM is major target of the attack on VCCI. However, to achieve secure VMM, we describe several techniques applied by various researchers to secure VCCI. However, the security must be applied at different layers of resources such as storage, network, and applications by considering to resource management issues such as SLAs (Service Level Agreements) are concerned in delivering software for a million users to use as a service via a data center, which is a lot more complex, as compared to distributing software for a million users to run on their individual personal computers. Our future work would investigate new models and techniques for securing VMM, VCCI depending on resources efficiency and cost of cloud computing providers.

REFERENCES

1. Kulkarni, G., et al. (2012) Cloud Security Challenges. 7th International Conference on Telecommunication Systems, Services, and Applications (TSSA), India, October 2012, 88-91.
2. Zhang, L.J., et al. (2009) CCOA: Cloud Computing Open Architecture. IEEE International Conference on Web Services, IBM T.J. Watson Research Center, New York, 6-10 July 2009, 607-616.
3. Mehra, P., Katsaros, D., Vakali, A., Pallis, G. and Dikaiakos, M.D. (2009) Cloud Computing: Distributed Internet Computing for IT and Scientific Research. IEEE Internet Computing, 13, 10-13.
4. Shengmei, L., et al. (2011) Virtualization Security for Cloud Computing Service. International Conference on Cloud and Service Computing, China, 174-179.
5. Fu, W. and Li, X. (2011) The Study on Data Security in Cloud Computing Based on Virtualization. International Symposium on IT in Medicine and Education (ITME), Chongqing College of Electronic Engineering, 9-11 December 2011, 257-261.
6. Buyya, R., Garg, S.K. and Calheiros, R.N. (2011) SLA-Oriented Resource Provisioning for Cloud Computing: Challenges, Architecture, and Solutions. International Conference on Cloud and Service Computing, IEEE Computer Society, Washington DC, 1-10.
7. Liang, C., Zhang, Y. and Han, Z.H. (2013) Quantitatively Measure Access Control Mechanisms across Different Operating Systems. 7th International Conference on Software Security and Reliability, Beijing, 18-20 June 2013, 50-59. https://doi.org/10.1109/sere.2013.12
8. Berger, S., et al. (2006) vTPM: Virtualizing the Trusted Platform Module. Security'06: 15th USENIX Security Symposium, Vancouver, BC, 31 July-4 August 2006, 305-320.
9. Brohi, S.N., Bamiah, M., Brohi, M.N. and Kamran, R. (2012) Identifying and Analyzing Security Threats to Virtualized Cloud Computing Infrastructures. Proceedings of International of Cloud Computing, Technologies, Applications & Management, 151-155.
10. Griffin, J.L., Jaeger, T., Perez, R., Sailer, R., van Doorn, L. and Cáceres, R. (2005) Trusted Virtual Domains: Toward Secure Distributed Services. The 1st Workshop on Hot Topics in System Dependability, Yokohama, 30 June 2005, 1-6.
11. Iqbal, A., Pattinson, C. and Kor, A.-L. (2015) Performance Monitoring of Virtual Machines (VMs) of Type I and II hypervisors with SNMPv3. World Congress on Sustainable Technologies (WCST), Leeds, 14-16 December 2015, 98-99.

CHAPTER 14

Security Awareness of the Digital Natives

Vasileios Gkioulos [1,*,†], Gaute Wangen [1,†], Sokratis K. Katsikas [1,2,†], George Kavallieratos [2,†] and Panayiotis Kotzanikolaou [3,†]

1.Department of Information Security and Communication Technology, Norwegian University of Science & Technology, 2802 Gjøvik, Norway,

[2]Department of Digital Systems, University of Piraeus, 18532 Piraeus, Greece

[3]Department of Informatics, University of Piraeus, 18532 Piraeus, Greece

ABSTRACT

Young generations make extensive use of mobile devices, such as smartphones, tablets and laptops, while a plethora of security risks associated with such devices are induced by vulnerabilities related to user behavior. Furthermore, the number of security breaches on or via portable devices increases exponentially. Thus, deploying suitable risk treatments requires the investigation of how the digital natives (young people, born and bred in the digital era) use their mobile devices and their level of security awareness, in order to identify common usage patterns with negative security impact. In this article, we present the results of a survey performed across a multinational sample of digital natives with distinct backgrounds and levels of competence in terms of security, to identify divergences in user behavior due to regional, educational and other factors. Our results highlight significant influences on the behavior of digital natives, arising from user confidence, educational background, and parameters related to usability and accessibility. The outcomes of this study justify the need for further analysis of the topic, in order to identify the influence of fine-grained semantics, but also the consolidation of wide and robust user-models.

Keywords: security; mobile devices; digital natives; security awareness; user behavior; education

1. INTRODUCTION

Mobile devices (i.e., cellphones, laptops, tablets) have become an indispensable part of our everyday life, since they fulfill the increasing users' desire for Internet connectivity and access to information, social and private networks at any time and place. Owing to the proliferation of "smart" devices and the escalating dependency on them with respect to the execution of everyday tasks, they have evolved from a communication medium to a multifunctional equipment. The reduced cost, in combination with the increasing computational and storage capacity of mobile devices, allow them to accommodate critical functionalities with significant security and safety related impact such as e-banking, control systems and Internet of things architectures. Such devices do not simply store information related to their owners, but also receive data on people and infrastructure related in some way to them. As a result, they can retrieve, store and modify extensive quantities of diverse and potentially sensitive information.

Furthermore, the users are accustomed to the notion of continuous connectivity, even across networks with potentially unknown configurations. Such transmissions are likely to be vulnerable to unauthorized access and, consequently, they constitute a security risk. In many cases, these risks materialize as direct criminal attacks, such as privacy intrusions or unauthorized disruptions of communication. Moreover, they can expose the users to more complex types of malicious activity, such as identity theft, blackmailing, active data collection, or defamation. In light of the increasing risks due to the aforementioned use of mobile devices, it is important that users are aware of the risks they are exposed to and, more importantly, that they are informed about how to protect themselves.

Therefore, the aim of this study is to investigate the user behavior of digital natives from distinct educational backgrounds and levels of security competence. We seek to identify how user confidence, security awareness and background affect their decisions, in aspects related to the use of their mobile devices that can inflict significant security related impact. More specifically, this study investigates how the background and technical competence influences the digital natives' security awareness within five focus areas: (i) Use of Mobile devices; (ii) Connectivity and Network Access; (iii) Management of Credentials; (iv) Knowledge and Fear of Risks; and (v) Self-evaluation of security awareness. With this study, we aim to understand how young people use their mobile devices, how well they know them, and what their concerns are, in order to help improve the secure and safe use of these devices. Our results outline the generic properties of the whole sample and the categorical differences across the groups (see Section 3) within the focus areas.

The results of this study are useful both for designing educational and awareness campaigns, but also for purposes of user behavior modeling. With this article, we aim to highlight areas in which current security related knowledge dissemination is sufficient, areas where there is a clear difference in behavior across the digital natives, and areas where they lack knowledge as a whole or they choose usability over security. The remaining of the paper is structured as follows: Section 2 discusses related work, while Section 3 presents the methodology used for this study. Subsequently, in Section 4, we present the results of the executed surveys, identifying categorical differences across the groups and discussing their origins. Finally, Section 5 summarizes the results extracted from our analysis, while we conclude with presenting the limitations of our study and potential paths for future work.

2. RELATED WORK

Since 2014, mobile devices have been becoming the leading digital platform, displacing the desktop PC [1]. Prensky [2] writes that the digital natives have radically changed their way of thinking by being exposed to technology almost since birth, while other scholars [3] have contested such claims. However, there is no denying that the digital natives have a different view of technology than older generations.

The scope of this article is the digital natives and their security awareness, related in particular to mobile devices. A considerable number of studies concerning user behavior, with regards to selecting and installing applications on smartphones, have found that users do not consider security and privacy issues during app selection, as they tend to ignore privacy policies and EULAs (End-user license agreement) [4]. Furthermore, Android users were found not to pay attention, understand, and act on permission information during installation [5,6]. Mylonas et al. [7] have explored the security awareness metrics of smartphone users who download applications from official application repositories.

The authors of that study applied these to measure how the security background affects the smartphone security awareness of their sample, concluding that security background has a slight impact on awareness. The key differences between the current study and Mylonas et al. is that the latter applied self-rating as the independent variable for determining skill level, did not explicitly target the digital natives and investigated different areas of smartphone security awareness.

Furthermore, Mylonas et al. [8] explore the security awareness of smartphone users who download applications from official application repositories. The findings from said study show that users are complacent in their smartphone security behavior and display high levels of trust towards smartphone application repositories. In addition, they rarely consider privacy and security when installing new applications, and do not install adequate protection mechanisms [9]. Additional research into users and protection mechanisms partially contradicts the idea that smartphone users are not security aware, and finds several correlations between security awareness and smartphone OS, language, and gender [10]. However, the said study [10] does not specifically target the digital natives, despite them being the majority of users. More related to the topic are the studies conducted by Markel and Bernik [11] and Markel and Zgaga [12]. These papers report the findings of a survey carried out in 2011 among 281 students of Slovenian faculties, investigating threat perception on mobile devices [11] and in cyberspace [12]. The findings show that the sample student population had a low awareness of security threats and security measures, and the authors suggest that education and awareness levels must be increased in Slovenia to counter this development.

A common argument towards the reviewed studies is that, although they address a similar topic, they are geographically limited [11,12,13] or they investigate behaviors in relation to subsets of technologies [5,6,9] and problems [4,7,8,9] that are not specifically related to the digital natives. Ariu et al. [14] have worked on filling this gap by studying the level of awareness and perception of IT security amongst university students, paying particular attention to the world of mobile devices. Their report analyses the answers given by 1012 students from over 15 Italian universities to a multiple-choice questionnaire.

The analysis shows that students' perception of their knowledge is generally wrong and that they are unaware of the risks arising from their behavior. This paper builds on the Ariu et al. results and supplements with two additional datasets, thus expanding the knowledge base. The second data set targeted generic computer science students, while the third dataset targeted information and cyber security students specifically.

3. METHODOLOGY

This article builds on a previous study [14] on the topic of security awareness of the digital natives, and was conducted to investigate the differences in risk perception across three distinct groups categorized by their technical background. This section has the following structure: the first sub-section addresses the choice of data collection method and instrument, followed by the sample description, and a brief overview of the statistical methods used for data analysis.

3.1. Data Collection and Instruments

The survey aimed to explore the security awareness of the digital natives addressed to students of the digital age, i.e., persons who were born in the years of the technological boom in Information Technology and Communications (ICT), between 1987–1997. Universities are ideal since they comprise a diverse population. Thus, the sample of this study comes from students born within range. We found the online questionnaire to be the best option for data gathering as it reaches a broad audience and provides a strong level of anonymity; therefore, the presented datasets were collected using Google Forms.

The original survey was developed by Ariu et al. and initially ran in multiple Italian universities [14]. The survey had 60 questions that investigated security awareness aspects within the five areas outlined in the introduction. As for the level of measurement, the questionnaire had categorical, ordinal, and continuous type questions. Category type questions are used here mainly for demographics, while the main bulk of the questionnaire was designed using several mandatory scale and ranking questions.

3.2. Sample and Analysis

This study utilises three distinct samples:

- The data set collected by Ariu et.al., which was targeted at the Italian digital natives, is included in this study and corresponds to our general security competence group (GSCG). The sample consists of 1012 respondents from various university departments (Including law, engineering, computer science, humanitarian, marketing, and multiple other faculties not directed to IT education), which are mapped for the purposes of this study to the general population of digital natives.

- Secondly, we collected data for the medium security competence group (MSCG) by targeting digital natives from Greece with education exclusively in computer science. This group is expected to a have wider knowledge over the use of mobile technologies and increased awareness over security related aspects due to their educational background. The sample consists of 303 responders in total at the undergraduate (234), postgraduate (54), and doctoral (15) levels.
- Finally, the target population for the high security competence group (HSCG) was undergraduate, postgraduate and doctoral students of information security from Norway. These were expected to have a higher security awareness regarding the four main areas than the medium and generic groups, due to their specialized education. For this group, we had 35 respondents in total, of which 21 are undergraduate students, 10 postgraduate, and four doctoral students.

The difference in quantity of respondents for each survey reflects the scarcity of each group in the general population; for example, there are more respondents in GSCG than MSCG, and more in MSCG than HSCG, with the latter group was large enough for the central limit theorem to apply [15]. For the descriptive data analysis, we primarily consider differences in the frequency distributions, while we used the security competence groups as categorical data for bi-variate analysis. The questionnaire primarily asked categorical and ordinal multiple-choice questions, while, as a measure of central tendency for ordinal questions, we considered the median, variance, and range.

4. ANALYSIS OF RESULTS AND DISCUSSION

The individuals participating in the survey, across all competence groups, were requested to self-evaluate their knowledge on aspects related to information security, both before and after participating in the survey (Table 1 and Figure 1). A degradation is noticeable at the "before" and "after" responses across the groups, with the exception of HSCG group participants that selected "Insufficient". In conjunction with the results presented in the following sections, this is attributed to the increased user confidence that characterizes the everyday use, when security threats are not prioritized or not directly visible. This contributes to the unjustified perception of being secure, hence intensifying the security risk, and necessitates increased effort towards educating and making the users aware of the risks.

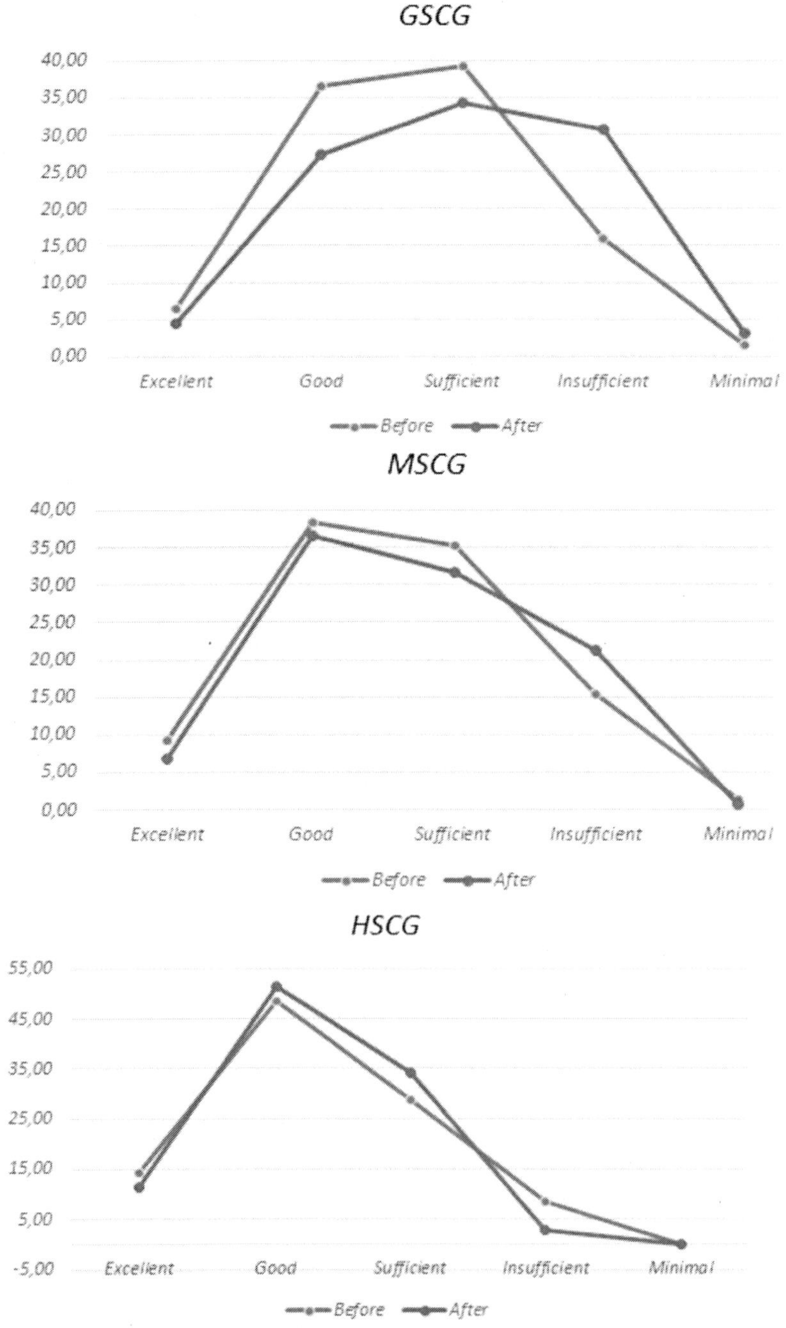

Figure 1. How do you assess your knowledge on information security?

Table 1. How do you assess your knowledge on information security?

		Excellent	Good	Sufficient	Insufficient	Minimal
Before	*GSCG*	*6.5%*	*36.6%*	*39.3%*	*16.0%*	*1.6%*
	MSCG	9.3%	38.5%	35.3%	15.4%	1.3%
	HSCG	14.3%	48.6%	28.6%	8.6%	0.0%
After	*GSCG*	*4.4%*	*27.4%*	*34.4%*	*30.7%*	*3.1%*
	MSCG	6.7%	36.5%	31.7%	21.2%	0.6%
	HSCG	11.4%	51.4%	34.3%	2.9%	0.0%

GSCG: general security competence group; MSCG: medium security competence group; HSCG: high security competence group.

4.1. Use of Mobile Devices

This section includes questions related to the use of mobile devices and applications, as well as questions related to user behavior when selling or losing a mobile device, and modifying its operating system.

We asked the digital natives what they store on their mobile devices, while a section of the question referred to personal passwords. As presented in Table 2, despite the frequent warnings, an average of 29.1% of the responders stores personal passwords in their mobile devices, regardless of their security related competence or background.

Table 2. Do you store personal passwords on your mobile device? (in plaintext).

	Yes	No
GSCG	*27.7%*	*72.3%*
MSCG	31.1%	68.9%
HSCG	28.6%	71.4%

Subsequently, we asked the digital natives if, in the case of loss/theft of their mobile device, they reported the event to the authorities. The results that are presented in Table 3 highlight the fact that the users are not widely aware of the ability to deny access to wireless networks based on the IMEI (International Mobile Equipment Identity) and other misuse countermeasures. Additionally, some of the differences in the responses between the GSCG and the MSCG/HSCG groups are likely caused due to regional variations in legislation, trust in the efficiency of the authorities, and the awareness of related countermeasures.

Table 3. Have you reported the loss/theft of your device to the authorities?

	Yes	**No**
GSCG	*68.5%*	*31.5%*
MSCG	33.5%	66.5%
HSCG	28.6%	71.4%

The next question focused on software updates on cellphones/tablets and laptops. The results for each category of mobile devices are presented in Table 4 and Figure 2 and Figure 3. It is noticeable that 14.5% of the GSCG group state that they do not update anything in their laptops, while across all groups, updating only the applications ranks higher than updating only the operating system. Furthermore, comparing the results of the two categories, we observe that the GSCG and MSCG groups better maintain the software of their cellphones/tablets in comparison to their laptops.

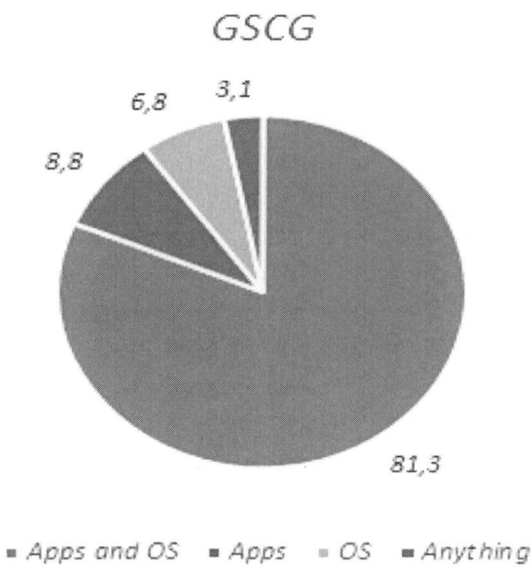

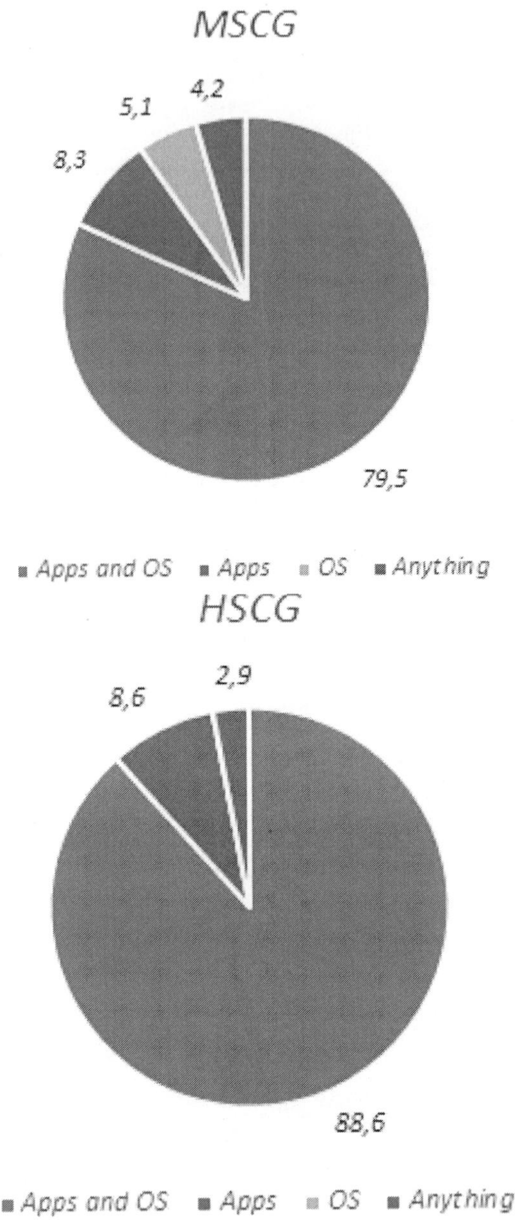

Figure 2. Do you regularly update the software on your mobile device? (cellphone/tablet).

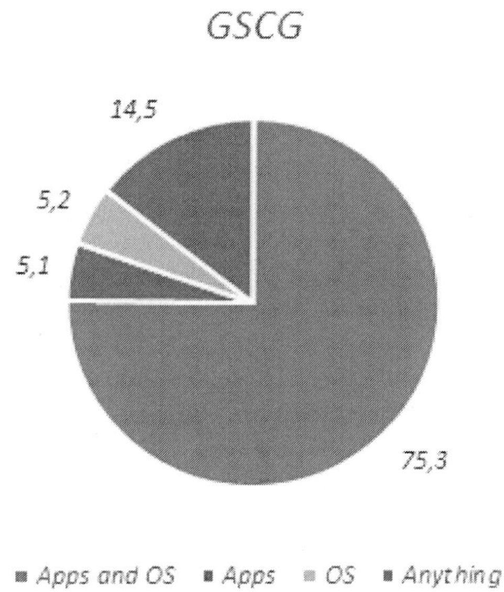
GSCG
14,5
5,2
5,1
75,3
Apps and OS
Apps
OS
Anything

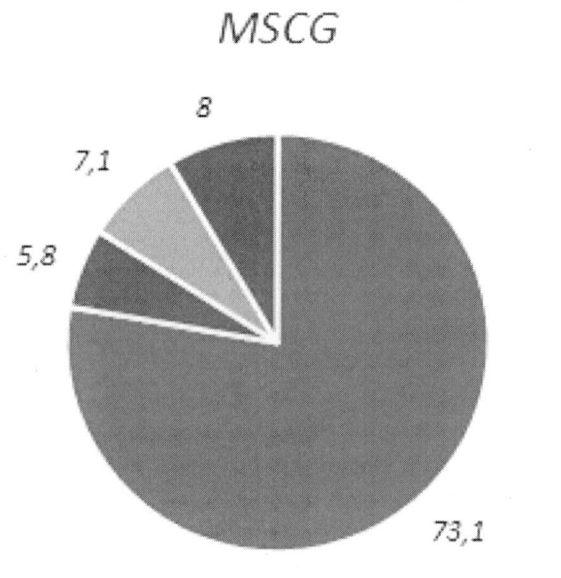
MSCG
8
7,1
5,8
73,1
Apps and OS
Apps
OS
Anything

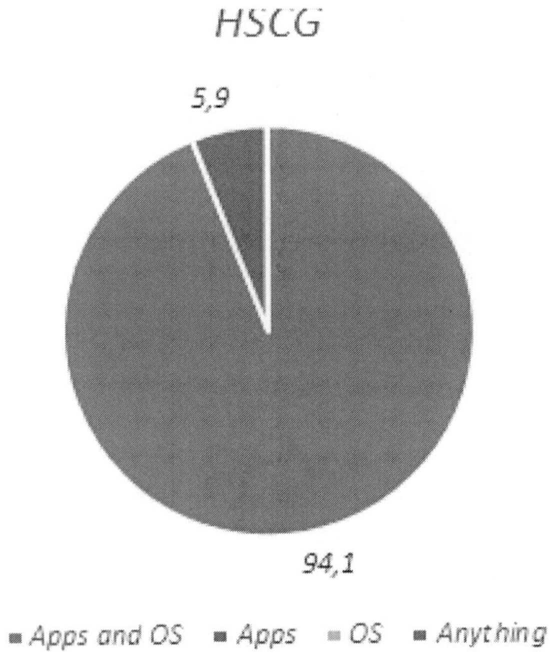

Figure 3. Do you regularly update the software on your mobile device? (laptop).

Table 4. Do you regularly update the software on your mobile device?

		Apps and OS	Apps	OS	Anything
Cellphone/tablet	GSCG	81.3%	8.8%	6.8%	3.1%
	MSCG	79.5%	8.3%	5.1%	4.2%
	HSCG	88.6%	8.6%	0.0%	2.9%
Laptop	GSCG	75.3%	5.1%	5.2%	14.5%
	MSCG	73.1%	5.8%	7.1%	8.0%
	HSCG	94.1%	5.9%	0.0%	0.0%

Regarding the use of applications, the next question focused on the sources that the digital natives use in order to download applications from, as presented in Table 5. Over 80% of the digital natives primarily use the official store, while an average of 12.3% across groups consciously uses non-official sources, regardless of the potential security threats. However, there is a positive correlation between security competence and application source.

Table 5. Where do you download applications from?

	Official Store	Other Sources
GSCG	*83.1%*	*16.9%*
MSCG	85.9%	11.5%
HSCG	91.4%	8.6%

Focusing on the behavior of the digital natives in terms of the application usage patterns, we asked how they manage their credentials when they have finished using an application. The results that are presented in Table 6highlight that, regardless of knowledge on the potential privacy and other implications, they select usability over security, since only an average of 24.5% logs out. Furthermore, there is a notable difference between the MSCG and HSCG regarding saving the credentials, where the HSCG group more frequently chooses to save the credentials to stay logged in. Another notable finding is that a significant percentage of participants states that logging-out is "not important".

Table 6. As soon as you have finished using an application, you..?

	Save Credentials to Stay Logged in	Log out	Forget to Log out	Do Not Log out Because It Is Not Important	Do Not Log out Because I Do Not Know How
GSCG	40.3%	24.1%	19.6%	10.3%	5.6%
MSCG	30.8%	26.6%	16.7%	20.5%	1.9%
HSCG	48.6%	22.9%	14.3%	14.3%	0.0%

Another aspect of application usage patterns with significant security implications is the control of application access rights. Thus, we asked the digital natives how frequently they check the permissions that an application requires prior to accepting its installation. The results, in Table 7, show significant differences across the groups with a positive correlation between competence and security behavior. Analyzing these responses, in conjunction with the results of Table 6, highlights that expertise and knowledge can affect user behavior when security is not in conflict with usability.

Table 7. How frequently do you check the permissions (access rights) that the application requires before completing the installation?

	Never	Rarely	Often	Always
GSCG	*15.6%*	*38.2%*	*25.5%*	*20.7%*
MSCG	8.0%	26.3%	27.6%	34.9%
HSCG	5.7%	14.3%	40.0%	40.0%

A set of questions in this section focused on technical knowledge regarding mobile devices, in particular jail breaking and rooting, as presented in Table 8 and Figure 4. The respondents across all groups seem to be familiar with these practices, and despite justifiably considering them potentially hazardous in terms of security, an average of 41.6% has used them in their mobile devices. The results show a difference between the groups where the competence level correlates positively with having a jail broken or rooted mobile device, while the HSCG is slightly (8–10%) less likely to consider these practices as risky. It is evident, from the second data set presented in this table, that individuals with computer science/engineering background are less reluctant in applying such methods. This has also been traced across the GSCG group, when filtering the digital natives according to their academic background [14].

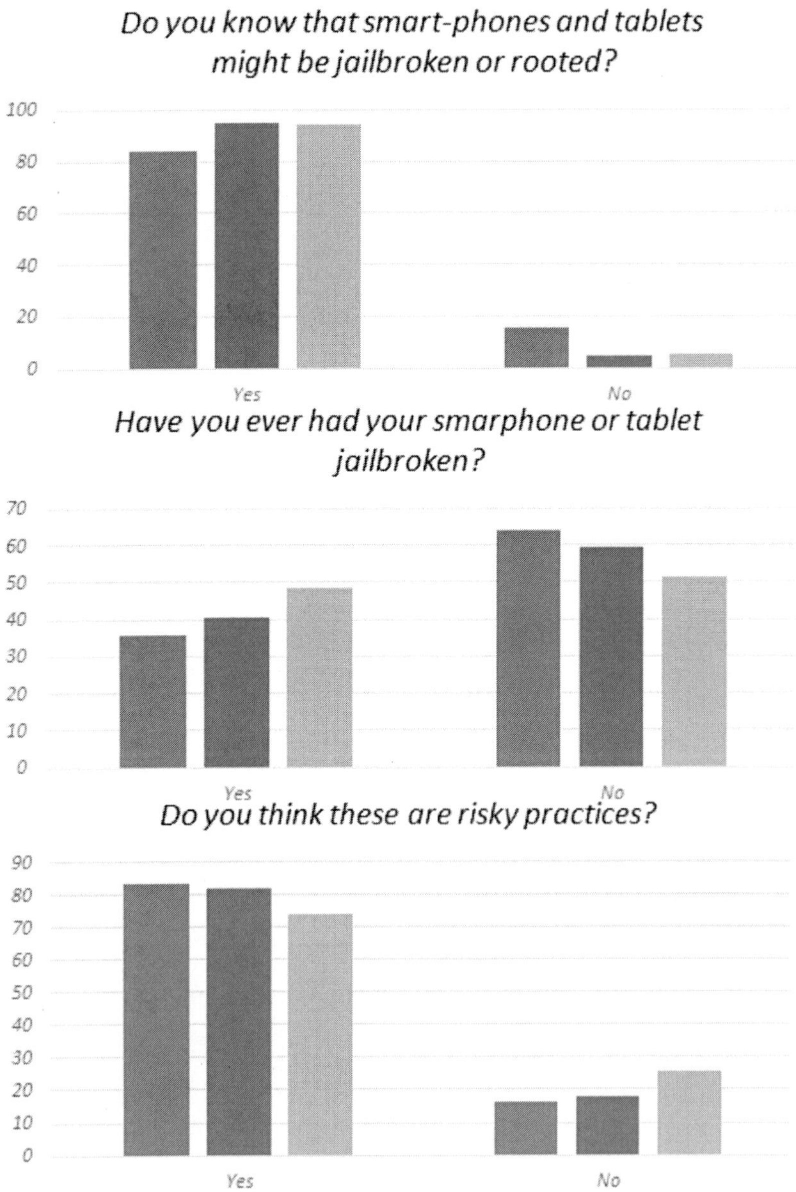

Figure 4. Visualization of Table 8 results.

Table 8. Jailbreaking and rooting mobile devices.

Do you know that smartphones and tablets might be jailbroken or rooted?		
	Yes	No
GSCG	84.2%	15.8%
MSCG	94.9%	5.1%
HSCG	94.3%	5.7%
Have you ever had your smarphone or tablet jailbroken?		
GSCG	35.7%	64.3%
MSCG	40.4%	59.6%
HSCG	48.6%	51.4%
Do you think these are risky practices?		
GSCG	83.5%	16.5%
MSCG	82.1%	17.9%
HSCG	74.3%	25.7%

Additionally to these results, the questionnaire included a number of propositions regarding the security of these techniques (jailbreaking, etc.), which the respondents had to evaluate as "True", "False", or "Unknown". An example of the investigated propositions is: *"Some Jailbreaking methods delete some operating systems' protections, which can be exploited by malicious code"*. In the majority of cases, these propositions have been answered incorrectly by all groups, suggesting that the digital natives are willing to apply such methods on their mobile devices, despite being aware of the involved security risks and without the required experience/ knowledge.

4.2. Connectivity and Network Access

This section was focused on analyzing the behavior of digital natives towards connectivity and network access. The results show significant variations across the groups, while one of the most notable differences relates to user behavior when they have the opportunity to connect to an unsecured wireless network, as presented in Table 9.

As presented in Figure 5, there exists a significant difference between the GSCG and the other two groups when it comes to connecting to free Wi-Fi, with both mobile devices and laptops, the former having the largest divergence. The MSCG are more likely to connect their mobile devices, but restrict the use of activities that require credential authentication. Moreover, the HSCG stands out with 42.9% opting not to connect with mobile devices at all, which represents a 20% difference from the two other groups. It is also noticeable that a larger portion of the HSCG (45.7%) opts to connect their laptops, rather than their mobile devices, to unsecured Wi-Fi with restricted activities.

Table 9. If you find free Wi-Fi, what do you do with your mobile device?

		I Connect and Use the Internet without Restrictions	I Connect but Only Do Activities that Do Not Require Credential Authentication	I Do Not Connect
Cellphone/tablet	GSCG	43.6%	33.4%	23.0%
	MSCG	26.0%	44.9%	21.8%
	HSCG	22.9%	34.3%	42.9%
Laptop	GSCG	43.6%	33.4%	23.0%
	MSCG	28.0%	46.9%	25.1%
	HSCG	25.7%	45.7%	28.6%

The results across all types of mobile devices, show that user background and knowledge of the involved risks can affect their behavior, according to the significant differences across groups in response to the "I connect and use the Internet without restrictions" question. However, the results highlight that only with small exceptions across people with a security related background do users disregard or are unaware of the involved risks. Furthermore, users tend to be less reluctant when using their laptops in comparison to other mobile devices, potentially due to a falsely increased trust level in the security of such devices.

4.3. Management of Credentials

This section presents results in questions related to the management of credentials and the use of protection technologies. Initially, the digital natives have been asked about the solutions they use, in order to enforce access control to their mobile devices. The results revealed that 40.1% of the GSCG group, 19.9% of the MSCG group and 8.6% of the HSCG group choose to not use any access control mechanism in their mobile devices, while the pattern lock and PINs (Personal Identification Numbers) were the most popular solutions among the GSCG–MSCG groups and biometrics for the HSCG group. The results showed that the users' background can significantly affect related decisions regarding the overall use of access control mechanisms, while the exact choice of technologies can also be affected by financial or cultural agents.

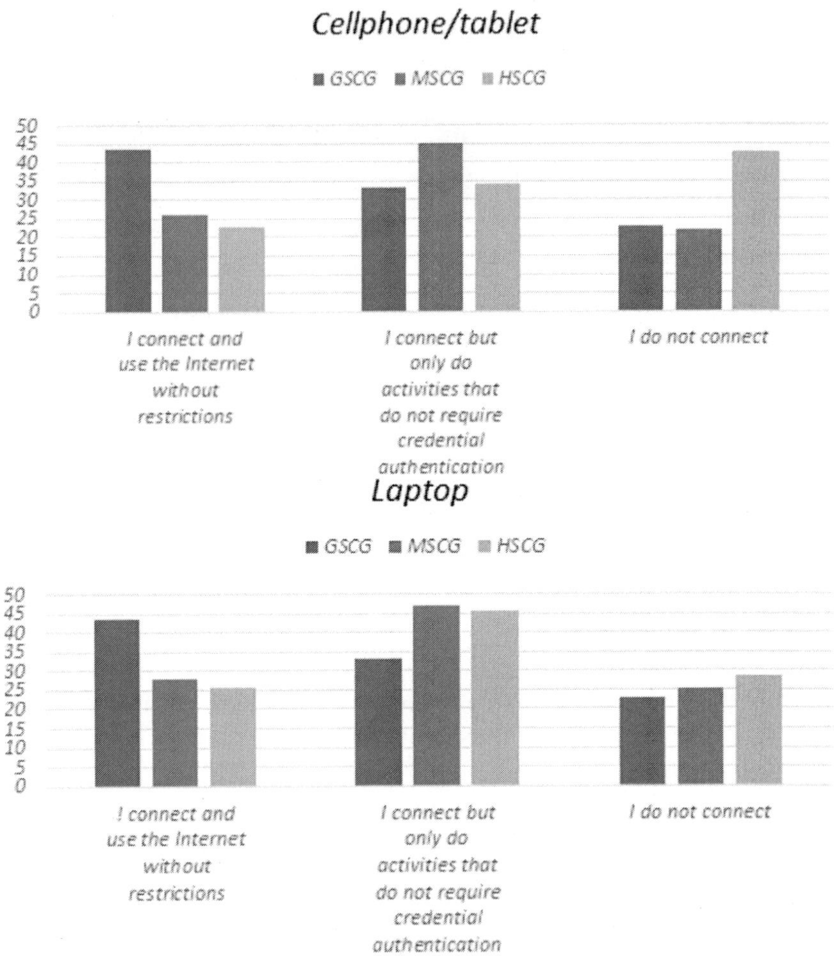

Figure 5. If you find free Wi-Fi, what do you do with your mobile device?

Aiming to identify potential external influences on these results, we asked the digital natives to identify the reasons behind the decision to not utilize an access control mechanism. The results that are presented in Table 10show that the usability of these mechanisms can significantly affect this decision. For the HSCG group, the use of access control was at 91.4%, with biometrics used in 54.3% of the sample, which highlights that users who are aware of the involved risks and provided with usable solutions (biometrics) will increasingly incorporate access control mechanisms.

Table 10. If you do not use a mechanism to protect access to your mobile device, why is that so?

	I Know Them but Never Thought About Using Them	I Know Them but I Am Not Interested in Using Them	I Know Them but They Make the Use of My Device Uncomfortable	I Do Not Know Them
GSCG	13.6%	27.7%	52.5%	6.3%
MSCG	3.0%	41.5%	51.0%	5.0%
HSCG	16.7%	33.3%	50.0%	0.0%

A further set of questions was dedicated to analyzing the use of passwords for authentication purposes. The results in Table 11 and Table 12 show that a mixture of best and worst practices is implemented across the groups, with significant variations among the different password types. Lasting and persistent awareness campaigns focused in the past several years on educating the public and raising awareness about best practices. However, these results show that, despite the visible positive influence, the system did not reach a stable state yet, while educating the users on security best practices requires sending a simple and clear message.

Table 11. For applications that require a password.

	I Always Use the Same Password for All the Applications	I Use Small Variations of the Same Password for Different Applications	I Always Use Different Passwords	I Do Not Use Applications that Require Passwords
GSCG	20.6%	41.3%	31.7%	6.3%
MSCG	8.7%	41.7%	39.1%	6.7%
HSCG	5.7%	51.4%	40.0%	2.9%

Table 12. What type of password are you most likely to use?

	The passwords that I use are at least 8 characters long	
	Yes	No
GSCG	*87.0%*	*13.0%*
MSCG	83.7%	11.5%
HSCG	100.0%	0.0%
	I use passwords that contain personal information	
GSCG	*36.5%*	*63.5%*
MSCG	36.8%	63.2%
HSCG	17.1%	82.9%
	I use passwords that contain simple strings of characters (1234, qwerty, etc.)	
GSCG	*8.7%*	*91.3%*
MSCG	29.5%	80.5%
HSCG	0.0%	100.0%
	I use passwords that contain meaningful words	
GSCG	*45.0%*	*55.0%*
MSCG	27.8%	72.2%
HSCG	34.3%	65.7%
	I use passwords that contain numbers and special characters	
GSCG	*74.6%*	*25.4%*
MSCG	9.1%	90.9%
HSCG	97.1%	2.9%
	If the system allows it, I do not use a password	
GSCG	*6.2%*	*93.8%*
MSCG	9.4%	90.6%
HSCG	14.3%	85.7%

4.4. Knowledge and Fear of Risks

This section included questions aiming to identify how the users perceive security related risks, their level of confidence in using their mobile device and their concerns. A summary of the results is presented in Figure 6 and Figure 7, showing that the background affects the confidence of users in respect to security related risks, especially regarding laptop usage. However, a difference between the distributions corresponding to cellphones/tablets and laptops is noticeable. In correlation with the network access results presented in Section 4.2, this can be traced both to the maturity of the technologies and the roles of the distinct devices in daily use. Additionally, it is evident that, despite their increased computational capacity, access to personal data, and incorporation into critical systems, the users, to a great extent, seem to still perceive smartphones and tablets in a more liberal fashion.

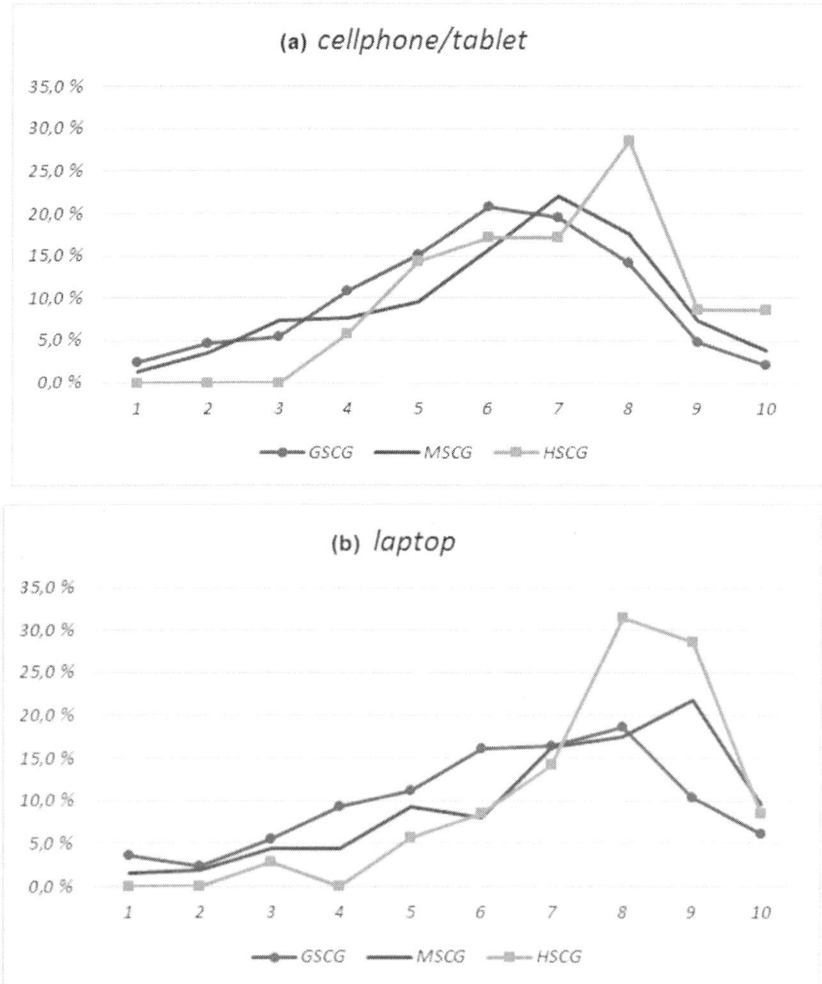

Figure 6. On a scale from 1 (none) to 10 (excellent), how do you assess your knowledge of issues and risks associated with the use of your—(a) cellphone/tablet, (b) laptop?

5. SUMMARY OF RESULTS

The most significant findings of this study can be summarized as follows:

- Users tend to have increased confidence in the daily use of their mobile devices, leading them to negligent behavior towards actions with potential security related impact. However, the digital natives seem to adopt a more constrained stance when security threats become directly visible. It would be interesting to investigate the variations in user behavior prior and after a major security incident, along with analyzing the duration and extent of this phenomenon.

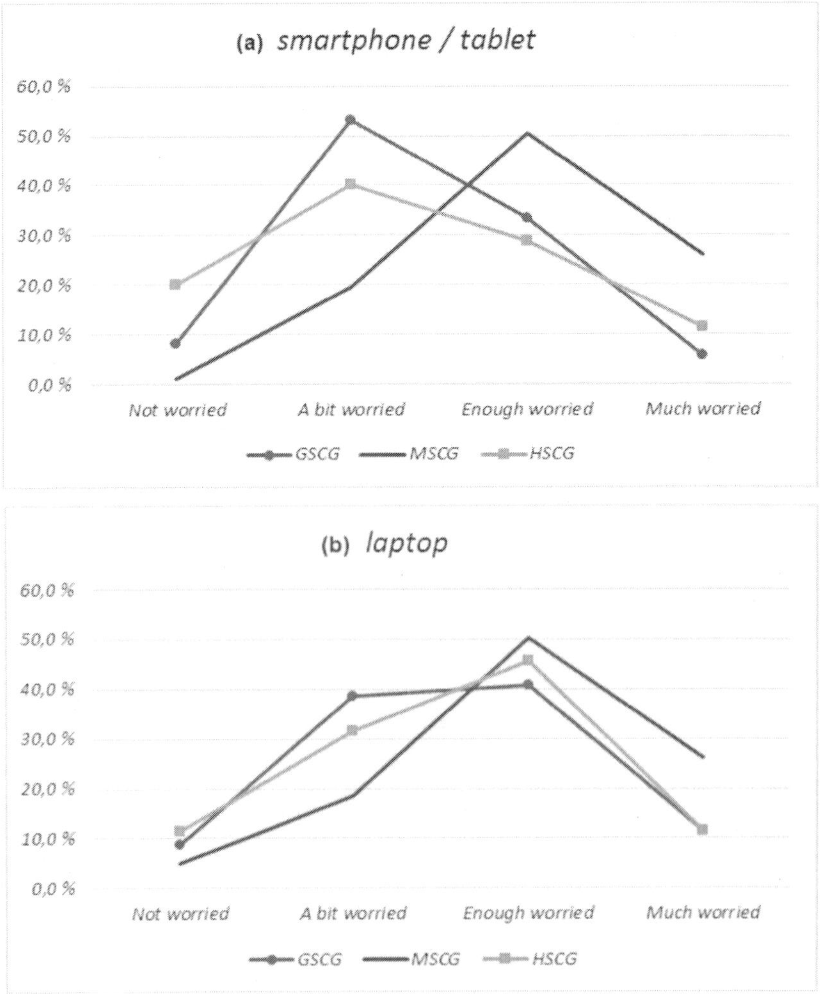

Figure 7. How concerned are you about the security of your—(a) cellphone/tablet, (b) laptop?

- Specific areas of user behavior (such as the storage of plaintext passwords in mobile devices) are not significantly affected by their security awareness or background, with a consistent percentage of digital natives remaining willing to accept the risk. Aiming to facilitate further security improvements in such areas would require not only informing the users about the potential threats, but also channeling those who persist in the practicality of such actions into more secure alternatives (e.g., password managers).
- The digital natives still remain unaware of some countermeasures that are available at their disposal and could improve their user experience while maintaining higher security standards.
- Variations in user behavior have been identified to originate not only from their level of security awareness, but also from regional, financial and cultural agents. Thus, regional studies and campaigns aiming to raise security awareness, must be scoped and adapted accordingly.
- Users tend to prioritize access to services and the usability of their mobile devices over the enforcement of security measures, without major differentiations based on their background. However, the results of this study have shown that users who are aware of the security risks are willing to opt for security when usable solutions become available.
- Digital natives are willing to accept risks despite of their concerns about security (e.g., jailbreaking/rooting, unofficial application sources) in order to obtain access to additional services. This decision is not significantly affected by their overall knowledge about security, while users with backgrounds in engineering, computer science or information security are less reluctant due to their increased confidence.
- The users of mobile devices seem to feel more confident and less constrained in terms of security when using their laptops in comparison to smartphones and tablets. This is attributed to the maturity of the technologies, but also the lack of recognition of the increased computational capacity and criticality of tasks allocated to smartphones and tablets.
- In some aspects, such as the selection of secure passwords, the digital natives seem to be informed of the appropriate practices. However, the results highlight that, despite the noticeable improvement, a precise framework still needs to be consolidated across the users' mindsets.

6. LIMITATIONS

This study has been conducted under the limitation that the dataset referring to the GSCG was collected in a prior investigation. Therefore, access to the raw data was not possible, something that restricted the possibility for deeper statistical analysis. Inherently, expanding the samples' geographic distribution for this study carries interlacing cultural influences. Therefore, future work in this field should also consolidate an understanding of the influences arising from such fine-grained cultural divergences.

7. CONCLUSIONS

The purpose of this study was to investigate how the digital natives use their mobile devices, their level of security awareness, and how these relate to their background and educational influences. Our goal was to identify common usage patterns with negative security impact in order to facilitate the deployment of suitable risk treatments. To this end, an initial study of students across Italian Universities has been extended, totaling 1350 participants across three countries, mirroring distinct educational backgrounds and security related competence levels. Categorical differences have been identified between the groups within all five investigated areas, allowing the extraction of findings referring to the modeling of digital natives both across and within the investigated groups.

The results of this study open multiple paths for future work. Regarding risk understanding, the digital natives tend to have increased confidence in the daily use of their mobile devices, but seem to adopt a more constrained stance when security threats become directly visible. A path for future work would be to investigate the variations in user behavior prior and after a major security incident as stated earlier. Our results may also contribute to targeted user-modeling validation studies, specifically regarding the correctness of how developers and security experts perceive the user behavior of the digital natives.

ACKNOWLEDGMENTS

We extend our thanks to Francesca Bosco for giving us access to the questionnaire used in [14]; to Elisavet-Maria Katsika for translating it from Italian to Greek; and to Marte Lunde for suggesting to extend the survey to Norwegian students.

REFERENCES

1. Lella, A.; Lipsman, A. The US Mobile App Report. 2014. Available online: http://www.comscore.com/Insights/Presentationsand-Whitepapers/2014/The-US-Mobile-App-Report (accessed on 8 April 2015)
2. Prensky, M. Digital natives, digital immigrants part 1. *On the Horizon* 2001, *9*, 1–6
3. Bennett, S.; Maton, K.; Kervin, L. The 'digital natives' debate: A critical review of the evidence. *Br. J. Educ. Technol.* 2008, *39*, 775–786
4. Chin, E.; Felt, A.P.; Sekar, V.; Wagner, D. Measuring user confidence in smartphone security and privacy. In Proceedings of the Eighth Symposium on Usable Privacy and Security, Washington, DC, USA, 11–13 July 2012
5. Felt, A.P.; Ha, E.; Egelman, S.; Haney, A.; Chin, E.; Wagner, D. Android permissions: User attention, comprehension, and behavior. In Proceedings of the Eighth Symposium on Usable Privacy and Security, Washington, DC, USA, 11–13 July 2012
6. Kelley, P.G.; Consolvo, S.; Cranor, L.F.; Jung, J.; Sadeh, N.; Wetherall, D. A conundrum of permissions: Installing applications on an android smartphone. In Proceedings of the International Conference on Financial Cryptography and Data Security, Kralendijk, Bonaire, 27 February–2 March 2012; Springer: Berlin/Heidelberg, Germany, 2012; pp. 68–79
7. Mylonas, A.; Gritzalis, D.; Tsoumas, B.; Apostolopoulos, T. A qualitative metrics vector for the awareness of smartphone security users. In Proceedings of the International Conference on Trust, Privacy and Security in Digital Business, Prague, Czech Republic, 28–29 August 2013; Springer: Berlin/Heidelberg, Germany, 2013; pp. 173–184
8. Mylonas, A.; Kastania, A.; Gritzalis, D. Delegate the smartphone user? Security awareness in smartphone platforms. *Comput. Secur.* 2013, *34*, 47–66
9. Ophoff, J.; Robinson, M. Exploring end-user smartphone security awareness within a South African context. In Proceedings of the 2014 Information Security for South Africa, Johannesburg, South Africa, 13–14 August 2014
10. Parker, F.; Ophoff, J.; Van Belle, J.P.; Karia, R. Security awareness and adoption of security controls by smartphone users. In Proceedings of the 2015 Second International Conference on Information Security and Cyber Forensics (InfoSec), Cape Town, South Africa, 15–17 November 2015
11. Markelj, B.; Bernik, I. Safe use of mobile devices arises from knowing the threats. *J. Inf. Secur. Appl.* 2015, *20*, 84–89
12. Markelj, B.; Zgaga, S. Comprehension of cyber threats and their consequences in Slovenia. *Comput. Law Secur. Rev.* 2016, *32*, 513–525
13. Sheila, M.; Faizal, M.; Shahrin, S. Dimension of mobile security model: Mobile user security threats and awareness. *Int. J. Mob. Learn. Organ.* 2015, *9*, 66–85
14. Ariu, D.; Bosco, F.; Ferraris, V.; Perri, P.; Spolti, G.; Stirparo, P.; Vaciago, G.; Zanero, S. Security of the Digital Natives. 2014. Available online: https://ssrn.com/abstract=2442037 (accessed on 13 October 2016)
15. Norman, G. Likert scales, levels of measurement and the "laws" of statistics. *Adv. Health Sci. Educ.* 2010, *15*, 625–632

CHAPTER 15

BBDS: Blockchain-Based Data Sharing for Electronic Medical Records in Cloud Environments

Qi Xia *, Emmanuel Boateng Sifah, Abla Smahi, Sandro Amofa and Xiaosong Zhang

Center for Cyber Security, Computer Science and Engineering, University of Electronic Science and Technology of China, Chengdu 610054, China

ABSTRACT

Disseminating medical data beyond the protected cloud of institutions poses severe risks to patients' privacy, as breaches push them to the point where they abstain from full disclosure of their condition. This situation negatively impacts the patient, scientific research, and all stakeholders. To address this challenge, we propose a blockchain-based data sharing framework that sufficiently addresses the access control challenges associated with sensitive data stored in the cloud using immutability and built-in autonomy properties of the blockchain. Our system is based on a permissioned blockchain which allows access to only invited, and hence verified users. As a result of this design, further accountability is guaranteed as all users are already known and a log of their actions is kept by the blockchain. The system permits users to request data from the shared pool after their identities and cryptographic keys are verified. The evidence from the system evaluation shows that our scheme is lightweight, scalable, and efficient.

Keywords: cloud computing; blockchain; data sharing; privacy; access control; electronic medical records

1. INTRODUCTION

The migration of medical records to cloud-based platforms has facilitated the sharing of medical data between healthcare and research institutions, enabling faster and more convenient exchange in a manner previously not possible [1]. The advantages of collaboration range from gaining new insights into already existing treatments, analysing new ones, and better management of population health. However, the risks and challenges associated with the practice are significant and cannot be ignored [2,3,4].

Typically, the data is stored in cloud repositories which are protected with traditional access controls in order to comply with the many policies and frameworks that govern its sharing [5,6,7,8,9]. These measures have several shortcomings as they have been breached time and again. First, they aim to protect the data by the penalties to be inflicted in the event of a breach; Second, users can exercise no control over the data once it leaves the sharing institution; Third, no technical barrier exists to prevent the recombination of data shared from different sources and hence the risk of re-identification of individuals remains when dealing with anonymised data sets [10]. Techniques like K-anonymity [11], ℓ-Diversity [12], t-closeness [13,14], and others developed to guarantee privacy in such instances have not been sufficient. Patients who are unsure about adequate protection measures for the data they provide may avoid treatment altogether or make full disclosure of their medical condition a non-option.

Existing electronic medical data sharing schemes generally have one of two challenges: the first achieves good data sharing but comes with poor control. In effect, the institution that shares the data loses the ability to control it. This raises privacy concerns as there are several ways to narrow down data sets and to re-identify individuals even where anonymizing was carried out prior to sharing. The second retains strong control of the data and remains poor at sharing. This defeats the paradigm of sharing in order to facilitate the derivation of greater value from already available data sets. Therefore, strict accountable access control to the shared cloud repository is paramount.

Generally, implementing access control in systems is usually achieved in three steps: identification, authentication, and authorization. Aside from permitting only legitimate users' entry, access control also ensures accountability: the ability to track which user carried out what action in a system. In traditional access control systems, security administrators determine which user(s) can access a particular piece of information. With that said, these current systems are more vulnerable to hacking as well as anonymous intrusions [15].

Blockchain technology is relatively new and has seen advanced developments of its most significant application in cryptocurrencies (Bitcoin currently being the best known of them all) [16,17]. Aside from the use of the blockchain technology in the aforementioned area, developers are already hard at work building applications and services (identity management, proof of existence for intellectual property, decentralised DNS services, and others) that leverage the power and versatility of the blockchain [18].

There is therefore the urgency to develop a blockchain based access control method that sufficiently controls the access to medical data stored and processed on cloud systems and securely provides efficient data sharing. Blockchain technology offers secure cryptographic techniques to identify and authenticate users and systems and thereby contrive access control in a scalable, distributed, and secure manner [19]. The blockchain in such a system will be used for data control.

In this paper, we propose a secure, scalable access control system for sensitive information. We employ secure cryptographic techniques (encryption and digital signatures) to ensure efficient access control to sensitive shared data pool(s) using a permissioned blockchain for added security and a closely monitored system. We design a blockchain-based data-sharing scheme that permits data users/owners to access electronic medical records from a shared repository after their identities and cryptographic keys have been verified. The requests after verification and onward servicing form part of a closed, permissioned blockchain. Our system succeeds where traditional access control methods of passwords, firewalls, and intrusion detection systems fail.

2. RELATED WORKS

In this section, research trends pertaining to access control with emphasis on the improving blockchain technology are outlined.

Guy Zyskind et al. [19] addressed privacy preservation when using third party mobile services. When signing up to a mobile application for the first time, a set of permissions (such as location, list of contacts, camera, etc.) are required to be granted for the proper functioning of the app. Unlike existing applications, the proposed platform allows only users to change the permissions in accordance with the access control policies stored on the blockchain. The proposed decentralised system consists of three entities: mobile phone users, service providers (applications), and the nodes maintaining the blockchain. In the blockchain network, two types of transactions are accepted; T_{access} for access control management and T_{data} for data storage and retrieval. For every user of a service, identity and the associated permissions are generated and sent to the blockchain in a T_{access} transaction. Data collected from the user's mobile phone is encrypted and stored off-blockchain; only hashes of the data are stored in the public ledger. Both the user and service can query the data in a T_{data}transaction.

Xiao Yue et al. [20] in their research briefly tackled access control management within the healthcare data sharing systems. The authors propose the one purpose-centric access control model. Two kinds of data users were distinguished; r-users denote users seeking to read raw data and p-users denote users who attempt to read data and retrieve results. For every data request, a transaction is made up of a requester who wants to access data of a specific category within a limited period depending on their purpose.

Guy Zyskind et al. [21] used the blockchain for access control management and for audit log security purposes, as a tamper proof log of events. Enigma is a proposed decentralized computation platform based on an optimized version of the secure multiparty computation (sMPC). The different parties altogether store and run computations on data while keeping the data completely private.

Blockchain-based access control management was described in more detail in Thomas and Alex's system [22]. The ChainAnchor system provides anonymous but verifiable identity to entities trying to perform transactions to a permissioned blockchain. The Enhanced Privacy ID (EPID) zero-knowledge proof scheme is used to achieve and prove the participants' anonymity and membership. Entities can then register—as many times as they desire—their self-asserted public key for transacting on the blockchain. Based on these public keys, miners (consensus nodes) sieve the transactions; the transactions having their origin from unknown public keys are ignored or dropped.

On the other hand, access control for Internet of Things (IoT) applications has been gaining considerable attention in recent years. Affaf Ouaddah et al. [23] proposed the FairAccess system that relies on the bitcoin blockchain technology and smart contracts for access control management in an IoT-based environment. Related to the IoT, much research on Wireless Sensor Network (WSN)-based access control has been done [24,25,26]. Fan Wu et al. [24] addressed the access control in secure group communication (SGC) of WSNs. In this framework, node access privileges are assigned by the network's administrator to ensure the adaptability and the flexibility of the system.

Table 1 below presents a comparison between different access control schemes presented in the literature.

Table 1. Comparison between proposed access control schemes from the literature.

References	Blockchain-Based	Scalability	Identity Management	Distant-Access
[24]	N	Y	N	N
[26]	N	Y	Y	N
[20]	Y	N	N	Y
[19]	Y	N	Y	N
Our proposed BBDS	Y	Y	Y	Y (in case parties have already joined the system)

Our main contribution is to provide a transparent blockchain-based Data Sharing for Electronic Medical Records system. It should be mentioned that our system relies on identity-based authentication to achieve the users' membership. Moreover, a lightweight block format has been—for the first time—proposed to improve the system's efficiency compared to the existing blockchain implementations (e.g., bitcoin).

3. PRELIMINARIES

In this section, we formally define the preliminaries used in our blockchain-based scheme for electronic medical records, including the blockchain network, blocks, and cryptographic keys.

3.1. Blockchain Network

The blockchain is a distributed database that contains an ordered list of records linked together through a chain, on blocks. Blocks can be described as sets of individual entities that hold information pertaining to some transactions, for example, financial transactions. The blockchain maintains a continuously growing list of records which are distributed and immutable. It is for this reason that many systems built on the blockchain technology achieve secure distribution of assets amongst untrusted clients.

For a client "A" who wants to transfer an asset to a client "B", the asset is verified by sets of nodes and ownership of such an asset is tagged to the client "A". The client transfers the asset through a channel to "B" who becomes the new owner of this asset. All these records of verification, transfer, and change of ownership are recorded in a public database for future transactions and references. In cases where there is a malicious activity, verifying nodes can trace the attributes of the record and resolve the issues. For such systems, there is a need for a database that is highly immutable and provably secure. For transactions between clients who have no idea of the identities of each other, there is an equal need for a system to allow a trust-less but secure transaction between such parties. The blockchain is a perfect fit for resolving these problems associated with trust and change in data in cloud storage. It is highly distributed; meaning every single client part of the network has records of every valid transaction completed on the network. The properties of the blockchain that make it attractive for secure sharing of data are its immutability and "trust-less" transaction execution.

In relation to our work, the blockchain network is made up of individual blocks which are formed from events chained together from the genesis (first block) to the current or broadcast block. When blocks which contain details of an entire event (which spans from the time the user sends a request until the time he gets the data) are broadcast into the network, the blocks form a chain and can never be changed, updated, or removed. This enables data forensics and enhances data traceability in events where a user abuses the policies of data handling in the group or when there is a malicious threat in the system.

A block is made up of a single event and an event spans from the moment a request was created to when the block was broadcast into the blockchain. In instances where an authorized body needs to investigate irregularities in the system, a request is sent and access is granted to probe into the irregularities. The consensus node bears the responsibility to mine and report on the results of such irregularities. This is easy due to the blocks being linked together with an attractive property of the blockchain's immutability.

In summary, the blockchain network acts as an immutable ledger. Processed and authorised blocks are only allowed into the blockchain network if and only if the block is broadcast by an appropriate authorised entity. No other entity has the permission to broadcast blocks into the network.

3.2. Cryptographic Keys

Cryptographic keys denote the sets of keys established to perform tasks pertaining to the security of a system. For the blockchain-based scheme we propose, we establish such keys which perform roles in relation to user authentication and membership, user verification, request generation, and request authentication. These keys help to guarantee a level of security of the scheme. The keys include:

- Membership issuing Keys: Generated and sent to a user who requests to join a data sharing system and allows access to the membership verification key with adequate parameters necessary to generate the transaction private and public key. Without the membership issuing key, users are not allowed to join the system.
- Membership verification Key: Used to authenticate a user's validity in a system and consents to a user's access to the membership private key. The membership verification key is used to generate the user's membership private key.
- Membership private key: Used to create a request which later develops into blocks. Without access to a membership private key, a user can never create a request.
- Transaction private key: Used to digitally sign requests created from a membership private key.
- Transaction public key: Used to verify signatures on a block. For a request whose signature cannot match to the appropriate public key, such a request is considered as invalid.

3.3. Membership Authentication and Verification

For a user to join the permissioned blockchain, there is the need for membership authentication. The verification and acquisition of a user's identity used to generate specific keys in relation to the user needs to be secure through already established systems. In our work, we adopt an efficient and secure identity-based authentication and key agreement protocol which guarantees user anonymity as a means to which membership authentication is achieved. Methods necessary to setup a new user as a member into the system is categorised into two parts.

The first section is based on an existing cryptographic techniques adopted from Wu et al.'s work [27]. The authentication phase includes system setup, key exchange, and authentication and key agreement. System setup involves generating parameters necessary to compute the shared key for the system. These parameters are drawn from the identities of the users and random numbers. Key exchange is based on sets of computations drawn from the system setup with strong emphasis on random variables that both the user and the issuer exchange with each other. Authentication and key agreement which includes the first section describes the creation of the shared, symmetric key for the user and issuer. The shared key computed by the user and issuer is used to encrypt and decrypt information pertaining to account registration and verification for the user to be a member of the system.

The second section is based on the sharing of information for account registration and verification for the user. The issuer sends an encrypted form which requires pre-set regulations (can be described as sets of policies of a system) and user details pertaining to the group concatenated with a proof of verification. Proof of verification (Pv) defines the validity of the response for the encrypted form containing user registration details. This encryption is denoted as $Enc[Fp\|Pv]$ The user decrypts this encrypted file with their shared key and sends an encrypted, completed form concatenated with the valid proof of verification value, back to the issuer, $Enc[Fp\|Pv]$. The issuer creates the membership issuing key from the user's identity and sends this key to the user making the user a member of the group, KMK (Key Membership issuing Key). The user requests for verification of correctness of the information provided to the issuer for the formation of the key, Correctness [KMK]. The issuer confirms the correctness of the key and sends parameters (Param) associated with the ID and a concatenation of the correctness to the user. The user uses the parameters to create a transaction key pair. The verification process described beforehand is denoted as $Verify[KMK\|Param]$.

Membership verification is important to set up the rights of users to be involved in the access of data. The verification mechanisms used to achieve the blockchain-based data sharing scheme is achieved between the User and the Verifier. The user sends a request to the verifier for verification of membership into the group. The user first sends a request to the verifier for membership verification. The verifier sends a challenge with a concatenation of a random number created from the membership issuing key. The user performs computations based on the challenge and the random number and sends a response to the verifier signing the message with the membership verifying key. In addition to the response, the user sends a generated random number to authenticate the verifier's identity. The verifier compares the signature and computations with a value saved in memory associated with the shared verification keys. The verifier sends a proof of membership and a hash of the random number to the user. The user confirms the identity of the verifier and sends the verifier his transaction public key. The verifier upon receiving this stores the transaction public key in a private database. The verifier computes the membership private key from the membership verification key and sends this to the user.

3.4. Pool of Unprocessed Requests

The pool of unprocessed requests is a data pool of blocks which contain requests created by the user for the purpose of contributing data or accessing data from the storage. The consensus node is the entity that fetches data from the pool for processing. Attention should be drawn to the fact that blocks found in the pool are not chained together. They are tagged with a timestamp of when they arrived in the pool. A suitable algorithm is necessary to define the order at which such blocks will be fetched and processed. A point worth noting is that the pool of unprocessed requests and the blockchain network are two separate entities which are not linked together in any way. The only characteristic between them is the consensus node.

4. SYSTEM DESIGN

We formulate a data sharing mechanism used by the blockchain-based medical data sharing scheme for electronic medical records. There are three entities, namely the user, system management, and storage, as shown in Figure 1 and Figure 2. These are elaborated below.

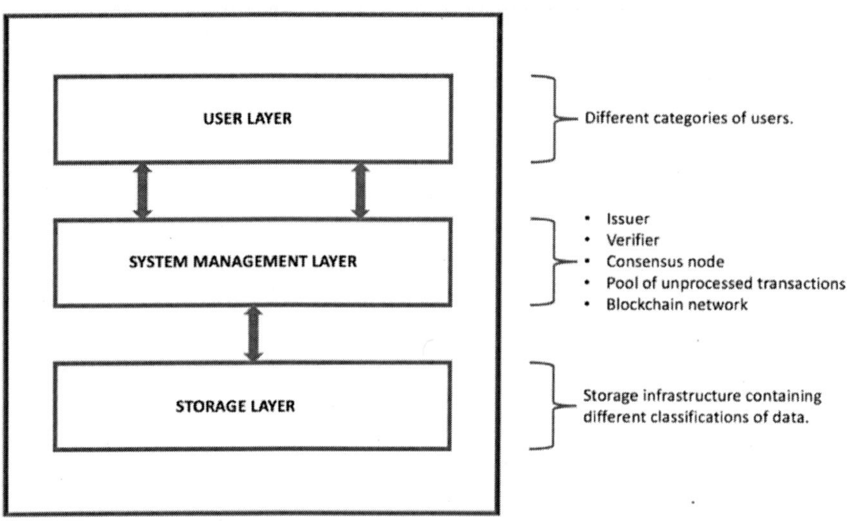

Figure 1. BBDS ecosystem.

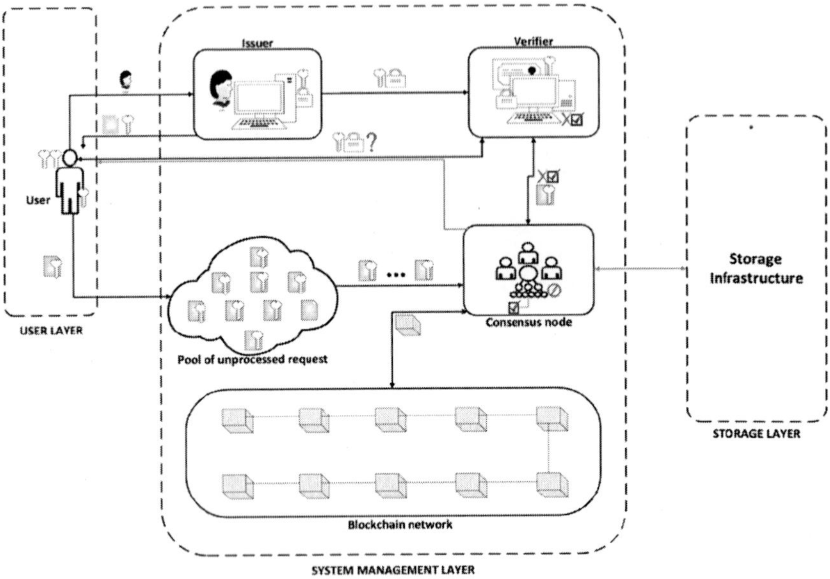

Figure 2. Proposed BBDS system architecture.

- User: Users consist of individuals or organizations that want to access or contribute data from and to the closed system. The intent of most users is to help analyze data for research purposes. Examples of users can be healthcare organizations such as hospitals, research institutions, as well as universities, individual research personnel, and governmental bodies.
- System Management: The system management is composed of individual connected entities responsible for the secure establishment, efficient running, as well as optimization of the scheme. The different entities in the system management are;
  - Issuer: The issuer forms part of the data management layer of the group by authenticating users required to join the group. The issuer sends out required details and accepts users who request to join the group based on a criterion.
  - Verifier: The verifier forms part of the data management layer by further authenticating the user and receives the user's transaction key which is kept in a private database. The verifier later validates blocks which have been signed by the user. This enables a block's authenticity in the system to form part of the blockchain. The verifier creates and sends the user the

membership private key which is used by the user to create a block.

- Consensus nodes: Consensus nodes fetch unprocessed blocks from the pool of unprocessed requests. The consensus node is tasked to process and verify the authenticity and details relating to a block. Processed blocks are broadcast into the blockchain by the consensus node. An important role of the consensus node is the processing and publishing of results based on irregularities in the system. The consensus node is the only entity allowed to access the pool of unprocessed requests.

- Storage: The storage layer encompasses the cloud-based data storage and processing infrastructure where data is securely kept for future reference, research, and other diverse purposes.

In this work, we refer to data requests as either

1) Contributing data to the shared existing data stored in the cloud repository or

2) Accessing data from the cloud repository for modification, research, or analysis purposes.

Data contributors permit the aggregation and analysis of data which leads to value derivation. Verification and auditing trails of requests are necessary to permit the continued efficient functioning of the system.

5. SYSTEM IMPLEMENTATION

The goal of this section is to provide a framework for the BBDS construction while analysing secure structures implemented to facilitate data sharing. At the end of Section 5, Figure 3 describes the entire Blockchain-Based Data Sharing Scheme for Electronic Medical Records system logic.

- System setup

The issuer generates a set of membership issuing keys and membership verification keys. The issuer then shares the membership verification keys with the verifier. A user who wants to join this permissioned group sends a request to the issuer. The issuer is tasked to authenticate the user and accept the user into the group or deny user entry into the group. After successful authentication, the issuer completes this process by sending the user a membership issuing key. The user requests a key confirmation from the issuer by sending the issuer the membership key along with a generated tag of when the user entered the group. The issuer verifies whether the key is formed correctly and sends a verification key along with some other parameters to the user. The user uses the parameters to generate their transaction key pair, that is, the transaction private and public key.

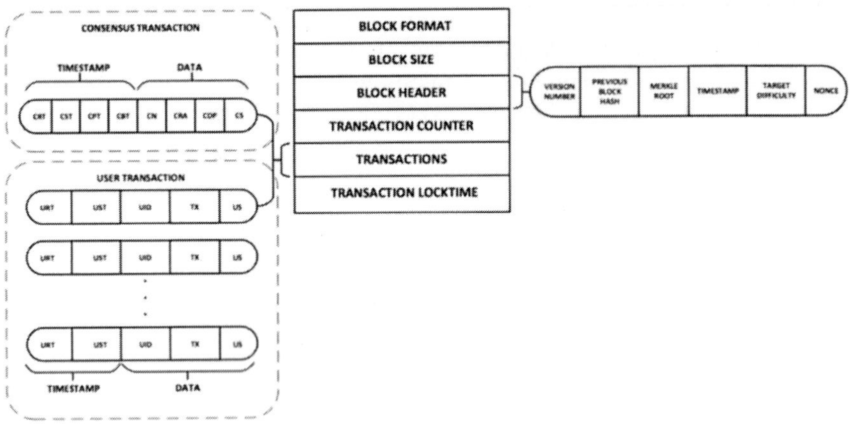

Figure 3. Proposed BBDS block structure.

The user requests for membership verification from the verifier by sending the membership verification key obtained from the issuer. The verifier verifies the user's membership in the group by sending the user a challenge. The user responds accordingly to the challenge. After successfully confirming the user's membership in the group, the verifier sends the user a membership private key. This membership private key is created from the verification keys and parameters by the verifier. The user in turn sends the verifier the transaction private key. The verifier keeps the transaction public key in a private database maintained by the verifier.

- Request file

The user sends a request for data contribution or data access into the system. The request is created by the membership private key obtained from the verifier during membership verification. Particular attention should be drawn to the fact that a block is first created when the user sends a request. The user uses the membership private key to create the block (request), sign the request with the transaction private key, and send it to a pool of unprocessed requests. The pool of unprocessed requests is made up of blocks which are not yet processed by the consensus nodes. For a request to be valid, the consensus node fetches the request from the pool and prepares it for validation.

A block is made up of a single event and an event spans from the moment a request was created to when the block was broadcast into the blockchain. In instances where an authorized body needs to investigate irregularities in the system, a request is sent and access is granted to probe into the irregularities. The consensus node bears the responsibility of mining and reporting on the results of such irregularities. This is easy due to the blocks being linked together with an attractive property of the blockchain, immutability. As shown in Figure 4, the suitable block that would suit the functions of the system is designed and highlighted.

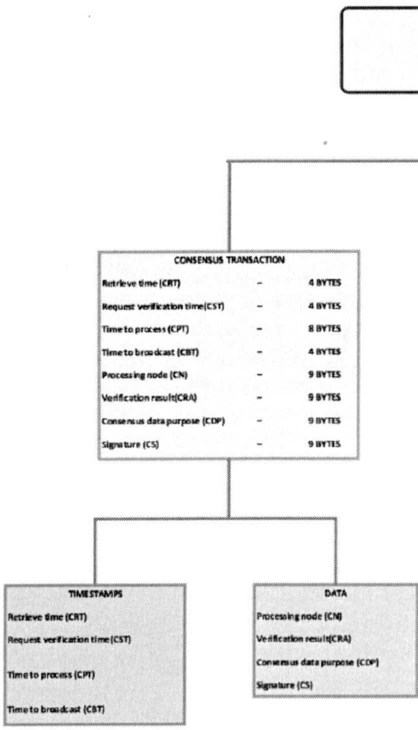

Figure 4. Transaction structure.

The abbreviations used in the block structure are described in the section of Abbreviations.

A block is made up of a format which uniquely identifies the block. This is followed by the block size which contains the size of a block. The next structure is the block header. The block header is hashed with *sha*256(*sha*256()) as done in the Bitcoin headers [16]. The block header plays a significant role in the blockchain network by ensuring immutability. By changing a block header, an attacker should have to change all block headers starting from the genesis block in order to falsify a block's record. This significantly ensures security on the network since there is a maximum assurance of an impossibility of achieving this task. Block mismatch will alert the system of a suspicious ongoing event which triggers data forensics.

The block header contains the version number which indicates the validation rules to follow. The header is also made up of the previous block's hash which is a $sha256(sha256())$ hash whose function is to ensure that no previous block header can be changed without changing this block's header. The Merkle root hash forms part of the header by ensuring that none of the blocks in the blockchain network can be modified without modifying the header. This is achieved by taking the hashes of all the events in the blockchain network and appending the output to the current block. The final output is a $sha256(sha256())$. The header includes a timestamp of when the block was created. The header contains target difficulty which is a value of how processing is achieved by the consensus nodes. This is unique to the system to make processing difficult for malicious nodes but efficient and solvable by verified consensus nodes in the system. Finally, the header consists of a nonce which is an arbitrary number the consensus nodes generate to modify the header hash in order to produce a hash below the target difficulty. The block header is therefore made up of six components.

The block has a transaction counter whose function is to record the total number of transactions in the entire block. The transaction is made up of the consensus transaction and the user transaction in relation to the purposes and processing of records as explained in the transaction section. The consensus transaction is categorized into two parts that are the timestamps and the data. The timestamps are made up if CRT, CST, CPT, and CBT whilst the data part is made up of CN, CRA, CDP, and CS. This is a standard model for a consensus transaction. The user transaction is also categorized into two parts that are the timestamps and the data. The timestamps are URT and UST whilst the data part is made up of UID, TX, and US. This forms the transaction for the user. User transactions are designed to accommodate multiple but limited events for user transaction instances that are not accounted for.

Finally, the structure that defines the entire block is the blocklocktime. This is a timestamp that records the last entry of transaction as well as the closure of a block. When conditions for this field are met, the block is ready to be broadcast into the blockchain network. The blocklocktime generally signifies the time the block enters the blockchain. The size of an entire block is 679 bytes. Figure 4 presents the detailed transactions' structure. Table 2 shows the size of the individual structures in the block.

Table 2. Block format and component size

Structure Name	Size in Bytes
Block format	4
Block size	4
Block header	80
Transaction counter	9
Transactions	578
Transaction LockTime	4

- Grant request

The user sends a request for data contribution or data access into the system. Particular attention should be drawn to the fact that a block is first created when the user sends a request. The user uses the membership private key to create the block (request), sign the request with the transaction private key, and send it to a pool of unprocessed requests. The pool of unprocessed requests is made up of blocks which are not yet processed by the consensus nodes. For a request to be valid, the consensus node fetches the request from the pool and prepares it for validation.

A hash of when this incident occurred is recorded in the timestamp section of the block header. Again, the key triggers the block format to record a standard format in the form of a sequence of digits generated from the key to the block. The transaction layer of the block is now triggered as the request is formed as part of a user transaction, by adequately satisfying the format of the user transaction model. The URT is set along with the UID and TX to signify the purpose of the request. The user signs the data, which is recorded in US and sends the request. A timestamp recording the exact time the data was sent is captured by UST. These actions complete a single transaction for a user.

The consensus node fetches a request that triggers the target difficulty, nonce, and consensus transaction. The consensus node solves a mathematical puzzle whose answer is updated by the target difficulty and nonce. This allows the consensus node to process the request. The completion of this triggers the consensus transaction since the consensus node sends the request for user verification by the verifier. CRT records the exact time of the data retrieval by the node. The action of sending the signature for verification is recorded at CST and the action for verification of a user is captured by CRA. The total time for processing is recorded by CPT with the processing node's identity executed by CN.

- Access file

After a user's request (data contribution or data access) is granted, access is given to the user pertaining to the data request or contribution and the verified request is ready for broadcast which is recorded by CBT with a record of purpose and the user in addition to the purpose for the creation of this block. This is recorded by CDP. A signature to verify proof of processing is recorded by CS. During the processing, the format layer of the block is completed by appending a sequence number to the generated format by the user key to identify the current position of this block. As part of processing, the version number of the block is recorded in the header. The hash of the previous block is also recorded in the header and the Merkle root is formed which includes the current block. The hash of the header is formed, readying the block for broadcast. The block length is recorded and the BlockLockTime then locks the block with a timestamp. At this time, there is an assurance of the block being a constituent of the blockchain network and forming part of a chain.

The block is now part of a chain system and adds to the height of the blocks in the blockchain system. For occurrences where other blocks are formed after this block, the hash of the header of the last block in the network is taken and appended in the header of the newer block, which is yet to be part of the chained blocks in the network. The whole process is shown in Figure 5 that bellows.

6. PROTOCOLS USED TO COMPLETE THE SYSTEM

As demonstrated in Figure 6, the interactions between both user-issuer and issuer-verifier are described in this section.

6.1. User-Issuer Protocol

For communication between the user and the issuer, there is the need for authentication and verification. This section describes the protocols necessary to setup a new user as a member into the system. Part of the formation of the protocol is adopted from Wu et al. [27] regarding their research based on an efficient and secure identity-based authentication and key agreement protocol which guarantees user anonymity.

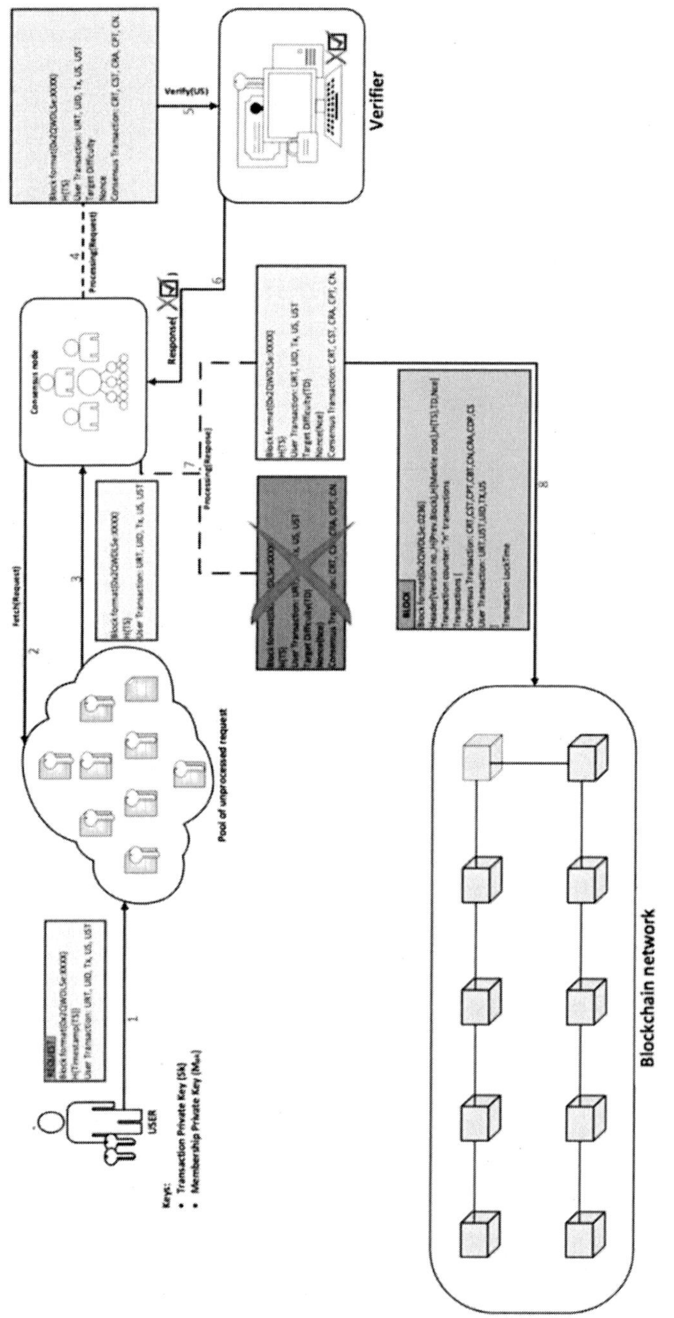

Figure 5. Proposed BBDS system logic.

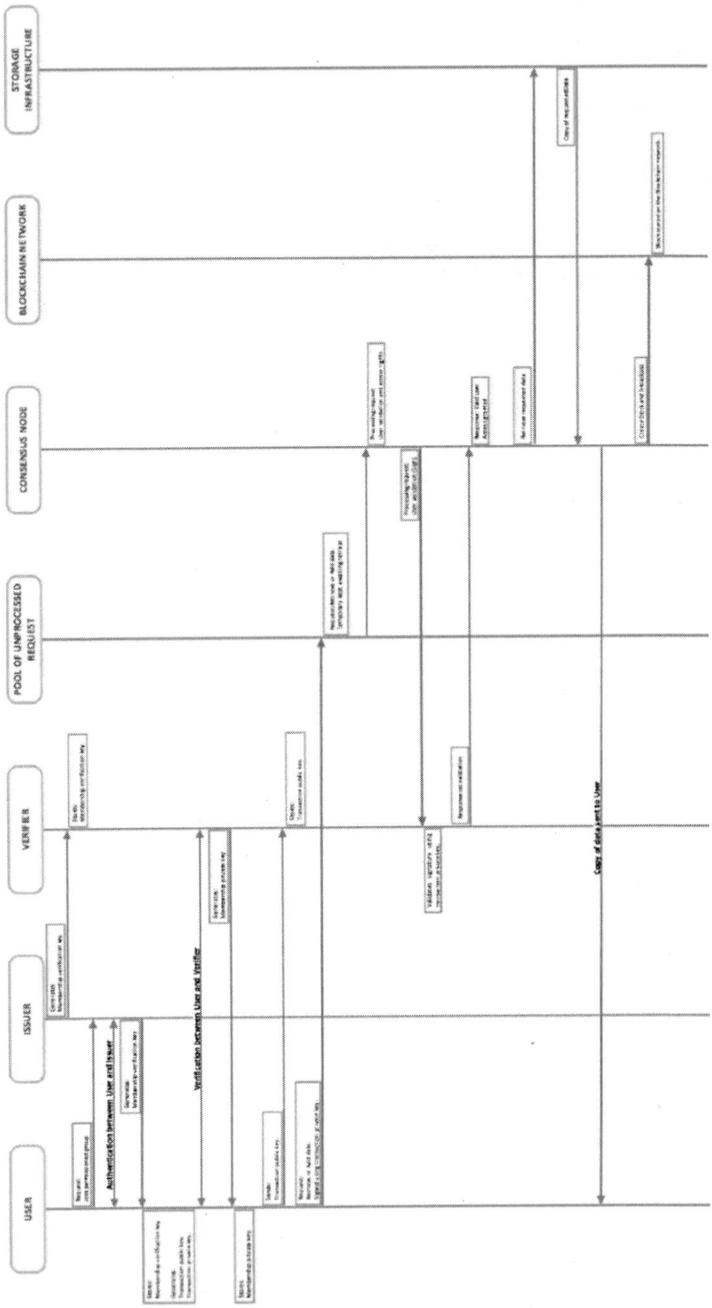

Figure 6. Protocols used to complete the system.

Part 1:

The protocol between the user and the issuer is divided into two parts. The first section is based on existing cryptographic techniques adopted from Wu et al.'s work [27]. The authentication phase of our protocol from the adopted work is further divided into three phases:

A. System setup phase (generating parameters necessary to compute the shared key for the system)

B. Key exchange phase (sets of computations and keys that both the user and the issuer exchange with each other)

C. Authentication and key agreement phase (creating the shared key for the user and the issuer)

Part 2:

The shared key computed by the User and Issuer is used to encrypt and decrypt information pertaining to account registration and verification for the user to be a member of the system:

1) The issuer sends an encrypted form which requires pre-set regulations and user details pertaining to the group concatenated with a proof of verification. Proof of verification defines the validity of the response for the encrypted form containing user registration details, $Enc[Fp||Pv]$.

2) The user decrypts this encrypted file with their shared key and sends an encrypted, completed form concatenated with the valid proof of verification value, back to the issuer, $Enc[Fp||Pv]$.

3) The issuer creates the membership issuing key from the user's identity and sends this key to the user making the user a member of the group, KMK.

4) The user requests for verification of correctness of the information provided to the issuer for the formation of the key, Correctness [KMK].

5) The issuer confirms the correctness of the key and sends parameters associated with the ID and a concatenation of the correctness to the user.

6) The user uses the parameters to create a transaction key pair, $Verify[KMK||Param]$.

6.2. User-Verifier Protocol

The user sends a request to the verifier for verification of membership into the group. This section discusses the protocols necessary for the establishment of verification by the user and verifier:

1) The user first sends a request to the verifier for membership verification.
2) The verifier sends a challenge with a concatenation of a random number created from the membership issuing key.
3) The user performs computations based on the challenge and the random number and sends a response to the verifier signing the message with the membership verifying key. In addition to the response, the user sends a generated random number to authenticate the verifier's identity.
4) The verifier compares the signature and computations with a value saved in memory associated with the shared verification keys.
5) The verifier sends a proof of membership and a hash of the random number to the user.
6) The user confirms the identity of the verifier and sends the verifier his transaction public key.
7) The verifier upon receiving this stores the transaction public key in a private database. The verifier computes the membership private key from the membership verification key and sends this to the user.

7. EVALUATION

Scalability is one of the major challenges facing the current bitcoin networks whose underlying technology is the blockchain. The block structure described in Section 5 is proposed as a solution to the scalability problem.

To determine the size and scalability of the blockchain network (compared to the blockchain currently implemented within bitcoin) in this system, tests based on calculated assumptions derived from different vendor transactions per unit time have been simulated. For clarity, the transactions of existing vendor networks have been explained and the number of users on this system has been adopted to exaggerate the entire size of the blockchain in our blockchain-based data-sharing scheme for a given period of time.

The fast-growing Bitcoin network, processes on average a single transaction per second with a theoretical maximum of seven transactions per second [28]. Considering the number of transactions processed by other vendors, implementing such numbers on the Bitcoin blockchain network leads to scalability issues. Bitcoin's blockchain has a size of over GB, with an increase of several GB in 2015. Considering an increased throughput of about 2000 transactions per second, the supplementary transactions would result in a growth of about several PB/year. At 150,000 transactions per second, the size of the blockchain would overwhelm the network. The generation of such huge amounts of data per year is due to the fact that a block size is 1 MB in Bitcoin's blockchain.

The number of transactions processed by Visa is 2000 transactions per second with a maximum of 10,000 transactions per second at peak times such as holidays. With respect to other vendors, the number of transactions processed by Twitter is 5000 transactions per second with a maximum of 15,000 transactions per second at peak times. Advertising networks, trading networks, and email networks process a minimum of 500,000 to 2,100,000 transactions per second [29]. Ideally, a carefully designed block structure on a blockchain network will support these massive amounts of data generated each second without being concerned with the scalability of the networks.

By carefully structuring the block size in our system, we adopt the use cases of user transactions per second to create an over-exaggerated value for users sending such requests per second. The importance is to prove the scalability of the blockchain network in our system in exaggerated conditions. The following formulas are used in the calculation for all vendor transactions per second and can be used for real case scenarios.

- **Calculations**

Tx(B×ts) used to calculate data size per second

Tx(B×60(tm)) used to calculate data size per minute.

Tx(B×36×102(th)) used to calculate data size per hour.

Tx(B×864×102(td)) used to calculate data size per day.

Tx defines the number of transactions sent per period of time

B defines the block size, 679 MB

ts defines the time in seconds

tm defines the time in minutes

th defines the time in hours

td defines the time in days

- **Example**

Assuming the system consists of 1000 users with a maximum of 200 users sending transactions each second, the size of the blockchain network would be: 135 bytes/s, 7.77 MB/min, 466.23 MB/h, and 10.29 GB/day.

- 200(679×1) = 135,800 bytes per second = 132.62 KB per second
- 200(679×60(1)) = 8,148,000 bytes per second = 7.77 MB per minute
- 200(679×36×102(1)) = 488,880,000 bytes per second = 466.23 MB per hour
- 200(679×864×102(1)) = 11,733,120,000 bytes per second = 10.29 GB per day

Using the example above as a guide, Table 3 shows an assumed over-exaggerated number of user transactions per second. The total size in bytes of the results shown in the table below are outputs pertaining to blocks generated in this system. Data sizes generated are represented in megabytes (MB), gigabytes (GB), terabytes (TB), and petabytes (PB). The transaction column illustrates the number of transactions per period of time. Data generated per period in relation to the design block represents the amount in size for the blockchain network over a period of time.

Table 3. Estimated blockchain network growth.

	Data Generated Per Period in Relation to Designed Block			
Transaction	Per Second	Per Day	Per Year	Per 10 Years
2000	1.29 MB	108.84 GB	38.79 TB	387.90 TB
10,000	6.47 MB	545.91 GB	194.59 TB	1.95 PB
15,000	9.71 MB	819.28 GB	292.03 TB	2.92 PB
500,000	323.77 MB	26.68 TB	9.74 PB	97.40 PB
2,100,000	1.33 GB	112.22 TB	40.96 PB	409.60 PB

8. CONCLUSIONS

In this paper, we proposed a blockchain-based mechanism to mediate access between users and a pool of shared (sensitive) data. Compared to the Bitcoin blockchain network, we constructed a scalable (redesigned to allow speedy transactions) and lightweight blockchain to demonstrate the efficiency of our design which permits data sharing in a secure manner and protects the privacy of data. In the proposed system, communication and authentication protocols and algorithms between entities were not fully investigated. It would be interesting to extend this work by fully exploring these in future studies. We state that the architecture described in this paper is a top layer of the blockchain-based access control system that is under implementation and testing. In our future work, an experimental study will be conducted to improve the system's efficiency and to obtain empirical data for further studies.

ACKNOWLEDGMENTS

The Fundamental Research Funds for the Central Universities (ZYGX2015J154), Key research and development projects of high and new technology development and industrialization of Sichuan Province (2017GZ0007). The paper was approved by Ke Huang after the authors collectively reviewed it.

REFERENCES

1. Longo, D.L.; Drazen, J.M. Data Sharing. *N. Engl. J. Med.* **2016**, *374*, 276–277.
2. Davis, J. 7 Largest Data Breaches of 2015. *Healthcare IT News*. 11 December 2015. Available online: www.healthcareitnews.com/news/7-largest-data-breaches-2015 (accessed on 14 April 2017).
3. Higgins, K.J. Healthcare Data Breaches From Cyberattacks, Criminals Eclipse Employee Error For The First Time. *Information Week DarkReading*. 5 July 2015. Available online: http://www.darkreading.com/attacks-breaches/healthcare-data-breaches-from-cyberattacks-criminals-eclipse-employee-error-for-the-first-time/d/d-id/1320315 (accessed on 14 April 2017).
4. IBM-Security. *Reviewing a Year of Serious Data Breaches, Major Attacks and New Vulnerabilities: Analysis of Cyber Attack and Incident Data from IBM's Worldwide Security Services Operations*; IBM Security: Somers, NY, USA, 2016.
5. Sladić, G.; Milosavljević, B.; Konjović, Z. Modeling context for access control systems. In Proceedings of the 2012 IEEE 10th Jubilee International Symposium on Intelligent Systems and Informatics (SISY 2012), Subotica, Serbia, 20–22 September 2012; pp. 37–42.
6. Elliott, A.; Knight, S. Start Here: Engineering Scalable Access Control Systems. In Proceedings of the 21st ACM on Symposium on Access Control Models and Technologies, Shanghai, China, 5–8 June 2016; pp. 113–124.
7. Maw, H.; Xiao, H.; Christianson, B.; Malcolm, J. A Survey of Access Control Models in Wireless Sensor Networks. *J. Sens. Actuator Netw.* **2014**, *3*, 150–180.
8. Brucker, A.D.; Hang, I.; Lückemeyer, G.; Ruparel, R. SecureBPMN: Modeling and Enforcing Access Control Requirements in Business Processes. In Proceedings of the 17th ACM Symposium on Access Control Models and Technologies (SACMAT'12), Newark, NJ, USA, 20–22 June 2012; pp. 123–126.

9. Chen, H.; Bhargava, B.; Zhongchuan, F. Multilabels-based scalable access control for big data applications. *IEEE Cloud Comput.* **2014**, *1*, 65–71.
10. Anonymous. Data Breaches Cost the Healthcare Industry an Estimated $6.5 Billion. *Micrographics* **2011**, *29*, 3–5.
11. Sweeney, L. K-Anonymity: A model for protecting privacy. *Int. J. Uncertain.* **2002**, *10*, 557–570.
12. Machanavajjhala, A.; Gehrke, J.; Kifer, D.; Venkitasubramaniam, M. L-Diversity: Privacy beyond k-anonymity. In Proceedings of the International Conference on Data Engineering, Atlanta, GA, USA, 3–7 April 2006; Volume 2006, p. 24.
13. Ninghui, L.; Tiancheng, L.; Venkatasubramanian, S. T-Closeness: Privacy beyond k-anonymity and L-diversity. In Proceedings of the International Conference on Data Engineering, Istanbul, Turkey, 11–15 April 2007; pp. 106–115.
14. Soria-Comas, J.; Domingo-Ferrert, J. Differential privacy via t-closeness in data publishing. In Proceedings of the 2013 11th Annual Conference on Privacy, Security and Trust (PST 2013), Tarragona, Spain, 10–12 July 2013; pp. 27–35.
15. Ausanka-Crues, R. Methods for Access Control: Advances and Limitations. Available online: https://www.cs.hmc.edu/~mike/public_html/courses/security/s06/ projects/ryan.pdf (accessed on 14 April 2017).
16. Nakamoto, S. Bitcoin: A Peer-to-Peer Electronic Cash System. Available online: www.bitcoin.org (accessed on 14 April 2017).
17. Sasson, E.B.; Chiesa, A.; Garman, C.; Green, M.; Miers, I.; Tromer, E.; Virza, M. Zerocash: Decentralized anonymous payments from bitcoin. In Proceedings of the IEEE Symposium on Security and Privacy, San Jose, CA, USA, 18–21 May 2014; pp. 459–474.
18. Schneider, J. Blockchain—Putting Theory into Practice. Available online: https://t.co/CLJJf0tGp0 (accessed on 14 April 2017).
19. Zyskind, G.; Nathan, O.; Pentland, A.S. Decentralizing privacy: Using blockchain to protect personal data. In Proceedings of the 2015 IEEE Security and Privacy Workshops (SPW 2015), San Jose, CA, USA, 21–22 May 2015; pp. 180–184.
20. Yue, X.; Wang, H.; Jin, D.; Li, M.; Jiang, W. Healthcare Data Gateways: Found Healthcare Intelligence on Blockchain with Novel Privacy Risk Control. *J. Med. Syst.* **2016**, *40*, 218.
21. Zyskind, G.; Nathan, O.; Pentland, A. Enigma: Decentralized Computation Platform with Guaranteed Privacy. *arXiv* **2015**.
22. Hardjono, T.; Pentland, A.S. Verifiable Anonymous Identities and Access Control in Permissioned Blockchains. Available online: www.w3.org/2016/04/blockchain-workshop/interest/hardjono-pentland.html (accessed on 14 April 2017).
23. Ouaddah, A.; Elkalam, A.A.; Ouahman, A.A. Towards a novel privacy-preserving access control model based on blockchain technology in IoT. *Adv. Intell. Syst. Comput.* **2017**, *520*, 523–533.
24. Wu, F.; Pai, H.T.; Zhu, X.; Hsueh, P.Y.; Hu, Y.H. An adaptable and scalable group access control scheme for managing wireless sensor networks. *Telemat. Inform.* **2013**, *30*, 144–157.
25. Wang, Y.W.Y.; Attebury, G.; Ramamurthy, B. A survey of security issues in wireless sensor networks. *IEEE Commun. Surv. Tutor.* **2006**, *8*, 1–23.
26. Huang, H.F. A novel access control protocol for secure sensor networks. *Comput. Stand. Interfaces* **2009**, *31*, 272–276.
27. Wu, L.; Zhang, Y.; Xie, Y.; Alelaiw, A.; Shen, J. An Efficient and Secure Identity-Based Authentication and Key Agreement Protocol with User Anonymity for Mobile Devices. *Wirel. Pers. Commun.* **2016**.
28. Luu, L.; Narayanan, V.; Baweja, K.; Zheng, C.; Gilbert, S.; Saxena, P. SCP: A Computationally-Scalable Byzantine Consensus Protocol For Blockchains. *IACR Cryptol. ePrint Arch.* **2015**, *2015*, 1168.
29. McConaghy, T.; Marques, R.; Muller, A.; de Jonghe, D.; McConaghy, T.; McMullen, G.; Henderson, R.; Bellemare, S.; Granzotto, A. BigchainDB: A Scalable Blockchain Database (DRAFT). Available online: https://pdfs.semanticscholar.org/1c0c/5640e2efcd32480f 940 20bf857 c261acdae4.pdf (accessed on 14 April 2017).

CHAPTER 16

Cybersecurity: Integrating Information into the Microeconomics of the Consumer and the Firm

Scott Farrow

Department of Economics, UMBC, Baltimore, USA

ABSTRACT

The connectivity of information has changed many things but not the way economists model consumers, firms and government. Information is here newly modeled as a fundamental element of microeconomic choices and utility, cost and tax functions. The results are more clearly defined metrics for losses due to cyber breaches or productivity gains from cyber investments. The integration of information into standard microeconomics also allows use of econometric and other tools to analyze the empirics of the consumer and the firm. In particular, the results identify ways in which losses in the Gordon and Loeb [1] model can be specified in more detail.

Keywords: Microeconomics, Utility, Cost, Cyber Losses

1. INTRODUCTION

Capital and labor are the time honored categories for production inputs which are transformed into marketable goods and services. But the economy is more virtual now with information occupying a central place in economic activity. Economics has primarily dealt with information as an issue in information gathering for decision-making under uncertainty as in Bikhchandani, Hirshleifer and Riley [2]. A major area of application includes labor market signaling as in Rogerson, Shimer and Wright [3]. However, maintaining the abstraction that information is an imprecise signal for a decision or simply changes the quality or quantity of (computer) capital does not capture the many ways that information itself is an input into production. Shutting down a website and a consumer's virtual access to a business is damaging; intellectual property and personal identity are stolen virtually, production processes can be controlled by or destroyed by changes in the information running the machines. Motivated by issues in cybersecurity, this note investigates the ways information alters fundamental structures of the consumer, firm and government. Analyzing those structures more clearly identifies microeconomic definitions of cybersecurity losses even in the absence of a decision involving uncertainty

Gordon and Loeb [1] obtained significant insight by abstracting cyber information sets from the remainder of the economic activity of the firm or organization. Information sets were interpreted broadly; potentially including data sets, websites, accounting information, algorithms, intellectual property, electronic communications and so on. In their model and extensions as in Farrow and Szanton [4] , the effect of a cyber information breach results in a conditional loss, L, to the firm. The loss is a part of an expected value objective function where probabilities of loss are modeled separately. In Gordon, Loeb, Lucyshyn and Zhou [GLLZ, [5]], the losses include external effects beyond the firm. There is however, value in re-integrating their sparsely defined conditional loss into the more detailed but standard microeconomic modeling of the firm, the consumer, and government. Such reintegration facilitates the decomposition of losses due to a breach, the differentiation of types of attacks, and the distinction between what GL refer to as private and external costs of an attack[1].

Microeconomics builds from an individual consumer and firm up to the market and general equilibrium levels. However, research on cyber losses to both consumers and firms has taken a more ad-hoc approach. Prior research seems to have taken two alternative approaches. One approach in the information technology literature is to develop taxonomies of types of attacks, potentially distinguished by their method of attack or the outcome as in Undercofer, et al. [8]. A second approach has focused on cost categories. Detica [9] focused on the costs associated with various stages of cyber-attacks, identifying categories of costs in anticipation, in consequence, in response, and indirect costs. Anderson, et al. [7] organize their cost analysis using direct, indirect, and defensive costs with the cost to society being the sum of these categories.

In contrast to the existing cyber focused work, the standard sequence of firm and consumer modeling is developed here in order to explicitly identify the pathways losses can occur. Such a delineation may encourage more detailed empirical modeling given the methodologies already developed for analyzing microeconomic structures. While the focus here is on the mechanism of losses due to some type of cyber activity, the dominant impact of cyber activity has been gains through many of the same mechanisms capable of generating losses.

2. MODELING INFORMATION AS AN INPUT

2.1. Information and the Consumer

Begin with the consumer who, for example, can be directly affected by breaches of Personal Identifying Information (PII) and whose choices create demand for a firm's product.

A deterministic model identifies goods Q_i that may have characteristics dependent on embedded cyber information and capabilities, I, as is common with many consumer goods. Furthermore, transactions are facilitated by cyber information and processes typically embedded in computers, phones or other devices and linked to the internet. Consequently the good itself and its purchase is partially defined by cyber information, $Q(I)$. Prices, P_i, are here assumed parametric in the budget constraint, Y such that:

Max Utility $(Q_1(I), Q_2(I), Q_3(I), \cdots, Q_n(I))$

w.r.t. Q_i

Subject to: $\sum_1^n P_i(I)Q(I) = Y$

Cyber breaches can then affect the consumer's utility through various pathways. The direct theft from a consumer, perhaps from the loss of PII, can be modeled as a discrete decline in income[2], $Y(I)$. More complexly, consider that characteristics of differentiated goods are identified both by their embedded use of cyber information through software, displays, controls and so on while the transaction cost and purchase context is also influenced by cyber information. To the extent that there are changes in the cyber information embedded in the good, prices[3], or income then the consumer's demand, $Q_i(I) = f(P_i(I), P_j(I), Y(I), I)$, changes. The total derivative of demand, Equation (1), thus identifies specific chains or pathways of effects from changes in information to observable quantities based on consumer behavior.

$$\mathrm{d}Q(\boldsymbol{I}) = \frac{\partial f}{\partial P_i}\frac{\partial P_i}{\partial \boldsymbol{I}}\mathrm{d}\boldsymbol{I} + \frac{\partial f}{\partial P_j}\frac{\partial P_j}{\partial \boldsymbol{I}}\mathrm{d}\boldsymbol{I} + \cdots + \frac{\partial f}{\partial Y}\frac{\partial Y}{\partial \boldsymbol{I}} + \frac{\partial Q}{\partial \boldsymbol{I}}\mathrm{d}\boldsymbol{I} \tag{1}$$

The consumer's problem can also be written in terms of household production where household labor and purchased inputs yield household output as in Becker [10] or Gronau and Hammermesh [11]. For instance, loss of an individual's time to re-establish identity or time involved with personal malware leads one to a household production model where time has a shadow price primarily measured by household labor. While not fully developing that model here, household labor can be affected, both positively and negatively, by cyber information, $H(I)$. Other household inputs such as electricity and water are information dependent, $HE(I)$ and $HW(I)$, and are of concern due to potential cyber-physical infrastructure damage.

An information set (or just information) augmented consumer model thus captures: a) changes due to loss of income, b) costs associated with household production including unpaid time, c) changes in the quality of goods including the process of obtaining them, and d) potential changes in the utility function itself. For instance, the result of stolen PII from a retailer may involve changes in utility (and associated monetized value of that utility loss) reflected in a tighter budget constraint, having to spend time and other household inputs to restore their identity and changing their demand for products from that source or similar sources. In the latter case, there could be a public bad of decreased quality across multiple goods, a topic investigated in more detail below. Alternatively, the primary effect of cyber information change can be positive for the consumer (as it typically has been from non-criminal use of cyber information).

2.2. Information in the Firm and the Government

Firms are linked to consumers via the market demand (or inverse demand) function, shown above to depend on cyber information and upon aggregation across consumers. But the firm's output also depends on its production function, f. Begin with a classical production function in which output, Q, is a function of capital and labor, $f(K, L)$. Consideration is given first to the situation where no network or other externalities exist. The role of (ostensibly) internal cyber information, I, can be modeled as both a stand-alone input and an intermediate input embedded in and affecting the productivity of K and L. The usefulness of considering the stand-alone portion occurs for instance, when considering theft of PII or intellectual property. The capital and labor within the firm would still operate with the same productivity, but a loss occurs. Examples of an effect mediated through capital and labor is malware which can affect the productivity of both inputs. Within a firm, initially augment a production function as $Q(I) = f(L(I), K(I), I)$. Cyber security from the firm's perspective, absent externalities, is to consider how the production process is damaged if the I input is compromised, as from attacks which may affect confidentiality, integrity, authenticity, availability to users and so on. Further, I may affect the very definition of the output such that differentiated products may viewed by the consumer differently if they are secure or not.

Now consider the role of public goods (or bads) which is the mechanism through which externalities occur. Current production typically depends not only on the firm's own cyber information input, I, but also that of the external cyber system to which it is connected, I, comprised at least of all the linkages the firm uses on the internet or more indirect effects as through communications, control of utilities, and so on. Such a public good input may affect production directly or indirectly through other inputs. For instance, infrastructure damage to I may both impair the firm's internal cyber information input as well as capital. Further, an attack over the internet may result in technological adaptation or response by the firm. While this could be considered an entirely new production function, here such responsive actions are modeled as direct shifts in output or shifts mediated through capital and labor with resulting implications for costs. A production function including both types of internal and external cyber information can then be written as $Q(I, I) = f(L(I, I), K(I, I), I(I), I)$. There is also the standard cost function—representing the minimum cost of producing a level of output given the production function and input prices—here shortened to focus on the role of information as $C(I, I)$.

The final element affected by cyber information is demand for the firm's product which, in perfect competition, is pre-determined at the firm level but jointly determined by supply and demand at the market level. At the market level, the internal cyber information is presumably so small as to not affect the price, but an external impact of cyber information may exist at the market level. Hence a competitive market price depends on external cyber information $P(I)$. For an imperfectly competitive firm the price is a function of the firm's marginal revenue and marginal cost and, given the prominent role of internet sales and communication, hence characterized as a function of both the internal and external cyber information, $P(I, I)$.

Consequently the pre-tax profit function for a firm can be written as $\pi(I, I) = P(I, I)\ Q(I, I) - C(Q(I, I))$ with some of the internal cyber information possibly irrelevant to a competitive firm. However, government and industry also interact in a variety of ways. The production function itself may be constrained by various regulatory policies. Changes in such policies can result in a changed production function perhaps but not necessarily related to cyber information. More directly, a number of taxes transfer money from industry (and the consumer) to Government. The bi-directional impact of cyber information on taxes and tax revenue is here modeled by a tax on profits, $\tau(\pi(I, I))$, although the focus below will be on the effect of the external effects. Including the tax effect allows for losses in government revenue potentially due to loss of intellectual property, or gains if government imposes taxes or fines on a firm due to cyber information breaches and or other actions.

Define the total potential private supply side loss due to information as the total derivative of the profit function:

$$\begin{aligned} \mathrm{d}\pi(I,\boldsymbol{I}) &= \frac{\partial \pi}{\partial I}\mathrm{d}I + \frac{\partial \pi}{\partial \boldsymbol{I}}\mathrm{d}\boldsymbol{I} \\ &= \left[\frac{\partial P}{\partial I}Q + P\frac{\partial Q}{\partial I} - \frac{\partial C}{\partial Q}\frac{\partial Q}{\partial I}\mathrm{d}I - \tau\frac{\partial \pi}{\partial I}\mathrm{d}I\right] + \left[\frac{\partial P}{\partial \boldsymbol{I}}Q + P\frac{\partial Q}{\partial \boldsymbol{I}} - \frac{\partial C}{\partial Q}\frac{\partial Q}{\partial \boldsymbol{I}}\mathrm{d}\boldsymbol{I} - \tau\frac{\partial \pi}{\partial \boldsymbol{I}}\mathrm{d}\boldsymbol{I}\right] \end{aligned} \tag{2}$$

Each term in Equation (2) represents a pathway through which changes in information can affect profit where the key pathways are through price, quantity, cost, and taxes. One may also ask, what about financial dimensions of firms such as stock market prices, net worth, and borrowing costs? These financial dimensions are considered here as derivative of the profit position of the firm.

If profit expectations decline due to cyber breaches, that decline is expected to affect the financial condition of the firm including its forecast net worth, stock value and so on. Such links could be analyzed through the impact on the profit function as in Campbell et al. [12].

Finally, Government is potentially affected by cyber information both through its own production and through its financing from taxes on firms and consumers.

Regarding government production, the same pathways occur as with private firms with the caveat that neither costs are assumed to be minimized nor is social profit maximized. Hence government output is affected by both its internal and external cyber information, $G(I,I)$ through the processes similar to those above.

3. DEFINING LOSSES

3.1. Deterministic Losses

The literature on cyber costs uses various loss categories such as direct, indirect, defensive and so on. Such categories may be informative for particular data sets but are not economically well defined terms. Table 1 presents several candidate classifications based on widely used language from accounting, microeconomics and macroeconomics.

The accounting terms "direct" and "indirect" have little classification power as cyber information losses (or gains) are spread across both production and "back office" processes which is central to the accounting definition. The distinction between private, external, and pecuniary effects from microeconomics has some classification power, although cyber losses are almost always initiated through an externality; they are not the result of a voluntary exchange. Like the spread of disease however, there can be an initial loss which is spread as an additional externality, as through malware. Pecuniary externalities can exist as markets are affected. Finally, macroeconomic terms have some classification power by incorporating the production and market linkages across industries. For instance, the banking sector may incur losses from re-issuing cards as the result of a PII data breach in another industry. In short, the macroeconomics reminds us of industry interactions such as when an information loss in industry j causes a change in industry i. That change may operate through the price mechanism, the legal system or other mechanisms. Similarly, interactions may occur through the endogeneity of the household sector as with induced effects. Finally, there may be political economic effects through government, including regulation.

The modeling of Section 2 allows loss definitions to depend on the partial derivatives that are affected. Consequently, direct effects are here taken to be the partial derivatives in the consumer, firm, and government problems that are not mediated through market prices or through non-market responses such as regulation. Secondary (or indirect including induced) effects are those responses mediated through the market. The direct effects identified above are then the partial derivatives: $\partial Y/\partial I, \partial Q/\partial I, \partial HL(I)/\partial I, \partial HX(I)/\partial I$ for the consumer and $\partial Q/\partial I, \partial C/\partial I, \partial I/\partial I, \partial Q/\partial I, \partial C/\partial I$ for the firm, noting that $\partial \pi/\partial I$ (associated with taxation) is affected by both direct and indirect changes to be further defined below. These direct effects are identified by the economic actor and the mechanism of impact rather than whether the actor chooses, for instance, to alter their production function via changes in software, capital, labor or some other aspect. Consequently, in the case of PII, both damages incurred by a consumer and monitoring or re-issue costs in the financial sector would be deemed direct, while possible changes in interest rates charged would be indirect as that latter is mediated through the market mechanism.

Table 1. Loss categories from different professional framings.

Professional Framing	Categories and Meaning
Accounting: direct and indirect	Direct associated with production or identifiable cost sector, compared with widely spread indirect costs.
Microeconomics: private and external	Private: the result of voluntary exchanges while external effects are involuntarily incurred (positively or negatively) by third parties. Pecuniary externalities are third party effects mediated through market prices.
Macroeconomics: direct, indirect, induced	Whether at the industry level or firm level, direct output effects are identified with a change in output of a specific firm or industry while indirect effects are those from industry production or market linkages. Induced effects occur when households are endogenous to the system and expand or contract activity as part of a general equilibrium system. Secondary effects can be either or both of indirect or induced.

The secondary or indirect effects are then $\partial P_i/\partial I, \partial P_j/\partial I, \partial P_i/\partial \boldsymbol{I}, \partial P_j/\partial \boldsymbol{I}, \partial G/\partial I, \partial G/\partial \boldsymbol{I}$ reflecting the interactions through the marketplace or regulation.

Illustrative components of loss from two types of cyber breaches, payment card fraud and intellectual property, are presented in Figure 1 for direct costs and Figure 2 for indirect costs. The type of cyber breach is identified on the left with arrows leading to categories of effects—the partial derivatives—and a partial linkage to categories identified in Anderson, et al. [7].

This enumeration of core pathways for cost in standard economic terms has the potential to identify costs typically ignored, such as potentially positive or negative price effects, and to provide a structure in which to identify other pathways and elements of loss.

Economists are familiar with estimating elements of consumer demand and firm costs and production. The proposed framing of losses into a standard economic framework may facilitate the transition of empirical methodologies to cyber loss estimation and estimation of the partial derivatives based on data.

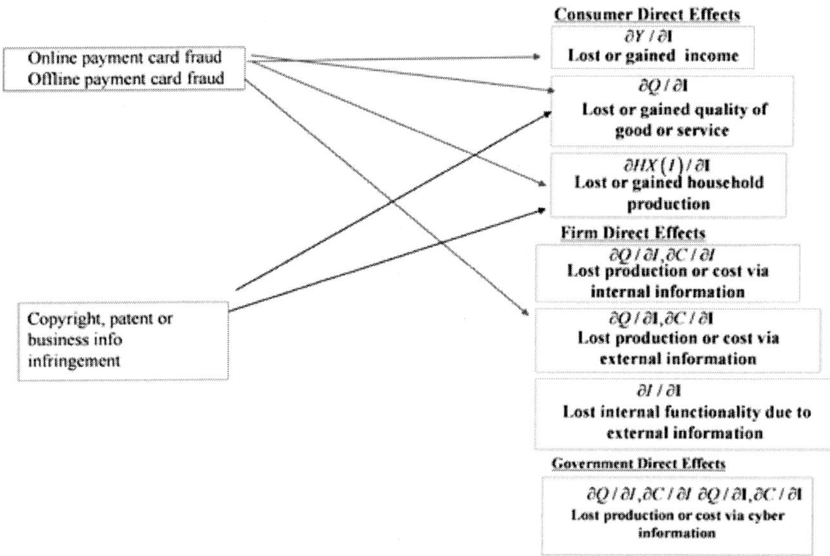

Figure 1. Direct effects of illustrative cyber online fraud and intellectual property breach.

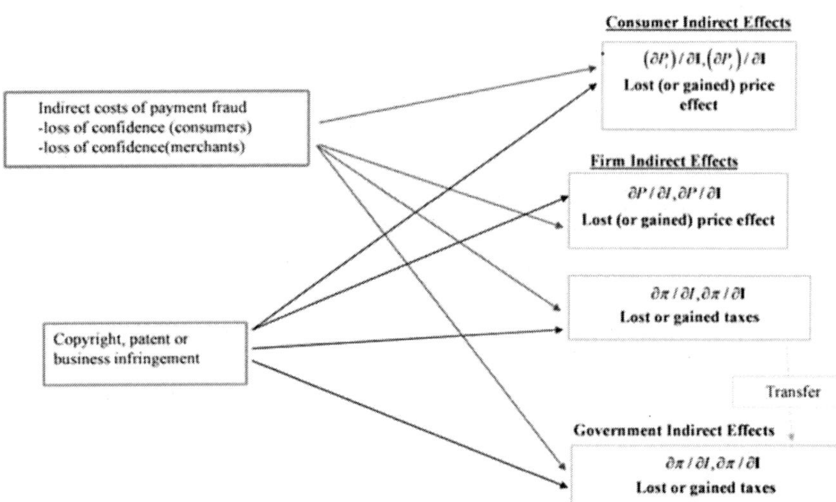

Figure 2. Indirect effects of illustrative cyber payment fraud or intellectual property breach.

3.2. Some Effects of Uncertainty in Defining Losses

The loss estimates in Gordon and Loeb [1] and Gordon, Loeb, Lucyshyn and Zhou [5] are part of the objective function where the expected net benefit of a cyber investment is maximized. The losses, elaborated upon above, are the conditional losses where cyber security investment expenditures affect the probability of a successful attack. Continuing to focus on losses, the model of the consumer and firm has long been extended to conditions with uncertainty based on the expected utility model and more recently, non-expected utility models.

A natural extension to expected value optimization is expected utility maximization. To the extent that losses are potentially large so that a significant gamble is involved, then some risk aversion may be present as in Eeckhoudt, Gollier and Schlesinger [13]. Numerous methods exist in economics and decision analysis to elicit utility functions subject however, to the more restrictive assumptions that imply cardinal instead of ordinal utility (e.g. [14] [15]). The concern by some firms for a reputational effect from a cyber breach or intellectual property theft may well warrant extending the model of losses to expected utility instead of expected value. Consideration of risk aversion leads naturally to consideration of insurance as a risk management strategy in addition to prevention which has indeed occurred.

However, the descriptive validity of the expected utility model is being questioned by behavioral economists and psychologists with a rich and rapidly evolving literature on consumer and firm behavior under uncertainty (Della Vigna, [16]). That literature identifies a number of outcome anomalies such as the importance of reference points and asymmetric treatment of gains and losses as well as more complex treatment of probability than in the expected utility model. An analyst seeking a descriptive model of cyber losses may wish to include consideration of such factors. In empirical practice, such consideration can simply involve a different specification of an assumed utility function as compared in Farrow and Scott [17].

Although this note has focused on defining conditional losses, cyber investments are often modeled as directly affecting the probability of the loss. Given that framework, the dynamic aspect of cyber security—new weakness are constantly being found and defenses are evolving—may best be incorporated into the probability function rather than making production functions dynamic although the latter remains a possibility. Similarly, behavioral models of probability as with cumulative prospect theory may be descriptively appropriate to consider as synthesized by Waaker [18].

4. CONCLUSION

Previous categories of costs from cyber improvements and losses have conformed to general professional categories but have not been specific about the pathways through which gains and losses can occur. This paper brings information, both internal and external, into the canonical structure of microeconomic models of the consumer, the firm, and government. Impacts are then identified through the full set of partial derivatives for utility, price, quantity, profit, and taxes. The increased definitional detail facilitates the use of statistical tools to study the behavior of consumers and the firm.

ACKNOWLEDGEMENTS

Appreciation is extended to Anupam Joshi, Matt Shabat and Jules Szanton for comments and discussion. Funding was provided by the Department of Homeland Security National Center on the Risk and Economic Analysis of Terrorism Events (CREATE).

REFERENCES

1. Wakker, P. (2010) Prospect Theory for Risk and Ambiguity. Cambridge University Press, Cambridge.http://dx.doi.org/10.1017/CBO9780511779329
2. Farrow, S. and Scott, M. (2013) Comparing Multi-State Expected Damages, Option Price and Cumulative Prospect Measures for Valuing Flood Protection. Water Resources Research, 49, 2638-2648. http://dx.doi.org/10.1002/wrcr.20217
3. Della Vigna, S. (2009) Psychology and Economics: Evidence from the Field. Journal of Economic Literature, 47, 315-372. http://dx.doi.org/10.1257/jel.47.2.315
4. Keeney, R.L. and Raiffa, H. (1976) Decision Making with Multiple Objectives Preferences and Value Tradeoffs. Wiley, New York.
5. Clemen, R.T. and Reilley, T. (2001) Making Hard Decisions. Duxbury Press, Belmont.
6. Eeckhoudt, L., Gollier, C. and Schlesinger, H. (2005) Economic and Financial Decisions Under Risk. Princeton University Press, Princeton.
7. Campbell, K., Gordon, L.A., Loeb, M. and Zhou, L. (2003) The Economic Cost of Publicly Announced Information Security Breaches: Empirical Evidence from the Stock Market. Journal of Computer Security, 11, 431-448. http://dx.doi.org/10.3233/JCS-2003-11308
8. Gronau, R. and Hammermesh, D. (2006) Time vs. Goods: The Value of Measuring Household Production Technologies. Review of Income and Wealth, 52, 1-16. http://dx.doi.org/10.1111/j.1475-4991.2006.00173.x
9. Becker, G. (1965) A Theory of the Allocation of Time. Economic Journal, 75, 493-517. http://dx.doi.org/10.2307/2228949
10. Detica and the Office of Cyber Security and Information Assurance (2011) The Cost of Cybercrime, February. https://www.gov.uk/government/publications/the-cost-of-cyber-crime-joint-government-and-industry-report

11. Undercofer, J., Joshi, A. and Pinkson, J. (2003) Modeling Computer Attacks: An Ontology for Intrusion Detection. Proceedings of the Sixth International Symposium on Recent Advances in Intrusion Detection. http://dx.doi.org/10.1007/978-3-540-45248-5_7
12. Anderson, R., Barton, C., Boehme, R., Clayton, R., van Eeten, M., Levi, M., Moore, T. and Savage, S. (2012) Measuring the Cost of Cyber Crime. Workshop in the Economics of Information Security (WEIS).
13. Levinson, D. (2002) Encyclopedia of Crime and Punishment. Vol I, Sage Publications.
14. 14. Gordon, L., Loeb, M., Lucyshyn, W. and Zhou, L. (2015) Externalities and the Magnitude of Cyber Security Underinvestment by Private Sector Firms: A Modification of the Gordon-Loeb Model. Journal of Information Security, 6, 24-30. http://dx.doi.org/10.4236/jis.2015.61003
15. Farrow, S. and Szanton, J. (2016) Cybersecurity Investment Guidance: Extensions of the Gordon and Loeb Model. Journal of Information Security, 7, 15-28. http://dx.doi.org/10.4236/jis.2016.72002
16. Rogerson, R., Shimer, R. and Wright, R. (2005) Search-Theoretic Models of the Labor Market: A Survey. Journal of Economic Literature, 959-988. http://dx.doi.org/10.1257/002205105775362014
17. Bikhchandani, S., Hirshleifer, J. and Riley, J.G. (2013) The Analytics of Uncertainty and Information. 2nd Edition, Cambridge University Press, Cambridge. http://dx.doi.org/10.1017/CBO9781139016209
18. Gordon, L. and Loeb, M. (2002) The Economics of Information Security Investment. ACM Transactions on Information and System Security, 5, 438-457. http://dx.doi.org/10.1145/581271.581274

NOTES

[1]The economics literature on crime typically defines attacks as externalities as there is no voluntary exchange (Levinson [6]). Most cyber breaches can be viewed as types of crime enabled by computers or that are uniquely possible with computers (Anderson et al. [7]). The crime literature further debates whether "thieves" have standing for costs and benefits with the usual but not universal conclusion that they do not. This is especially important for issues such as intellectual property or international cybercrime.

[2]As governments heavily depend on income taxes; such taxes could be modeled as depending on income and cyber information. For simplicity, such tax modeling is omitted here but included in the description of the firm.

[3]Note that to the extent effects are mediated through market price changes, then there can be usual income and substitution effects.

CHAPTER 17

A Survey on M2M Service Networks

Juhani Latvakoski [1,*], Antti Iivari [1], Paul Vitic [2], Bashar Jubeh [3], Mahdi Ben Alaya [4], Thierry Monteil [4], Yoann Lopez [5], Guillermo Talavera [6], Javier Gonzalez [6], Niclas Granqvist [7], Monir Kellil [8], Herve Ganem [9] and Teemu Väisänen [1]

[1]*VTT Technical Research Centre of Finland Kaitoväylä 1, Oulu 90571, Finland*

[2]*Vektor Telematics Necatibey Caddesi, Akçe Sokak, No: 6 Karaköy Istanbul, 34420 Turkey*

[3]*Bull, 207, Cours du Medoc, Bordeaux 33000, France*

[4]*CNRS-LAAS, 7 Avenue du Colonel Roche BP 54200 31031 Toulouse cedex 4, France*

[5]*Thales Communications S.A. 160, Boulevard de Valmy—BP 82. 92704 Colomber, France*

[6]*UAB, Celphis Etse Campus, 08193 Bellaterra (Cerdanvola del Valles), Barcelona, Spain*

[7]*Polar Elektro Oy. Professorintie 5, Kempele 90440, Finland*

[8]*CEA. Saclay DRT/LIST/DIASI/LSC Bat 528, Boite courrier 94. 91191 Gif-sur-Yvette, Cedex, France*

[9]*Gemalto. 6, rue de la Verrerie, Meudon 92197, France*

ABSTRACT

The number of industrial applications relying on the Machine to Machine (M2M) services exposed from physical world has been increasing in recent years. Such M2M services enable communication of devices with the core processes of companies. However, there is a big challenge related to complexity and to application-specific M2M systems called "vertical silos". This paper focuses on reviewing the technologies of M2M service networks and discussing approaches from the perspectives of M2M information and services, M2M communication and M2M security. Finally, a discussion on technologies and approaches potentially enabling future autonomic M2M service networks are provided. According to our conclusions, it is seen that clear definition of the architectural principles is needed to solve the "vertical silo" problem and then, proceeding towards enabling autonomic capabilities for solving complexity problem appears feasible. Several areas of future research have been identified, e.g., autonomic information based services, optimization of communications with limited capability devices, real-time messaging, creation of trust and end to end security, adaptability, reliability, performance, interoperability, and maintenance.

Keywords: machine to machine communication; Internet of things; cyber-physical systems

1. INTRODUCTION

The number of embedded devices has continuously increased in recent years. Traditionally, such devices have worked locally in an independent way and provided services for human users. Advances in radio communication technologies have enabled even mobile connectivity for the referred devices over the Internet. These trends are now visible as the increasing number of application cases which rely on the services exposed from physical equipment, such as sensors, actuators, RFID tags, machines, vehicles and industrial embedded devices. Such service systems are described here as Machine to Machine (M2M) service networks, and they can also be called Internet of Things (IoT), Web of Things, Wireless Sensor Networks and Actuator Networks (WSANs) or Cyber Physical Systems [1,2].

Usually, such M2M service networks include capabilities for remote measurements and remote control of embedded devices. Remote measurements consist of sensing physical phenomenon, storing, sending, receiving and processing of measured information. Remote control of devices includes access control, mutual exclusion, sending, receiving and processing of control commands. The basic enabler for such functionality is M2M connectivity, which links various kinds of embedded devices into the Internet based M2M services. The added value is created by the enabled M2M services based on the use of the measured information in a smart way, reasoning, and execution of smart remote control actions with the M2M asset devices. The real benefits of such smart M2M services will be realized when connecting them with the core processes of the companies. This can enable real-time situation awareness in the company processes, and create opportunities for novel services for customers, increase service quality and enable cost savings, e.g., in maintenance processes. Furthermore, this is also an enabler for transition from product centric to service centric businesses.

The main problems in these M2M service networks arise from the complexity and the vertical fragmentation of M2M markets. This complexity is due to the number of embedded devices, connectivity means, and service platforms and especially to their heterogeneity. Establishing and maintaining an interactive system capable of interoperating with the human user is here expected to go beyond human capabilities soon. M2M market is fragmented to multiple vertical industries, and the resulting systems are usually domain or vendor specific closed systems, also called “vertical silos”. In addition, the natural needs of businesses to protect themselves seem to lead such systems that require special access rights for each specific system, resulting in vendor specific closed systems. This has caused problems, for example in residential home environments, and prevented the emergence of home automation to a large extent. Smart grid solutions cannot interoperate with infrastructure and buildings/homes, even if it would be strongly required to reach higher level energy efficiency. Therefore, it is observed here that the technological complexity and vertical M2M silos are the cause of a *grand research challenge* for the development of a modern ecosystem.

It is assumed here that the referred challenge is so fundamental that it requires novel approaches for the system architectures and application of novel paradigms. It is seen that Internet “IP everywhere” cannot alone solve the problem with industrial M2M systems. Something more is needed, such as horizontal approach and autonomic computing, which may have potential to create basis for solving this sizable challenge. Most of the existing vertical M2M solutions have difficulty in scaling, and therefore enabling the *horizontal model* is important for realizing embedded M2M [3]. Autonomic computing is a concept inspired from biological systems that aims to develop systems capable of automatic management for solving the complexity problem [4,5].

There are multiple attempts to build such autonomic systems, e.g., [6,7], and different design approaches such as externalization and internalization [8]. According to IBM, the evolutionary path to autonomic computing is represented by five levels [9], starting from basic, through managed, predictive, adaptive and finally to autonomic. Such approaches as software agents [10], active networks [11] and policy-based systems [12] have been developed to automate the management tasks to achieve higher response times with less management cost. Attempts have been made to solve the communication complexity problem by using be solved by built-in mechanisms to let systems manage their own communications [13]. The self-management capability aims to solve the rapidly growing complexity of computing system management and enable dynamic future growth of the system. There are four properties that enable autonomic capabilities in a system: self-configuration, self-optimization, self-healing and self-protection [14]. Self-Configuration is the ability of the system to perform configurations according to pre-defined high level policies and seamlessly adapt to change caused by automatic configurations. Self-Optimization is the ability of the system to continuously monitor and control resources to improve performance and efficiency. Self-Healing is the ability of the system to automatically detect, diagnose and repair faults. Self-Protection is the ability of the system to pro-actively identify and protect itself from malicious attacks or cascading failures that are not corrected by self-healing measures. An autonomic system should satisfy these properties through a reactive or a proactive behavior. A reactive autonomic system tries to detect problems or meaningful events and then finds an appropriate action or solution after the problem has been already detected. A proactive autonomic system [15] uses preventive measures to maintain, improve or optimize the system performance. Those measures are based on the analysis of the current state, anticipated events and the predicted system reaction to them.

Thus, we review here the technologies to evaluate their capabilities to solve the grand challenge in the context of M2M service networks. The approaches for M2M service networks are first discussed in Chapter 2 and the taxonomy for the review is defined. Then, the related M2M standards and technologies for each category are reviewed as follows: Chapter 3 M2M information and services, Chapter 4 M2M communication and Chapter 5 M2M security. After the review, a discussion is provided in Chapter 6, and finally concluding remarks are provided in Chapter 7.

2. M2M SERVICE NETWORKS

2.1. M2M System

A M2M system usually consists of a set of M2M asset devices attached in a M2M capillary network, a kind of M2M gateway, M2M communication infrastructure and a set of M2M services and applications as shown on Figure 1. The red line represents a typical scenario related to the remote monitoring and control process in M2M service networks. Such a scenario requires operation of the complete M2M system including the functionalities of M2M information and service, M2M communication and

M2M security, which are therefore included in a sensible level into this survey.

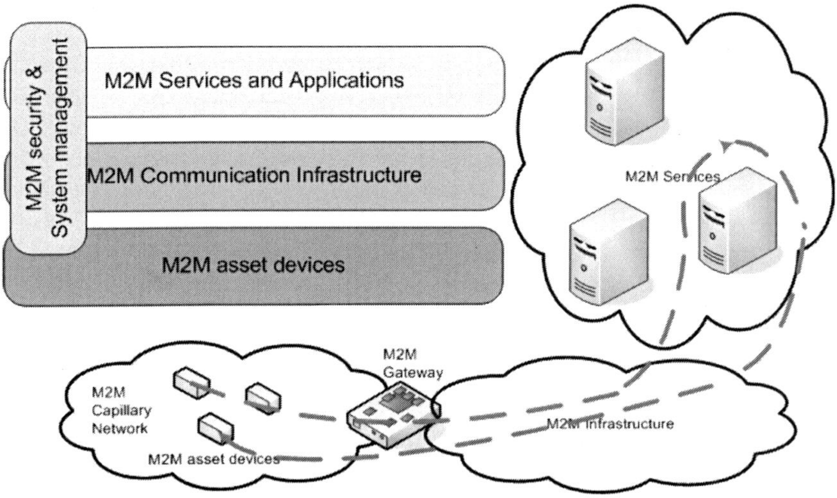

Figure 1. A view of a Machine to Machine (M2M) system.

M2M services and applications can be divided further to multiple levels such as, e.g., information, service platform and applications. The applications are usually domain specific business logic, high level management of the M2M system, devices, and domain specific information. The *information level* usually contains information management services and exchange transactions between the stakeholders of the system. A standardized common information model can enable smooth information exchange and business interactions between stakeholders of the domain. An example of this kind of common information model is CIM standardized for energy grid [16]. *M2M Service Platform* includes service solutions and frameworks, which may be applied in multiple domains. The service solutions can contain generic service elements such as e.g., event notification, environment monitoring, service discovery and delivery, generic profiling, access control, generic storage and device management [17]. ETSI M2M has specified a set of service capabilities related to application, communication, reachability, addressing and repository, remote management, security, history and data containers [18]. A standardized M2M service platform could enable smooth application development and interaction between service platforms of different vendors, and services of M2M asset devices to be applied in multiple cases.

M2M communication infrastructure contains heterogeneous networks including local M2M asset network (M2M capillary network) such as personal/body area network, vehicular network and wireless sensor network (WSN), and Internet including various overlay networks. The overlay network can logically connect the M2M asset devices, M2M gateways, infrastructure servers and user with each other to hide the heterogeneity of physical networks and solve such problems as mobility, device power saving features, security including firewalls and NAT restricted networks. Thus the overlay network is a logical network operating on top of physical networks like, e.g., the Internet. The local asset network can contain M2M gateway(s), which may be needed to connect the local area network to the wide area network. If the local M2M asset devices are able to handle communication themselves such a gateway device is not necessarily needed. Several standardized short range radio technologies such as Bluetooth, ZigBee, RFID, *etc.*, can be utilized locally, but also as vendor specific and optimized radio technologies for WSNs. The wide area and Internet connectivity can be provided by, e.g., Telecom operator and/or ISP using, e.g., Ethernet, DSL, GSM, 3GPP, WiFi, WiMax, *etc.* There are a number of standardization bodies such as IETF, 3GPP, Bluetooth, *etc.*, whose works are related to specific areas of connectivity.

M2M asset devices consist of a huge number of heterogeneous embedded devices, which can be general purpose sensors, actuators, tags or M2M gateways in addition to domain, or even business case specific, heterogeneous devices. These devices, ranging from miniaturized sensors to large industrial machinery, operate with different technologies, operational characteristics and environments. It is obvious that all these devices cannot have the same type of interface because the purpose and capabilities can be very different. However, there are usually dependencies with the domain specific application, information, M2M service platform and M2M connectivity levels in the M2M asset devices. This may lead to a need to make changes into various levels of the M2M system, if, e.g., an M2M asset device manufacturer is changed. Therefore, application of standard based technologies in M2M service networks is very important.

In addition, the system needs to scale, be interoperable, flexible and extensible during the complete life-cycle [3,19].

Last but not the least is security and management of the complete M2M system. They are seen to be cross issues, which mean that these features shall be built-in to the levels of the system applying widely approved standards. In addition, the needs of ensuring services provided by industrial companies needs to be taken into account.

2.2. Related M2M Standardization Approaches

An analysis of some M2M standardization approaches is provided in Table 1. At least a tiny IP stack is required in the end-to-end Internet based approach to enable connectivity for small devices. If such a stack is available, then this approach may be possible. However, the challenge is that also the embedded devices which are not necessarily Internet-capable are required to be connected to the Internet. The M2M gateway based approach may enable also their connectivity; however, the challenge may be dynamic behavior of the wireless systems and need to adapt with different kinds of service back-end systems.

A number of industry associations have been established to cover some specific category of M2M asset devices, such as electronic product codes, generic identification numbering, RFID tags, video devices, electricity, gas, water and heat meters and different kind of sensors (e.g., Geospatial) and devices for specific applications (e.g., medical devices).

The capability of user interface to adapt to the dynamic behavior of wireless devices has been a challenge. UIML type of approach seems to be too heavy to be applied with the UIs of embedded M2M asset devices. It is also possible to apply the natural need of the M2M asset device manufacturers to make drivers and UIs for their products, and connect these SW components into the dynamic configuration and discovery process [20].

Dynamic configuration and discovery methods have been applied in large scale within peer to peer (P2P) content delivery systems, e.g., Napster, KaZaA, Gnutella, Morpheus and BitTorrent [32].

Table 1. M2M Standardization approaches.

Approach/Focus	Forums	Contributions
End-to-End Internet based approach	- IPSO Alliance—Enabling the Internet of Things [21] - The Internet Engineering Task Force (IETF) [22]	- Network related standards, e.g., IPv6 over Low Power WPAN (6LoWPAN) - Constrained RESTful Environments (CoRE) - Routing Over Low power and Lossy Networks (ROLL) - RPL for tiny battery operated devices
M2M gateway based approach	- ETSI M2M/Smart M2M Technical Committee [23] - One M2M forum [24]	- Generic horizontal service capability layer with standard interfaces - M2M concept and architecture
Electronic product codes	EPC Global [25]	Usage of electronic product codes with RFID technology
Generic identification numbering	uID center [26]	Identification of objects and places uniquely, and association of information with them
	Coordination And Support	- Global Coding System (GCS) in relation to

RFID coordination	Action For Global RFID-related Activities and Standardization (CASAGARAS)	RFID systems - Ontologies for identification - IoT architectural components
Video devices	ONVIF [27]	ONVIF defines a common protocol for the exchange of information between network video devices including automatic device discovery, video streaming and metadata
Electricity, gas, water and heat meters	Openmeter [28]	Development of open standards for advanced meter interface (AMI)
Sensors	OGC Sensor Web Enablement (SWE) [29]	Sensor web enablement standards to enable developers to make all types of sensors, transducers and sensor data repositories discoverable, accessible and usable via Web
User interfaces	UIML [30]	User Interface Mark-up Language (UIML), which allows dynamic change of the UI content by enabling UI generation
Devices and their services	Universal Plug and Play (UPnP) [31]	Configuration and discovery of the devices and their services, UPnP
(Building) automation and control networks	For BACnet: ASHRAE Standing Standard Project Committee (SSPC)	- A data communication protocol for building automation and control networks. - BACnet, Modbus, DNP3, CAN, *etc.*
Radio access protocols for IoT and M2M	IEEE, NFC Forum, ZigBee Alliance, Bluetooth SIG	ZigBee, NFC, Bluetooth, WiFi, *etc.*
Semantic access to IoT and M2M data	W3C	- Ontology Web Language (OWL) - Darpa Agent Mark-up Language (DAML) - Resource Description Framework (RDF)
Medical devices	- Center for Integration of Medicine and Innovative Technology (CIMIT) - Continua Health Alliance	Standards and/or profiles for health related or medical devices

However, content delivery differs essentially from the discovery of services exposed from M2M asset devices. There are some service discovery systems targeted to local scale and embedded devices such as UPnP and Bluetooth SDP. However, there is lack of solutions for large-scale wireless and hybrid networks [33].

Overlay networking is based on the virtual communication layer, which is built on top of other transport media and/or physical network [34]. Overlay networking has been applied to improve the robustness and availability of Internet paths between hosts (e.g., MIT RON), enable smooth transition to the improved technology (e.g., 6Bone) or to reduce network load by peer assisted data delivery (e.g., BitTorrent). Overlays have been used to route control messages and connect different entities (e.g., SIP and XMPP), and also to implement data forwarding and dissemination (e.g., Chord, Tapestry, and Pastry). Another motivation for overlay networking arises from security challenges. For example, Virtual Private Ad Hoc Networking (VPAN) has been developed to create virtual overlay networks between trusted IP capable devices [35].

In an M2M system, M2M asset devices, network and users can be mobile. In these conditions, information exchange with the M2M asset device need to solve such challenges as unreliable communication channels, temporal presence, limited power and computing capabilities. Solutions for wireless sensors networks in some specific domain and application have been developed [36]. Usually, these solutions have vendor dependent optimized solutions for computing platform, radio technology, communication and services. However, there is at least one potential emerging standard for low power communication between wireless sensors called as Bluetooth 4.0 [37], Bluetooth Smart, which may be applicable for multiple domains. However, there is still a need for generic standard based communication and service protocols working with limited capability embedded M2M assets and mobile gateways.

2.3. Discussion

The M2M standardization approaches demonstrate the heterogeneity of the M2M service networks area. The area is very large; our aim is to review the available technological solutions at least from the following perspectives: M2M Information and services, M2M communication and M2M security. In this review we categorize the available technologies into these perspectives. Within each category, the key contribution of each technology is analyzed. After the review, the potential contributions of the technologies to support horizontal and autonomic M2M are discussed.

3. M2M INFORMATION AND SERVICES

M2M Information and Service technologies are reviewed in this chapter. After the review, two potential technologies: sensor web enablement (SWE) and ETSI M2M service capability layer are shortly overviewed. Finally, autonomic features and related technologies are discussed.

3.1. M2M Information and Service Technologies

The selected set of M2M information and service level technologies are reviewed in Table 2, and some of them are shortly analyzed in the following.

ETSI M2M service capability layer has been defined to be horizontal in the sense that the service capabilities have been specified to be applied with multiple application domains. It uses a resources tree structure to represent the service capabilities layer of each M2M device [18,38]. This tree describes information such as registered SCLs, registered applications, access rights, subscription, groups, data containers, *etc.* ETSI

M2M describes only data containers without specifying any information content, which means that information content is transparent and out of scope from ETSI M2M. In addition, device descriptions are not properly included, but interfaces with OMA DM and BBF TR069 device management are specified. Therefore, it is necessary to decide the containers, information content and device management of the devices and applications beforehand.

Table 2. Review of M2M Information and Service Technologies.

Technology	Forum(s), References	Main Contribution
ETSI M2M	ETSI M2M service capability layer [18,23,38]	Specification of a Horizontal M2M service capability layer. RESTful approach to represent information by resources which are structured as a tree. The content of the information is transparent and out of scope.
OMA DM data model	Open Mobile Alliance [39,40]	Information model for management and dynamic service provisioning of OMA DM enabled devices.
BBF TR069 data model	Broadband forum [41,42]	Information model for Auto-configuration and dynamic service provisioning of TR069 enabled customer premise equipment.
UPNP data model	Universal Plug and Play [31,43]	Information model based on XML to describe device and its provided services for UPNP enabled devices.
DPWS data model	Devices Profile for Web Services (DPWS) [44]	Information model defined in the WSDL file based on the XML Schema specification for DPWS enabled devices.
oBix data model	Open building information Xchange [45]	Restful approach based on an object oriented data model to represent data for the mechanical and electrical systems in commercial buildings.
OPC UA data model	OPC Foundation [46,47]	Information model based on object-oriented technics to represent data for Object Linking and Embedding for Process Control (OPC).
OWL-S ontology	Semantic Markup for Web Services [48,49]	Semantic web services ontology that enables users and software agents to automatically discover, invoke, compose, and monitor Web resources offering services, under specified constraints.
SSN ontology	W3C Semantic Sensor Networks [50,51]	Ontology that defines the capabilities of sensors and sensor networks, and to develop semantic annotations of a key language used by services based sensor networks.
FIPA-device ontology	FIPA Device Ontology Specification [52,53]	Semantic device profile and service ontology that can be used by agents when communicating.
Sensor Web Enablement	Sensor Web enablement [54–56]	Overlay architecture for integrating sensor networks and applications on the Web.
OSGi	OSGi Alliance [57]	Modular system and service platform for Java.
Service Delivery Framework (SDF)	TM Forum [58]	Providing a reference in the industry on management of "next generation services".

The devices offering services can be managed by Device Management Servers in OMA DM [39]. OMA DM devices are identified by a model number, and represent services as management objects in the OMA DM data model (Device Management Tree). These service objects are just service representations which contain nodes. These nodes contain properties for the actual service which can be managed by the ACS. The calls to configure the management objects are done over SyncML. Devices offering services can be managed by Auto Configuration Servers in TR-069 [41]. TR-069 devices are identified by a serial number and a type, and represent services as service objects in the TR-069 data model. These service objects are just service representations which contain parameters for the actual service which can be managed by the ACS. Service objects can be classified by profiles which are specified by the DSLForum.

UPnP devices [43] are represented by XML device descriptions, which contain a device ID, the device type and the list of provided services. Each entry in this service list points to an XML service description which contains a service ID, the service type and the actions and states which specify the functionalities of the service. Service description is handled with WSDL file in DPWS [59]. A service's metadata includes information about its relations with other services, such as the hosting service's relationship to the hosted service and vice versa. The application payload data model is defined in the WSDL by means provided by the XML Schema specification, which is an XML based language that can be used to define the properties of other XML based languages.

OBix [45] proposes a restful data model based on a highly extensible full-blown object oriented model. It includes classes and even method signatures and objects composed of other objects. It offers a standard library providing the base object types and special purpose classes such as watch, history, batch operations, *etc.* In classic OPC, only pure data was provided, such as raw sensor values, with only limited semantic information, such as the tag name and the engineering unit. OPC UA [46,47] offers more powerful capability for semantic modeling of data. It uses object-oriented techniques, including type hierarchies and inheritance, to model information. The OPC UA Node model allows for information to be connected in various ways, by allowing for hierarchical and non-hierarchical reference type. This facilitates exposing the same information in many ways, depending on the use case.

OWL-S [48,49] is an OWL-based Web service ontology, which supplies Web service providers with a core set of markup language, constructs for describing the properties and capabilities of their Web services in unambiguous, computer-interpretable form. OWL-S markup of Web services facilitates the automation of Web service tasks, including automated Web service discovery, execution, composition and interoperation. The SSN ontology [50] describes sensors, the accuracy and capabilities of such sensors, observations and methods used for sensing. Also, concepts for operating and survival ranges are included, as these are often part of a given specification for a sensor, along with its performance within those ranges. Finally, a structure for field deployments is included to describe deployment lifetime and sensing purpose of the deployed macro instrument. Fipa-Device ontology [52,53] can be used as reference to express the capabilities of different devices in a ubiquitous computing system. Some concepts of FIPA are: Device, Hardware Description, Software Description and Connection Description. FIPA can be used by agents when communicating about devices. Agents pass profiles of devices to each other and validate them against the Fipa-Device ontology.

Data transmitted in M2M networks need both, the semantics and the level of abstraction, that could make it possible to provide them as a pool of common data available in a given environment and to share them between different applications, without needing to know beforehand the specifics of these data. The physical entities that are sensed and acted need to be modeled with a level of abstraction allowing the M2M system to treat them as generic entities, intrinsic to the environment and not tied to a specific M2M application.

Open Geospatial Consortium (OGC) Sensor Web Enablement (OGC SWE) initiative is focused on developing an infrastructure which enables an interoperable usage of sensor resources by enabling their discovery, access, tasking, as well as events and alerting on the Web from the application level. It hides the underlying layers, the network communication details, and heterogeneous sensor hardware, from the applications built on top of it, but does not provide sensor network management functionality [54,55,56].

3.2. Sensor Web Enablement

The term *Sensor Web* refers to a wireless network of sensor nodes which autonomously share the data they collect and adjust their behavior based on this data [60,61]. Today, it refers in practice into WWW overlay for integrating sensor networks and applications [62,63,64]. The view of *Sensor Web* has been largely influenced by the architecture that is being developed by OGC SWE work group [56]. The SWE architecture represents a *logical view-point* of the *Sensor Web*, as an infrastructure which enables an interoperable usage of sensor resources by enabling their discovery, access, tasking, as well as events and alerting, in a standardized way [63]. The SWE architecture consists of two main blocks: Interface model and Information model.

The information model, formalized as XML schema documents, consists of the conceptual data models. The interface model (services model), is the specification of services in the form of Web service interface specifications (WSDL). Figure 2and Figure 3 show the new generation

SWE standards (Version 2.0) which were published in the second half of 2011. Green boxes are specifications approved as standards (or in standardization process), grey boxes are discussion papers and dashed arrows point to dependencies.

SWE Common specifies low level data models for exchanging sensor related data between SWE framework nodes. It defines the representation, nature, structure and encoding of sensor related data [65]. Observations & Measurements (O&M) defines a conceptual schema for observations, and for features involved in sampling when making observations. These provide models for the exchange of information describing observation acts and their results, both within and between different scientific and technical communities [66]. SWE services use SensorML as a format for describing their associated sensors [67]. The model provides information needed for discovery of sensors, location of sensor observations, processing of low-level sensor observations, and listing of configurable sensor properties. A sensor is defined as a process which is capable of observing a phenomenon and returning an observed value. For example, a process can be a measurement procedure conducted by a sensor or the post processing of previously gathered data. Event Pattern Markup Language (EML) defines subscription filters to SWE framework nodes that provide publish/subscribe type services. Currently, the Sensor Event Service (SES) is the first prototype within OGC SWE that supports EML. Both the O&M and SensorML models extend the OGC's Geographic Markup Language (GML) which is a standard XML encoding for expressing geographical features. This provides the functionality to integrate sensors into Spatial Data Infrastructures (SDI).

SWE Service Model defines packages with data types and operation request and response types for common use across SWE services [68]. Sensor Observation Service (SOS) provides standardized access to sensor observations and sensor metadata [69]. The service acts as a mediator between a client and a sensor data archive or a real-time sensor system. The heterogeneous communication protocols and data formats of the associated sensors are hidden by the standardized interface of SOS. SOS defines O&M as its mandatory and default response format for sensor data and recommends the usage of SensorML for sensor metadata exchange. Sensor Planning Service (SPS) is a web service interface that allows clients to submit tasks to sensors for operations such as the configuration of the sampling rate or the steering of a movable sensor platform [70].

SPS operations derive from the abstract request type defined by SWE Service Model and aggregates operations covering the complete process of controlling and planning sensor tasks.

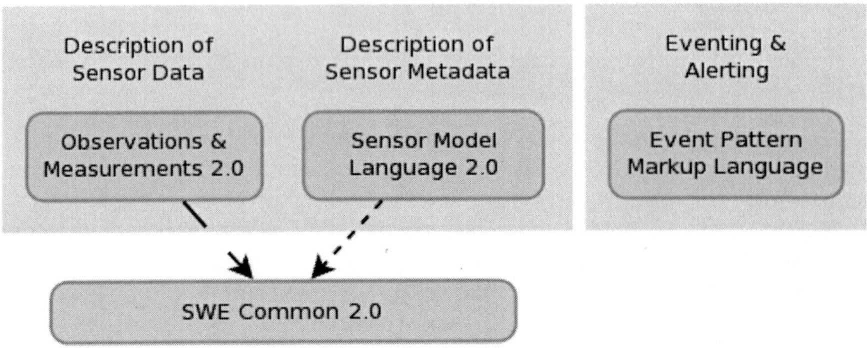

Figure 2. Sensor web enablement (SWE) common.

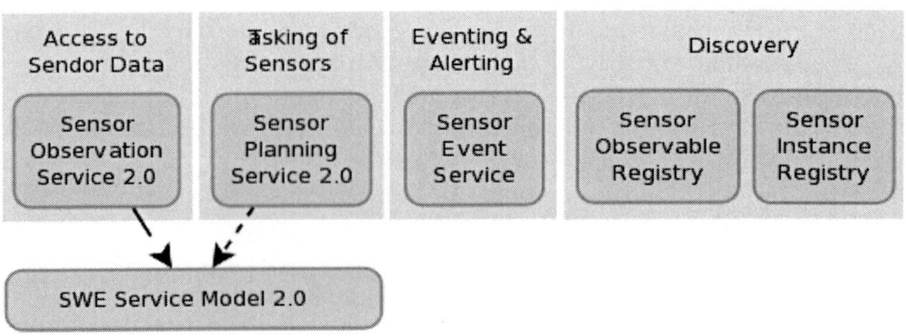

Figure 3. SWE Service Model.

Sensor Event Service (SES) is a SWE service specification at discussion phase. It provides a push-based access to sensor data as well as functionality for sensor data mining and fusion inside a spatial data structure. SES uses the OASIS WS-Notification (WS-N) standard for the definition of the service operations needed for a publish/subscribe communication. This suite of standards defines operations for subscription handling and notifications (WS-BaseNotification), for the brokering of notifications (WS-BrokeredNotification) and for the use of event channels (WS-Topics). Event channels allow a grouping of notifications with respect to a specific topic, for instance weather forecasts. Instead of defining the filter for forecasts in each consumer's subscription, a consumer can simply subscribe for all notifications on the weather channel. Consumers may also use filter criteria while subscribing to sensor data. Depending on the filter type used these criteria operate on single observations or on observation streams, potentially aggregating observations into higher-level information (which itself can be regarded as observation data).

Sensor Instance Registry (SIR) provides functionality to collect, manages, transform and transfer sensor metadata through SensorML as well as extended discovery functionality and sensor status information. It is intended to close the gap between the SensorML based SWE world and conventional Spatial Data Infrastructures (SDIs). In the future it is expected that the functionality of the SIR interface will partly be covered by other existing SWE services (e.g., SOS for retrieving sensor status information and the SES for filtering sensor status updates).

Sensor Observable Registry (SOR) is designed in order to support users when dealing with identifiers pointing to phenomenon observed by a sensor (observable) which is very important when searching for sensors. Usually such parameters are expressed within SensorML documents through some kind of identifier (*i.e.*, URIs). Figure 4 depicts two scenarios where the SWE architecture is in action: sensors without embedded IP stack, and sensors with embedded IP stack. The scenarios have been simplified in order to clarify the basic idea. More details can be found in the standards specifications and the SWE white papers.

SWE is a standard M2M architecture that focuses primarily on the requirements of the scientific community dealing with remote sensor and sensor data management. Certain features of the SWE architecture pose a barrier for its widespread adoption for this purpose. For example, the complexity of the SOAP based SWE service interface specification and other extension specifications (e.g., OASIS WS-Notification, *etc.*) are one of these barriers. Future versions add a lightweight HTTP GET binding for certain operations with the aim of improving ease of adoption. Another issue is the tight coupling of the information model with GML which binds spatial data infrastructure across all data ubiquitously. While this feature makes it easy to relate sensor data with other spatial-temporal resources (e.g., maps, raster as well as vector data) at the application level, this is not a requirement in all M2M scenarios. However, adaptation of the SWE information model may provide useful solutions within the context of M2M service networks.

Scenario 1—Sensors without Embedded IP Stack

1.1 Multiple sensor nodes connect to a SWE Gateway. Sensor networks that utilize various network topologies and low level communication protocols may be connected to the SWE architecture in this manner. The Gateway layers the sensor network data with Internet and Web protocols and relays it to a SES server. Initially the gateway calls the RegisterPublisher operation to add sensors to the SES. The request includes a SensorML which describes the sensor and its capabilities.

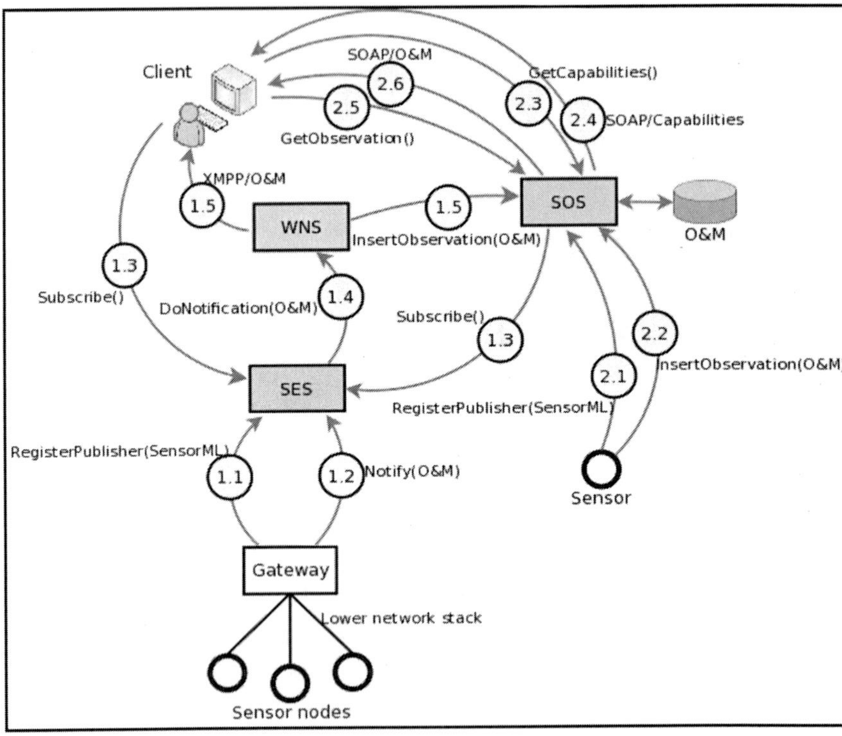

Figure 4. SWE Architecture in action.

1.2 Sensor data is published to the SES via the Gateway. Notify operation, which contains sensor data in the O&M standard, is used.

1.3 A SOS server and a user application subscribe to sensor data using the Subscribe operation. The requests include the topic and the filtering specifications, as well as the information about the endpoint to which the filtered sensor data should be delivered. The step would probably be preceded by GetCapabilities and DescribeSensor operations which allow the consumers to collect information about the available sensor data that is being brokered by the SES. Note that while the SOS acts as a consumer in this interaction it is in fact a broker of sensor data. In SWE any service, application or process may act as a consumer as long as it provides an endpoint where notifications can be delivered to. Thus, even chaining of information brokers is possible.

1.4 SES forwards the sensor data that conforms to the subscription filters; to the WNS by invoking the DoNotification operation. The request includes the id of the delivery endpoint account.

1.5 WNS delivers the sensor data to the intended consumers. It must be noted that to receive notifications consumers have to be registered to the WNS beforehand. In this scenario the SOS consumer receives the data via HTTP POST while the user application receives it via XMPP.

Scenario 2—Sensors with Embedded IP Stack

2.1 A sensor registers itself to an SOS server by invoking the RegisterSensor operation. The request includes a SensorML document that describes the sensor capabilities. In this scenario the sensor system includes an embedded IP stack that allows it to communicate directly with the SOS server over the Internet.

2.2 The sensor sends streaming observation data to the SOS by invoking its InsertObservation operation. The data is encoded in O&M format and it is persisted on the SOS backend.

2.3 A SWE client invokes the GetCapabilities operation of the SOS. This operation allows clients to retrieve service metadata about a specific service instance.

2.4 SOS responds with the response with an XML encoded document. This document provides clients with service Filter Capabilities which indicate what types of query parameters are supported by the service and Contents Section in the form of Observation Offerings. These are sets of sensor observation groupings that can be queried using the GetObservation operation. Note that the response will not only include metadata that describe observations collected from the sensor mentioned in this scenario but also the observations received from the sensor nodes in the previous scenario.

2.5 Based on the information gained in the previous steps the client requests sensor observations by invoking the GetObservation operation. The request parameters are based on the Filter Capabilities information received in the previous GetCapabilities request. This may be a one-off operation or the client may poll the SOS periodically.

2.6 The response to a GetObservation request is an O&M Observation, an element in the Observation substitution group, or an ObservationCollection. These are historical sensor observations retrieved from the SOS backend.

The SWE Common and O&M which are data models for exchanging heterogeneous sensor data at low and higher levels respectively allow applications and/or servers to structure, encode and transmit data in a self-describing and semantically enabled way. O&M, which is based on Martin Fowler's Observation & Measurements analysis pattern [71], is a dynamic model that can adapt smoothly to new requirements without necessarily needing to change implementation or the way objects interact.

It is therefore, a particularly interesting solution for the description of device data across different business domains.

One of the key requirements of M2M systems is the ability to fuse, interpret or transform device data into higher level information, required by various M2M applications. A mechanism that enables such on-demand processing, using generic software that utilizes standard process descriptors, simplifies M2M application development and facilitates interoperability. The view-point of the sensor as a process or a chain of processes in the SensorML model with detailed process input, output, parameter, and method descriptions makes it a possible candidate for such a generic process descriptor.

The ongoing work on SensorML 2.0 is planning additional functionalities such as the Sensor Interface Descriptor (SID) extension. SID enables the precise description of a sensor's protocol and interface. This work may be used as a basis to develop generic device drivers carrying protocol definitions of legacy devices which in turn would allow on-the-fly, plug-and-play integration of such non-compliant devices into the standard M2M service network without the need for manual ad-hoc development for each device type [3].

3.3. ETSI M2M Service Capability Layer

ETSI provides an M2M network architecture specification with a generic set of service capabilities. The idea of the architecture is to provide horizontal service capability layer that can be applied to several vertical M2M application domains with standardized reference points. The ETSI M2M Network is composed of two domains: (1) The Device and Gateway domain with M2M devices and Gateways and (2) the Network domain with core network access, M2M service capabilities, M2M applications and management functions, see Figure 5 and Figure 6.

Three different Service Capability Layers are specified: a Device Service Capability Layer, a Gateway Service Capability Layer and a Network Service Capability Layer. Each SCL exposes the services required by the M2M applications residing in the underlying M2M Network. The ETSI adopted a RESTful [72] architecture style for the M2M Applications and/or M2M SCL information exchange [18].

Each SCL is comprised of several services groups: Application Enablement Capability (AEC) for providing M2M point of contact for using the M2M applications of the corresponding SCL, Generic Communication Capability (GCC) for interfacing between the different SCL available on a given M2M Network, Reachability, Addressing and Repository Capability (RARC) for managing events relative subscriptions and notifications as well as for handling applications registration data and information storage, Communication Selection Capability (CSC) for network selection and alternative communication service selection after a communication failure, Remote Entity Management Capability (REM) for remote provisioning, Security Capability (SECC), History and Data Retention for archiving data (HDR), and Interworking Proxy (IP) for integrating non ETSI compliant systems.

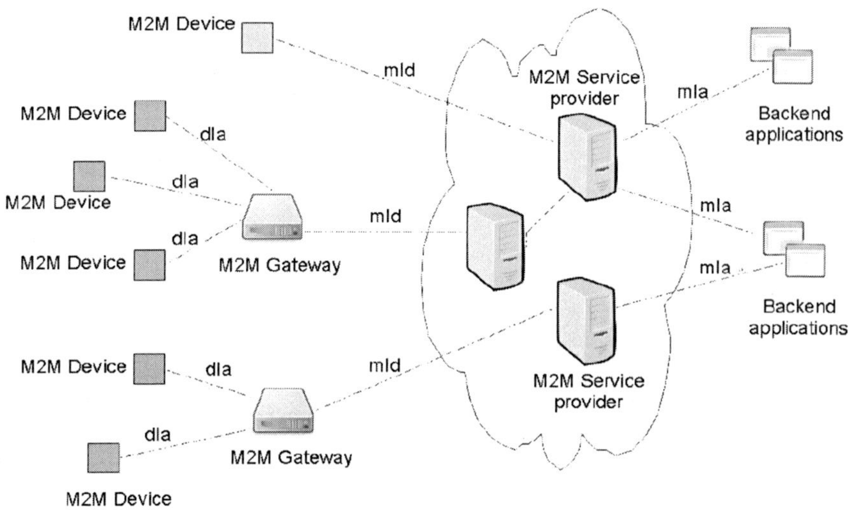

Figure 5. M2M system with ETSI M2M standard reference points.

The presented service capabilities are logical groups of functions identified by ETSI, but all of them are not mandatory [18]. Only the external reference points, dIa, mId and mIa, between the M2M applications and SCLs are mandatory. Where the dIa interfaces devices applications and Gateway or Device Service Capability Layer, the mId interfaces the M2M Gateway or Device Service Capability Layer and the M2M Network Service Capability Layer and the mIa interfaces backend M2M Applications and the M2M Network Service Capability Layer. These interfaces aim to be applicable to a wide range of network technology and application and access independent [35].

The ETSI M2M architecture indicates that it does not explicitly specify means for integrating legacy devices or other already existing non-ETSI compliant systems, but it presents integration points (Interworking Proxy) on the Gateway and Network Service Capability Layers [15]. Figure

7 presents the different M2M Service Capability Layers that comprise the ETSI M2M Network as well as the related reference points.

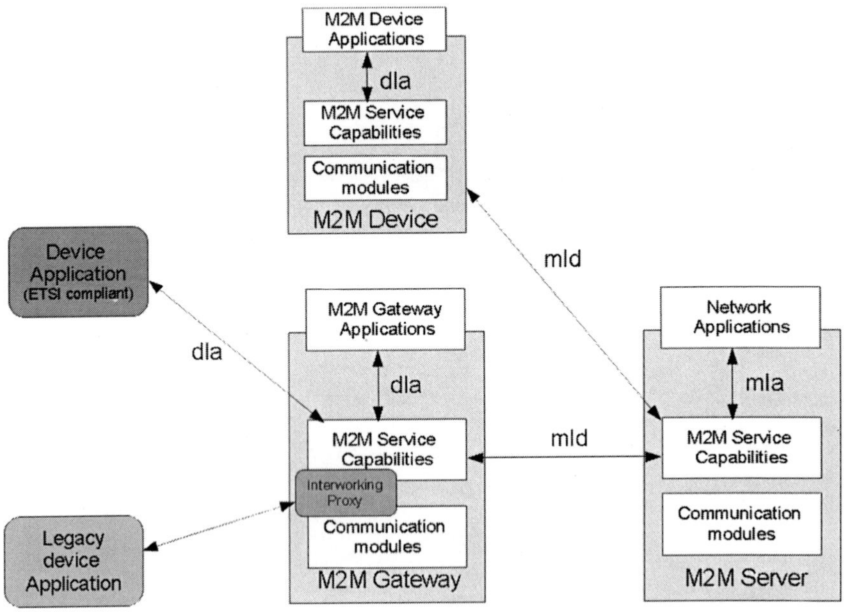

Figure 6. Interfaces of ETSI M2M system.

According to the ETSI M2M architecture, an M2M Gateway can act as a proxy for M2M devices available in the same local area network. Once M2M devices applications are registered on a given GSCL, they become available to the registered SCLs and M2M applications if they acquire the appropriate access rights. Ex: Network applications can subscribe to information produced by a sensor (Device application) registered on a reachable GSCL. Figure 8 explains how this can be done.

We presume that the GSCL is registered to the NSCL and that the Device Application is registered to the GSCL. First the Network application registers to the NSCL (001). Then Network Application Enablement capability checks if the issuer is authorized to be registered and treats the request (002). The registration information is then stored by the Network Reachability, Addressing and Repository Capability. After it Network Application receives a positive answer (003). The Network Application subscribes to the data produced by the desired sensor (Device application) (004). This data can also follow a certain criteria specified by the issue. If the issuer is authorized to subscribe to the given Device

Application, the Gateway Reachability, Addressing and Reachability capability treat the request (005). Network application receives a positive response (006). Device application sends information to the Gateway (007). Then Gateway Reachability, Addressing and Repository Capability identify an event that needs to be reported to a subscriber (008). Finally, The GRAR Capability notifies the subscribers (009).

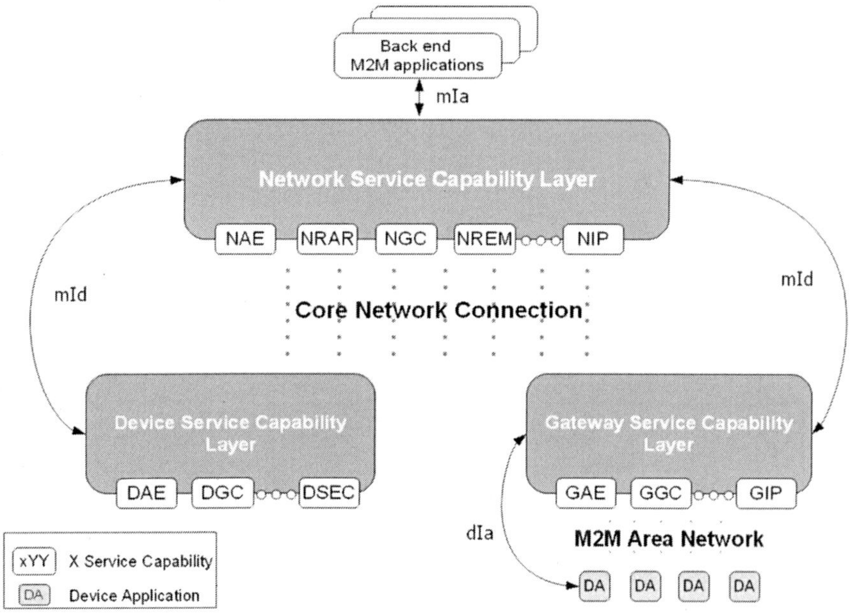

Figure 7. Architecture of ETSI M2M Service Capabilities.

3.4. Autonomic M2M Services

Autonomic computing has been inspired from biological systems including both centralized and decentralized approaches, which have been proposed to enable autonomic behavior in computer systems. The centralized approach focuses on the role of human nervous system as a controller to regulate and maintain the other systems in body [73]. Decentralized approaches take inspiration from local and global behavior of biological cell and ant colony networks [74]. Another area focuses on developing self-managed large scale distributed systems and databases. One such project is Oceano [75], a project of IBM providing a pilot prototype of a scalable, manageable infrastructure for a large scale utility power plant. OceanStore [76], a project of University of California Berkeley describes a global persistent data store for scaling billion of users. IBM's SMART [77] offers a solution to reduce complexity and improve quality of service through the advancement of self-managing capabilities. Similarly, Microsoft's AutoAdmin [78] makes database system self-tuning and self-administering by enabling them to track the usage of their system and gracefully adapt to application requirements. Agent architecture has been frequently used to develop infrastructures supporting autonomic behavior based on a decentralized approach. Unity [79] makes use of this approach to achieve goal-driven self-assembly, self-healing and real-time self-optimization. Similarly, Autonomia [80] is a University of Arizona project providing the application developers with all the tools required to specify the appropriate control and management schemes to maintain any quality of service requirements.

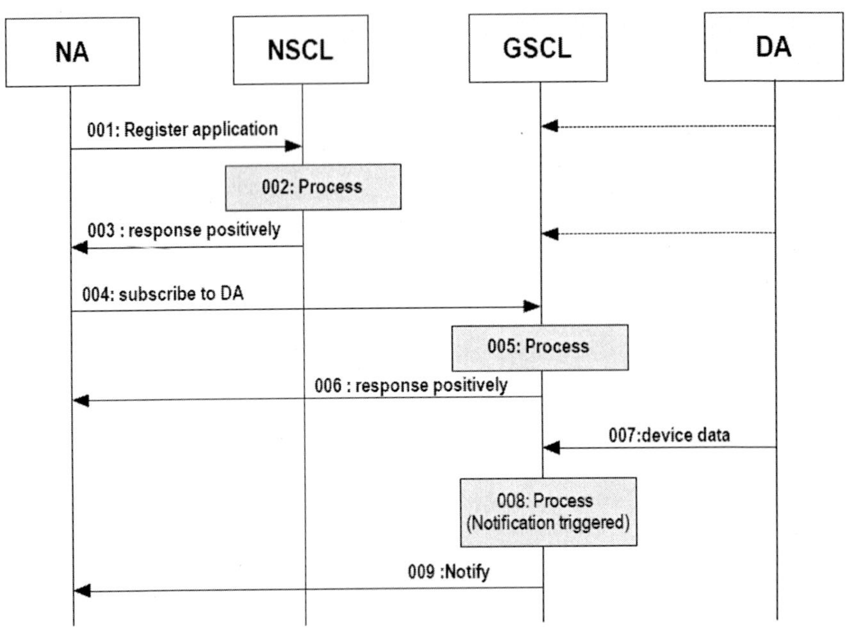

Figure 8. Sequence diagram for a network application subscription to device data.

Component based frameworks have been suggested for enabling autonomic behavior in systems. The Accord framework [81] facilitates development and management of autonomic applications in grid computing environments. It provides self-configuration by separating component behavior from component interaction. Selfware [82] models the managed environment as a component based software architecture which provides means to configure and reconfigure the environment and implements control loops which link probes to reconfiguration services and implement autonomic behaviors. A number of frameworks make use of techniques such as artificial intelligence (AI) and control theory. In [83] an AI planning framework based on the predicate model has been presented. It achieves user defined abstract goals by taking into account current context and security policies. Another area focuses on modifying control theory technique [84] and presents a framework to address resource management problem. A mathematical model is used for forecasting over a limited time horizon. Service Oriented Architecture has been also used to design architecture with autonomic behavior. In [85], autonomic web services implement the monitoring, analysis, planning and execution life cycle. The autonomic web service uses log file provided by a defective functional service to diagnose the problem and consults the policy database to apply appropriate recovery action. Infrastructures have been proposed to inject autonomic behavior in legacy and non-autonomic system, where design and code information is unavailable [86]. Some of the identified frameworks make use of layered architecture [87], case based reasoning (CBR) [88], and a rule driven approach [89] to enable automaticity in existing systems.

Different techniques can be used to achieve the capabilities described in each of the four major self-* properties. There are more system specific techniques to achieve self-configuration such as hot swapping [90] and data clustering [91], and techniques that make use of more generic approaches such as machine learning, ABLE [92] and case-based reasoning [93]. Many applications that require continuous performance improvement and resource management make use of control theory approach demonstrated in the Lotus Notes application [94], learning based self-optimization techniques such as LEO [95], and active learning based approach [96] based on building statistical predictive models. Self-healing is the property that involves problem detection, diagnosis and repair. CBR [93] performs problem detection in the analysis phase, finds a solution in planning phase and performs problem repair in execution phase. Hybrid approach [97] to create a survivability model provides more robust survivability services. Active probing and Bayesian network [98] is a problem diagnosis technique that allows probes to be selected and sent on demand. The heartbeat failure detection algorithm [99] enables detecting problem when the monitor experiences a delay in receiving of message. Another technique to detect problems in distributed systems is to use tools like Pip [100] that expose structural errors and performance problems by comparing actual system behavior and expected system behavior. Performance Query Systems (PQS) [101] can be used to enable user space monitoring of servers. Component level rebooting is a technique that recovers from defects, without disturbing the rest of the application as shown in Microreboot [102]. Another safe technique to quickly recover programs from deterministic and non-deterministic bugs is demonstrated in Rx [103]. It rolls back the program to a recent checkpoint upon a software failure, and then re-executes the program in a modified environment. Some notable techniques that enable systems to enable self-protection make use of component models such as Jade [104] and self-certifying alerts as demonstrated in Vigilante [105].

4. M2M COMMUNICATION

M2M Communication technologies are reviewed in this chapter. Afterwards, a set of potential technologies is shortly overviewed: Constrained Application Protocol (CoAP), EXtensible Messaging and Presence Protocol (XMPP), 6LowPAN and RPL, and Bluetooth Smart. Finally, autonomic features and communication technologies are discussed.

4.1. Overview on M2M Communication Technologies

A set of M2M communication technologies is reviewed in Table 3. M2M applications impose several new constraints on communication solutions. They generate a type of traffic which is most likely to be comparatively small but with a larger number of involved devices. Even if the messages are usually quite short, in most cases there are strong requirements on the reliability and delays. In addition, the embedded asset devices may have computing and power constraints, which challenge the traditional communication protocols.

Thus reliable and delay aware transfer of messages over the network is very important for M2M applications. The hypertext transfer protocol (HTTP) is usually applied to transfer messages in client-server manner in World Wide Web. There are protocols such as SMTP, POP and IMAP for electronic mail systems. In addition, protocols like XMPP and SIP/SIMPLE have enabled capabilities such as instant messaging and presence to be applied in more real-time communication. XMPP uses decentralized client-server architecture to keep clients simple, and pushes most of the complexity into the servers [106]. The architecture is different than WWW in the sense that it supports inter-domain connections called federations. In addition, email network uses multiple hops between servers to deliver messages but the XMPP architecture uses direct connections. When taking the communication requirements set by M2M applications into concern, it is seen that XMPP type of architecture has succeeded to enable real-time messaging with support for simple clients.

Table 3. Review of the M2M Communication technologies.

Technology	Forum(s), References	Main Contribution		
Sensor-Over-XMPP	XMPP Extension (protoXEP) [107]	a payload format for communicating sensor and actuation information		
Data Distribution Service for Real-Time Systems (DDS)	Object Management Group (OMG)	Scalable, real-time		
Advanced Message Queuing Protocol (AMQP)	OASIS AMQP standard	Broker-based messaging, publish-subscribe		
STOMP	STOMP	Simple broker-based text-based protocol		
MQ Telemetry Transport (MQTT)	MQTT Eclipse M2M Industry Working Group	Lightweight publish/subscribe binary messaging protocol		
ZeroMQ	ZeroMQ protocol [108]	An openly published simple and lightweight publish-subscribe type of messaging protocol designed for constrained devices and low-bandwidth, high-latency or unreliable networks.		
COAP usage for REsource LOcation And Discovery (RELOAD)	Proposed as IETF Internet-draft	peer-to-peer federation of geographically distributed WSN islands		
Content-Centric Network	CCNx	Content-based networking. Security by design.		
Websocket protocol	IETF RFC 6455	two-way communications with Low-overhead transport (single TCP connection)		
CoAP	IETF's Constrained RESTful environments (CoRE) working group	An application layer protocol designed for constrained devices allowing them to communicate over the Internet.		
		Wired	Radio	Full IP
Cellular	3GPP	No	Yes	Yes
Bluetooth	Bluetooth Special Interest Group	No	Yes	No
Bluetooth LE	Bluetooth Special Interest Group	No	Yes	No
Ant/Ant+				
ZigBee	ZigBee Alliance (and IEEE)	No	Yes	No
ZigBee IP	ZigBee Alliance (and IEEE and IETF)	No	Yes	Yes
6LowPan	IETF	No	Yes	Yes
Z-Wave	Z-Wave alliance	No	Yes	No
WiFi low power	IEEE	No	Yes	Yes
Modbus	Modicon (society)	Yes	No	No
BacNet	ASHRAE	Yes	No	No
LonWorks	ANSI	Yes	No	No
KNX	ISO/IEC	Yes	Yes	No

The websocket protocol (a part of HTML5 initiative) which relies on HTTP for handshake and negotiation, is message-based and has been designed to allow bidirectional communications. The related message queues protocols can be broker-based (e.g., DDS, AMQP, and STOMP) or broker less (e.g., ZeroMQ) and allow asynchronous communications and operate at the same level as HTTP. MQTT is a message queue designed with M2M applications in mind to enable lightweight publish/subscribe messaging transport.

A challenge is related to application of HTTP within constrained local M2M asset network. To solve this problem, IETF CoRE (Constrained RESTful Environments) working group has specified Constrained Application Protocol (CoAP) standard with the goal of supporting REST-like applications in constrained environments. The second challenge is related to the sizes of IP packets and headers. To solve this problem, IETF has created the 6lowpan (IPv6 Low Power wireless Area Networks), which describes an adaptation layer between IPv6 and a layer 2 protocol, such as (but not limited to) IEEE 802.15.4, to handle MTU sizes and compress IPv6 headers from 60 bytes to 7 bytes. There are also other challenges arising from heterogeneity of M2M devices and local M2M asset networks, and coding and integration of M2M application content.

4.2. Low Power and Lossy Networks

A Low Power and Lossy Network (LLN) is a network between constrained embedded devices, in which the communication links may change frequently, or even disappear. In order to face the challenges in those networks, the IETF has set working groups to elaborate standards which guarantee that such an infrastructure is scalable, secure and reliable in terms of communications between each device. One of the most important aspects of these standardization activities is the use of the IP layer as the reference layer. Using this reference, new protocols have been developed for routing, transport, and applications in LLNs. IPv6 brings some outstanding benefits such as an addressing scheme which allows identifying billions of devices and supporting point-to-point communications between a device and a PC connected to Internet. However, the IPv6 protocol is inadequate for LLNs in terms of network overhead. As a result, the IETF 6LowPAN WG [109] proposes adaptations of the IPv6 protocol when the underlying network is constrained. For example, standards have been proposed for the transmission of compressed IPv6 packets over IEEE 802.15.4 networks [110]. IPv6 and 6LowPAN network stacks are natively available on common operating systems for embedded devices (e.g., Contiki and TinyOS), therefore making them able to communicate with both Internet and LLNs devices.

Another aspect or LLNs is the strong constraints on routing protocols, which must be different from those used in traditional IP networks. First of all, link conditions may change frequently during time; therefore a routing protocol must react quickly to these changes. Second, the nodes have really strong storage constraints; therefore, a routing protocol should work even if a node has not stored all the routes to each of the other nodes in the network. Third, since the nodes have severe energy constraints, the exchange of control messages should be kept as low as possible.

One solution to the above-mentioned LLNs limitations is provided by the RPL routing protocol. It has been developed to have really limited control traffic, to fit harsh and constrained environments, with limited data rate and potentially elevated error rate. RPL is a distance-vector protocol based on the creation of a routing tree, referred to as Destination Oriented Acyclic Directed Graph (DODAG), where the cost of each path is evaluated according to the metrics defined in an objective function. The goal of this protocol is the creation of a collection tree protocol, as well as a point-to-multipoint network from the root of the network to the devices inside the LLN.

In order to keep the status of the network updated, the root of the RPL tree sends periodical messages, referred to as DODAG Information Object (DIO). The receiving nodes may relay this message or just consume it, if configured as leaves of the tree. The RPL protocol also introduces a *trickle* mechanism which allows reducing the transmission frequency of DIO messages according to the stability of the network. In addition, RPL offers several advanced functionalities, the detection of loops in the routes, and the management of local faults (via local or global repair).

4.3. Constrained Application Protocol (CoAP)

The IETF CoRE (Constrained RESTful Environments) working group [111] has defined the Constrained Application Protocol (CoAP) standard with the goal of supporting REST-like applications inside constrained environments like those identified by the RoLL [112] and 6lowPAN working groups. Application domains include LLNs and more generally M2M communications, and span over a large range of business use cases such as smart energy or building automation. The specification defines a binary message structure between CoAP endpoints as well as the interaction protocol. By following REST architectural principles [71], CoAP exposes a representation of the information available on a constrained device as a set of identifiable resources. This way, any CoAP endpoint may interact with it remotely using the interaction methods used by the HTTP protocol: GET, POST, PUT, and DELETE.

In order to make the resources discoverable, the CoAP protocol standard advises to expose CoAP endpoint's resource metadata using the CoRE Link Format [113] at a specific URI. CoAP messages rely on the UDP transport protocol between endpoints. This is to accommodate the potentially unreliable and lossy wireless environments that render the TCP protocol inefficient in terms of network resource usage. In order to meet eventual QoS requirements, since UDP is natively unreliable, CoAP has introduced the use of confirmation messages, which correspond to an acknowledgement that a CoAP message has been received.

Collection of data from a CoAP-enabled device is achieved by sending a CoAP request message (GET method) to the CoAP server hosted on the device: as soon as the CoAP server receives such a request, it replies with a CoAP response with data requested by the CoAP client or notifies that the response will be sent in a separate response. Another interaction scheme supported by the CoAP protocol is the publish/subscribe paradigm. Instead of sending periodical requests to a CoAP server to be kept updated on the status of a resource, the CoAP client may subscribe, through specific exposed end-points, to a CoAP server, which will be in charge of periodical updating all the subscribed clients of the status of a given resource.

RESTful architectures make caching of the data possible within the network. Caching is supported by CoAP and makes it possible to optimize the data delivery over potentially constrained wireless links. For each CoAP observed value a lifetime is defined; if two consecutive requests are received by a CoAP server or proxy in a period of time smaller than that defined by the lifetime parameter, the former request will be sent querying the resource, whereas the latter will be served using the cached value. Using caching, some optimizations can be easily foreseeable for M2M communications. By serving fresh information from a cache instead of querying the endpoint itself, one could experience a shorter delay or a better QoS on a particular request. Also, caching may help reduce the overall consumption of an energy-constrained network by reducing the number of wireless transmissions required for collecting data.

A low-power version of CoAP has been implemented for Contiki [114]. The implementation leverages the ContikiMAC low-power duty cycling mechanism to provide power efficiency. Based on the results of the CoAP request/response, cycles are most energy-efficient when each message fits into a single 802.15.4 frame. When messages are bigger than frames, the interoperation of information models, data encoding/decoding, and segmentation/reassembly with constrained M2M capillary networks and M2M asset devices need to be carefully considered. HC (HTTP/CoAP) proxies provide the interworking functionalities for application spanning across LLNs (potentially running CoAP/UDP/IPv6/IEEE 802.15.4 protocol stack) and the Internet (HTTP/TCP/IPv6).

CoAP base specifications identify DTLS [115] and IPsec [116] as mechanisms to offer data origin authentication, integrity and replay protection, and encryption for the CoAP messages. In addition to these, an alternative [117] to IPsec and DTLS has been presented.

4.4. Extensible Messaging and Presence Protocol (XMPP)

XMPP has been developed to enable message oriented communication services applicable in the Internet context on top of TCP/IP. The XMPP communicatio0n architecture is based on distributed client-server model; however, also client-to-client (peer to peer) communication is enabled. The core services of XMPP includes support for presence information, secure messaging (TLS), overlay communication over IP, near real-time messaging, authentication, contact list management, and service discovery. Each XMPP client has an account hosted by a XMPP server, and the client can be addresses by unique Jabber ID (JID). XMPP JID contains three parts: user, domain and resource as shown in Table 4, RFC 6122/RFC3921 [118]. In XMPP, network domain-part of JID must be a fully qualified domain name or IP address. Each domain presents one logical groups with one user account database. Each domain may present own user account policies. The device owner is usually considered to be also a user of the M2M domain and an owner of at least one XMPP user id. All devices share same user id (local-part and domain-part) with their owner. Separation of devices is done by examining the resource part of JID.

Table 4. An example of Extensible Messaging and Presence Protocol (XMPP) Jabber ID.

JID: Matt@home.com/heating-regulator		
Local-part	Domain-part	Resource
Matt	home.com	heating-regulator

A client connects to the server to send and receive messages, the servers routes messages to the others enabling client-to-client communications over multiple servers, Figure 9. The procedure for M2M client establishing connection with the XMPP server is shown in Figure 10. Discovery can be done directly using a domain part as a server address or discovering server address with SRV lookup from DNS. All clients connect to only their own server specified by JID. Connections are persistent XML streams over TCP and optionally encrypted by Transport Layer Security (TLS) layer. Encryption of TCP stream is strongly recommended, but not required. An administrator of a domain may specify that encryption is mandatory and it is up to administrator or designer to choose whether TLS certificates should be checked. Most client libraries accepts self-signed certificates, this should be taken into account when considering security aspects of client-to-server connections. The availability of each client can be detected with the aid of presence messages. Presence information is shared only with XMPP users that are in the roster/address book of the client sending the presence information.

Server to server connection is an XML stream over a TCP connection, similar to client to server connections. The most important difference is that server to server connections are not authenticated because they happen in between different domains that do not share a common user database. XMPP servers may use XMPP Dial back (XEP-0220), to verify the domain of the connecting server.

The domain administrator may require stronger identification verification by using TLS certificates and Simple Authentication and Security Layer (SASL). When M2M clients located in different domains would like to exchange messages, routing of messages will be done by the domain specific servers, see Figure 11. Then, a communication link between servers of the domains is negotiated to enable messaging between the referred M2M clients.

The capability for handing presence information has been developed for XMPP. The availability of each client can be detected with the aid of presence messages. XMPP offers mechanisms to select how, when and to whom presence information is shared to, as described in requirements listed in [119]. For example, presence can be shared only with contacts that are in roster/address book of client sending the presence information. The related presence information (JIDs) is critical information in the system and it is stored in the roster database. Another useful feature is the publish-subscribe model (XEP0060), which can be used by XMPP entities to subscribe information of the presence of other entities, and receive notifications accordingly.

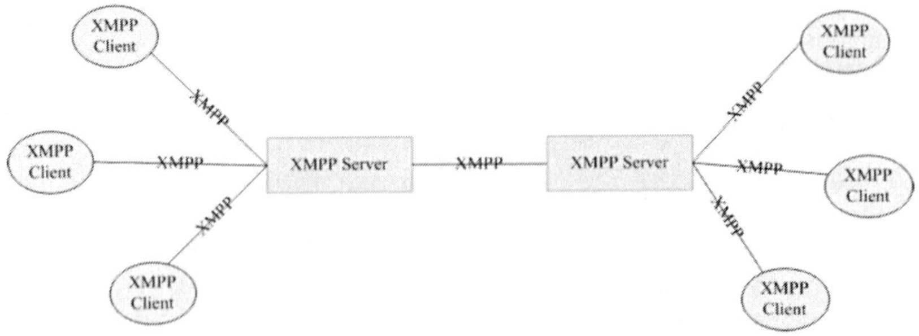

Figure 9. XMPP architecture.

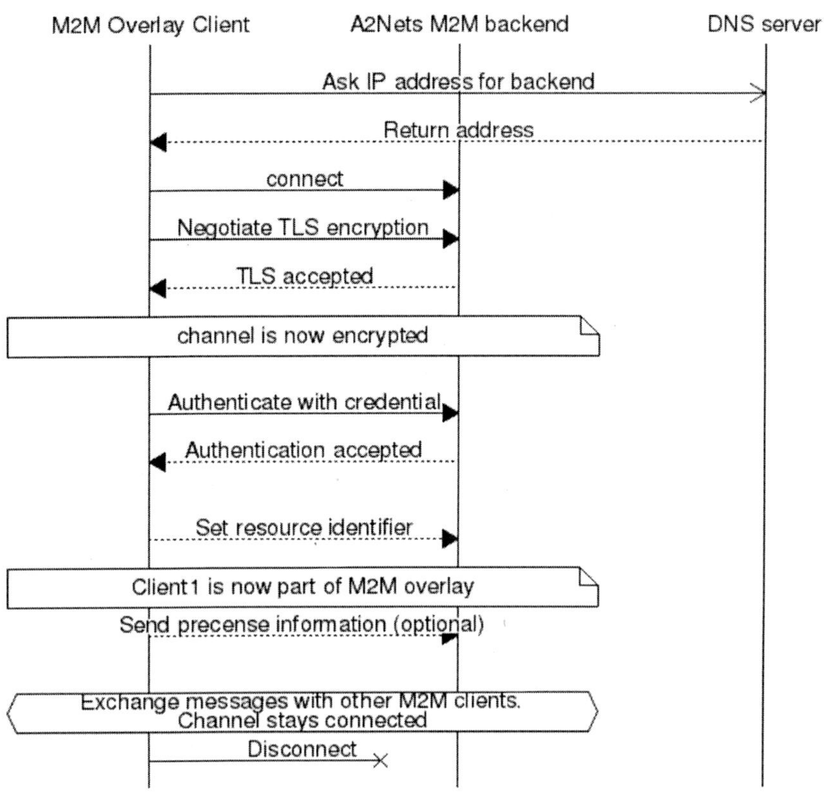

Figure 10. M2M client connecting to XMPP Server.

4.5. Bluetooth Low Energy

Bluetooth SMART v. 4.0 [120] is a PAN technology that was introduced to the market by the Bluetooth Special Interest Group in 2010. Bluetooth SMART consists of two distinctly different transports called Basic and Enhanced data rate (BR/EDR) and Low energy (LE). The following focuses briefly on the LE technology and use for web applications in battery operated sensor applications.

LE supports two modes of connection: Non-connected, unidirectional advertisements (broadcast, unicast and scan support), and Connected, bidirectional and reliable (maximum application throughput is 270 kbit/s). The network topology for connection is star/bus where the collector device is typically a master and sensors are slaves. LE uses three channels for advertisements and 37 channels for data. One reason for having the master role assigned to the collector is that collocation of multiple radios in a handset requires operation between all radios. The Bluetooth co-existence controller is specified in Core specification addendum 4 (CSA4) [121] and it is particularly important in combination with 4G networks as LTE TDD. LE also improves co-existence and robustness with nearby networks by using adaptive frequency hopping (AFH).

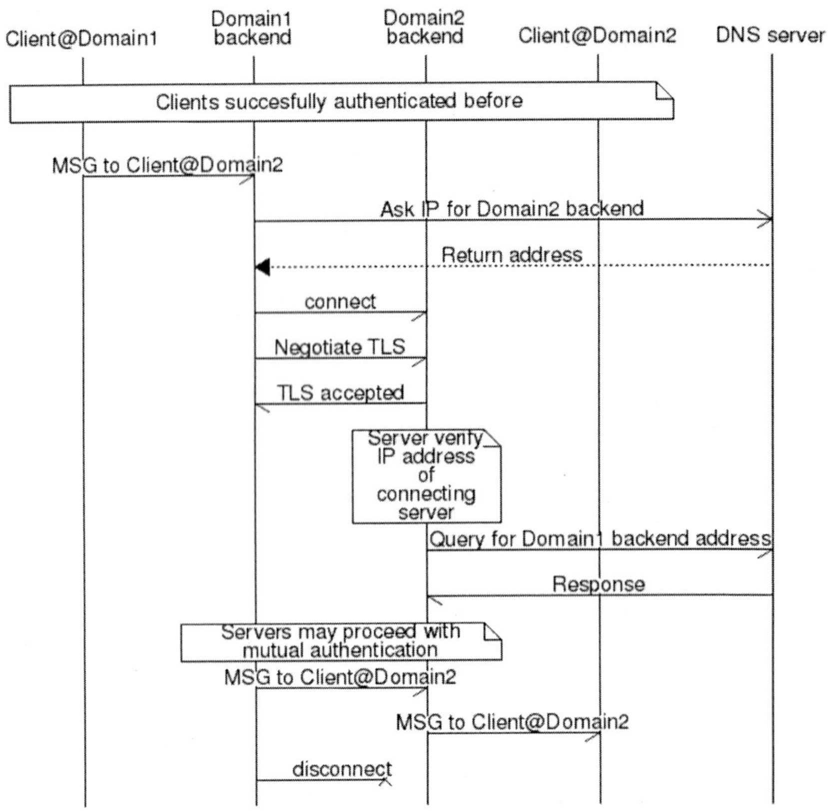

Figure 11. Server to server interdomain communication.

The main layers of Bluetooth are shown in the following Figure 12 and consist of the following components: Radio and link layer (LL) with an AES-128 bit encryption unit, Multiplexer—Logical link control and adaption layer protocol (L2CAP) providing fixed and connection oriented channels together with fragmentation and reassembly (FAR), Security Manager (SM), Host Controller Interface (HCI)—Connects application processor and Bluetooth controller, The General Access profile (GAP)—Contains a collection of standard procedures, and Generic attribute profile (GATT), which provides an interoperable framework with service discovery and operation. Bluetooth SIG defined service data is characterized by 16 bit universally unique identifiers (uuids) while proprietary extensions use randomized 128 uuids.

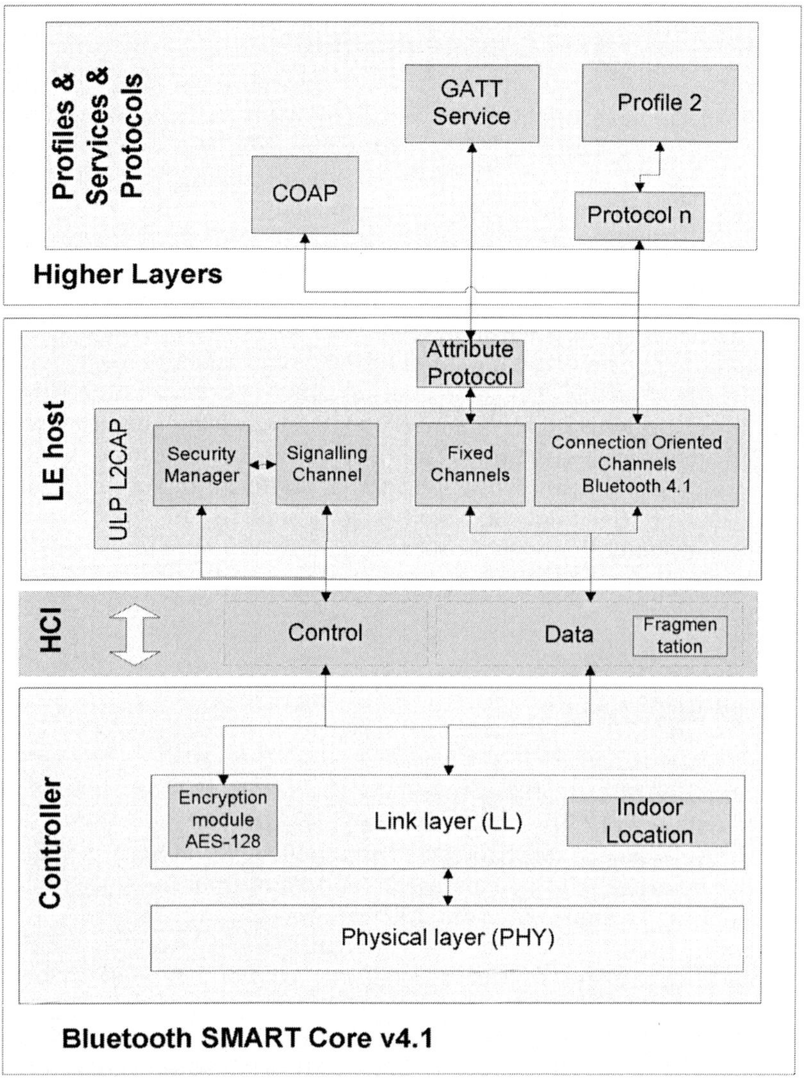

Figure 12. The Bluetooth SMART core 4.0.

All packets in LE have the same layout and the maximum length of a packet is 47 Octets. Depending on mode of connection the payload may be max 31 Bytes, for an advertisement, implying an efficiency of 31 Bytes/47 Bytes * 100% = 66%. A connection can have max 27 Bytes per packet implying an efficiency of 27 Bytes/47 Bytes * 100% = 57% for a raw L2CAP channel without encryption. The efficiency drops to 20 Bytes/41 Bytes * 100 = 49% when using GATT with notification and encryption.

4.6. Autonomic M2M Communication

Several projects have targeted autonomic network and communications. Some examples are DASADA [122], Autonomia [80], ACCORD [123], ANA [124] and the IoT-A [125]. The University of Bologna is building a framework [126] to support the design, implementation and evaluation of peer-to-peer Internet applications using Swarm Intelligence; the University College London is working on different projects inspired on bio-approaches for autonomous configuration of distributed systems. All those projects and research groups treat the Internet as an ecosystem and study the relations between the different network elements from a cross-disciplinary perspective. The main goals of every approach are to achieve efficiency in a self-CHOP manner in a large-scale heterogeneous communication infrastructure. The autonomic communication final objective is to provide an evolving network platform for communication between devices (including decision making and reacting) with a high degree of autonomy to decrease to the minimum the human intervention providing a high level of efficiency for both users and telecommunication industry.

5. M2M SECURITY

The emergence of the M2M ecosystem has led to the revision of the conventional network security paradigm [127]. The M2M communication systems, by essence, interconnect heterogeneous network segments, where the heterogeneity is expressed in terms of functional capabilities and capacities. This encompasses, for instance, the interconnection of a WAN with low-power network segments like WSNs in multihop communication schemes. The security of communications involving several hops is usually addressed using hop by hop security where each segment of the communication path from source to destination is secured using distinct credentials possibly managed by distinct parties involving rekeying operations at each transmission node. Credential management with this model may be complex. Furthermore, in order to provide reasonable security, the various parties involved in credentials distribution and management needs to trust each other. This requirement is often difficult to achieve in the case of M2M communications and it is generally accepted that end to end security involving the use of a single set of credential from source to destination is a better model. However the deployment of end to end security is a challenging task as it requires solving the problem of credential distribution at a global level.

A typical network security service (e.g., authentication, access control, data confidentiality, *etc.*) is made up of two phases: bootstrapping and enforcement. Providing an end-to-end security service in M2M requires thus exploring methods for both phases, where the said methods should take into account both the interoperability and trust issues.

Security service bootstrapping comprises authentication and key agreement methods needed for the security enforcement phase. Therefore, given the interoperability and trust challenges in M2M systems, a flexible and adaptive bootstrapping phase is needed in order to guarantee the enforcement of an efficient end-to-end security service.

M2M communications are commonly classified into three main communication domains: M2M device, network and application domains. Those three domains are associated to three distinct security domains involving generally distinct business actors to perform credential management.

Thus, the device domain corresponds to M2M capillary communications occurring in a LAN or PAN proximity network. Generally the owner of this network has the responsibility to manage the credentials used to secure those communications occurring between the devices and the gateway.

In some cases there is a need to secure the connection between the Gateway/device and the point of entry to the Internet (WAN). This is the case when using 3GPP communications to protect the radio transmission. In this case, the SIM card holding credentials used to secure the access to the wide area network is managed by the mobile network operator to achieve "network access security".

Table 5 lists the major security technologies used in the LAN (device) domains to offer, e.g., authentication, integrity and confidentiality. Table 6 lists the major network technologies, or security technologies used to secure the network access. These technologies provide, e.g., interoperability for secure communication in WANs but in some cases also secure and interoperable communication between devices in WANs and devices in LANs. Table 7 lists security technologies that have been or can be used at application layer, e.g., in M2M services, and also in M2M architectures.

Table 5. Review of security technologies used in the LAN device domains to offer, e.g., authentication, integrity and confidentiality.

Technology, What to Solve?	Forum(s), References	Main Contribution
- Security technologies of Bluetooth - To enable authentication and pairing of Bluetooth devices, to encrypt the transmitted data, and to check integrity of transmitted data packets in Bluetooth network.	Bluetooth Special Interest Group (SIG)	- Frequency-hopping spread spectrum - Master clock is shared to slaves - Binding of devices is done through selected pairing mechanisms - Different security modes - Link keys to establish authenticated and/or encrypted ACL links - SAFER+ block cipher (not for encryption!) - E0 stream cipher - Secure Simple Pairing (SSP) with Elliptic Curve Diffie-Hellman (ECDH).
- Security technologies of Bluetooth low energy - Similar problems to solve as in BT.	Bluetooth Special Interest Group (SIG)	- AES-CCM block cipher - Data can be signed with Connection Signature Resolving Key (CSRK), MAC, counter - Privacy feature to change private address on a frequent basis
- Security technologies of ZigBee - Authentication, encryption, integrity checking, countermeasures against replay-attacks.	ZigBee Alliance	- 16 channel hopping - Key establishment, key transport, frame protection, ad device management implemented mostly at the network (NWK) and application support sub-layer (APS). - AES-CCM to offer confidentiality and authentication, AES-CBC-MAC to offer authentication or AES-CTR to offer confidentiality. 32-, 64-, or 128-bit MAC and 128-bit key. - Key sequence counter
Security technologies of ZigBee RF4CE (Even lower power and simplified version of ZigBee)	ZigBee Alliance	- 3 channel hopping - Simpler pairing mechanism than in ZigBee - AES-CCM with 128-bit key.
- Security technologies of Wi-Fi - Authentication, encryption, integrity, replay protection		- WPA2 that uses Counter Mode with Cipher Block Chaining Message Authentication Code Protocol (CCMP) based on 128-bit AES-CCM block cipher - Cryptographic hash function - Key management - Replay protection - WPA2 can be used in two modes: - Shared key: relying upon the use of a key shared by all Wi-Fi clients and access point. - Enterprise, relying upon the use of an external AAA server
- Default security technologies of EPCglobal UHF Class 1 Generation 2(v1.2.0) RFID tags - To prevent unauthorized writing and disabling and counterfeiting of RFID tags.	EPCglobal	- 32-bit KILL and ACCESS passwords - (perma)locking of memory - Unique unprogrammable TID numbers

Table 6. Network related security technologies used to enable secure network access.

Technology, What to Solve?	Forum(s), References	Main Contribution
IPsec	IETF's IP Security Protocol (IPsec) concluded working group	IPsec WG developed a security protocol in the network layer to provide cryptographic security services to support combinations of authentication, integrity, access control, and confidentiality. IPsec has been implemented, e.g., over 6LoWPAN [128].
- EAP based authentication - EAP/TLS - EAP/TTLS - EAP/SIM - EAP/AKA - EAP/PEAP	IETF network working group	EAP is an authentication protocol commonly used to secure access to wireless networks and point to point connections.
- TLS/DTLS - To choose cipher suites for providing (mutual) authentication of end-points, encryption and integrity of transmitted data.	IETF's Transport Layer Security (TLS) working group	Specifying new TLS and DTLS protocols and extensions to them. They run on top of transport layer protocols and provide, e.g., confidentiality and data integrity between two communicating applications. Both has been implemented, e.g., over 6LoWPAN.
- WTLS - To offer data integrity, confidentiality and authentication of end-points.	Open Mobile Alliance (OMA)	Similar to TLS but originally meant to be used devices without TCP/IP. Works over UDP or WAP Datagram Protocol (WDP)
3GPP	3rd Generation Partnership Project's (3GPP) Service and System Aspects (SA) working group 3	- IMS security - Security of multimedia broadcast and multicast service (MBMS) - Generic Bootstrapping Architecture (GBA) - Key establishment mechanisms - Ongoing: security for system improvement for machine-type communications - Lawful interception

The security of group communications is an important problem that has been addressed for more than a decade. Most of the research efforts focused on conventional Internet (*i.e.*, Internet Multicasting) both in the wired and wireless environments (e.g., [129,130,131]). Protocol scalability and the security-performance tradeoff are the major concerns in the group communications security topic. Furthermore, a number of standards have emerged in the IETF [132], and some of them have even been adopted by a number of technology standardization bodies (e.g., 3GPP's MBMS [133] and ETSI's SES [134]).

Group communication security is particularly important in the WSN context when implementing end to end security given the critical resources of WSN networks (CPU, memory, battery, and bandwidth) (e.g., [135,136,137,138]). If the data has to be secured from the source, then it is quite important to send a single protected data stream from the device.

Unfortunately, asymmetric cryptographic techniques usually involve ciphering the data stream with the public key of the receiver, creating the need for redundant data transmission, which in the case of WSN creates an unbearable load upon the device. Group communication security techniques must therefore be used, involving the distribution of a group key to all parties involved in the communication scheme.

The other aspect that needs to be considered in M2M is the interoperability problem due to network heterogeneity in terms of capacity (e.g., WAN *vs.* LAN) and supported protocols. This interoperability problem requires defining dynamic configuration mechanisms and adaptive protocols to ensure end-to-end security for M2M group communications.

Table 7. Security technologies applicable for applications layer.

Technology, What to Solve?	Forum(s), References	Main Contribution
- JSON security - To provide authentication, integrity and confidentiality, access control and resource control	- IETF's JavaScript Object Signing and Encryption (JOSE) working group - Used, e.g., in/by SAML 2.0, WS-Federation, OpenID, OAuth 2.0, XMPP, ALTO and to provide integrity of exigent (alarms)	Standardizing integrity protection and encryption security services, in order to increase interoperability of security features between protocols that use JSON.
- XML security - To provide authentication, integrity and confidentiality.	W3C's XML security working group	XML Signature provides integrity, message authentication, and/or signer authentication services for data. XML Encryption specifies a process for encrypting data and representing the result in XML. XKMS specifies protocols for distributing and registering public keys.
HTTP Strict Transport Security (HSTS)	IETF's Web Security (websec) working group	HSTS is designed to allow web sites or http servers to tell users' browsers or http clients that they want to communicate only over an encrypted connection.
- DNSSEC - To provide secure DNS.	IETF's Domain Name System Security (dnssec) working group	Enhancements to the secure DNS protocol.
ETSI M2M security architecture	ETSI	- Pre-provisioned device/gateway credential types, e.g., SIM/AKA or X.509v3 certificates. - Defining M2M bootstrap procedures based on GBA, TLS or EAP/PANA. - Securing M2M service connection by GBA, TLS or EAP/PANA. - Securing mId by TLS or DTLS, XML security or relying access network security.
- SASL - To provide authentication.	IETF's Simple Authentication and Security Layer (SASL) concluded working group	A framework for authentication and data security in Internet protocols. Application protocol that uses SASL can in theory use any authentication mechanisms supported by SASL.

- HTTPS - Authentication of end-points, protection against MitM attacks, encryption of communication	IETF	Usage of TLS to secure HTTP connections
- AAA protocols - To authenticate entity's identification - To authorize the entity - To account aka track a network resource consumption	- IETF's Authentication, Authorization and Accounting (AAA) concluded working group, RADIUS Extensions (radext) working group, Diameter maintenance and Extensions (dime) working group - 3GPP	- Diameter - Radius - 3GPP EPS AAA
- Trusted Key Distribution Centers (KDC) - Authentication and key exchange, sometimes also access control	- MIT (Kerberos) - OpenID Foundation	- Kerberos 5 - OpenID - Single Sign-On (SSO)

Finally, most of the M2M devices are involved in applications producing or consuming data which need to be secured from the source to the destination, either using hop by hop or end-to-end security. This is addressing "application domain security", and the application providers or the M2M service providers are typically responsible to manage the associated credentials.

6. DISCUSSION

M2M Service networks are inherently multiple stakeholder systems, which usually consist of parts evolving in different timescales. For example, the generations of cellular radio systems may evolve 10 years, while novel M2M applications may be born even every month. However, the M2M service system lifecycles are required to be even longer than 20 years. If a part of the system is dependent on a single provider, then it is a strong risk for system being operational for such a long lifecycle. Therefore, the system should be based on open standards, and horizontal layering shall be kept clear. If autonomic M2M solutions are developed for the systems where horizontal layers are mixed, the challenge with such solutions is that their application is likely to be limited to the special case only.

In this survey we categorize the available technologies into M2M Information and services, M2M communication and M2M security. According to the review, this categorization could act as a starting point for horizontal architectures of the M2M service networks. However, it is seen that principles and guidelines for the architectures are needed to be defined in order to establish a solid basis for multiple stakeholder system. In addition, it is seen that both end-to-end Internet approach, and M2M gateway based approach are needed to enable horizontally capable M2M service networks. These are needed for solving the heterogeneity of technologies to enable communication between objects and applications, which are not initially been designed to communicate together. It is also seen that the horizontal architecture of the system should be defined first, and then proceeding into the solving of complexity would be feasible. Otherwise, the solutions for solving the complexity may prevent the horizontal approach and thus the basis for a multiple stakeholder system.

6.1. M2M Information and Services

When looking at the reviewed M2M information and service technologies, several subcategories can be found. ETSI M2M defines horizontal M2M service capabilities, which are agnostic for the information content. There are several technologies defining data models (e.g., oBix), ontologies (e.g., OWL) and device management (e.g., OMA DM, UPnP). Open service frameworks (e.g., OSGi) and specification of overlay architectures for integrating sensor networks and applications on the Web (e.g., OGC SWE). The review shows that this area contains a huge amount of technologies which are not necessarily interoperable, and mix at least in the subcategory level. In addition, there are multiple projects working in the area and have defined their own proposal for the architecture and technologies. For example, Hydra [139], Runes [140], IoT-A [141], iCore [142], Sofia [143] and Fi-Ware [144]. It is seen here that there are some essential starting points, such as e.g., having horizontal M2M service capabilities which could be applied with multiple domain M2M applications. However, more detailed analysis and synthesis are needed to establish solid basis for subcategories to enable multiple stakeholder system within M2M information and service level. It is clear that technologies in this area are not ready for this, because for example, ETSI M2M assumes that M2M applications know all details of the device installation and data interpretation, which is challenging for application developers. It is also important to enable means for information level interaction with multiple stakeholders, and enabling autonomic decision making with applications which have not initially been designed for such a purpose. This kind of system is expected to be able to monitor the system in information level, analyze the situation, plan the required actions, and execute the control events towards the system automatically or at least semi-automatically. In addition, interacting systems need to understand the meaning of the received events, and be able to create actions in such a way that the other player understands it accordingly. This area is still mostly open for future research, and solutions are needed to make *autonomic* M2M service networks a reality. There is a need to develop self-active decision engines enabling autonomic monitoring, analyzing, planning and executing responses to M2M systems. This includes need for smart and adaptive technologies for reasoning based on the complex events and state changes happening in the system. In addition, the autonomic decision engines need to be connected with generic service capabilities in a horizontal way to enable basis for interoperation in a services level.

6.2. M2M Communication

When looking at technologies for M2M communications, subcategories related to M2M communication overlays (e.g., MQTT, HTTP/Coap, XMPP), Internet technologies (e.g., IPv6, 6LowPan), and radio access technologies for WAN (e.g., cellular 3G), LAN (e.g., WiFi) and sensor networks (e.g., Bluetooth Smart) can be found. M2M applications are usually based on messaging with M2M devices. Traditionally, such messaging is done with short message service (SMS) or Email systems. It is seen that real-time messaging, capabilities to handle not always on mobile devices and capabilities for more dynamic topologies are needed. Therefore, technologies such as, e.g., XMPP to enable real-time M2M messaging, presence management and dynamic topologies are potential for M2M systems. In addition, there is need for virtualization of communications, and having a kind of M2M communication overlay hiding the heterogeneity of underlying networks and ensuring security. This is because of, e.g., the need to connect M2M asset devices with limited power and computing capabilities into the system. In addition, the referred M2M asset devices ownership set limits for the communication. When connecting such resources into system, also lower levels of communication need optimization. Examples of potential areas of research may be related to novel Bluetooth profiles, IPv6 over Bluetooth low energy, energy efficient IPv6 multicast, Coap, 6LowPAN and RPL including optimized M2M gateway and M2M messaging solutions.

6.3. M2M Security

There are huge amount of technologies, which could be applied for enabling M2M security as shown by the review. There is very strong need for defining guidelines for the use of M2M security technologies also because M2M applications are usually very sensitive on misuse there are high requirements for reliability. When both ends of the communication are mobile, there is need e.g., for advanced credential management, creation of trust, bridging mobile asset network and WAN security, adaptive M2M secure elements and horizontal end to end security solutions. For example, creation of trust is traditionally established in hop by hop manner between M2M asset devices and M2M applications. This kind of model can be challenging in M2M systems, because of M2M information content may be business critical and it may contain high privacy requirements. Therefore, these areas are also open for future research and novel solutions.

6.4. Interoperability

According to the review, it can be seen that there are technologies available for M2M service communications between remote physical objects over the network infrastructures with virtual world services. However, there are still challenges related to adaptability, reliability, performance, security, smartness, interoperability, and cost of development, manual operation and maintenance during the life-cycle of M2M products. Interoperability with existing systems and resource constrained embedded devices are usually approached via gateways of some sort. For example, the functional architecture designed by ETSI M2M [145], Cisco [146], AnyBridge [147], Systech [148], Alcatel Lucent [149] and IOT-A [141] relies on the use of a kind of M2M gateway mainly because of challenges related to communication with constrained devices. Such a M2M gateway can handle, e.g., the issues related to communicating with a system based on an incompatible communication protocol, low-power devices which are unable to communicate with the rest of the system directly due to limited resources or capabilities, or communication with a domain in which the access is otherwise restricted by some service provider. Such a gateway can take care of mapping of protocols to be more applicable for embedded capillary networks and devices, and enable interoperability between various proprietary networks. For example, the M2M gateway (which may also be called a border router) can translate HTTP to CoAP, IPv6 to 6LowPan, XMPP to Bluetooth Smart and 6LowPan to Bluetooth Smart messages. In addition, the gateway can act as a translating and security element, which can interconnect two systems having different protocols and data formats and perhaps belonging to different security domains. Such gateway component may not be optimal from communication point of view, but it is required in some cases because of interoperability and security.

A gateway may also prevent message flooding from devices to the backbone network, enable management of M2M asset devices in groups, make maintenance and configuration smooth, enable usage of unlicensed frequency bands and/or optimized radio technologies for specific M2M asset devices. Typically, a gateway is then connected to a back-end server which is taking care of data storages, management, centralized control and enforcement of security policies. The use of back-end servers have a crucial role in combatting the various scalability and reliability issues found in pure peer-to-peer and ad-hoc -type systems [150,151,152].

There seems to be multiple communication options for realization of M2M gateways: M2M gateway as an Internet protocol (IP) router, M2M gateway as a service gateway and direct connection to M2M devices without any M2M gateway. When M2M gateway is acting as an IP router, it makes possible to establish end-to-end IP connectivity if M2M asset devices are supporting IP. In that case, the local radio access technology needs to have mapping to IP communication. If M2M asset devices are not supporting IP, then there is a need to have an M2M service gateway, which is able to act as a bridge/protocol translator between M2M asset network and M2M infrastructure. There are also multiple options for making protocol translation from WAN connectivity to LAN connectivity in M2M gateways. For example, the service capable M2M gateway is able to make protocol adaptation between proprietary protocol stack, and ETSI M2M SCL. Communication with constrained M2M devices can apply several options, however, there are several practical challenges which require optimization within the local M2M asset network such as, e.g., application of web services within constrained local M2M asset network, sizes of IP packets and headers, power consumption of radio access protocols, heterogeneity and mobility of M2M devices and local M2M asset networks, and coding and integration of M2M application content. Some solutions for these challenges (e.g., Coap, 6LowPAN, Bluetooth LE) are already available; however, there are still several open issues for future research in these areas.

6.5. Horizontal and Autonomic M2M

Based on the review, it is seen that principles for the architecture need to be defined in order to establish a solid basis for multiple stakeholder system for M2M service networks. In addition, architecture principles for solving the heterogeneity of technologies are needed to enable communication between objects and applications, which are not initially been designed to communicate together.

An approach may be horizontal approach for the system architecture and application of autonomic computing principles [153]. Such horizontal architecture is based on open standards to enable connectivity and interoperation with multiple M2M domains and heterogeneous devices and to enable reaching wide acceptance as a basis of multiple stakeholder M2M systems. In such a way, several different M2M domains could become capable of deploying the architecture, enabling interoperability, lowering the development cost and boosting the arising M2M markets by contributing towards transferring from vertical towards more horizontal M2M markets.

7. CONCLUDING REMARKS

This survey provides an overview of the potential technologies enabling future autonomic M2M service networks. However, a clear definition of the architectural principles for horizontal M2M system is needed first, which must then proceed towards enabling autonomic capabilities in a feasible way. Otherwise, the solutions for solving the complexity may prevent the horizontal approach and thus the basis for multiple stakeholder system and enablers for autonomic M2M. In addition, it is important to enable interoperation with multiple application domains.

Solving the complexity in future M2M systems opens several areas for future research, such as, e.g., autonomic decision engines, reasoning, generic service capabilities for autonomic computing, virtualization of M2M communications, optimization of communications with limited capability devices, M2M messaging, and last but not the least M2M security for advanced credential management, creation of trust, bridging mobile asset network and WAN security, adaptive M2M secure elements and horizontal end to end solutions.

According to the review, there are technologies available for M2M service communications between remote physical objects over the network infrastructures and virtual world services. However, there are still challenges related to adaptability, reliability, performance, security, smartness, interoperability, and cost of development, manual operation and maintenance during the life-cycle of M2M products.

ACKNOWLEDGMENTS

This review is related to deliverables of ITEA2 A2Nets project dealing with autonomic M2M service networks. The authors wish to thank all contributors of A2Nets project, and especially the A2Nets ITEA2 reviewers and public research funding organizations in Spain, France, Turkey and Finland for making this work possible.

REFERENCES

1. Miorandi, D.; Sicari, S.; de Pellegrini, F.; Chlamtac, I. Internet of things: Vision, applications and research challenges. *Ad Hoc Netw.* **2012**, *10*, 1497–1516.
2. Akyildiz, I.F.; Su, W.; Sankarasubramaniam, Y.; Cayirci, E. Wireless sensor networks: A survey. *Comput. Netw.* **2002**, *38*, 393–422.

3. Wu, G.; Talwar, S.; Johnsson, K.; Himayat, N.; Johnson, K.D. M2M: From mobile to embedded internet. *IEEE Commun. Mag.* **2011**, *49*, 36–43.
4. Kephart, J.O.; Chess, D.M. The vision of autonomic computing. *Computer* **2003**, *36*, 41–50.
5. Horn, P. Autonomic Computing: IBM's Perspective on the State of Information Technology. Availableonline: http://people.scs.carleton.ca/~soma/biosec/readings/autonomic_computing.pdf (accessed on 11 November 2014).
6. Salehie, M.; Tahvildari, L. Autonomic computing: Emerging trends and open problems. *ACM SIGSOFT Softw. Eng. Notes* **2005**, *30*, 1–7.
7. Parashar, M.; Hariri, S. Autonomic computing: An overview. In *Unconventional Programming Paradigms*; Springer: Berlin/Heidelberg, Germany, 2005; pp. 257–269.
8. Garlan, D.; Cheng, S.-W.; Huang, A.-C.; Schmerl, B.; Steenkiste, P. Rainbow: Architecture-based self-adaptation with reusable infrastructure. *Computer* **2004**, *37*, 46–54.
9. Nami, M.R.; Bertels, K. A survey of autonomic computing systems. In Proceedings of the 3rd International Conference on Autonomic and Autonomous Systems (ICAS'07), Athens, Greece, 11–13 February 2007; pp. 26–30.
10. Karmouch, A. Mobile software agents for telecommunications. *IEEE Commun. Mag.* **1998**, *36*, 24–25.
11. Boutaba, R.; Polyrakis, A. Projecting advanced enterprise network and service management to active networks. *IEEE Netw.* **2002**, *16*, 28–33.
12. Calo, S.; Sloman, M. Guest Editorial: Policy-Based Management of Networks and Services. *J. Netw. Syst. Manag.* **2003**, *11*, 249–252.
13. Murch, R. *Autonomic Computing*; Prentice Hall: Upper Saddle River, NJ, USA, 2004.
14. IBM Corporation. An Architectural Blueprint for Autonomic Computing, White Paper. 4th ed. October 2004. Available online: http://www-03.ibm.com/autonomic/pdfs/AC%20Blueprint%20White%20Paper%20V7.pdf (accessed on 30 October 2014).
15. Want, R.; Pering, T.; Tennenhouse, D. Comparing autonomic and proactive computing. *IBM Syst. J.* **2003**, *42*, 129–135.
16. IEC 61970. Common Information Model (CIM)/Energy Management. Available online: http://www.iec.ch/smartgrid/standards/ (accessed on 30 October 2014).
17. Pakkala, D.; Latvakoski, J. Distributed service platform for adaptive mobile service. *Int. J. Pervasive Comput. Commun.***2006**, *2*, 135–147.
18. ETSI Technical Specification 102 690 Machine to Machine communications (M2M) Functional Architecture. V2.1.1. Available online: http://www.etsi.org/deliver/etsi_ts/102600_102699/102690/02.01.01_60/ts_102690v020101p.pdf(accessed on 30 October 2014).
19. Chang, K.; Soong, A.; Tseng, M.; Xiang, Z. Global Wireless Machine-to-Machine Standardization. *IEEE Internet Comput.* **2011**, *15*, 64–69.
20. Latvakoski, J.; Pakkala, D.; Paakkonen, P. A communication architecture for spontaneous systems. *IEEE Wirel. Commun.* **2004**, *11*, 36–42.
21. IPSO Alliance. Available online: http://www.ipso-alliance.org/ (accessed on 29 October 2014).
22. The Internet Engineering Task Force (IETF). Available online: http://www.ietf.org/ (accessed on 29 October 2014).
23. ETSI M2M/Smart M2M. Available online: http://www.etsi.org/ (accessed on 29 October 2014).
24. One M2M forum. Available online: http://www.onem2m.org/ (accessed on 29 October 2014).
25. Electronic Product Codes (EPCglobal). Available online: http://www.gs1.org/epcglobal/ (accessed on 29 October 2014).
26. uID center. Available online: http://www.uidcenter.org/ (accessed on 29 October 2014).
27. ONVIF. Available online: http://www.onvif.org/ (accessed on 29 October 2014).
28. Openmeter. Available online: http://www.openmeter.com/ (accessed on 29 October 2014).
29. OGC. Sensor Web Enablement (SWE). Available online: http://www.opengeospatial.org/ogc/ markets-technologies/swe (accessed on 29 October 2014).

30. OASIS User Interface Markup Language (UIML). Available online: http://www.uiml.org (accessed on 29 October 2014).
31. Universal Plung and Play (UPnP). Available online: http://www.upnp.org/ (accessed on 29 October 2014).
32. Li, J. On peer-to-peer (P2P) content delivery. *Peer-to-Peer Netw. Appl.* **2008**, *1*, 363–381.
33. Meshkova, E.; Riihijärvi, J.; Petrova, M.; Mähönen, P. A survey on resource discovery mechanisms, peer-to-peer and service discovery frameworks. *Comput. Netw.* **2008**, *52*, 2097–2128.
34. Tarkoma, S. *Overlay Networks—Towards Information Networking*; Auerbach Publications, Taylor & Francis Group: Boca Raton, FL, USA, 2010; p. 245.
35. Hoebeke, J.; Moerman, I.; Dhoedt, B.; Demeester, P. An Overview of Mobile Ad Hoc Networks: Applications and Challenges. *J. Commun. Netw.* **2004**, *3*, 60–66.
36. Yick, J.; Mukherjee, B.; Ghosal, D. Wireless sensor network survey. *Comput. Netw.* **2008**, *52*, 2292–2330.
37. Bluetooth 4.0. Available online: https://www.bluetooth.org/apps/content/ (accessed on 29 October 2014).
38. ETSI. ETSI Technical Specification 102 921: "Machine to Machine Communications (M2M); mla, dla and mld interfaces". Available online: http://www.etsi.org/deliver/etsi_ts/102900_102999/102921/02.01.01_60/ts_102921v020101p (accessed on 30 October 2014).
39. Open Mobile Alliance (OMA). OMA Device Management Tree and Description Serialization Specification, Version 1.2.1 Open Mobile Alliance. Available online: http://technical.openmobilealliance.org/Technical/release_program/docs/DM/V1_2_1-20080617-A/OMA-TS-DM_TND-V1_2_1-20080617-A.pdf (accessed on 30 October 2014).
40. Open Mobile Alliance. Available online: http://openmobilealliance.org/ (accessed on 29 October 2014).
41. Broadband Forum. TR-181 Device Data Model for TR-069. Available online: http://www.broadband-forum.org/technical/download/TR-181_Issue-2.pdf (accessed on 30 October 2014).
42. Broadband Forum. Available online: http://www.broadband-forum.org/ (accessed on 29 October 2014).
43. Jeronimo, M.; Weast, J. *UPnP Design by Example: A Software Developer's Guide to Universal Plug and Play*; Intel Press: Santa Clara, CA, USA, 2003.
44. OASIS. Devices Profile for Web Services (DPWS). Available online: http://docs.oasis-open.org/ws-dd/ns/dpws/2009/01 (accessed on 29 October 2014).
45. Open building information Xchange (oBIX). Available online: http://www.obix.org/ (accessed on 29 October 2014).
46. Hannelius, T.; Salmenpera, M.; Kuikka, S. Roadmap to adopting OPC UA. In Proceedings of the 6th IEEE International Conference on Industrial Informatics, Daejeon, Korea, 13–16 July 2008; pp. 756–761.
47. OPC Foundation. Available online: http://www.opcfoundation.org/ (accessed on 29 October 2014).
48. Martin, D.; Burstein, M.; Mcdermott, D.; Mcilraith, S.; Paolucci, M.; Sycara, K.; Mcguinness, D.L.; Sirin, E.; Srinivasan, N. Bringing Semantics to Web Services with OWL-S. 2007. Available online: http://link.springer.com/article/10.1007%2Fs11280-007-0033-x (accessed on 30 October 2014).
49. Semantic Markup for Web Services. Available online: http://www.w3.org/Submission/OWL-S/ (accessed on 29 October 2014).
50. Compton, M.; Barnaghi, P.; Bermudez, L.; García-Castro, R.; Corcho, O.; Cox, S.; Graybeal, J.; Hauswirth, M.; Henson, C.; Herzog, A.; *et al.* The SSN ontology of the W3C semantic sensor network incubator group. *Web Semant. Sci. Serv. Agents World Wide Web* **2012**, *17*, 25–32.
51. W3C Semantic Sensor Networks. Available online: http://www.w3.org/ 2005/Incubator/ssn/ (accessed on 29 October 2014).
52. Bandara, A.; Payne, T.; de Roure, D.; Clemo, G. An Ontological Framework for Semantic Description of Devices. In Proceedings of the International Semantic Web Conference (ISWC), Hiroshima, Japan, 7–11 November 200.

53. FIPA Device Ontology Specification. Available online: http://www.fipa.org/ specs/ fipa00091/PC00091A.html (accessed on 29 October 2014).
54. Bröring, A.; Echterhoff, J.; Jirka, S.; Simonis, I.; Everding, T.; Stasch, C.; Liang, S.; Lemmens, R. New Generation Sensor Web Enablement. Open Access-Sensors ISSN 1424–8220. Available online: http://www.mdpi.com/1424-8220/11/3/2652 (accessed on 30 October 2014).
55. Botts, M. *OpenGeo Sensor Web Enablement (SWE) Suite*; Botts Innovative Research Inc., June 2011. Available online: http://boundlessgeo.com/whitepaper/opengeo-sensor-web-enablement-swe-suite/ (accessed on 30 October 2014).
56. Sensor Web Enablement (SWE). Available online: http://www.ogcnetwork.net/swe (accessed on 30 October 2014).
57. OSGi Alliance. Available online: http://www.osgi.org/ (accessed on 29 October 2014).
58. TMForum. Available online: http://www.tmforum.org/ (accessed on 29 October 2014).
59. Jammes, F.; Mensch, A.; Smit, H. Service-oriented device communications using the devices profile for web services. In Proceedings of the 3rd International Workshop on Middleware for Pervasive and Ad-Hoc Computing, Grenoble, France, 28 November–2 December 2005.
60. Delin, K.; Jackson, S.; Some, R. Sensor Webs. *NASA Tech. Briefs* **1999**, *23*, 90.
61. Gibbons, P.; Karp, B.; Ke, Y.; Nath, S.; Seshan, S. Irisnet: An Architecture for a Worldwide Sensor Web. *IEEE Pervasive Comput.* **2003**, *2*, 22–33.
62. Shneidman, J.; Pietzuch, P.; Ledlie, J.; Roussopoulos, M.; Seltzer, M.; Welsh, M. *Hourglass: An Infrastructure for Connecting Sensor Networks and Applications*; Technical Report; Harvard University: Columbia, MA, USA, 2004.
63. Moodley, D.; Simonis, I. A New Architecture for the Sensor Web: The SWAP Framework. In Proceedings of the 5th International Semantic Web Conference (ISWC 2006), Athens, GA, USA, 5–9 November 2006; Cruz, I., Decker, S., Allemang, D., Preist, C., Schwabe, D., Mika, P., Uschold, M., Aroyo, L., Eds.; Lecture Notes in Computer Science. Volume 4273.
64. Botts, M.; Percivall, G.; Reed, C.; Davidson, J. OGC Sensor Web Enablement: Overview and High Level Architecture. In Proceedings of the 2nd International Conference on GeoSensor Networks, GSN 2006, Boston, MA, USA, 1–3 October 2006; Nittel, S., Labrinidis, A., Stefanidis, A., Eds.; Lecture Notes in Computer Science. Springer: Berlin, Germany, 2008; Volume 4540, pp. 175–190.
65. Open Geospatial Consortium Inc. OGC SWE Common Data Model Encoding Standard (OGC SWE Common). 2011. Available online: http://www.opengis.net/doc/IS/SWE/2.0 (accessed on 30 October 2014).
66. Open Geospatial Consortium. Observations and Measurements—XML Implementation (OGC O&M). 2011. Available online: http://www.opengis.net/doc/IS/OMXML/2.0 (accessed on 30 October 2014).
67. Open Geospatial Consortium. (*Sensor Model Language (SensorML). OpenGIS Implementation Specification* (OGC SensorML). Version 1.0.0. 2007. Available online: http:// portal.opengeospatial.org/files/?artifact_id=21273 (accessed 30 October 2014).
68. Open Geospatial Consortium. OpenGIS SWE Service Model Implementation Standard. 2011. Available online: http://www.opengis.net/doc/IS/SWES/2.0 (accessed on 30 October 2014).
69. Open Geospatial Consortium. Sensor Observation Service Implementation Standard. SOS, Version 1.0. 2007. Available online: http://www.opengeospatial.org/ (accessed on 30 October 2014).
70. Open Geospatial Consortium. OGC Sensor Planning Service Implementation Standard SPS. 2011. Available online: http://www.opengis.net/doc/IS/SPS/2.0 (accessed on 30 October 2014).
71. Fowler, M. *Analysis Patterns: Reusable Object Models*; Addison-Wesley: Indianapolis, IN, USA, 1997.
72. Fielding, R.T. Architectural Styles and the Design of Network-based Software Architectures. Ph.D. Thesis, University of California, Irvine, CA, USA, 2000.
73. Hariri, S.; Khargharia, B.; Chen, H.; Yang, J.; Zhang, Y.; Parashar, M.; Liu, H. The autonomic computing paradigm. *Clust. Comput.* **2006**, *9*, 5–17.

74. Chakravarti, A.J.; Baumgartner, G. The organic grid: Self-organizing computation on a peer-to-peer network. In Proceedings of the 1st International Conference on Autonomic Computing (ICAC), New York, NY, USA, 17–18 May 2004.
75. Appleby, K.; Fakhouri, S.; Fong, L.; Goldszmidt, G.; Kalantar, M.; Pazel, D.; Pershing, J.; Rochwerger, B. Oceano—SLA based management of a computing utility. In Proceedings of the 2001 IEEE/IFIP International Symposium on Integrated Network Management, Seattle, WA, USA, 14–18 May 2001; pp. 855–868.
76. Rhea, S.; Wells, C.; Eaton, P.; Geels, D.; Zhao, B.; Weatherspoon, H.; Kubiatowicz, J. Maintenance-free global data storage. *IEEE Internet Comput.* **2001**, *5*, 40–49.
77. Lohman, G.M.; Lightstone, S.S. Smart: Making DB2 (more) autonomic. In Proceedings of the 28th International Conference on Very Large Data Bases, Hong Kong, China, 20–23 August 2002; pp. 877–879.
78. Chaudhuri, S.; Narasayya, V. Self-tuning database systems: A decade of progress. In Proceedings of the 33rd International Conference on Very large data bases, Vienna, Austria, 23–27 September 2007; pp. 3–14.
79. Chess, D.; Segal, A.; Whalley, I.; White, S. Unity: Experiences with a prototype autonomic computing system. In Proceedings of the International Conference on Autonomic Computing, TeX90 CD '04, ICAC, New York, NY, USA, 17–18 May 2004; pp. 140–147.
80. Dong, X.; Hariri, S.; Xue, L.; Chen, H.; Zhang, M.; Pavuluri, S.; Rao, S. Autonomia: An autonomic computing environment. In Proceedings of the Performance, Computing, and Communications Conference, Phoenix, AZ, USA, 9–11 April 2003; pp. 61–68.
81. Liu, H.; Parashar, M. A component based programming framework for autonomic applications. In Proceedings of the International Conference on Automatic Computing, New York, NY, USA, 17–19 May 2004; pp. 10–17.
82. Sicard, S.; Boyer, F.; de Palma, N. Using components for architecture-based management: The self-repair case. In Proceedings of the 30th International Conference on Software Engineering, Leipzig, Germany, 10–18 May 2008.
83. Ranganathan, A.; Campbell, R.H. Autonomic pervasive computing based on planning. In Proceedings of the International Conference on Autonomic Computing, New York, NY, USA, 17–19 May 2004; pp. 80–87.
84. Abdelwahed, S.; Kandasamy, N.; Neema, S. Online control for self-management in computing systems. In Proceedings of the 10th IEEE Real-Time and Embedded Technology and Applications Symposium (RTAS 2004), Toronto, ON, Canada, 25–28 May 2004; pp. 368–375.
85. Gurguis, S.A.; Zeid, A. Towards autonomic web services: Achieving self-healing using web services. *SIGSOFT Softw. Eng. Notes* **2005**, *30*, 1–5.
86. Kaiser, G.; Gross, P.; Kc, G.; Parekh, J.; Valetto, G. An approach to autonomizing legacy systems. In Proceedings of the Workshop on Self-Healing, Adaptive and Self-Managed Systems, New York, NY, USA, 23 June 2002.
87. Kaiser, G.; Parekh, J.; Gross, P.; Valetto, G. Kinesthetics extreme: An external infrastructure for monitoring distributed legacy systems. In Proceedings of the Autonomic Computing Workshop Fifth Annual International Workshop on Active Middleware Services (AMS'03), Seattle, WA, USA, 25 June 2003; pp. 22–30.
88. Anglano, C.; Montani, S. Achieving self-healing in autonomic software systems: A case-based reasoning approach. In Proceedings of the International Conference on Intelligent Computing, Qingdao, China, 21–24 August 2007; pp. 1–19.
89. Stanfel, Z.; Hocenski, Z.; Martinovic, G. A self-manageable rule driven enterprise application. In Proceedings of the 29th International Conference on Information Technology Interfaces (ITI 2007), Cavtat/Dubrovnik, Croatia, 25–28 June 2007; pp. 717–722.
90. Appavoo, J.; Hui, K.; Soules, C.; Wisniewski, R.; Silva, D.; Krieger, O.; Marc, D.; Auslander, A.; Gamsa, B.; Ganger, G.; *et al.* Enabling autonomic behavior in systems software with hot-swapping. *IBM Syst. J.* **2003**, *42*, 60–76.
91. Kcman, E.; Wang, Y.-M. Discovering correctness constraints for self-management of system configuration. In Proceedings of the International Conference on Autonomic Computing, New York, NY, USA, 17–19 May 2004; pp. 28–35.

92. Mesnier, M.; Thereska, E.; Ganger, G.R.; Ellarda, D.; Seltzer, M. File classification in self-* storage systems. In Proceedings of the 1st International Conference on Autonomic Computing (ICAC-04), New York, NY, USA, 17–19 May 2004; pp. 44–51.
93. Khan, M.J.; Awais, M.M.; Shamail, S. Achieving self-configuration capability in autonomic systems using case-based reasoning with a new similarity measure. In Proceedings of the 3rd International Conference on Intelligent Computing, Qingdao, China, 21–24 August 2007; pp. 97–106.
94. Hellerstein, J.L.; Gandhi, N.; Parekh, S.S. Managing the Performance of Lotus Notes: A Control Theoretic Approach. In Proceedings of the 27th International Computer Measurement Group Conference, Anaheim, CA, USA, 2–7 December 2001; pp. 397–408.
95. Markl, V.; Lohman, G.M.; Raman, V. LEO: An autonomic query optimizer for DB2. *IBM Syst. J.* **2003**, *42*, 98–106.
96. Shivam, P.; Babu, S.; Chase, J.S. Learning application models for utility resource planning. In Proceedings of the International Conference on Automatic Computing, Dublin, Ireland, 13–16 Jun 2006.
97. Park, J.; Chandramohan, P. Static *vs.* Dynamic recovery models for survivable distributed systems. In Proceedings of the 37th Annual Hawaii International Conference on System Sciences, Big Island, HI, USA, 5–8 January 2004; pp. 1–9.
98. Rish, I.; Brodie, M.; Odintsova, N.; Ma, S.; Grabarnik, G. Realtime problem determination in distributed systems using active probing. In Proceedings of the Network Operations Management Symposium (NOMS 2004), Seoul, Korea, 23 April 2004; pp. 133–146.
99. Mills, K.; Rose, S.; Quirolgico, S.; Britton, M.; Tan, C. An autonomic failure-detection algorithm. *ACM SIGSOFT Softw. Eng. Notes* **2004**, *29*, 79–83.
100. Reynolds, P.; Killian, C.; Wiener, J.L.; Mogul, J.C.; Shah, M.A.; Vahdat, A. Pip: Detecting the unexpected in distributed systems. In Proceedings of the conference on Symposium on Networked Systems Design and Implementation, San Jose, CA, USA, May 2006; pp. 1–14.
101. Roblee, C.; Berk, V.; Cybenko, G. Implementing large-scale autonomic server monitoring using process query systems. In Proceedings of the Second International Conference on Automatic Computing, Seattle, WA, USA, 13–16 June 2005; pp. 123–133.
102. Candea, G.; Kawamoto, S.; Fujiki, Y.; Friedman, G.; Fox, A. Microreboot—A technique for cheap recovery. In Proceedings of the 6th Symposium on Opearting Systems Design and Implementation, San Francisco, CA, USA, 5 December 2004; pp. 31–44.
103. Qin, F.; Tucek, J.; Sundaresan, J.; Zhou, Y. Rx: Treating bugs as allergies- A safe method to survive software failures. *ACM Trans. Comput. Syst.* **2007**, *25*.
104. Claudel, B.; Palma1, N.D.; Lachaize, R.; Hagimont, D. Self protection for distributed component-based applications. In Proceedings of the 8th Symposium on Stabilization, Safety, and Security of Distributed Systems, Dallas, TX, USA, 17–19 November 2006; pp. 184–198.
105. Costa, M.; Crowcroft, J.; Castro, M.; Rowstron, A.; Zhou, L.; Zhang, L.; Barham, P. Vigilante: End-to-end containment of internet worms. In Proceedings of the ACM symposium on Operating systems principles, Brighton, UK, 23–26 October 2005; pp. 133–147.
106. Saint-Andre, P.; Smith, K.; Tronçon, R. *XMPP: The Definitive Guide*; O' Reilly Media Inc.: Sebastopol, CA, USA, 2009; p. 306.
107. Sensor over XMPP. Available online: http://xmpp.org/extensions/inbox/sensors.html (accessed on 30 October 2014).
108. MQTT protocol. Available online: http://mqtt.org (accessed on 30 October 2014).
109. IETF. IPv6 over Low Power WPAN (6LowPAN) WG. Available online: http://tools.ietf.org/wg/6lowpan (accessed on 30 October 2014).
110. Hui, J. Compression Format for IPv6 Datagrams over IEEE 802.15.4-Based Networks. IETF RFC 6282. September 2011. Available online: http://tools.ietf.org/html/rfc6282 (accessed on 30 October 2014).
111. Constrained RESTful Environments (CoRE) WG. Available online: http://tools.ietf.org/wg/core/ (accessed on 30 October 2014).
112. IETF. Routing Over Low power and Lossy networks (ROLL) WG. Available online: http://tools.ietf.org/wg/roll/(accessed on 30 October 2014).

113. Constrained RESTful Environments (CoRE) Link Format. IETF RFC 6690. Available online: http://tools.ietf.org/html/rfc6690 (accessed on 30 October 2014).
114. Kovatsch, M.; Duquennoy, S.; Dunkels, A. A Low-Power CoAP for Contiki. In Proceedings of the Workshop on Internet of Things Technology and Architectures (IEEE IoTech 2011), Valencia, Spain, 17 October 2011.
115. Rescorla, E.; Modadugu, N. "Datagram Transport Layer Security". IETF RFC 4347. April 2006. Available online: http://tools.ietf.org/html/rfc4347 (accessed on 30 October 2014).
116. Kent, S. "IP Encapsulating Security Payload (ESP)". RFC 4303. December 2005. Available online: http://tools.ietf.org/html/rfc4303 (accessed on 30 October 2014).
117. Yegin, A.; Shelby, Z. CoAP Security Options. Internet-Draft, October 14, 2011, Expired April 16, 2012. Available online: http://www.ietf.org/archive/id/draft-yegin-coap-security-options-00.txt (accessed on 30 October 2014).
118. Saint-Andre, P. Extensible Messaging and presence protocol (XMPP): IETF RFC 3921. Available online: https://tools.ietf.org/html/rfc3921 (accessed on 30 October 2014).
119. Instant Messaging/Presence Protocol Requirements. RFC 2779. February 2000. Available online: https://tools.ietf.org/html/rfc2779 (accessed on 30 October 2014).
120. Bluetooth SIG. The Bluetooth Core specification v4.0. 2010. Available online: https://www.bluetooth.org/docman/handlers/downloaddoc.ashx?doc_id=229737 (accessed on 11 November 2014).
121. Bluetooth SIG. Core specification addendum 3. 2012. Available online: https://www.bluetooth.org/docman/handlers/DownloadDoc.ashx?doc_id=269452 (accessed on 11 November 2014).
122. Parekh, J.; Kaiser, G.; Gross, P.; Valetto, G. Retrofitting Autonomic Capabilities onto Legacy Systems. *J. Cluster Comput.* **2006**, *9*, 141–159.
123. Liu, H.; Parashar, M. Accord: A programming framework for autonomic applications. *IEEE Trans. Syst. Man Cybern. Part C Appl. Rev.* **2006**, *36*, 341–352.
124. ANA: Autonomic Network Architecture. Available online: http://www.uio.no/ studier/emner/matnat/ifi/INF5090/v08/undervisningsmateriale/D.1.4-5-6.Blueprint.pdf (accessed 30 October 2014).
125. Initial IoT Protocol Suite Definition. Available online: http://www.iot-a.eu/public/public-documents/documents-1/1/1/d3.3/at_download/file (accessed on 30 October 2014).
126. The Anthill Project. Available online: http://www.cs.unibo.it/projects/anthill (accessed on 30 October 2014).
127. Inhyok, C.; Shah, Y.; Schmidt, A.U.; Leicher, A.; Meyerstein, M. Security and trust for M2M Communications. *IEEE Veh. Tech. Mag.* **2009**, 69–75.
128. Raza, S.; Chung, T.; Duquennoy, S.; Yazar, D.; Voigt, T.; Roedig, U. Securing Internet of Things with Lightweigth IPsec. Available online: http://soda.swedish-ict.se/4052/ (accessed on 30 October 2014).
129. Judge, P.; Ammar, M. Security issues and solutions in multicast content distribution: A survey. *IEEE Netw.* **2003**, *17*, 30–36.
130. Challal, Y.; Bettahar, H.; Bouabdallah, A. A Taxonomy of Multicast Data Origin Authentication: Issues and Solutions. *IEEE Commun. Surv.* **2004**, *3*, 34–57.
131. Kellil, M.; Romdhani, I.; Lach, H-Y. Multicast Receiver and Sender Access Control and its Applicability to Mobile IP Environments: A Survey. *IEEE Commun. Surv.* **2005**, *7*, 46–70.
132. Hardjono, T.; Weiss, B. The Multicast Group Security Architecture. Available online: https://tools.ietf.org/html/rfc3740 (accessed on 30 October 2014).
133. ETSI. Security of Multimedia Broadcast/Multicast Service (MBMS). Available online: http://www.etsi.org/deliver/etsi_ts/133200_133299/133246/10.01.00_60/ts_133246v100100p.pdf (accessed 30 October 2014).
134. ETSI. Satellite Earth Stations and Systems (SES); Broadband Satellite Multimedia (BSM). Availableonline: http://www.etsi.org/deliver/etsi_ts/102400_102499/102466/ 01.01.01_ 60/ts_102466v010101p.pdf (accessed on 30 October 2014).
135. Ben Jaballah, W.; Meddeb, A.; Youssef, H. An efficient source authentication scheme in wireless sensor networks. In Proceedings of the Proceedings of IEEE/ACS AICCSA Conference, Hammamet, Tunisia, 16–19 May 2010; pp. 1–7.

136. Lim, S.Y.; Lim, M.H. Energy-Efficient and Scalable Group Key Management for Hierarchical Sensor Network. *J. Ubiquitous Syst. Pervasive Netw.* **2011**, *2*, 39–47.
137. Alexander, R.; Tsao, T. Adapted Multimedia Internet KEYing (AMIKEY): An extension of Multimedia Internet KEYing (MIKEY) Methods for Generic LLN Environments. Available online: http://tools.ietf.org/html/draft-alexander-roll-mikey-lln-key-mgmt-04 (accessed on 30 October 2014).
138. Keoh, S.; Kumar, S.; Garcia-Morchon, O.; Dijk, E.; Rahman, A. DTLS-based Multicast Security for Low-Power and Lossy Networks (LLNs). Available online: http://tools.ietf.org/html/draft-keoh-dice-multicast-security-04 (accessed 30 October 2014).
139. Hydra Project. Available online: http://www.hydramiddleware.eu (accessed on 17 April 2014).
140. Runes Project. Available online: http://www.ist-runes.org (accessed on 17 April 2014).
141. IoT-A Project. Available online: http://www.iot-a.eu (accessed on 17 April 2014).
142. ICore Project. Available online: http://www.iot-icore.eu (accessed on 17 April 2014).
143. Sofia Project. Available online: http://www.artemis-ia.eu/project/index/view?project=4 (accessed on 17 April 2014).
144. Fi-Ware Project Architecture. Available online: http://forge.fi-ware.eu/plugins/mediawiki/ wiki/ fiware/index.php/FI-WARE_Architecture (accessed on 17 April 2014).
145. ETSI. Machine to Machine Communications. Available online: http://www.etsi.org/website/technologies/m2m.aspx(accessed on 17 April 2014).
146. Cisco. Available online: http://www.fiercebroadbandwireless.com/story/cisco-introduces- small-m2m-gateway-businesses/2011-08-25 (accessed on 17 April 2014).
147. AnyBridge. Available online: http://www.anybridge-m2m.nl/home (accessed on 17 April 2014).
148. Systech. Available online: http://www.systech.com/ (accessed on 17 April 2014).
149. Alcatel-Lucent. Available online: http://www2.alcatel-lucent.com/blogs/techzine/ 2011/getting-ready-for-m2m-traffic-growth/ (accessed on 17 April 2014).
150. Androutsellis-Theotokis, S.; Spinellis, D. A survey of peer-to-peer content distribution technologies. *ACM Comput. Surv.* **2004**, *36*, 335–371.
151. Zheng, H.; Yan, M. Research and Analysis of the Optimization of the Unstructured P2P Overlay Networks. In Proceedings of the 5th International Conference on Wireless Communications, Networking and Mobile Computing (WiCOM'09), Beijing, China, 24–26 September 2009; IEEE Press: Piscataway, NJ, USA, 2009; pp. 4376–4379.
152. Lua, E.K.; Crowcroft, J.; Pias, M.; Sharma, R.; Lim, S. A survey and comparison of peer-to-peer overlay network schemes. *IEEE Commun. Surv. Tutor.* **2005**, *7*, 72–93.
153. Latvakoski, J.; Alaya, M.B.; Ganem, H.; Jubeh, B.; Iivari, A.; Leguay, J.; Bosch, J.M.; Granqvist, N. Towards Horizontal Architecture for Autonomic M2M Service Networks. *Futur. Internet* **2014**, *6*, 261–301.

INDEX